THE ROOT OF ALL EVIL

For Brigid

Dr Cormac Moore is an historian-in-residence with Dublin City Council and a columnist with *The Irish News* who also edits its 'On This Day' segment. He has published widely on Irish history, including the books *Laois: The Irish Revolution, 1912–1923* (Four Courts Press, 2025), *Birth of the Border: The Impact of Partition in Ireland* (Merrion Press, 2019), *The Irish Soccer Split* (Cork University Press, 2015), and *The GAA v Douglas Hyde: The Removal of Ireland's First President as GAA Patron* (The Collins Press, 2012).

THE ROOT OF ALL EVIL

THE IRISH BOUNDARY COMMISSION

CORMAC MOORE

IRISH ACADEMIC PRESS

First published in 2025 by
Irish Academic Press
10 George's Street
Newbridge
Co. Kildare
Ireland
www.iap.ie

© Cormac Moore, 2025

978 1 78855 177 9 (Paper)
978 1 78855 178 6 (eBook)
978 1 78855 179 3 (PDF)

A CIP catalogue record for this book is available from the British Library.

All rights reserved. No part of this publication may be reproduced, stored in a retrieval system, or transmitted, in any form or by any means (electronic, mechanical, photocopying, recording or otherwise), without the prior written permission of both the copyright owner and the publisher of this book.

Typeset in FreightText Pro 11/16 pt

Cover design by Fiachra McCarthy

Front cover: Detail of map from *The Morning Post*, 7 November 1925.
Back cover: Members of the Irish Boundary Commission, courtesy of the National Library of Ireland

Irish Academic Press is a member of Publishing Ireland.

CONTENTS

Acknowledgements vi

Introduction 1

1. 'I do not know who will die for Tyrone and Fermanagh' 4
2. 'The root of all evil' 29
3. *Festina Lente* (Make Haste Slowly) 52
4. '... stereotyping the existing boundary' 77
5. 'Delay defeats Equity' 97
6. '... the Government will nominate a proper representative' 120
7. '... the primary but not the paramount consideration' 157
8. '... inertia, incapacity, and appalling ineptitude' 195
9. Craig 'had won all down the line' 215

Conclusion 238

Endnotes 247

Bibliography 285

Index 293

Acknowledgements

Firstly, I wish to thank the people who assisted me greatly in reading the draft and suggesting changes that have made this a better book, particularly Marie Coleman, Mike Cronin, Gráinne Daly, John Dorney, Tara Doyle, Kieran Glennon, Brian Hanley, Martin Mansergh, David McCullough, Ronan McGreevy, Mary Muldowney, Paddy Mulroe, and Margaret O'Callaghan. I want to thank Kieran Rankin for allowing me to use his NEBB map.

I am indebted to the staff members of the Newry and Mourne Museum, the National Archives of Ireland, the Public Record Office of Northern Ireland, the National Library of Ireland, the University College Dublin Archives, the Trinity College Dublin Archives, the UK National Archives and the Bodleian Archives and Manuscripts, Oxford University for all their help while researching this book.

I am very grateful for the help I have received from the staff of Irish Academic Press throughout the publishing process, particularly from Wendy Logue and Conor Graham.

I would like to thank all my family and friends for their encouragement and help throughout the process. To Brigid and Oisín, I am thankful for your love and support and for putting up with me while I was researching and writing this book. I dedicate this book to you, Brigid.

Introduction

ARTICLE 12 OF THE 1921 Anglo-Irish Treaty states:

> a Commission consisting of three persons, one to be appointed by the Government of the Irish Free State, one to be appointed by the Government of Northern Ireland, and one who shall be Chairman to be appointed by the British Government shall determine in accordance with the wishes of the inhabitants, so far as may be compatible with economic and geographic conditions, the boundaries between Northern Ireland and the rest of Ireland, and for the purposes of the Government of Ireland Act, 1920, and of this instrument, the boundary of Northern Ireland shall be such as may be determined by such Commission.[1]

The Irish Boundary Commission was offered by the British government as a concession to Sinn Féin and Irish nationalism during negotiations on the Anglo-Irish Treaty, in the hope of bringing about a permanent peace between Britain and Ireland. The Sinn Féin plenipotentiaries accepted the Boundary Commission as a way to limit the consequences of the partition of Ireland, while for the British signatories it offered a path to an agreement on the troublesome Irish question that had dominated British party politics for decades.

Ireland had been arbitrarily partitioned by the British government under the Government of Ireland Act 1920 to appease Ulster unionists, whose opposition to a Home Rule government had been resolute since the Third Home Rule crisis ten years earlier. Irish nationalists had never accepted this partitioning, but once the already established Northern Ireland government rejected British calls for the inclusion of the six counties in an all-Ireland parliament, the Treaty negotiations pivoted towards the establishment of a boundary commission on Ulster to overcome the impasse and go some way to meet the demands of the nationalists. Although boundary commissions had helped to resolve border disputes in post-First World War Europe, the nature and wording of the commission agreed to by Sinn Féin was at the heart of many of the subsequent problems Irish nationalists encountered. The devil was in the details.

Under the Treaty, the Irish Boundary Commission was to consist of three commissioners, one appointed by the Irish Free State government, one by the Northern Ireland government, and the chairman by the British government. The job of the commissioners was to deliberate on the boundary question in Ireland. They were afforded full powers to redraw the boundary line based on those deliberations. The vague wording of Article 12 gave great latitude to the commissioners to interpret the Boundary Commission's terms of reference as they saw fit, and with the Free State and Northern government representatives cancelling each other out, considerable control was vested with the British-appointed chairman.

The Boundary Commissioners worked intensively for a year, receiving submissions, interviewing witnesses, visiting contested areas and using different tools and data to reach a decision on a new boundary line. Most of their work, as with the work of the governments beforehand, particularly that of the Free State government and its North Eastern Boundary Bureau, came to nought as there was no change to the border from the one provided for under the Government of Ireland Act 1920. Despite those efforts and the considerable political controversy that surrounded the Irish Boundary Commission throughout its existence, not one person or acre of land was transferred under the Commission's remit.

While the tale of the Irish Boundary Commission could be accused of being one about nothing, given the ultimate outcome, the complex and fascinating story reveals much about the nature of Ireland's partition and about the Free State's attempts to assert its independence on the one hand and the British government's efforts to maintain the reach of its global empire on the other. The Irish Boundary Commission, in the words of Kieran Rankin, 'served as a crucial catalyst in defining the Irish Free State's relationship with the British State and in entrenching the territorial framework of Northern Ireland's six counties that exists to this day'.[2] The Boundary Commission was a crucial high-stakes matter for the British, Free State and Northern Irish governments from the moment it became a component of the Treaty in late 1921 through to its termination four years later.

Nevertheless, this is not only a story of high politics but one of how the decisions from above impacted on people on the ground. Through the different reactions and inputs of people from multiple perspectives, who engaged with the Boundary Commission before and during its convening, the rich source material provides key information on the consequences of the partition of Ireland on day-to-day life, particularly for those who lived close to the border.

The Boundary Commission saga also revealed much about the Irish Free State's efforts to forge its identity as a newly independent nation of the world while attempting to increase the size of its territory and the amount of people who resided in it, with an ultimate aim of ending partition. For Ulster unionists, the Commission was seen as an existential threat that required unity within and use of all their experience and allies from Britain to overcome the threat it posed to the territorial integrity of Northern Ireland. For British stakeholders, most desired that the Commission would disappear altogether or cause the minimum amount of damage to party politics there.

The aim of this book is to explain this incredibly complex, but captivating and important saga in modern Irish and British history. Published in the year of the hundredth anniversary of its collapse, it sheds more light on the intriguing and, particularly for Northern nationalists, infuriating story behind the Irish Boundary Commission, the results of which still resonate deeply today.

Chapter One

'I do not know who will die for Tyrone and Fermanagh'

ON 7 SEPTEMBER 1921 THE British Prime Minister, David Lloyd George, hosted a Cabinet meeting in Inverness Town Hall in North Scotland. Being hauled to a far-flung corner of Scotland did not impress the Cabinet nor its advisers, with one Cabinet member, Austen Chamberlain, remarking, 'I simply splutter with rage.'[1] At that Cabinet meeting, in proposing a conference with Sinn Féin to reach a settlement on the Irish question, Lloyd George stated that he did not want any such event to 'become entangled in the Ulster problem; that [Sinn Féin president Éamon] de Valera would raise the question of Fermanagh and Tyrone, where we had a very weak case, the Conference might break on that point, a very bad one. He would rather break – if there was to be a break – now, on allegiance and Empire.'[2] He added, 'Men will die for the Throne and Empire. I do not know who will die for Tyrone and Fermanagh.'[3]

In many ways, the boundary dispute, which became a key component of the Irish question at the time of the 1912–14 Third Home Rule Crisis, hinged on Counties Fermanagh and Tyrone. The Ulster unionist case – that areas of Ulster which did not want to be part of a Dublin-based Home Rule parliament should be excluded – was severely undermined by their insistence that Tyrone and Fermanagh must be excluded also, despite both counties having Catholic majorities and consistently electing nationalist public representatives.

The 'how and where a border might be drawn',[4] and for how long, dominated much of the talks and negotiations from the moment Liberal backbencher Thomas Agar-Robartes tabled an amendment to the Third Home Rule Bill in June 1912 to exclude the four counties of Antrim, Armagh, Derry and Down from the scheme.[5] For Ulster unionists and British politicians, mainly from the Conservative Party, the exclusion of some or all of Ulster went from being a 'wrecking amendment' of the entire Bill, to being 'supported on the grounds of logic'.[6]

Different schemes of exclusion were devised that could have seen from four to all nine counties of Ulster omitted from the Home Rule Bill.[7] The Irish Parliamentary Party (IPP) leader John Redmond was under increasing pressure from the Liberal prime minister Herbert Asquith to accept some form of exclusion of some areas in Ulster for some length of time. Asquith, in turn, was under intense pressure from within and outside his own party to deal separately with some or all of Ulster, including from a sometimes shrill monarch, King George V, who, in correspondence with Asquith, actively promoted the permanent exclusion of six counties.[8] On one occasion he wrote to Asquith fearing that the crisis in Ireland 'all point [sic] towards rebellion if not Civil War, &, if so, to certain bloodshed'. He was also worried about 'alienating the Ulster Protestants from me probably for ever, & whatever happens the result must be most detrimental for me personally & for the Crown in general'. He complained to Asquith that 'I cannot help feeling that the Government is drifting & taking me with it.'[9] He proposed a conference to attempt to prevent a civil war in Ireland.

The king's suggested conference, the Buckingham Palace Conference of July 1914, held as a far more deadly war in Europe loomed large, resulted in a breakdown, as many had predicted beforehand, over whether the excluded area should comprise 'six counties or four'.[10] While the Ulster unionist leader Edward Carson insisted 'he would certainly never agree to leave out Tyrone or Fermanagh', Redmond found it 'absurd and intolerable that while a majority of Unionists can exclude a county from the Irish Parliament, a majority of Nationalists should be refused the right to vote for their inclusion'.[11] The IPP was aghast that all the focus was on the large Protestant minorities in Tyrone and Fermanagh, while there was little mention of the larger Catholic minority in County Armagh. According to the 1911 census, Armagh had a higher percentage of Catholics (45.33 per cent) than Tyrone, Fermanagh or Derry city had of other denominations (44.6 per cent, 43.8 per cent and 43.8 per cent respectively).[12]

Table 1: 1911 Census of Ireland Religious Denominations in Ulster[13]

	Total	Catholic	Non-Catholic
County			
Antrim (exc. Belfast city)	193,864	39,751 (20.5%)	154,113 (79.5%)
Armagh	120,291	54,526 (45.33%)	65,765 (54.67%)
Cavan	91,173	74,271 (81.5%)	16,902 (18.5%)
Derry (exc. Derry city)	99,845	41,478 (41.5%)	58,367 (58.5%)
Donegal	168,537	133,021 (78.93%)	35,516 (21.07%)
Down	204,303	64,485 (31.6%)	139,818 (68.4%)
Fermanagh	61,836	34,740 (56.2%)	27,096 (43.8%)
Monaghan	71,455	53,363 (74.68%)	18,092 (25.32%)
Tyrone	142,665	79,015 (55.4%)	63,650 (44.6%)
Borough			
Belfast city	386,947	93,243 (24.1%)	293,704 (75.9%)
Derry city	40,780	22,923 (56.2%)	17,857 (43.8%)
Overall			
Ulster	1,581,696	690,816 (43.7%)	890,880 (56.3%)
Six Counties (NI)	1,250,531	430,161 (34.4%)	820,370 (65.6%)

As the First World War commenced, Home Rule was put on the statute book with two important provisos: 'on the one hand, a Suspensory Bill stipulated that the Home Rule Act would not come into operation until the end of the war; secondly, parliament had the Prime Minister's assurance that special provision must be made for Protestant Ulster.'[14]

Despite their previous reservations, in the summer of 1916 Redmond and the IPP leadership agreed to the temporary exclusion of six counties as Lloyd George tried to introduce a Home Rule scheme to be immediately implemented following the fallout from the Easter Rising. Opposition from Southern unionists and in Britain, as well as the discovery by the IPP of the duplicitous dealings of Lloyd George, who had promised Carson the permanent exclusion of the six counties, ended the agreement. However, divisions within Ulster nationalism started to appear openly due to the fact that parliamentary nationalists had agreed to the exclusion of Tyrone and Fermanagh, albeit temporarily, and that this exclusion would likely form the basis of any future proposals.[15]

Divisions appeared within Ulster unionism, too, as unionists from Counties Cavan, Donegal and Monaghan believed that the 1912 Solemn League and Covenant oath was compromised after the Ulster Unionist Council (UUC) supported the exclusion of six instead of all nine Ulster counties in Lloyd George's 1916 scheme.[16] This sense of abandonment was felt even more acutely in 1920 when, under the Government of Ireland Bill, instead of accepting the nine counties offered by the British government to form the devolved entity of Northern Ireland, the UUC insisted on six counties again. As Belfast-based MP Thomas Moles explained, the three counties had to be sacrificed in order to save the six: 'In a sinking ship, with life-boats sufficient for only two-thirds of the ship's company, were all to condemn themselves to death because all could not be saved?'[17]

Ulster unionists desired the largest area possible that would provide a secure permanent majority for unionists, but not too large an area that might threaten their control and leave them faced with the prospect of being 'outbred' by Catholics.[18] To avoid a nine-county parliament, leading Ulster unionist James Craig, who went on to become Northern

Ireland's first prime minister, even proposed a boundary commission. In December 1919, in a private conversation with the Conservative Minister for Pensions Laming Worthington-Evans, Craig suggested:

> [The establishment] of a Boundary Commission to examine the distribution of population along the borders of the whole of the six counties and to take a vote in districts on either side of and immediately adjoining that boundary in which there was a doubt whether they would prefer to be included in the Northern or Southern area. This proposal, carefully limited in its application, was commended as being in accord with the practice and principles adopted in the Peace Treaties.[19]

Another prominent Ulster unionist, Colonel Frederick Crawford, chief organiser of the 1914 Larne gunrunning, also favoured a boundary commission. In agreeing with Crawford in February 1920 that 'the Boundary Commission may be the best way out', Carson felt, however, 'a great deal of anxiety as to what they may do with portions of Co. Down, Fermanagh and Tyrone'.[20] Responding to another Crawford letter relating to a boundary commission in May 1920, he wrote, 'I greatly fear if we once begin to raise the question of partition of the County [of Donegal] there would be an attempt to take away parts of the Six Counties where the Nationalist majority prevails.'[21]

While the British government in late 1919/early 1920 considered the boundary commission proposal favourably, the issue was not pursued further due to fears that 'enquiries would produce unrest'. The 'consequences of that omission', historian Nicholas Mansergh argued in 1991, 'are with us to this day'.[22]

The British government acceded to the UUC's wishes to confine the Northern Parliament to six counties in the spring of 1920, just as the Government of Ireland Bill was being brought before the House of Commons.[23] Having not been consulted on a settlement that was less favourable than the 1914 Home Rule Act, which by 1920 was far below the minimum demanded by most of the Sinn Féin-supporting Irish public, unsurprisingly the Government of Ireland Act 1920 was rejected by the vast majority of the people in Ireland. Despite the considerable opposition, however, the British government carried on with the Act, but its provisions only ever became applicable to Northern Ireland. The British remained at war with the rest of Ireland, finally agreeing a truce with Sinn Féin in July 1921, shortly after Northern Ireland had been established two months earlier, in May.

Even though Northern Ireland was in existence and Ulster unionists believed they had secured their final settlement, its durability, even its continuance, was fluid. As Margaret O'Callaghan has written, 'at its very base, the status of Northern Ireland was ambivalent'.[24] The vulnerability of Northern Ireland's position was made apparent to James Craig just days after the Truce. Once the Truce came into force on 11 July, negotiations for a settlement began almost immediately between Sinn Féin and the British government. Four meetings were held in London between their respective leaders, Éamon de Valera and David Lloyd George, with the first one taking place on 14 July. Lloyd George offered de Valera dominion status for Southern Ireland 'with all sorts of important powers, but no Navy, no hostile tariffs, and no coercion of Ulster'.[25] Agreement was not reached, though, due mainly to Ulster. The leading Conservative, Andrew Bonar Law, who was recovering from a prolonged illness at the time, believed the biggest problem 'as always in the past, to be Ulster. I greatly fear that de Valera will find it impossible to treat Ulster as entirely outside his sphere.'[26] Bonar Law, who had played a prominent role in Ulster unionism's resistance to being included in a Dublin parliament during the Third Home Rule crisis, feared that Lloyd George might force unionists into one. This is exactly what Lloyd George attempted.

Craig was not involved in the talks between de Valera and Lloyd George that summer. He informed Alfred Cope, assistant under-secretary in Dublin Castle, 'I'm going to sit on Ulster like a rock, we are content with what we have got – let the Prime Minister and Sinn Fein settle this and if possible leave us out.'[27] He wanted to make Northern Ireland 'a new impregnable Pale'.[28] Craig believed that 'no coercion of Ulster' was among Lloyd George's non-negotiable commitments. On 18 July, however, Lloyd George put forward 'five suggestions to Craig and his ministers as to how they might accommodate de Valera's requirement of Irish unity with local autonomy for the north devolved from Dublin'.[29] However, the concerted efforts of Lloyd George, Conservative leader Austen Chamberlain, South African leader Jan Smuts and Alfred Cope to budge Craig were all in vain. After Craig and his colleagues emphatically rejected the suggestions, Lloyd George backed down.

In the British government's official offer of dominion status to de Valera on 20 July, the document stated that a settlement 'must allow for full recognition of the existing powers and privileges of the Parliament of Northern Ireland, which cannot be abrogated except by their own consent'.[30] This sentence was subsequently used extensively by Craig and his colleagues to refuse to co-operate with the Boundary Commission as it did not have the Northern government's consent.[31]

In rejecting the British government proposals on 2 August, de Valera demanded that any offer of dominion status would include Northern Ireland as part of the Irish dominion. Failing this, he demanded complete independence for Southern Ireland. De Valera was adamant that 'we cannot admit the right of the British government to mutilate our country, either in its own interest, or at the call of any section of our population'. He also ruled out the use of force against Ulster.[32] He followed up by stating in Dáil Éireann on 22 August, that they 'had not the power, and some of them had not the inclination, to use force with Ulster. He did not think that policy would be successful. They would be making the same mistake with that section as England had made with Ireland. He would not be responsible for such a policy.' For de Valera, 'if the Republic were recognised, he would be in favour of giving each county power to vote itself out of the Republic if it so wished'.[33]

According to John Bowman, the 'one "certain result" of the county option would have been the gain of Counties Tyrone and Fermanagh to the south at the expense of the north', something the Southern unionist

Lord Midleton 'believed that the Sinn Féin leadership was especially covetous of' and that there would be 'no more trouble' if they were transferred.[34]

While no agreement was reached between de Valera and Lloyd George, both sides remained engaged, the Truce held, and they agreed to a conference in London to negotiate a settlement. During the impasse between de Valera's talks with Lloyd George in July and the negotiations that started in October 1921, Sinn Féin established a committee to 'collect, compile and arrange ... statements of fact and argument bearing on the position of Ulster'. It had the remit to address the 'challenge which Ulster posed to the Sinn Féin cabinet' and 'devise a policy tolerable both to their own supporters and to the British government and which could also be imposed on the Ulster unionists'.[35] The suggestion by some Northern Sinn Féin members to set up an advisory body of experts on the North, to support the negotiation team in London, was not taken up, however.[36]

Much has been written about the Treaty negotiations from October to December 1921, with many arguing that Sinn Féin was primarily interested in issues related to sovereignty and the Crown, and not in the issue of partition. In Lord Longford's account of the Treaty, *Peace by Ordeal*, for example, he contended that, for Sinn Féin, 'Ulster was not the main issue, as can be seen from the negligible time spent in the Dail debate over the Ulster provisions of the Treaty' and was instead 'a strange abstract factor in tactics'.[37] Given the amount of time and energy spent on Ulster before and during the negotiations, most of it instigated by Sinn Féin, this stance does not bear up under scrutiny. It is important to note, though, that while Sinn Féin cared deeply about the essential unity of Ireland, it lacked a coherent policy on Ulster and was unable to press home its advantage on the British government's reluctance to break up the negotiations over the province.

During the Treaty negotiations, the two primary issues discussed were Ulster and the Crown. Despite Northern Ireland being an established polity since May 1921, the Irish plenipotentiaries, led by

Arthur Griffith and Michael Collins, were successful in reopening the Ulster question. The Irish delegation's position was that 'the unimpaired unity of Ireland is a condition precedent to the conclusion of a Treaty of Association between Ireland and the nations of the British Commonwealth' as articulated in a memorandum it presented to the British in late October.[38]

With the Treaty negotiations commencing on 11 October, partition formed the basis for discussion during the fourth and fifth sessions, held on 14 and 17 October respectively.[39] At the session on 14 October, Collins was the first person to mention the possibility of a boundary commission being constituted to deal with Ulster, saying, 'There might be a plan for a boundary commission, or for local option, or whatever you may call it. It is not intended to use force, not because Ulster would not be defeated in a fight, but because defeat would not settle the matter.'[40]

At the fifth session it was apparent that the Irish delegates' focus was on the areas in Northern Ireland with large nationalist majorities. Griffith claimed that if the Northern government refused their 'reasonable proposals, then people must be entitled to choose freely whether they will come with us or remain under the Northern Parliament'. Another Irish delegate, George Gavan Duffy, stated, 'If the Orange Party in Belfast knew that they could not retain Fermanagh and Tyrone it would be much easier for us to come to terms with them at a round table,' adding that the 'English Government should say that there had been a mistake and that the six counties could not be retained … every capital town in the six counties, except Belfast, was controlled by us.' Collins stated, 'freedom of choice must be secured in order to enable the people to say whether they would come with us or remain under the Northern Parliament'.[41]

In a memorandum the Irish delegation sent to the British negotiators on 24 October, its policy on Ulster was further crystallised: 'Should we fail to come to an agreement [with Ulster unionists], and we are confident we shall not fail, then freedom of choice must be given to electorates within the area.' On the same day Griffith wrote to de Valera in Dublin, saying that the British must fight on the Crown, but 'I told them that the only possibility of Ireland considering Association of any kind with Crown was in exchange for essential Unity.'[42]

With the Irish delegation stating that its allegiance to Crown and Empire was contingent on Ireland's 'essential unity', Lloyd George and others within the British government pushed to change Northern Ireland's status. Lloyd George told Griffith and Collins that 'he could carry a six county parliament subordinate to a national Parliament'.[43] He was probably being disingenuous here, as James Craig had emphatically rejected similar proposals by him in July. Lloyd George also assured Griffith and Collins that he would resign 'if Ulster proved unreasonable', rather than use force against Ireland.[44] But his secretary, fellow Welshman Thomas (Tom) Jones, added the threatening caveat that the returning Bonar Law would then probably form a government and would introduce Crown colony government for the South for a couple of months.[45]

During the negotiations, Lloyd George had to expend as much energy in soothing unionist (both Ulster and Conservative) fears as he did in negotiating with Sinn Féin. While, as Ronan Fanning has written, Craig and Bonar Law were not 'the elephants in the room', they were 'the elephants outside the door'.[46] Lloyd George's government had been re-elected in a landslide in December 1918. However, most of the seats in the coalition were won by the Conservatives: 339 in contrast to 136 seats for Lloyd George's Coalition Liberals. Afterwards Lloyd George 'was sensitive to his own vulnerability in the House and felt himself on occasion to be a prisoner of the Coalition'.[47] This was apparent during the Treaty negotiations. The make-up of the British negotiation team suited Lloyd George, as many of the diehards within the Conservative Party were absent. Bonar Law was absent due to illness. Walter Long, who had delivered the Government of Ireland Act 1920, had retired earlier in 1921, and Arthur Balfour, arguably the most intransigent Tory, was sent away for the final phases of the Treaty negotiations by Lloyd George to a naval conference in Washington from November 1921 to February 1922. Even though they were considered diehards, Winston Churchill and Lord Birkenhead (F.E. Smith) were included because 'they were too dangerous to leave out'.[48]

Lloyd George himself was ambivalent about what terms would be agreed – he just wanted an agreement, reminding his colleagues, 'We are after a settlement – that [is] our objective.'[49] He was hampered, though, by elements within the Conservative Party who supported the Ulster unionists. In the House of Commons on 7 November, Lloyd George was asked for assurances by Antrim-born Conservative MP Sir William Davison that he would not force the government and people of Northern Ireland 'into surrendering any of the territory or rights granted to them by the Government of Ireland Act'.[50] Lloyd George had survived a censure vote just days earlier, after 'roughly three dozen Tory MPs tabled a motion demanding that the government abandon its talks with Sinn Fein and work the 1920 Act'.[51]

Working in tandem with diehard Tory opposition was the diehard Tory press. *The Morning Post* devoted much of its 31 October edition to 'British Generosity and Irish Ingratitude' since 1916. It wrote of 'the foul methods of the Sinn Fein rebels' who used men, woman and children as shields while the rebels 'fire at Crown forces or throw bombs'. After 'The Great Surrender' (the Truce), the newspaper was astonished that some of 'these men are now of the Downing Street tea party'. De Valera was described as 'an alien', born 'in a low quarter of New York'. Against the name of Collins, formerly known as 'Mysterious Mike', 'stand charged several ambushes in Dublin with their cost of over 70 lives'. Rounding off its invective was an editorial describing the situation

> as that of 'a motor-car with one wheel over a precipice'; and yet the cry is still 'Go forward!' Ulster is now to be dragged in, and Tyrone and Fermanagh are to be offered to the rebels in a desperate attempt to placate them ... The motor-car is hanging over a precipice, or, as we put it the other day, is foundered above the axles in an Irish bog.[52]

Even though, as Churchill explained, 'We can't give way on the six counties ... we are not free agents,' Lloyd George met and corresponded with

Craig in November to try and squeeze him into accepting an all-Ireland parliament.[53] Austen Chamberlain thought it was possible for the British government to convince Craig to accept an all-Ireland parliament, saying at the time to his wife, Ivy, that it would be difficult, if not impossible, for Craig to govern Tyrone and Fermanagh 'with their Sinn Fein majorities'.[54]

In a letter from Lloyd George to Craig on 10 November, he proposed that the 'Government of Northern Ireland would retain all the powers conferred upon her by the Government of Ireland Act', but the 'unity of Ireland would be recognised by the establishment of an all-Ireland Parliament'.[55] He emphasised the financial disadvantages of staying out of such a parliament, writing, 'Customs barriers would have to be established between Northern and Southern Ireland over a jagged line of frontier,' adding that the 'difficulty of working any such arrangement would be unceasing, the cost considerable, and the vexation to traders continuous.' Moreover, 'the finance of the Government of Ireland Act would necessarily have to be recast' and the 'people of Northern Ireland would have to bear their proportionate share of all Imperial burdens, such as the Army, Navy and other Imperial Services, in common with the taxpayer of the United Kingdom'.[56]

In explaining his rationale for potentially imposing financial 'penalties' on the North for staying out of an all-Ireland parliament, Lloyd George told his secretary and mistress, Frances Stevenson, 'They have their hands on their hearts all the time, but if it comes to touching their pockets, they quickly slap their hands in them. I know ... My wife is a Presbyterian.'[57]

Craig did not budge, writing to Lloyd George on 11 November emphatically rejecting an all-Ireland parliament, stating, 'Such a Parliament is precisely what Ulster has for many years resisted by all the means at her disposal, and her detestation of it is in no degree diminished by the local institutions conferred upon her by the Act of 1920.' He added, 'The feelings of the loyal population of Ulster are so pronounced and so universal on this point that no Government representing that population could enter into any Conference where this point is open to discussion.'

Much to the annoyance of Lloyd George and others in the British government, including Bonar Law, Craig suggested that Northern Ireland should also have dominion status, showing there was some flexibility in the North on its relationship with the Empire.[58] When Griffith heard about Craig's desire for Northern Ireland to have dominion status, he claimed it was proof of 'Ulster's sordidness', all 'for the sake of a lower income tax'.[59]

Writing at the time to Craig, Fred Crawford stated, 'If there is any attempt made to put Ulster under Dublin, more than what is in the present Bill by the powers granted to the Council of Ireland, Ulster will not stand it, and there will be hell to pay.' The Council of Ireland, to be made up of twenty members from each Irish parliament, was to adjudicate on issues of common concern to the two Irish jurisdictions, such as railways, fisheries and diseases of animals. Crawford did express an openness to changing the boundary, saying, 'As I mentioned to the "Chief" [Carson] in 1916, if feasible, an alteration of the six county boundary could be offered – parts of Fermanagh and Armagh in exchange for a cut out of Cavan, Monaghan, and East Donegal.' He believed it was 'quite possible the Sinn Feiners in Tyrone will try and be cut out by a corridor similar to what the Allies have arranged in Siliesa [sic]. Of course this will be a most difficult point to settle, even if it be not quite impossible.'[60]

As Lloyd George was trying to convince Craig to allow Northern Ireland to join an all-Ireland parliament, he granted him a considerable concession. Northern Ireland's vulnerable position at its inception was augmented by the non-transference of powers to the new political entity. It had no control over policing, local government or education, all powers needed for it to function as a viable government. However, on 5 November, Lloyd George agreed to transfer government services to the North, scheduled to be transferred from 22 November 1921 to 1 February 1922.[61]

The transfer of law-and-order powers gave the Northern government control over the Royal Irish Constabulary (RIC) in the six counties, as well as remobilising the Ulster Special Constabulary, established in late

1920, which had been partly demobilised since the Truce. The Specials were organised into three classes: the 'A' class were full-time uniformed police auxiliaries; the 'B' were employed on a part-time basis and allowed to keep their weapons at home; the 'C' were only to be called out for emergencies such as invasions. According to Robert Lynch, while officially Northern Catholics were allowed to join the force, few did or were actively encouraged to do so. Right from the beginning, Northern nationalists saw the Specials as being 'nothing more and nothing less that the dregs of the Orange lodges, armed and equipped to overawe Nationalists and Catholics, and with ... an inclination to invent "crimes" against Nationalists and Catholics'.[62] By early 1922, one in six Protestant males in the North were members of the Specials.[63]

The move to transfer services to the Northern government and its timing calls into question Lloyd George's genuine commitment to securing Irish unity. Why did he not hold out on transferring powers until he got something from Craig in return? Kevin Matthews has noted that to 'retain the loyalty of Tory backbenchers' during a Commons censure vote in late October, 'Lloyd George gave in to a demand for the transfer of executive power to the Northern Ireland government'.[64] But for such a skilful negotiator, he too readily transferred these vital powers to Northern Ireland without securing any concessions that could have progressed his negotiations with Sinn Féin.

The Irish delegation had been aware that the Northern jurisdiction was not fully functioning when the conference began in October, but it appeared unaware of how to use this to its advantage. Without the transference of services, such as policing and education, the Northern government was essentially a government in name only, and yet the Sinn Féin plenipotentiaries did not press the British on the topic during the negotiations. The significance of services being transferred to the North seems to have been lost on almost all of those back in Dublin too.[65]

With the avenue of reaching a settlement by pressurising Craig now closed, Lloyd George looked to squeeze the Sinn Féin delegation instead. In a meeting with Griffith and Collins on 8 November, Tom Jones 'threw out the suggestion of the Southern Parliament plus Boundary Commission'. Griffith responded that he would prefer a plebiscite and Collins said he 'did not like the suggestion at all because it sacrificed unity entirely'. As Griffith was not 'alarmed at the proposal', Jones promised 'to sound the PM upon it', and, seeing Griffith again the following day, told him 'that the PM was prepared to play the Boundary Commission as an absolutely last card if he could feel sure that Sinn Fein would take it, if Ulster accepted'. Griffith replied, 'It is not our proposal' and said that he would prefer a plebiscite, 'but in essentials a Boundary Commission is very much the same. It would have to be not for Tyrone and Fermanagh only but for the Six Counties.'[66]

Initially, the openness of Griffith to a boundary commission, by not rejecting it outright, was a tactical move 'to deprive "Ulster" of support in England by showing it was utterly unreasonable in insisting to coerce areas that wished to get out'.[67] He believed there would be benefits to it, writing to de Valera that a boundary commission 'would give us most of Tyrone, Fermanagh, and part of Armagh, Down, etc.'[68] Griffith naively interpreted his own assurances on a commission as a ploy to help Lloyd George secure Irish unity.

According to Matthews, the 'idea for a Boundary Commission was initially put to Griffith with only the six counties in mind. Jones was later told to make it plain that the Commission's writ must apply to all nine Ulster counties, and he claimed that he passed this information along to the Irish leader.'[69] In correspondence with de Valera on 12 November, Griffith mentioned he had a meeting with Lloyd George alone that afternoon. The prime minister showed Griffith the letter exchanges with Craig, with Griffith writing to de Valera that if Northern Ireland refused to join an all-Ireland parliament, 'their area would be delimited and the part that desired to remain in the British Parliament would have to bear the same taxation as England'.[70] While Lloyd George, in his letters to Craig, had mentioned harsher financial terms for the North if it was not part of a dominion with the rest of Ireland, there was no mention of delimiting any area, at least in the official letters. However, Tom Jones recorded that in a conversation between Lloyd George and Craig on 10 November, on Fermanagh and Tyrone, Lloyd George said 'it made all the difference whether you regarded the problem from the point of view of All-Ireland or two separate Parliaments. From latter standpoint, case of Sinn Fein was overwhelming. If All-Ireland, position of Tyrone and Fermanagh not so important.' Jones also mentioned that Edward Carson suggested a boundary commission was 'a defensible position', with Carson claiming, on balance, 'Ulster would gain'.[71]

According to Keith Middlemas, who edited Tom Jones's Whitehall diaries, Lloyd George asked Chamberlain and Jones to put what they were claiming was an agreement with Griffith over a boundary commission into a short memorandum, and when Lloyd George showed this document to Griffith on 13 November, the latter 'approved its contents'.[72] The contents of the paper were:

> If Ulster did not see her way to accept immediately the principle of a Parliament of all Ireland ... it would be necessary to revise the boundary of Northern Ireland. This might be done by a Boundary Commission which would be directed to adjust the line both by inclusion and exclusion so as to make the boundary conform as closely as possible to the wishes of the inhabitants.[73]

This seemingly trivial piece of paper came back to haunt Griffith and the rest of the Irish delegation as the negotiations reached their climax on 5/6 December. Regardless of whether Griffith consented to the proposals on Ulster or not, as Lord Longford has pointed out, 'the existence of a document made things so very much more definite'.[74] Believing the lead Sinn Féin plenipotentiary Griffith, at the very least, would not break on Ulster, the British were able to focus their energies on Crown and Empire.

There is some dispute about the supposed meeting and memorandum of 13 November, with Colum Kenny arguing that there is no evidence of any meeting taking place between Griffith and Lloyd George on that date or that Chamberlain and Jones drew up a memorandum. Instead, he believes that one drawn up by Lionel Curtis earlier in November was used to advance the boundary commission concept. Curtis was a Colonial Office advisor on Irish affairs from 1921 to 1924 who played a key role during the Treaty negotiations and subsequently on British government policy relating to the Boundary Commission. Kenny refutes Lord Longford's assertion that Griffith 'had been duped by Chamberlain', saying he 'was neither a dupe nor a knave, and made no such secret deal'.[75]

In the tentative suggestions for a Treaty presented by Jones to Griffith on 16 November, a boundary commission was included amongst the terms, stating that should Northern Ireland not join an all-Ireland parliament, 'a commission shall be appointed to determine in accordance with the wishes of the inhabitants the boundaries between Northern Ireland and the rest of Ireland'.[76] Unlike the actual Treaty, there were no economic or geographic conditions included in the wording, nor was there any specific reference to the British government appointing the chairman of a commission. According to Paul Murray, what was originally a straightforward process afterwards became 'open to an unpredictable variety of interpretations, and made to depend in the final analysis on the character and outlook of a chairman appointed by one of the parties'.[77]

John Chartres, who served as legal adviser to the Sinn Féin delegation, later claimed that during the negotiations in which the Boundary Commission was discussed, 'the limiting words as to economic and geographical considerations were introduced ... only to meet the difficulty of isolated "islands" as indicated by Mr. Lloyd George himself – e.g. the Nationalist district in the Glens of Antrim'. In a conference where the 'English delegates were present in full force', Chartres was adamant that the 'whole of the arguments of the Irish delegation, illustrated by a series of careful maps, went to show that there was no question of slight rectification and that the transfer of substantial areas was involved', a position that 'was fully accepted by the English representatives'.[78] One of the Sinn Féin plenipotentiaries, Robert Barton, also verified the understanding amongst the Irish delegates that economic and geographic limitations were added specifically for isolated 'islands', writing, 'We agreed that islands, such as West Belfast, would vote themselves into Southern Ireland, and we agreed that it would be administratively impossible for such an area to come into Southern Ireland. Voting in or out would have to be by contiguous areas.'[79]

The Sinn Féin delegation followed up on the British government's 16 November tentative Treaty suggestions with its own memorandum on 22 November, noting at the start of the document that 'the proposals are put forward on the assumption that the essential unity of Ireland is maintained'. It stated that if Northern Ireland accepted 'its position under the National Parliament', it would retain its existing powers. Ireland 'will undertake to provide the safeguards designed to secure any special interests of the area over which it functions'.[80] There was no mention of what would happen if Northern Ireland did not accept its position under an all-Ireland parliament. There also was no commitment to Crown or Empire. The British threatened to cancel the negotiations over the memorandum, with an outraged Lloyd George spewing, 'This time it is the Sinn Feiners. Last week it was the Ulsterites. They are both the sons of Belial!'[81]

The following day, in a meeting in Downing Street on Ulster and the Boundary Commission between Griffith, Collins and Barton on the Irish side and Lloyd George, Chamberlain and Lord Birkenhead on the British side, according to Griffith, 'Lloyd George declared that I had assured him I would not let him down, if he put up the proposals subsequently embodied in their memorandum to Craig, and we had not embodied them in our memorandum.' Griffith replied that he 'had given him that assurance and I now repeated it, but I told him at the time it was his proposal – not ours'.[82]

Despite the threats of a breakdown, both sides kept talking. The British government delivered a draft treaty to Griffith on 30 November. Under Article 13 of this draft treaty, if Northern Ireland chose to opt out of an all-Ireland parliament, 'a Commission shall be appointed by the British Government to determine in accordance with the wishes of the inhabitants, so far as may be compatible with economic and geographic conditions, the boundaries between Northern Ireland and the rest of Ireland'.[83]

While the economic and geographic limitations were included in this draft, the British government proposed that it alone would appoint the Commission. Annotated notes of a draft of this proposal, believed to be Arthur Griffith's, read, 'Suggest 1 man from us', one from the North-East and one, the chairman, from the British government.[84] While it was clearly better than having all the commissioners nominated by the British government, to suggest that the chairman, the most decisive role, should be nominated by the British government was a serious miscalculation by Griffith, particularly as other post-First World War boundary commissions in Europe had independent chairmen. They were 'presided over by a person chosen from a country which had no vested interest in the disposition of the territory in dispute'. In the case of Upper Silesia, 'the League of Nations commissioned a report from representatives of four countries without a vested interest in the Silesian question: Belgium, Brazil, China and Spain'.[85]

In a revision of the British proposed treaty, delivered on 2 December, in the Boundary Commission clause that was ultimately included in the Treaty, instead of the Commission being appointed by the British government, the clause was changed to 'a Commission consisting of three persons, one to be appointed by the Government of the Irish Free State, one to be appointed by the Government of Northern Ireland and one who shall be Chairman to be appointed by the British Government'. In Michael Collins's notes, he wrote 'No re Commission.'[86]

Lloyd George insisted on a deadline date of Tuesday 6 December for the talks to conclude. There is little evidence of much pushback on this deadline from the Irish side. All the exhausted Irish plenipotentiaries returned to Dublin for a Cabinet meeting on 3 December to discuss the draft treaty in the Mansion House. It turned out to be a very fractious meeting, a harbinger of what was to come just days later. While most of the division centred on the oath and Empire, Barton believed the 'Treaty would not give Dominion Status nor any guarantee re Ulster.' Collins said,

'Sacrifices to N.E. Ulster made for sake of essential unity and justified.' De Valera stated that the Treaty 'could not be accepted in its then form. He personally could not subscribe to the Oath of Allegiance nor could he sign any document which would give N.E. Ulster power to vote itself out of the Irish State.'[87] According to the Dáil Minister for Home Affairs, Austin Stack, de Valera 'said he might understand Mr. Griffith giving up Independence for National Unity, but "you have got neither this nor that"'.[88]

The Cabinet agreed that Griffith would 'inform Mr. Lloyd George that the document could not be signed, to state that it is now a matter for the Dail, and to try and put the blame on Ulster'. And all, except Austin Stack and Cathal Brugha, agreed 'that the Delegation be empowered to meet Sir James Craig if they should think necessary'.[89] This never happened.

Speaking in 1963, de Valera stated that if legal experts had looked at the Boundary Commission clause before the Treaty was signed, 'the trap in Article 12 would, I am sure, have been noticed – the trap by which the qualifying phrase "so far as may be compatible with economic and geographic conditions" was used ultimately to nullify, as a whole, the provision "in accordance with the wishes of the inhabitants"'.[90] While he was not minded to seek legal advice himself before the Treaty was signed, on 3 December, the day of the Cabinet meeting in Dublin, Griffith brought up the references to economic and geographic conditions in the Boundary Commission clause with John O'Byrne, legal adviser to the Sinn Féin delegation in London, who subsequently became attorney general of the Irish Free State. O'Byrne 'expressed deep reservations about this reading, explaining that the clause as it stood did not necessarily mean what Griffith thought it did, and that it was too vague to admit of a single unequivocal interpretation'. He 'suggested an alteration in the clause which would at least delimit the territorial units to be considered in applying it'.[91] There is no evidence that Griffith pursued the points raised by O'Byrne, and he ultimately accepted the ambiguous wording as it stood.

Much of the drama, as it unfolded from Sunday 4 December to just after 2 a.m. on Tuesday 6 December in London, centred around the

Boundary Commission clause. Lloyd George had a private meeting with Collins on 5 December, with Collins saying he was 'perfectly dissatisfied' with the British proposals, particularly 'with the position as regards the North East'. Afterwards Collins wrote:

> He [Lloyd George] remarked that I myself pointed out on a previous occasion that the North would be forced economically to come in. I assented but I said the position was so serious ... that for my part I was anxious to secure a definite reply from Craig and his Colleagues, and that I was as agreeable to a reply rejecting as accepting. In view of the former we would save Tyrone and Fermanagh, parts of Derry, Armagh and Down by the Boundary Commission.[92]

The belief of Collins, as well as Griffith, that the financial penalties Northern Ireland would incur were likely to force it into Irish unity, was based on the stereotype believed by many in the South of the hard-headed Ulster businessman who made his decisions based on his pocket rather than his heart. Lloyd George also appeared to share that belief, but like everything else with him, it is difficult to be sure. Even though Craig and his colleagues were always very conscious of economic matters and, as shown by Craig's proposal of the North obtaining dominion status, were willing to weaken core principles for financial benefit, their hatred of and insistence on having nothing to do with a Dublin parliament overrode everything else. This failure by Collins, Griffith and, indeed, de Valera, to grasp the revulsion that Ulster unionists felt towards Dublin, and to believe that divisions were caused solely by the British, led to a series of miscalculations before and during the Treaty negotiations. Their successors in the Cumann na nGaedheal Free State government would make the same mistake in their dealings with the Boundary Commission in subsequent years.

Lloyd George's notorious duplicity was on full display on 5 December. After leading Collins to believe that they shared the same interpretation of the Boundary Commission clauses, hours later 'he assured his Cabinet colleagues that the Boundary Commission would provide for nothing more than "a re-adjustment of the boundaries"'.[93]

With Collins appeased, the stage was set for the final act, which took place in the early hours of the morning of Tuesday 6 December. Lloyd George supposedly produced the memorandum written by Tom Jones on 13 November (as disputed by Kenny, see above) to which Griffith had in essence assented, a memorandum of which the other Irish plenipotentiaries were unaware. According to Keith Middlemas, Griffith, 'confronted with it as a matter of honour ... abandoned his attempt to break on this issue, and with superb artistry, Lloyd George then offered the Free State full fiscal autonomy – the right, if they wished, to impose a tariff'.[94] While little attention has been paid to the financial clauses of the Treaty, their impact was far-reaching. They allowed the Irish Free State to devise its own fiscal policies and tariffs separate from the United Kingdom, and resulted in the Free State being able to introduce customs barriers, which it did in 1923.[95] Collins subsequently stated it was 'the most valuable part of the Treaty'.[96]

Griffith was also very happy with gaining fiscal autonomy and vowed that he personally would sign the Treaty, regardless of whether Craig replied on the Ulster provisions or not. Ronan Fanning has given a damning indictment of that decision of Griffith's, writing, 'For the head of the delegation in a two-party negotiation suddenly to announce during the negotiations that he intends to sign the document under negotiation because his honour was allegedly impugned, regardless of whether the other members of his delegation did so, was as vain as it was naïve.'[97] After Lloyd George's last flourish of producing two letters for Craig, one for war within three days, the other for peace, and insisting that all the Irish plenipotentiaries must sign if there was to be peace, the rest followed Griffith and, without referring back to the Dáil Cabinet as agreed, signed the Anglo-Irish Treaty. Speaking of the drama of that night/morning, Churchill wrote, 'Michael Collins rose looking as if he was going to shoot someone, preferably himself. In all my life I have never seen so much passion and suffering in restraint.'[98] For Churchill, after the tumultuous years of the First World War, which had changed the world map, his government arrived back to where it was in July 1914, seeing 'the dreary steeples of Fermanagh and Tyrone emerge again'.[99]

The idea of a boundary commission was not a new one nor necessarily a bad one from Sinn Féin's perspective, although the belief which developed that the transfer of large areas from the North to the South would leave the remaining territory an unviable rump was deeply flawed, as the industrial heartbeat of Northern Ireland was Belfast and its hinterlands, not the west and south of the six counties. Northern Ireland could have survived economically without Tyrone and Fermanagh. Also, and paradoxically, the more the Boundary Commission favoured the nationalist case, the smaller the nationalist population that would remain in Northern Ireland, and thus the case for national unity would be diminished, something of which those nationalists farthest away from the border, in places like Belfast, were acutely aware.

While the Boundary Commission was viewed as a major concession to Sinn Féin, the details and wording of the clause agreed to in the Treaty would prove to be disastrous for the party and particularly for Northern nationalists close to the border. While the plenipotentiaries were not partitionists and genuinely sought a united Ireland, they erred greatly by acceding to such a vague clause, which was riddled with ambiguities. No timetable was mentioned, nor was a method outlined on how to ascertain the wishes of inhabitants, 'how exactly economic and geographic conditions would relate to popular opinion, and which would prove most important'.[100] Moreover, the areas and sizes of the units (small areas like district electoral divisions or entire counties) to be considered for transfer were not decided upon.

Although Lloyd George insisted during the negotiations that the Boundary Commission should cover nine rather than six counties and would involve exclusion as well as inclusion of Free State territory, this was not included in the wording of the Treaty. Even though there were some efforts by Collins and Griffith to seek a local plebiscite, this argument was not forcefully insisted upon. Given the importance of plebiscites for other boundary commissions happening at the time, particularly the one in Upper Silesia, which took place in March 1921, the Sinn Féin plenipotentiaries could and should have demanded such a vote to ascertain the wishes of the inhabitants of the areas in question. Essentially, the clause was open to many different interpretations, all to be decided ultimately by a British-appointed chairman.

What is particularly surprising is the lack of legal scrutiny the Sinn Féin plenipotentiaries gave to the vague Boundary Commission clause and how it compared or not to other boundary commissions in Europe. Recognising the defects of its drafting, Tom Jones later wrote that although 'there were half a dozen famous lawyers among the plenipotentiaries, it is notorious that a lawyer cannot draft his own Will clearly'.[101] Other than Griffith's conversation with John O'Byrne on 3 December, there is little evidence of any other legal advice being sought or offered. Considering the fact that the Treaty was an international treaty, a legally binding agreement, this is astonishing. Griffith and Collins just accepted that large parts of Northern Ireland would be transferred to the Irish Free State.

Some reasons have been put forward for 'the many loose ends' of Article 12. Tom Jones believed 'the article was hurriedly composed by the principal negotiators as opportunity offered and without officials (excluded because of [Erskine] Childers) and, as a result, despite the presence of the Lord Chancellor [Lord Birkenhead] and other lawyers, by inadvertence imprecisely and ambiguously drafted'.[102] Many believe the ambiguity was deliberate.

The Free State government and particularly Northern nationalists ended up being spurned by the 'loose draughtsmanship' of Article 12.[103] The Northern government, on the other hand, was able to take advantage of it. The article stipulated that each of the governments of Britain, the Irish Free State and Northern Ireland were to appoint a commissioner. Nothing was mentioned about what would happen if one or more of the governments chose not to appoint its commissioner, which the Northern government decided to do as it was not a party to, nor had it given its consent to, the Treaty. This, another example of clumsy draughting, endangered the British government more than anything else during the long Boundary Commission saga.

The British civil servant Lionel Curtis described Lloyd George's negotiating with the Irish as being 'like Augustus John drawing. Every stroke was made with precision and mastery, and never needed correction.' Tom Jones summarised Lloyd George's achievement: 'In essentials we have given nothing that was not in the July proposals.'[104] This was not entirely true, as there were some key differences between what was on offer in July and what was agreed in December. Firstly, on top of being offered full dominion status, the controversial oath Irish Members of Parliament had to take was not the 'full-blooded' oath that members in other dominions had to swear. Full economic independence with the ability to raise tariffs on British goods was also agreed. And the inclusion of a boundary commission under Article 12 of the Treaty was not on offer in July. But on the Boundary Commission, Lloyd George deftly lured Griffith and Collins into a trap. They took Lloyd George's word and the impression he gave that he agreed with their interpretation of the Commission, but the ambiguous wording of the clause allowed the British to change their interpretation, which they did almost immediately after the Treaty was signed, and continued to do right up until late 1925.

While the Treaty enhanced Lloyd George's reputation as a negotiator, it also confirmed to many his deceitful, duplicitous and dishonest persona. The Sinn Féin plenipotentiaries would not have signed the Treaty if they had not believed that large areas of the North were going to be transferred to the South. That they did sign was partly due to Lloyd George's deceitfulness but mostly due to their own foolishness. The mistakes they made effectively destroyed any chance of an acceptable solution to partition for many nationalists.

Chapter Two

'The root of all evil'

SPEAKING TO WINSTON CHURCHILL IN May 1922, James Craig claimed:

> The Boundary Commission is the root of all evil. If you picture Loyalists on the borderland being asked by us to hang on with their teeth for the safety of the Province, you can also picture their unspoken cry to us, 'if we sacrifice our lives and our property for the sake of the Province, are you going to assent to a Commission which may subsequently by a stroke of the pen, take away the very area you now ask us to defend?'[1]

Craig and most other Ulster unionists focused their opposition to the Treaty on the proposed Boundary Commission, which would be established once the North inevitably chose to opt out of the Irish Free State at the first opportunity, in December 1922. Although Ulster unionists were not party to the Treaty, they were now obliged to adhere to its clauses. The Boundary Commission reopened old wounds believed settled in 1920. As Robert Lynch has noted, unionists' fears over the Treaty, which heightened their growing mistrust of the British government, led them 'to a whole new focus on military solutions to the partition question in the first six months of 1922'.[2]

Craig's predecessor as the Ulster Unionist leader, Edward Carson, violently attacked the Treaty during his maiden speech to the House of Lords on 14 December 1921, although more so for the financial clauses than the Boundary Commission, criticising the British government for 'surrendering' to Sinn Féin by conceding too much to republicans in offering dominion status. However, the speech was not an anti-partition rant as many have since claimed. In it, Carson deplored 'the pressure being put on Ulster to join with the South', accusing the British government of betraying 'Ulster'.[3]

Lloyd George was bemused at Carson's bitterness, saying, 'He agreed, if he did not propose, the Boundary Commission.' He also claimed that Ulster had nothing to complain about: 'We have emancipated her and it was very unfair of Craig to talk of betrayal.'[4]

The Ulster unionist press, while reluctantly accepting elements of the Treaty, was opposed to the Boundary Commission provision and the threat it posed to the North. In its editorial on 7 December 1921, the *Belfast News-Letter* objected to any revision of the boundary line. It particularly objected to the idea that the Boundary Commission could revise the boundary based on population, as Lord Birkenhead alluded to, writing, 'The Unionists in Fermanagh and Tyrone Counties are a permanent population, while a large percentage of the other side are in temporary residence as farm servants, drawn from the border counties in Southern Ireland.' Using arguments that were later utilised by unionists when giving evidence to the Boundary Commission, the newspaper added, 'three-fourths of the taxation and rating valuation of these two counties is Unionist. The counting of heads is not the only factor in the matter.' Believing the Boundary Commission was imposed 'as a penalty upon Ulster for refusing to come under an All-Ireland Parliament', it concluded that those who signed the Treaty were 'men without conscience, and who do not intend justice'.[5]

The Northern Whig and Belfast Post was scathing of the Ulster provisions of the Treaty, writing that the British government had 'agreed to coerce Ulster for the satisfaction of their new Sinn Fein friends'. 'As soon as

Ulster's decision to remain mistress of her own household is given' by opting out of the Free State, a boundary commission would be set up, and on 'that body Ulster will be in a minority of one. It will have the power to cut and carve – not Tyrone and Fermanagh only, but the whole of the six counties. It might even allot the Falls district to the Irish Free State.' It concluded, 'Not by such despicable trickery and Judas-like treachery will the stalwart Loyalists of Northern Ireland be inveigled into a course antipathetic to their most deep-seated convictions, their most cherished ideals.'[6]

In its 8 December 1921 editorial, the *Belfast Telegraph* claimed that 'Ulster stands in a position of grave peril, and that we have been betrayed; that the great Unionist [Conservative] party has practically deserted us, and left us to our fate' by supporting the British government's proposals 'to emasculate the Parliament conferred upon us, truncate its powers and delimit its area'.[7]

Many unionists within Northern Ireland were apprehensive about the dangers posed by the Boundary Commission, with Lillian Spender, the wife of Northern Ireland Cabinet Secretary Wilfrid Spender, believing 'this past week, since the publication of the "Treaty" has been the most depressing I have ever known over here. Up to the last I don't think we ever really believed England would do this thing – would reward murder & treachery & treason & crime of all kinds, & penalise loyalty'. Her friend Mrs Erskine told her, 'It was the saddest day of her life. "England doesn't want us."' Spender feared that 'worse is to come, & further pledges are to be broken, for two of the six counties may be taken from us – Tyrone & Fermanagh'.[8]

Commenting on the Treaty negotiations when they were ongoing, Craig had said, 'that Ulster is not a cheese to be nibbled at. It is a rock of granite which will break the teeth of those mice who attempt to bite it, whether they are Sinn Feiners or any other.'[9] There was some flexibility to this 'not an inch' strategy in the days and weeks immediately following the Treaty, though. In meetings with Lloyd George and Chamberlain in December 1921, Craig's wife, Cecil, claimed that he insisted that 'on no account' would he give up part of the six counties. However, there is evidence that at the same time he considered appointing a commissioner if the British government would agree to provide 'full compensation' to any unionist being transferred to the Free State.[10] He was more forthright in a letter to Chamberlain on 15 December, writing, 'I could, I believe, have carried the people of Ulster with me towards a peaceful settlement had it not been for the inclusion in the terms of a proposal to set up a Boundary Commission.' He also threatened to use 'Loyalists and members of the "Loyal Orange Institution" in resisting coercion by the Irish Free State'.[11]

At a Northern Cabinet meeting on 10 January 1922, the first time it met after the Treaty was signed, the Unionist government ministers reflected on and weighed up their options for participating, or not, in the Boundary Commission. By not participating, although it would make the government 'very popular' in Northern Ireland for a time, having no input might mean that 'Ulster would lose a larger area than if she had a representative on the Commission' and resistance would be ineffective 'unless we were prepared to take up arms against British troops'. Such a move would 'be a reversal of Ulster's Unionist policy to obey the laws of Great Britain and would probably lose the support of the Unionist Party in Great Britain'. If they did take part, Bonar Law had obtained a promise from Lloyd George that either Lord James Clyde or Lord Dunedin (Andrew Murray), both Scottish politicians and judges within the Conservative Party, would act as the chairman of the Boundary Commission. Even though he was opposed to the Treaty, Edward Carson consented to act as Ulster's commissioner, saying 'a little modification of the boundary might be advantageous'.[12]

Craig 'thought the best course would be not to show our hand at the present time but to consider the matter very carefully during the few months that might elapse before the Boundary Commission would be established'.[13] This was agreed upon by the Cabinet and proved to be the correct decision from an Ulster unionist perspective, as a lot more time elapsed before the Commission finally met, and by then conditions were far more agreeable for unionists. Even though Craig claimed the

Boundary Commission was the 'root of all evil' for unionists, it resulted in uniting them.

For Northern nationalists, though, the Boundary Commission would turn out to be the root of much evil. It gave false hopes for the transfer of large areas of territory and many people from Northern Ireland to the Irish Free State. This assumption would lead to a catalogue of errors in the months and years ahead.

With the Treaty, nationalist leaders in the six and twenty-six counties were expectant that the entire counties of Tyrone and Fermanagh, as well as Derry city and Newry, and large parts of South Armagh and South and East Down would be transferred to the Free State. Denis Gwynn wrote that the 'suggestion of a Boundary Commission seemed naturally to imply that the Ulster Unionists would not be allowed to retain the full Six-County area if they did refuse to enter the Free State'.[14] His father, Stephen Gwynn, former IPP MP and persistent critic of Sinn Féin, believed that if the Dáil ratified the Treaty, 'then it is certain that before long Ulster will fall into its normal place ... Almost certainly Ulster will end as a counterpart to Quebec within the Irish Free State.'[15]

The nationalist optimism over the Boundary Commission, in many ways, explains the fraction of time devoted to partition during the acrimonious Dáil Éireann debates over the Treaty. Both the pro- and anti-Treaty sides supported the Commission to end, or at least limit, partition. Both sides were complacent about the vague terms of reference and the lack of provision for plebiscites, even in border areas. According to Mícheál Ó Fathartaigh and Liam Weeks, of the approximately half a million words spoken during the Treaty debates, Ulster and the Boundary Commission barely featured, with Ulster mentioned 113 times, North 80, unionist/ism 38, partition 29, Northern Ireland 25, James Craig 22, North-East 17, six counties 11 and Edward Carson 5 times. The border was mentioned just twice and the Boundary Commission once.[16]

One of the very few people to refer specifically to the dangers of the Boundary Commission, Belfast-born Monaghan TD Seán MacEntee, believed the purpose of Article 12 was

> to ensure that Ulster – secessionist Ulster – should remain a separate unit; and this is to be done by transferring from the jurisdiction of the Government of Northern Ireland certain people and certain districts which that Government cannot govern; and by giving instead to Northern Ireland, certain other districts – unionist districts of Monaghan, Cavan and Donegal, so that not only under this Treaty are we going to partition Ireland, not only are we going to partition Ulster, but we are going to partition even the counties of Ulster; and then I am told that these are not partition provisions.[17]

While some were claiming the provisions would force Northern Ireland into economic union with the rest of Ireland, MacEntee strongly disagreed, claiming that 'material or economic facts' are never the 'determining factors of nationality', and that England 'will find it much more profitable to subsidise Northern Ireland to remain out and weaken the Free State'.[18]

The leader of the anti-Treaty side, Éamon de Valera, did not appear to see at the time the dangers lurking within Article 12. In his alternative treaty, the so-called Document No. 2, there was no substantive difference between it and the Treaty on partition. The addendum on North-East Ulster read:

> [I]n sincere regard for internal peace, and in order to make manifest our desire not to bring force or coercion to bear upon any substantial part of the province of Ulster, whose inhabitants may now be unwilling to accept the national authority, we are prepared to grant to that portion of Ulster which is defined as Northern Ireland in the British Government of Ireland Act of 1920, privileges and safeguards not less substantial than those provided for in the 'Articles of Agreement for a Treaty' between Great Britain and Ireland signed in London on December 6th, 1921.[19]

The *Derry Journal* criticised de Valera's document, writing, 'It is advanced as an alternative to the Treaty, but it has not even the redeeming feature of effacing the worst flaw in that instrument, namely Partition.'[20]

Overall, the opposition in the Dáil to the Ulster provisions of the Treaty was scant, with both pro- and anti-Treaty TDs seeing the Boundary Commission as acceptable. Even for those who opposed, there was no comprehensive scrutiny of the vague and ambiguous wording of Article 12.

Arguably more harmful for Northern nationalists in the long term was the belief that they could continue to ignore and obstruct the institutions of Northern Ireland, particularly in areas of nationalist majorities. According to Patrick Buckland, 'it is beyond dispute that the prolonged controversy over the Boundary Commission kept alive nationalist hopes that Northern Ireland would collapse, so that most nationalists boycotted the Northern government and parliament'.[21] This policy was promoted and supported by senior Sinn Féin figures such as Michael Collins and Eoin MacNeill. MacNeill met a delegation of Northern nationalists in Dublin a day after the Treaty was signed, on 7 December, and asked them 'to adopt "a practical programme of passive resistance" to the Northern government's authority'.[22]

For Northern nationalists, the Treaty left many of them confused and dismayed. While those in the South were tearing themselves apart over the sovereignty issue, for Northern nationalists this was of secondary importance to the issue of partition. The role of the proposed Boundary Commission was of primary interest. It is important to note that Collins's assurances that the Treaty would end partition was pivotal in securing the support of many Northern nationalists and Irish Republican Army (IRA) members. Nationalists living in the border regions, particularly in Fermanagh and Tyrone, were optimistic that they would be quickly transferred to the Free State. However, most living in Belfast and east Ulster believed they would remain in Northern Ireland, regardless of the generosity of the Boundary Commission. One IRA member stated, 'The Treaty was a tragedy when it came. We all knew that. We knew in the North that we had been left out.'[23]

The Treaty resulted in differing opinions and strategies being adopted by nationalists within Northern Ireland. Unlike within Ulster unionism, there was a lack of consensus amongst Northern nationalists in general on the policy to be adopted towards partition and the Northern Ireland government. The split within Sinn Féin compounded the confusion and effectively prevented the formulation of a policy which might have unanimous support. In late 1921 the Northern government acted against 'recalcitrant' local authorities that refused to recognise it. It suspended both Fermanagh and Tyrone County Councils, with the police taking over the headquarters in Omagh and Enniskillen and impounding their records. While over twenty local authorities, such as Fermanagh County Council and those in South Down and South Armagh, remained defiant, others, such as Tyrone County Council, acknowledged the de facto jurisdiction of the Northern Parliament in view of what was described as 'the temporary period during which the northern parliament is to function in this area'.[24]

Derry City Corporation was divided between Sinn Féin members who urged unqualified allegiance to Dáil Éireann, and nationalists who believed the city would benefit from a nationalist-leaning mayor and corporation officially making the case through the Boundary Commission for the city's inclusion in the Free State. The main argument put forward by local authorities who believed in recognising the Northern jurisdiction, and by people like Arthur Griffith and W.T. Cosgrave in Dublin, was that if they did not, they would lose nationalist control and would 'rob whole nationalist tracts of effective representation in the face of the Boundary Commission'.[25] It was also, as Éamon Phoenix has argued, 'clear that any adoption of a full-blooded recognition policy would be opposed by a section of border nationalists who held that it would weaken their case before the Boundary Commission, and by a considerable anti-Treaty section in Belfast Sinn Féin'.[26]

Paid commissioners were put in place to run the affairs of the suspended local authorities.[27] The move by the Northern government was condemned by one of the British Treaty signatories, Lord Birkenhead. Speaking in Birmingham just hours after the Treaty was signed on 6 December, he stated that if Northern Ireland opted out of the Free State there must be a 'rectification of frontiers'. He said that the

Boundary Commission should examine the boundary lines, 'with a view to rendering impossible such an unhappy incident as that of a few days ago, in which the popularly-elected bodies of one or two of these districts were excluded from their habitations by representatives of the Northern Parliament, on the ground that they were not discharging their duties properly'.[28] Birkenhead's Birmingham speech demonstrated ambiguity similar to the wording of Article 12 itself. While claiming the boundary line would only be slightly rectified on either side of the then border, how could the Boundary Commission prevent the Northern government from interfering with the duties of Tyrone and Fermanagh county councils without large constitutional changes to both counties?

Speaking in the House of Commons on 14 December, Lloyd George gave a speech that could also be interpreted in different ways. He claimed that most people in Tyrone and Fermanagh 'prefer being with their Southern neighbours to being in the Northern Parliament. Take it either by constituency or by Poor Law unions, or, if you like, by counting heads, and you will find that the majority in these two counties prefer to be with their Southern neighbours.' He also stated that if 'Ulster is to remain a separate community, you can only by means of coercion keep them there, and although I am against the coercion of Ulster, I do not believe in Ulster coercing other units.' He added what turned out to be prophetic lines: that unless Northern Ireland dealt with its unhappy minority, it 'would be a trouble at her own door, a trouble which would complicate the whole of her machinery'.

But in recommending the 're-adjustment of boundaries', the prime minister said it could also mean an increase 'in the area of Ulster'. He explained his reasoning for insisting that the 'wishes of the inhabitants' was not the 'sole criterion', responding to his predecessor, Herbert Asquith, that 'you might take away a little corner of North-East Antrim. Therefore, you have also got to take into account geographical considerations and economic considerations.'[29] The speech is well described by Kevin Matthews as 'vintage Lloyd George, giving with one hand what the other promptly took away'.[30]

Ulster unionists certainly saw it as taking away, particularly Counties Tyrone and Fermanagh. Two days later, in response to criticism from Ronald O'Neill, MP for mid-Antrim and speaker of the Northern Parliament, Lloyd George somewhat retreated from some of his speech on 14 December, saying he never told 'the Sinn Feiners' that they would get the whole of Tyrone and Fermanagh. Interestingly, when further questioned by O'Neill about whether he, during the negotiations, had 'told the Sinn Feiners that all that was intended was a mere rectification of boundaries', he fudged the answer, saying, 'I did say to the Sinn Fein representatives that the representatives of Ulster who were at the Buckingham Palace Conference [of 1914], when there was a discussion of this kind, were under the impression that it would have the effect of increasing the population of Ulster.'[31]

For much of the four-year period from the signing of the Treaty to the tripartite government London Agreement of December 1925, to quote Lord Birkenhead, within Article 12 'there lurked the elements of dynamite', not only to cause widespread discord in Ireland but to wreak 'havoc in British affairs' too.[32] Primarily driven by domestic political concerns within the Conservative Party, most of the British signatories changed their views on Article 12 between the time they signed the Treaty in 1921 and that of the tripartite agreement. It was the ambiguous wording of Article 12 that allowed them to show this flexibility.

As colonial secretary, Winston Churchill was the British Cabinet minister with most responsibility for Irish affairs. He had to spend much of 1922 dealing with the fractious relationship between the two Irish governments (Northern Irish and the Provisional Government of the Irish Free State) in post-Treaty Ireland. A lot of his energy was focused on dealing with the fallout from the Treaty and the potential ramifications of the Boundary Commission.[33] As diehards in the Conservative Party tried to use the Treaty and the Boundary Commission clause to destabilise and ultimately bring down Lloyd George's government, Churchill had to walk a fine line between supporting all the Treaty articles and reassuring diehards and Ulster unionists that there was nothing to fear from the

Commission. He went from admitting in early 1922 that the Commission 'may conceivably affect' the Northern government 'prejudicially' to later dismissing the 'absurd supposition' that Northern Ireland would be reduced 'to its preponderatingly Orange areas'.[34] At this juncture, he was also wrestling with his own political future, moving away from the Liberals and looking to reconcile with the Conservatives, where many members still harboured a deep distrust of him for leaving the party in 1904. According to Liberal colleague Edwin Montagu, depending on the issues, 'Winston jumps from the diehard to the Liberal camp as he works from Egypt or India to Ireland.'[35]

As violence threatened to engulf Belfast and the area along the border at the start of 1922, Churchill facilitated meetings between Craig and Collins. Collins had recently become chairman of the Provisional Government of the Irish Free State after the ratification of the Treaty in the Dáil on 7 January. Showing the depths of naivety existing in Dublin at the time, Collins, the day before meeting with Craig in London, planned to 'suggest the convening of a meeting of representatives for all Ireland, either by Mr. Griffith or jointly by Mr. Griffith and Sir James to proceed with the drafting of a Constitution for Ireland'.[36] Meanwhile, on the same day, Craig and Wilfrid Spender, the Northern Cabinet secretary, visited the Carsons' home in England. While Spender and Lady Ruby Carson 'were longing to see De Valera's party & Collins' party at each other's throats & a real row, Craig said he thought peace in the south is better'.[37]

Collins's understanding of Ulster unionism at that juncture was partly influenced by the findings of Cork-born Diarmaid Fawsitt, who was commissioned by the Dáil Cabinet in November 1921 to 'undertake a special mission – to Belfast'. Based on Fawsitt's meetings and correspondence with Belfast-based businessmen from November 1921 to January 1922, a number of whom were prominent UUC members, Fawsitt believed many unionist-leaning businessmen were in favour of 'accepting an Irish Parliament'. While Fawsitt was arguably overly optimistic, it does confirm, as Brian Barton has asserted, that political attitudes in Belfast 'were less intransigent and monolithic, more amenable and nuanced, than is often assumed'.[38]

Collins spent three hours alone in a meeting with Craig in London on 21 January, after which they signed the first of their two 1922 pacts. Collins agreed to discontinue the Belfast Boycott, while Craig promised to 'facilitate, as far as economic conditions allowed, the return of expelled Catholic shipyard workers to their jobs'.[39] The Belfast Boycott, which the Dáil sanctioned in August 1920 in response to the expulsion of Catholics from Belfast-based businesses from the summer of 1920, was discontinued, but Craig failed to secure the return of many Catholics. Just twenty out of over 7,000 were reinstated in the shipyards by the end of January.[40]

The two men also endeavoured to find 'a more suitable system than the council of Ireland ... for dealing with problems affecting all Ireland'.[41] Craig told Collins that an 'All-Ireland Parliament was out of the question, possibly in years to come – 10, 20 or 50 years – Ulster might be tempted to join with the South'.[42] Remarkably, Collins agreed with Craig for them to 'deal with the question of the boundaries without help or interference from any British authority' and to nominate representatives reporting to Collins and Craig directly, with a view to 'mutually agree' borders.[43] Their agreement was even more vague than Article 12 of the Treaty. The main conclusion Collins drew from the conference was 'that north and south will settle outstanding differences between themselves. We have eliminated the English interference.'[44]

Northern nationalists generally were opposed to the pact, particularly those closest to the border, and annoyed that they were not consulted beforehand, with concerns raised over the removal of the chairman from the Boundary Commission, whom Northern nationalists hoped would act impartially. In the days following the pact, Collins received petitions and nationalist deputations to Dublin.[45] On removing the chairman from the Commission, he responded to the criticism by saying, 'first it was complained that an Englishman had been brought in – thereby making two votes to one in favour of the North East – now when the Englishman was left out they were not satisfied'.[46] Such was his distrust of the English it appears not to have dawned on him that he had granted Craig a veto on making any changes to the boundary. It was extremely naive of Collins to think he could get substantial border movement from an agreement with Craig. He also showed to Craig that the Treaty was not sacrosanct for one of its signatories.

The boundary element of the pact was primarily responsible for its undoing days later. On 2 February 1922 Craig arrived in Dublin and met Collins at City Hall. With 'Craig returning to his "not an inch" position and Collins to his claim to the two counties plus,' the pact broke down.[47] At the meeting Collins 'made the Provisional Government's position regarding the Boundary question clear to Sir James'. He suggested strongly to Craig 'the impossibility of two governments in Ireland and had put forward the proposal for a meeting of all Irish representatives to draft an Irish Constitution. Sir James Craig said it was too soon for this.'[48] An agreed press statement released after the meeting stated that 'no further agreement was reached, and a very serious situation has consequently arisen' due to the different interpretations given to both sides by Lloyd George, with Collins being told that 'large territories were involved in the Commission', while Craig was led to believe that 'merely a boundary line' was at stake.[49] Afterwards Collins said that 'we insist that majorities must rule and it is that principle for which the Treaty stands', adding, 'we will not coerce any part of Ulster which is desirous of remaining in the area controlled by the Northern Parliament, but neither will we allow the coercion of any part of Ulster which votes itself into the Irish Free State'.[50]

Despite the pact breaking down shortly after it was agreed, it was a useful exercise for Craig, who used it thereafter to insist, as per agreement with Collins, that a boundary line could only be reached by mutual agreement between both Irish jurisdictions. In the almost four years that followed, he never wavered from that stance.[51]

The main thrust of Craig and the Northern unionists' argument was that the Government of Ireland Act 1920 was a 'final settlement' as far as they were concerned. They were outraged that the institutions and area laid down in the 1920 Act were under threat by the Treaty, signed by the authors of the Government of Ireland Act 1920 and without their consent.⁵² Yet it was highly hypocritical of unionists to complain about a settlement being imposed on them when the Government of Ireland Act 1920 itself was a settlement imposed on Irish nationalists without their consent, particularly the one-third of the Northern population who detested the Act and had to live with its provisions. And while claiming that the Government of Ireland Act 1920, the 'supreme sacrifice', was now sacrosanct, Craig and his colleagues had no issues with removing or ignoring parts of it, such as the Council of Ireland and its provisions on the treatment of minorities.

On 4 February 1922 Craig's brother, Captain Charles Craig MP, demonstrated the direction in which Ulster unionism was heading on the issue of the Boundary Commission, saying, 'no other result would come about than civil war' if attempts were made 'to take away large pieces of the six counties'.⁵³ In many ways, a civil war was already happening in the North in the first half of 1922. While violence had increased in the border areas, most of it was concentrated in Belfast, as it had been since July 1920. According to Kieran Glennon, there were 502 people killed violently in Belfast from the summer of 1920 to late 1922. What marked the city out from other areas in Ireland at the time was the large number of civilian casualties, estimated at 84 per cent of the killings. The worst of the violence there was in the first half of 1922. In 'the four months from February to May, 231 people were killed, more than in the preceding nineteen months combined'.⁵⁴ Rural areas like Fermanagh and Tyrone were less violent than Belfast but were still highly militarised, with most adult male Protestants becoming members of the Specials, even though the IRA's presence in those counties was minimal. Numbering approximately 32,000 members at its peak, the Special Constabulary was, according to Seán Bernard Newman, 'Never a police force' but 'an uneasy combination of police, paramilitary and military elements'.⁵⁵

As chairman of the Provisional Government, Collins was now considered the spokesperson for Northern nationalists, at least by the British. He was under enormous pressure from many different groups who sought answers from him on how to deal with the ever-worsening situation in the North. In addition to Ulster unionists and the British government pressing him, Collins had to deal with the split within Sinn Féin and the IRA, with conditions in the South spiralling towards civil war, as well as the different outlooks within Northern nationalism on how best to deal with partition.

Compared to his government colleagues, Collins appeared to demonstrate a great interest in the plight of Northern nationalists and the ending of partition in 1922, with Lloyd George complaining to Churchill, 'we could get Mr. Collins to talk about nothing else'.[56] His strategies (if they could even be called that) on the North, however, were confusing, contradictory and often counterproductive. On the one hand he pursued political means, such as the pacts with Craig, and on the other he sought to militarily destabilise the North, aiming to end partition outright. He firmly believed it was essential to continue with the non-recognition of the Northern Parliament and its ministries, 'otherwise they would have nothing to bargain with Sir James Craig'.[57] An example of this obstructionist policy in practice was the financing by the Provisional Government of the salaries of teachers and school managers who refused to recognise the Northern educational ministry.[58]

The British and Northern Irish governments were deeply frustrated by the non-recognition of the six counties by Collins's administration.[59] Believing he was involved in military tactics, too, many claimed that he was in breach of the Treaty. In response to Gaelic footballers from County Monaghan (many of whom were in the IRA) being arrested by the Ulster Special Constabulary in Tyrone on 14 January on their way to a match in Derry, Collins ordered the kidnapping of some forty prominent loyalists from Tyrone and Fermanagh on the night of 7–8 February, who were taken across the border. The kidnappings caused a furore in the unionist community. Craig issued a statement to the 'People of Ulster' condemning the 'dastardly outrages' that 'will never be forgotten – it merely strengthens our determination that what Ulster has she holds'. He 'arranged for the immediate distribution of the arms necessary to protect our border'.[60] Despite both Collins and the Provisional Government's

Minister for Defence, Richard Mulcahy, denying any knowledge of the incident, Austen Chamberlain warned Griffith, 'I will consider myself absolved from the Treaty', unless the Provisional Government took steps to release the kidnapped men and end the border disturbances.[61] Chamberlain, who was looking to introduce the Irish Free State (Agreement) Bill at the time and had reports that up to 150 diehards from his own party would revolt against the bill in support of the Ulster unionists, was concerned that the kidnappings would damage the bill's prospects further.[62]

Lionel Curtis subsequently wrote to Churchill that the 'worst blot on their record is one we cannot now urge, one which the world has curiously overlooked, the raid on Ulster'. Curtis had 'no doubt that Collins was at least cognisant of this plot. You and I know that the kidnapped prisoners were held in his custody and that he traded with them in our negotiations. We should have been amply justified in treating that as a breach of the Treaty.'[63]

After the kidnappings, the Northern government bolstered the border areas with many more Specials. In Tyrone, five 'A' Special platoons joined the existing platoon in Aughnacloy. Similar reinforcements took up residence in other border counties. The 'roads crossing into the Free State were then made impassable by blowing up bridges or digging trenches and were covered by constabulary posts. Only the main roads were left open and on these there were permanent road blocks.'[64]

Even though the Northern government controlled the Specials, the British government financed the force with vast sums of money. In May 1922 Craig estimated that the annual cost of running the security for Northern Ireland was £2.75 million, with a special supplementary amount of £2.1 million needed for the threats posed in 1922.[65] British Imperial Secretary for the North Stephen Tallents was concerned about the bloated Specials doing 'the work of a soldier without police experience, whose name carries no weight in the country which seems destined to finance his plans. It has been subjected to no real criticism.'[66] In June 1922 James Masterson-Smith from the Colonial Office wrote:

The British government has armed and is paying for forces which it is told by the one who controls them, will in certain eventualities be turned against itself. If Ulster does not accept the award of the Boundary Commission the British Government will either have to pour in overwhelming forces and engage in a civil war of the most hateful kind, or else be accused in the presence of the civilised world of connivance with Ulster.[67]

By hiding the funding of the Specials through grants or easing off on Northern Ireland's imperial contribution for two years, 'these measures disguised a fundamental reordering of Northern Ireland's financial relations with Great Britain'. One member of the Irish Committee Churchill had set up to deal with affairs on the island pointed out, 'Ulster was being bribed to remain disassociated from the South, whereas in the negotiations with the Southern Irish the British Government had always stated that if Ulster chose to disassociate herself from the South, she would have to bear her full share of the financial burdens of the United Kingdom.'[68]

Despite the misgivings within British civil service circles, Craig was able to secure an agreement from the British government of continued financing of the Specials for an indefinite period, perhaps years, until the border was decided, partly due to the concerns of people such as Chamberlain over support within his own party for the Treaty.

Accused of Treaty breaches, Collins, in turn, became an accuser of such breaches by the British and, indirectly, by the Northern government. As violence escalated in the North, with most of the casualties being defenceless Catholic civilians in Belfast, his fury and exasperation were evident in exchanges with Craig and Churchill. In one fiery exchange with Craig, who had previously mocked the lack of experience of the Provisional Government, Collins, in mentioning atrocities such as the McMahon murders and the massacres on Weaver, Stanhope and Arnon Streets, replied, 'You suggest that we lack experience. If this be the test of "experienced government" then we are happy to be called "inexperienced".[69] Collins also believed that 'it should be made clear that the Border question is an artificial one engineered from Belfast to distract attention from the real issue', which was the violence against Catholics in Belfast.[70]

Minister for Foreign Affairs of the Provisional Government – and another Treaty signatory – George Gavan Duffy, in referring to the widescale violence perpetrated against Catholic civilians, in many cases by Northern police services, said the 'British Government is not blameless in this matter, for though, generally, it has observed the terms of the Treaty loyally, in this matter it is subsidising the armed gangs of Specials in Belfast'.[71] At a Provisional Government meeting in late May 1922, it was agreed that, on a forthcoming visit to London, Collins would bring up 'the attitude of the British Government towards North East Ulster', which 'was regarded generally as endangering the Treaty'.[72]

Collins also accused the British media of making matters worse and promoting Craig's stance on the boundary question. In a stinging attack on an editorial in *The Times* of 21 March 1922 entitled 'The Perils in Ireland', Collins sent a letter responding to it three days later, describing it as 'so inaccurate and so deliberately one-sided'. He condemned the paper for claiming that the people of Britain 'will be with Ulster in resisting any attempt at her coercion; they will be with her too in objecting to any change being made in her boundary except by mutual agreement', writing that the pro-Craig view of *The Times* was 'completely at variance with the best legal opinion of both countries, including Mr. Lloyd George's own statement against the incorporation and coercion of the Nationalist counties of Tyrone and Fermanagh'. He refuted *The Times*'s claim that the 'real truth' about the outrages in Belfast was unknown, claiming, of the thirty-nine people killed violently in the city from 11 February to 6 March, twenty-two were Catholics, who made up less than a quarter of Belfast's population. Of the close to 30,000 Specials available, Collins wrote that all of them had 'little or no discipline, and all open members of the Orange Society and fanatical partisans. How can peace be restored with this notorious force to restore it?'[73]

Many of Collins's criticisms were borne out on the day his article appeared in *The Times*, 24 March, when the home of Owen McMahon, a Catholic publican in Belfast, was attacked by five men dressed in police uniforms who broke into his house with a sledgehammer. They shot the males in the house, killing six: Owen, four of his sons and an employee, Edward McKinney.[74] So incensed were members of the Provisional Government by the McMahon murders, and particularly by the alleged involvement of the Specials in the killings, that some considered breaking the Treaty. Richard Mulcahy, the defence minister, described the Specials as 'a sectarian police force engaged in a very extensive campaign of murder and violence', saying 'the fact that the British government propose to finance the work of the Special Constabulary until 1 October next drives me to question [their] bona fides in respect of the agreement'.[75]

To stem the violence in the North, shortly after the McMahon murders Churchill convinced Collins and Craig to meet again in London, where a second pact was agreed on 30 March. Regarding the Boundary Commission, Clause 7 stated:

> During the month immediately following the passing into law of the Bill confirming the Constitution of the Free State (being the month within which the Northern Parliament is to exercise its option) and before any address in accordance with Article 12 of the Treaty is presented, there shall be a further meeting between the signatories to this agreement with a view to ascertaining:
>
> A. Whether means can be devised to secure the unity of Ireland.
>
> B. Failing this, whether agreement can be arrived at on the Boundary question otherwise than by recourse to the Boundary Commission outlined in Article 12 of the Treaty.[76]

Craig almost immediately threw cold water on the clause when speaking at the Northern House of Commons on 4 April. Referring to the 'unity of Ireland' clause and using similar words to what he had said to Collins in January, Craig said, 'If any person can be found in Ulster to lead the people into the Free State, Sir, it will not be me ... Even if I thought it beneficial to go into a Southern Parliament I would not be the person to do it.'[77]

With the violence continuing unabated after the pact, and an infuriated Collins accusing Craig of not sticking to it, it was over almost as quickly as it was signed. Collins's fury increased further as Craig sought to remove the proportional representation (PR) voting system from use in Northern elections. With no opposition present to delay its progress, due to the nationalist boycott of the Northern Parliament, the bill to abolish PR was ready to become law by 5 July 1922. Collins complained to Churchill, 'Do you not see ... the true meaning of all this?' He argued that the bill's purpose was 'to oust the Catholic and Nationalist people of the Six Counties from their rightful share in local administration' and, in anticipation of the Boundary Commission's work, 'to paint the Counties of Tyrone and Fermanagh with a deep Orange tint'.[78] The abolition of PR was also 'considered to be both actual and moral violations' of the Government of Ireland Act 1920.[79]

Churchill agreed with Collins and persuaded the Lord Lieutenant of Ireland, Viscount FitzAlan, to withhold royal assent. Craig and his Cabinet then threatened to resign, forcing Lloyd George's coalition to climb down and, after a two-month delay, royal assent was given on 11 September 1922.[80]

Due to their climbdown over PR, Churchill and Lloyd George would have expected problems from Collins. That wasn't to be. The two main Irish signatories of the Treaty, Griffith and Collins, died within ten days of each other in August 1922. Griffith died suddenly on 12 August, while Collins was shot dead on 22 August at Béal na Bláth in Cork. It was a huge blow to the fledgling Free State, and also to the nationalists' case before the Boundary Commission, particularly with the many interpretations that were attributed to Article 12 afterwards. The Civil War itself, of which Collins was the most high-profile casualty, did enormous reputational damage to the Free State and its case before the Boundary Commission. Lionel Curtis believed, though, 'that Collins' early death alone saved the Treaty', claiming his successor, W.T. Cosgrave, 'in substance reverted his policy. He has kept it in the letter and in the spirit except in so far as the insignia of the Crown are concerned.'[81] The change in the Provisional Government's policy towards Northern Ireland, which had started shortly before Collins's death, was accelerated to one without provocative actions against the North and instead became 'a policy of peaceful do-nothingness', a phrase coined by Kevin O'Shiel.[82] O'Shiel became the director of the North Eastern Boundary Bureau (NEBB) shortly after Collins's death.

The nationalist case was also hampered by the changing dynamics within British politics, which saw many of the British signatories of the Treaty becoming increasingly less popular as 1922 progressed, leading in turn to many of them hardening their views on the Boundary Commission. While their duplicity over the Treaty helped them in some ways to steer the Irish Free State Bill through the House of Commons, it did not help in gaining trust from the main Irish stakeholders.

As colonial secretary, Churchill insisted on 'fair play' between both Irish governments but added 'though we are impartial we cannot be indifferent. Naturally, our hearts warm towards those in the North who are helping, and have helped so long, to keep the old flag flying.'[83] Churchill had become more open in his support for the Northern government throughout early 1922, insisting that the Boundary Commission would only slightly rectify the border and not make wholescale changes. His financial backing of the Northern government had led to an angry exchange with Craig in May 1922. When Craig made an uncompromising statement, declaring he would have nothing to do with the Commission, Churchill responded:

> I do not consider your declaration made without any reference to the Government that in no circumstances would you accept any rectification of the frontier or any Boundary Commission as provided for in the Treaty is compatible with requests for enormous

financial aid and heavy issues of arms. While I was actually engaged in procuring the assent of my colleagues to your requests, you were making a declaration which was in effect in one passage little short of a defiance of the Imperial Government whose aid you seek.[84]

He concluded by stating, 'it is not within your rights to state that you will not submit to the Treaty which the British Government has signed in any circumstances, and at the same time to ask the British Government to bear the overwhelming burden of the whole of your defensive expenses'.[85]

Churchill was concerned, though, about the Treaty being used as a stepping stone to a republic, something Collins had frequently declared. In responding to Craig in July, shortly after the Civil War in Dublin had begun, Churchill had said, 'I see all your difficulties over the Boundary Commission.'[86]

In the 1922 UK general election campaign, Churchill's shift towards the diehard and Ulster unionist position was made public when he 'announced that he would "oppose all attempts to coerce Ulster" into joining the Irish Free State'. By then he was 'committed to resisting any Boundary Commission award which might endanger Northern Ireland's separate existence'.[87] After the November election, like others who signed the Treaty, including Lloyd George, Churchill was out of government, famously saying he was 'without an office, without a seat, without a party, and without an appendix', as he was suffering from acute appendicitis during his failed election campaign.[88]

While the British were going to the polls to elect a new government, the Free State was embroiled in a bitter civil war. Writing in September 1924 to Patrick McCartan, who had been a fellow TD in the Laois–Offaly constituency with him from 1921 to 1923, the Free State Minister for Justice, Kevin O'Higgins, claimed that if 'in January '22 we had sat down in grave council and considered how best we could destroy the prospect of union with those elements which were standing out in the North-East we could not have devised a better programme to that end than that which we have, in fact, carried out from January '22 to date'. They 'had an opportunity of building up a worthy State that would attract and, in time, absorb and assimilate' Ulster unionists. Instead, they 'preferred to practice [sic] upon ourselves worse indignities than the British had practised on us since Cromwell and Mountjoy and now we wonder why the Orange men are not hopping like so many fleas across the border in their anxiety to come within our fold and jurisdiction'.[89]

While O'Higgins was mainly referring to the devastating Civil War, which did untold damage to the Irish Free State, including in its aim of bringing about Irish unity, he could just as easily have been referring to the policies of the Provisional Government of which he was a member, and which was chaired by Collins before the Civil War commenced. Before his death, Collins's policies on the North had been contradictory and counterproductive. He, like the British government, through its support for Northern Ireland politically, financially and militarily, was in breach of the Treaty on more than one occasion. The most reckless example was his instigation and support for the 'May Offensive', a botched attempt by both pro- and anti-Treaty factions of the IRA to invade the six counties. His pact with Craig to settle the boundary question by mutual agreement was extremely naive, providing Craig with a platform to oppose any solution that was not through consent from then on.

Instead of trying to win over the nationalist minority, Craig's government took numerous draconian steps that enshrined a hostility between both communities that was played out while the boundary question remained unsettled. While occasionally demonstrating the veneer of an impartial arbitrator, the British government sided decisively with the Northern government in its quest to prevent the Boundary Commission from convening at all, but in this they failed, as the Commission, under the Treaty, was automatically triggered once Northern Ireland opted out of the Free State, which it did in December 1922.

Chapter Three

Festina Lente (Make Haste Slowly)

IN A MEMORANDUM TO THE Irish Free State's Executive Council in April 1923, the director of the NEBB, Kevin O'Shiel, wrote that the government's motto should be *Festina Lente* (make haste slowly), believing 'we have all to gain by going slowly and cautiously'.[1] Although almost at an end, the Civil War was still not over, and there was much preparatory work for O'Shiel and his team in the NEBB to do to ensure the Free State government had the best chance in presenting its case before the Boundary Commission.

On 2 October 1922, two months before the Northern Houses of Parliament had voted to opt out of the Free State, thus triggering the formation of the Boundary Commission, the NEBB was formed when the Provisional Government appointed O'Shiel to collect 'data in connection with the forthcoming Boundary Commission and that he should submit reports at frequent and regular intervals to the Government'.[2] O'Shiel, originally from Omagh in Tyrone, was a barrister who had served as the first judge of Sinn Féin's Dáil Courts before being appointed as assistant legal adviser to the Provisional Government. He was centrally involved in preparing the Free State's case for membership of the League of Nations and subsequently served as a land commissioner from 1923 to 1963. He worked closely with Collins on Northern affairs throughout 1922, acting as his 'proxy on the Sinn Féin Advisory Committee for Ulster, and acting as a member, but mainly as his agent on his own Provisional Government Advisory Committee in Ulster'.[3] His role as director of the NEBB was, according to his biographer Eda Sagarra, one of the 'potentially most important posts held by O'Shiel in a career of half a century'.[4]

O'Shiel immediately went about hiring staff for the bureau and organising it into divisions. When he appointed Edward Millington (E.M.) Stephens as secretary and the man in charge of the research and investigations division on an annual salary of £700, O'Shiel highlighted to Stephens that it was a temporary post with 'no guarantee of any permanence in connection with it, or even that it shall last longer than four months at the outside'.[5] Due primarily to the lengthy delay in the Boundary Commission convening, Dublin-born Stephens remained in the post for almost four years. The nephew of playwright John Millington Synge, and custodian and literary executor of his uncle's papers, Stephens was a barrister and civil servant. He had accompanied Michael Collins as legal draughtsman during the Treaty negotiations in London and served as a secretary on the Provisional Government committee appointed to draft the Free State constitution.[6]

To add heft to the government's economic arguments for transferring territory from Northern Ireland to the Free State, economist Dr Joseph Johnston was appointed economic adviser to the NEBB. A native of Tyrone like O'Shiel, Johnston was a lecturer in economics at Trinity College Dublin. He was subsequently elected to Seanad Éireann for Dublin University in 1938.[7]

Although O'Shiel wanted the TD Seán Milroy to head up the publicity division, Hugh A. MacCartan was appointed instead.[8] Down-born MacCartan was a poet and novelist of works such as *The Glamour of Belfast* and *Silhouettes: Some Character Studies from North and South*, as well as being a civil servant.[9] He, like many others who worked in the bureau, was on loan from other government departments. George A. Ruth, from the registrar-general's department, was responsible for the comprehensive statistical and mapping work completed by the bureau, and D. St P. Murphy took charge of the historical division, 'which subsequently proved comparatively unimportant'.[10]

One of the most interesting appointments was that of Bolton C. Waller, who was responsible for researching international precedents and procedures of other boundary commissions, particularly the ones in post-First World War Europe. Originally from Limerick, Waller was a civil servant, soldier, journalist and subsequently a Church of Ireland clergyman.[11] He was also an expert in international affairs. While employed by the bureau, in 1924 he 'won the Filene Prize of £1,000 for the best plan for securing world peace'.[12]

The NEBB also hired legal agents from Northern regions looking to be transferred to the Free State, whose job was 'to furnish the Bureau with the case for inclusion in the Free State of their respective areas, in brief form, setting out all local facts and circumstances'.[13] Some of those who were subsequently appointed as legal agents attended a fascinating meeting between a deputation of Northern nationalists and members of the Provisional Government on 11 October 1922, shortly after the formation of the NEBB. The deputation consisted of a combination of prominent clergy members and political and legal representatives from the North. They questioned the delay in pushing forward with work in connection with the Boundary Commission and suggested that the Provisional Government should 'set up an organisation to deal with the whole matter, and to finance it'. Nationalist MP for Fermanagh and Tyrone T.J. Harbison claimed that their 'Ulster' Orange friends 'hate us and we know they never will coalesce with us until they are pressed in, either by financial pressure or by the gun'. There was much comment on the impact the abolition of PR would have on the nationalist community and how 'the disastrous Civil War which has been raging has strengthened the hands of our enemies in the North'. Alderman John Bonner from Derry city said, 'What will be required now is a sort of standardisation of the information that can be collected all over these areas for your purposes. You will need counter propaganda against the propaganda of the

"Northern" Government.' There was much criticism of the Specials, with Father James McKenna, parish priest of Dromore in Tyrone, referring to them as 'the biggest blackguards up there'.[14]

Kevin O'Shiel was introduced to the deputation, proving that the body they were calling for had already been established. He provided a skeleton outline of his plans for the NEBB, saying he was mapping out a programme and preparing a scheme 'with a view to collecting and extracting all possible information we can get in connection with the Boundary Commission'. He recommended that there should be local committees in Northern areas that had a high chance of being transferred to the Free State, supervised by experts trained in similar work, such as solicitors, who would collect and collate information and send it to the bureau's headquarters in Dublin 'where it would be codified and where the main case would be made up'.

O'Shiel claimed that 'the scheme that I propose to work out is a very large one, and some people would consider it rather ambitious. But it is up to us to leave no stone unturned so as to see at any rate that we can get as big a share of the Six Counties into the Saorstat, as we possibly can.' He stated that the research and investigation division would deal with the matter under four headings: geography, economy, politics and history. The economic case would show 'that Derry City is really a Donegal City and not a Derry City at all, and that by every possible argument and justification Derry should be in the Saorstat. Clones is as much a South Fermanagh town as Monaghan is a Monaghan town.'

As part of leaving 'no stone unturned', the bureau planned to look at international partitions and boundary commissions, with particular emphasis placed on 'the Silesian question because the Article in the Treaty with reference to the Boundary Commission has been taken verbatim from the Silesian arrangement which rested there on manhood and womanhood suffrage'. O'Shiel believed it created 'a precedent that the British themselves were parties to in the Continent and if we get that Silesian precedent adopted for us it means that we would cut at the Six Counties to an extraordinary extent'.[15]

The Northern nationalist deputation was clearly impressed, with Michael Lynch, chairman of Omagh Urban District Council, saying, 'It seems to me that Mr. O'Shiel has put forward a very excellent programme' and Alderman Bonner of Derry city stating, 'You would nearly think he has anticipated our thoughts.'[16]

The Provisional Government then focused the meeting on its overall policy towards the North, a policy formulated by a committee comprised of Ernest Blythe, Patrick Hogan, J.J. Walsh, Desmond FitzGerald and Richard Hayes in August 1922. The government had decided to recognise the Northern government and to discontinue the obstructionist policies that had prevailed while Collins was still alive.[17] The steps of the new policy included discontinuing the payment of teachers in the Six Counties; urging Catholics in the North to recognise the Northern Parliament and local bodies; precautions to prevent border incidents from the Free State side; prisoners in the North to recognise the Northern courts; and that the '"Outrage" propaganda should be dropped in the Twenty Six Counties' as well as 'all kinds of minor nagging should cease'.[18]

In typically blunt fashion the Minister for Home Affairs, Kevin O'Higgins, told the meeting that the government had 'no other policy for the North East than we have for any other part of Ireland, and that is the Treaty policy'. O'Higgins spoke of the 'lack of cohesion among the people, who may be described generally as Nationalists in the Six County area', the 'conflict of interest between the men who has [sic] and the men who has [sic] not a dog's chance of getting out of the Boundary area. There is a conflict of interest between the men in Belfast, and the man down in the Border. And if we are not careful that conflict of interest will pretty well spoil things.' He recognised that many nationalists in the North felt they had 'been abandoned to some extent in this Treaty, and that their interests were not sufficiently looked to in this matter', but he believed they should 'hammer out some uniform policy. The people who know they have not a dog's chance under the Boundary Commission should be prepared to mark time, and give those who have a chance an opportunity of playing their hand.' He claimed the government planned to obtain the 'largest possible area' from the Boundary Commission.[19]

Showing that the obstructionist tactics of the Collins era were over, W.T. Cosgrave, who had replaced Collins as chairman of the Provisional Government as well as subsuming Griffith's role as president of the Dáil government, said to the Northern nationalist deputation that they had to make up their own minds whether they were to contest the upcoming UK general election or not. He added, however, that his government could not interfere, as they took 'very strong action here against people who don't give allegiance to the Government here. If we were to take the line that would be popular in the North and advise the people there not to give allegiance to that "Northern" Government it would be used against us down here; and it would also be used against us by the North.'[20]

O'Higgins's comments seemed to have the desired effect on one of the deputation at least, John Henry (J.H.) Collins, a solicitor from Newry, who subsequently wrote to Peadar Murney, a Northern republican from Newry, who was at the time incarcerated by Provisional Government authorities in the Curragh, saying all anti-partitionists 'should join and pull on the one rope, in the effort to reduce Craig's territory … To my mind at the present time, there is only one fight to hand, and that is on the Boundary question, and all other things should wait till that is decided.'[21]

J.H. Collins was appointed as a legal agent for the NEBB to cover Newry and surrounding districts, while others were appointed for Belfast, Magherafelt, Omagh, Cookstown, Armagh, Enniskillen and Derry. O'Shiel recommended that they should be paid 60 guineas to furnish the NEBB with their completed cases by 6 December, the day the Free State was officially established.[22] Although O'Shiel was against the appointment of Hugh O'Doherty, Derry city's first Catholic lord mayor since the seventeenth century, as the city's legal agent, he was advised that O'Doherty would be difficult to ignore as he 'possesses the Bishop's conscience'.[23] Ultimately, however, Derry-based solicitor John Tracy was chosen instead.

Under Article 14 of the Treaty, Northern Ireland was given a month to consider opting out of the Irish Free State once the latter jurisdiction was established. It was referred to as 'Ulster Month'. While the notion was fanciful, some within the Free State held out hope that Northern Ireland would use 'Ulster Month' to see the benefits of joining with the twenty-six counties and uniting Ireland. On the establishment of the Free State, Cosgrave declared, 'we are looking Northwards with hope and confidence that, whether now or very soon, the people of that corner of our land will come in with the rest of the Irish nation, and share with us its government, as well as the great prosperity and happiness which must certainly follow concord and union'.[24]

Craig believed it was important to opt out of the Free State immediately upon its establishment in order 'not to show the slightest hesitation to the world'.[25] Speaking to the Belfast Chamber of Commerce on 5 December 1922, a day before the Free State came into being, Craig said, 'that as they voted themselves out of the Free State and into a free Ulster, that Ulster would be free indeed, and that there would be encouragement to every right-thinking man to come along and help'.[26]

Accordingly, there was no 'Ulster Month', just a day, with the Northern Parliament's House of Commons and Senate deciding unanimously, at the first opportunity, to opt out of the Free State. Addressing King George V, the Northern House of Commons resolved:

> Most Gracious Sovereign, We, your Majesty's most dutiful and loyal subjects, the Commons of Northern Ireland in Parliament assembled, having learnt of the passing of the Irish Free State Constitution Act, 1922, being the Act of Parliament for the ratification of the Articles of Agreement for a Treaty between Great Britain and Ireland, do, by this Humble Address, pray Your Majesty that the powers of the Parliament and Government of the Irish Free State shall no longer extend to Northern Ireland.[27]

Using the parameters set out in the Treaty, and specifically referencing it in the resolution passed by both Houses of the Northern Parliament, was a demonstration that the Ulster Unionists accepted the Treaty, despite vowing to have nothing to do with it. The Free State government subsequently claimed that the Northern Parliament's address to the king opting out of the Free State 'rendered it an essential part of the fulfilment of the Treaty'.[28] Even though the Northern Minister of Home Affairs, Richard Dawson Bates, claimed there was no legal foundation for the Free State's contention, he still felt it prudent 'to consult his legal advisers on the matter'.[29]

Craig reiterated that he would have nothing to do with the Boundary Commission, which, under the terms of the Treaty, was triggered to convene once Northern Ireland opted out of the Free State. Craig described it as 'dirty work' and that the 'bargain had been entered into by the wrong people behind the back of the Northern Government; and in no manner would they be dragged into it'.[30] Speaking in Derry that same month, while still contending he would have nothing to do with the Commission, Craig believed the impasse could be overcome by a 'mutual accommodation' between both Irish governments. He stated he would not consider the transfer of a whole county, but 'if some fair give and take arrangement could be concluded – an arrangement, for instance, which would give East Donegal to the North – he would even take the whole County Donegal to-morrow if he got it'. This would be much more satisfactory 'than the boundary line fixed by a Commission which might leave both sides dissatisfied'.[31]

In December 1922 Lord Glenavy (James Campbell) sent Craig a secret letter on his own initiative, proposing a solution to the boundary question. Glenavy had been a Southern unionist who became chairperson of the Irish Free State Senate that same month. Even though the letter was marked 'private and confidential', it was soon in circulation in the press.[32] Kevin O'Shiel considered it 'an unfortunate episode'. In Glenavy's offer to Craig for Northern Ireland to enter an all-Ireland parliament, he proposed scrapping the Boundary Commission and 'that the Northern deputies in Dail Eireann, whilst retaining all their present powers over the Six Counties, would enjoy a right to veto any Bill concerning them'. O'Shiel believed it was 'highly unwise' and 'a diplomatic blunder of some magnitude', particularly given that the offer was probably 'far in excess of our ultimate maximum offer'.[33]

In the same memorandum, O'Shiel demonstrated his deep distrust of Joe Devlin, the influential West Belfast-based Northern nationalist politician, and his 'organ', *The Irish News*. Writing that no one 'knows Nationalist Ulster, its conditions, and particularly its prejudices, better than Mr. Devlin', O'Shiel claimed that Devlin 'hopes to bring off a special agreement, independent of us with Sir James Craig in lieu of the Boundary Commission, and on the basis of Established Partition', while using *The Irish News* to tell 'Northern Catholics that they have been betrayed by the Free State'. Devlin's 'propaganda is already having an effect on our people ... to the extent of increasing and making articulate their suspicion of us', adding that whatever harm 'Devlin has done or will do in his new gallop to power the delectable moment was afforded by the Glenavy episode'.[34] During the 'Glenavy Affair', *The Irish News* wrote a number of editorials critical of the Free State government's inaction on the Boundary Commission, claiming it was ignoring the 'puzzled and helpless' Northern nationalists, and urging that 'the issue of the Commission be put to the test without further hugger-mugger'.[35]

Shortly after Northern Ireland opted out of the Free State, Liberal MP William Wedgwood Benn asked Bonar Law, who had replaced Lloyd George as British prime minister in October 1922, in the House of Commons, 'Will Article 12 of the Treaty stand, and is it binding on the Government?' Much to the relief of the Free State government, Bonar Law replied that they stood by 'the whole of the Treaty'.[36] Many nationalists were fearful for the prospects of the Boundary Commission under the premiership of Bonar Law, as he was always a lukewarm supporter of the Treaty, while Ulster unionists felt they could 'rely upon him to see that no unfair advantage is taken of this Province in regard to the Council of Ireland or the Boundaries Commission', according to a *Belfast Telegraph* editorial.[37]

In December 1922 T.J. Harbison believed the Free State government 'should force a declaration from the British Government ... as to the person who is to fill the office of Chairman of the Boundary Commission'.[38] With some Northern nationalists insisting that the government 'must demand from Bonar Law an impartial chairperson', O'Shiel, however, believed their 'international credentials would suffer if we were so blunt with Bonar Law, showing we do not believe in his bona fides, which would be regarded as a deliberate insult'.[39]

The Free State government was not prepared to heed the calls for the Boundary Commission to immediately convene, primarily due to the ongoing Civil War. In a memorandum O'Shiel sent to the Free State Executive Council in February 1923, he wrote that it would be 'nothing short of folly on our part to raise the issue now or at any time until there is a decided change in general conditions'. He added, 'What a ridiculous figure we would cut – both nationally and universally – were we to argue our claim at the Commission for population and territory when at our backs, in our own jurisdiction is the perpetual racket of war, the flames of our burning railway stations, and the never failing lists of our murdered citizens!'[40]

Referring to the prospects of Northern Ireland uniting with the Free State as 'A Crazy Idea', the *Belfast Telegraph* described the conditions in the Free State:

> Wrong and outrage have stamped their bloody footprints over the whole country. Citizens are robbed, and are afraid to complain lest worse befalls them. The life and property of all decent people are completely at the mercy of lawless desperadoes who rob and plunder at will. The Executive are prisoners in their own offices, and can only venture abroad occasionally, at the imminent peril of their lives.[41]

The paper considered it ludicrous to suggest that 'Ulster' would 'abandon her position of security, and immunity, and happiness, and step into all this inferno'.[42] On a visit to the North in December 1922, NEBB member Bolton C. Waller wrote, 'People there are at present just thanking their stars they are out of the trouble in the S[outh]. Their own affairs are much better. Even those who expect to see union of some sort in the end are at the present inclined to wait and watch.'[43]

Were the Free State government to push for a Boundary Commission then, O'Shiel believed, the diehards in the Conservative Party would 'raise a storm about the British Government's being a party to any action which would result in cutting off large sections of the law-abiding people in the North and transferring them to the chaos disorder of the South'.[44] Later, a pamphlet issued by the NEBB took issue with republicans complaining about 'an unreasonable delay in having the Commission set up', calling it 'perhaps, the most dishonest and insincere in the whole range of Irregular propaganda … In complaining of the delay in the setting up of the Boundary Commission Mr. De Valera and his supporters are really condemning themselves, for they, and they alone, are responsible for the delay.'[45]

There was also a reluctance from some within the Free State government to propose the convening of the Boundary Commission while the Conservatives were in power. In May 1923 Andrew Bonar Law, who had been diagnosed with throat cancer, had been replaced as prime minister by Stanley Baldwin, who was an unknown quantity, particularly in relation to Ireland. Before his rapid political rise after being appointed Chancellor of the Exchequer by Bonar Law in October 1922, Baldwin had shown little interest in Ireland, describing himself as 'an ordinary rank-and-file member of the Unionist Party'.[46] Once he became prime minister, O'Shiel wrote that Baldwin was 'a person having strong Die-Hard sympathies' and had 'no doubt that he has strong pro-North-East sympathies and may have committed himself to these people by pledges in former days'. However, in contrast to some, he still felt that the Free State's best chance for a deal over the boundary question was with the Conservatives. Apart from being 'traditionally more straighter and honester [sic] in its dealings than the other parties', O'Shiel believed 'that by forcing a Conservative Government to deal with Article XII we eliminate from the British Parliament the largest possible measure of opposition ... it would be utterly impossible for the Conservatives to adopt a strong "pro-Ulster" and anti-Irish attitude, as their party is in power and has pledged itself to carry out the Treaty in good faith'.[47]

This was not a view shared by most within the Free State government or the NEBB. In a report outlining English attitudes to the Boundary Commission, Waller claimed it was highly unlikely that the public in England had heard of the Boundary Commission, writing, 'So far as the man in the street is concerned, it may be taken for granted that he is not thinking of Ireland at all.' He believed Baldwin's past record on 'Ireland has been uneventful, but not from our point of view very satisfactory'. With Baldwin and Bonar Law's governments owing their 'accession to power thanks to Conservative Die-Hards, opposed to the Treaty, and supporters of Ulster Unionist attitude', it did not bode well for the nationalist case. He singled out Lord Salisbury, Sir William Joynson-Hicks, Sir Thomas Inskip, Rupert Gwynne and Ronald McNeill as die-hards who were members of a ministry 'expected to have considerable bias in favour of Ulster'. He also highlighted that 'the presence in the House of a number of Ulster members gives them an advantage in stating their case and also of "Lobbying" with British Conservative members who are their personal friends'.[48]

O'Shiel believed that it would be better to delay the sitting of the Boundary Commission until after the Free State had joined the League of Nations, as the boundary question was an international rather than a domestic arbitration. If the Free State was a member, the League of Nations would be more likely to intervene if required. It would solidify the international dimension to the Boundary Commission and would 'make all the more evident that it is a Boundary dispute between a State internationally recognised and a province subordinate to another state'. He also felt it was important to make full use of the privileges and advantages of membership of the Imperial Conference, a sporadic gathering of the political leaders of the dominions and colonies of the British Empire, before pursuing the assembly of the Commission.[49]

Preparing the Free State's case for the Boundary Commission was another factor in that government delaying its pursuance. From October 1922 the NEBB was collecting and compiling data for the Commission, 'acting as a channel of communication between the Government and the Northern Nationalists for whom they were acting' and engaging in a publicity campaign in Ireland (North and South) and in Britain.[50] The huge volume of work carried out by the bureau is available in fifty-six boxes of files at the National Archives of Ireland. It published a wide range of leaflets and pamphlets that were distributed in different locations or published through the press.[51] Some of those distributed in Britain included ones entitled: 'England! Honour your Bond!', 'English Electors! Uphold the Treaty!' and 'Is the British Parliament Supreme in Northern Ireland?' For consumption in the North, the output included 'North-East: Numerical strength of the Nationalists', 'If "Ulster" Contracts Out – The Economic Case Against Partition' and 'Fair Play for Minorities?'[52] The bureau also issued weekly bulletins to the press, as well as 'Weekly Digests' to members of the Free State Executive Council, summarising the British and Irish media's coverage of the boundary question.[53]

The most comprehensive work completed by the NEBB was the *Handbook of the Ulster Question*, published in autumn 1923. It was divided into four sections: historical and political backgrounds; the wishes of the inhabitants; economic and geographic conditions; and analogous problems in other countries.[54] The book contained detailed statistics and maps; the maps were produced with the help of the Ordnance Survey Office in the Phoenix Park in Dublin.[55] It was compiled to 'facilitate the inhabitants of areas in Northern Ireland who sought inclusion in the Free State, and to make available for publication the salient facts of the case'[56] and was sent to leading newspapers in Ireland, Britain and the United States, and to statesmen and politicians, as well as being on sale to the general public. It was a book of reference for nationalists when preparing their cases for the Boundary Commission.

The extent of the work completed by the NEBB placed the Northern government in a quandary, with the secretary of the UUC, Alexander

Wilson (A.W.) Hungerford, querying the Cabinet on steps to be taken to combat the Free State propaganda. The Northern government's Cabinet Secretary, Wilfrid Spender, replying on behalf of Craig to Hungerford, said the position regarding the Boundary Commission was 'a very delicate one' and that Craig believed that by him not appointing a representative, the Commission could not be held. If the government instituted an enquiry 'in the various counties, etc. in order to obtain the statistics with which they could reply to the anti-partition propaganda of Southern Ireland it would provoke a feeling that the Government did not intend to stand by this course'. Spender acknowledged that the government 'would also welcome the preparation of statistics, provided it can be done without causing unsettlement along the boundary and provided that the Government is not in any way concerned in the preparation'. The government agreed to facilitate 'the supply of statistics to an outside organisation by any of their Departments' and would assist the UUC if it was 'ready to undertake such work on the above conditions'.[57] While publicly the Northern government proclaimed it would have nothing to do with the Boundary Commission, behind the scenes it worked closely with Hungerford and the UUC in assisting and coordinating unionist representations to the Commission.[58]

The NEBB was fully committed to obtaining the best possible outcome for the Free State and worked tirelessly to achieve that aim. It can also be argued that overall, the government, too, was committed and worked hard to get the best possible outcome. However, both institutions were severely hampered by the ambiguity of Article 12 and that the terms of reference for the Boundary Commission would in all probability be decided by a British-appointed chairman. Grappling in the dark forced the Free State government and the NEBB to make assumptions, many of them fundamentally flawed, which ended up damaging the Free State's prospects for success.

O'Shiel claimed that when he became NEBB director, he 'endeavoured to steer a course as near to the policy of the late General Michael Collins as was humanly possible'. He asserted that Collins frequently remarked that 'the Boundary Commission will settle nothing' and went out of his way to 'establish contact with the Belfast Authorities in the hope that such contact would lead to a better and more enduring settlement between Irishmen'. While this seemed at odds with the Free State government's pledges to carry out the entire Treaty, including Article 12, O'Shiel sought 'to reconcile these two somewhat disparate positions, which whilst enabling the Government to hold strongly to its pledges, yet allows ample room for the operations of statesmanship'. He explained the government's 'objective as not the securing of more territory but as the securing of National Union' and that 'the Boundary Commission must be regarded as a weapon, probably the most important weapon in this diplomatic war for National Union'.[59]

While O'Shiel's logic may have been sound, his understanding of the people with whom the Free State had to negotiate was not. One of the biggest flaws of the Free State government strategy during the period from the signing of the Treaty to the collapse of the Boundary Commission four years later was its lack of understanding of the Ulster unionist 'mindset'. Following on from previous Sinn Féin leaders, such as de Valera, Griffith and Collins, members of the Cumann na nGaedheal government believed the British government was the main obstacle to an agreement and clung on to the idea of seeking fruitless negotiations with Craig about Irish unity, despite Craig's very public utterances abhorring such a scenario. Speaking in 1926, nationalist MP for Fermanagh Cahir Healy wrote that it was because Northern nationalists 'knew the Northern mind much better than either Collins, Griffith or De Valera that we realised then that the big difficulty lay in Belfast and not in London. For years ... we have had the opposite preached.'[60] Stephen Gwynn, writing in *The Observer*, was even more emphatic: 'Sinn Féin in the North takes its orders from the South, which is more ignorant of Ulster than of Mesopotamia.'[61]

Cosgrave and others, such as O'Shiel, believed that unity was inevitable because of the internal squeeze that would force Northern Ireland into an all-Ireland parliament after its loss of territory through the Boundary Commission and through economic necessity. These assumptions underlay much of the preparatory work of the NEBB. Crucially, the bureau believed, erroneously as it transpired, that Article 12 laid down 'the wishes of the inhabitants as the primary consideration. Economic and geographic conditions are secondary matters.' Unlike Cosgrave, however, it accepted that territory and people from Ulster 'could be included in or excluded from the jurisdiction of either Government by the variation of the boundary line by the Commission'.[62] The Free State government, publicly at least, stuck to the stance that no territory of the Free State could be transferred to the North. Based on the government's assumption, the bureau drew up a maximum and minimum boundary line on what it expected from the Boundary Commission. The maximum claim would give the Free State 'all Ireland except Co. Antrim, the extreme north east corner of Co. Derry, portion of north and mid Armagh (excluding Armagh city) and north and mid Co. Down', whereas the minimum claim would give the Free State 'all Ireland except Co. Antrim, the extreme east portion of Co. Tyrone bordering on Lough Neagh, the eastern half of Co. Derry, the northern portion of Co. Armagh and the northern portion of Co. Down'.[63] Both projections were significantly more generous to the Free State than the award actually proposed by the Boundary Commission.

Those who were employed by the NEBB carried out extensive work in their efforts to advise the Free State government on their case for the Commission. The economist Joseph Johnston submitted a high volume of memoranda to the bureau on economic conditions in border areas, the development of County Donegal, Imperial preferences and fiscal changes, to name but a few.[64] In one of his documents, entitled 'Fiscal Independence – An Instrument of Irish Unity', he contended that the government should exercise its fiscal independence to the fullest, which in turn would see merchants from Derry, Newry and even Belfast putting pressure on the Northern government to agree to economic unity with the rest of Ireland, inevitably leading to eventual political unity.[65] This belief was one of the factors behind the Free State government's decision to erect customs barriers on the border in April 1923, a hugely consequential action that had largely negative results for the Free State's case before the Boundary Commission (see Chapter Four).

Bolton C. Waller was a highly important and respected member of the NEBB whose opinions on international precedents and procedures were generally adopted by the Free State government. Like Johnston, Waller completed significant research and wrote many memoranda for the bureau, producing documents such as 'Memorandum on European Precedents for the North Eastern Boundary Bureau', 'Memorandum on Ireland and the League of Nations, with reference to the Boundary Commission' and 'Reports on Methods of Conducting a Plebiscite'.[66] Due to the sensitive nature of the international boundary commissions, there were few reports Waller could access, so he travelled to London in January 1923, where he had lived before the Truce in July 1921, to investigate international precedents by interviewing many of his London contacts, including H.C. O'Neill from the Foreign Office, W. Molony and Miss Dugdale from the League of Nations Union, Delisle Burns from the Labour Party, S. Beresford, who had worked on the plebiscite for Upper Silesia, Lionel Curtis from the Colonial Office and Francis Bernard (F.B.) Bourdillon, a member of the Inter-Allied Commission in Upper Silesia. Waller found O'Neill and Bourdillon the most helpful, having 'more direct personal dealing with the Boundary question'.[67] Bourdillon was subsequently appointed secretary of the Irish Boundary Commission.[68]

During his visit to London, Waller obtained documents and information on procedures of continental boundary commissions, statements of claims, the use of plebiscites, customs frontiers and opinions on interpreting Article 12 of the Treaty. The people he spoke to 'were emphatic that in the plebiscite areas the "wishes of the inhabitants" have always been given preponderant weight, as against "economic and geographic conditions" – some thought in fact that the latter has been far too much overlooked'.[69] Waller looked primarily at the boundaries fixed to resolve territorial disputes in different European regions. Plebiscites had been used in five regions he examined: Upper Silesia, Allenstein and Marienwerder (disputes between Germany and Poland), Schleswig (between Germany and Denmark), and Klagenfurt (between Austria and Yugoslavia).[70]

The Schleswig dispute was decided in two parts: 'in the northern portion, a decision was to be reached by a majority vote of the whole. This resulted in a majority vote, 3 to 1 in favour of Danish sovereignty.' The more mixed southern zone's result was 'determined commune by commune by majority vote. The result there was a partitioning of the southern zone, creating the current Danish–German border.'[71] The Klagenfurt dispute between Austria and Yugoslavia was also put to a plebiscite of two areas, but the boundary commission in this instance decided if the zone consulted first, Zone A, chose to remain in Austria, there would be no vote in Zone B, which is what transpired.[72]

There were three plebiscites on the new Germany–Poland border, with two, the Allenstein and Marienwerder regions, relatively straightforwardly voting to remain in Germany with some slight adjustments. Upper Silesia was the most complex. It was divided into four districts under its boundary commission. Two voted heavily in favour of Germany, one for Poland and the other marginally for Germany. The 'Allied powers were unable to agree on how to implement a partition and left the issue for the Council of the new League of Nations. In a controversial decision, the League partitioned Upper Silesia, mostly on the basis of the vote but also taking into account geography and economics.'[73]

The one Waller found most like the Irish example was that of Upper Silesia. Even the wording for that commission was similar, stating, 'Regard will be paid to the wishes of the inhabitants as shown by the vote and to the geographic and economic conditions.' Waller felt this strengthened 'the case for applying self-determination in Ireland, since at Versailles the geographic and economic considerations were seemingly placed on a level with the wishes of the inhabitants, while in Ireland the words are plainly meant to be merely qualifying'.[74] He believed the phrase 'so far as may be compatible with economic and geographic conditions' meant 'that frontiers must be continuous. Isolated "islands" of Poles had to be left in Germany, and Germans in Poland.' Natural barriers like rivers were important and 'economic dislocations should be where possible avoided, for example a boundary may be so fixed as to keep a railway inside one country, or to avoid separating a town from its railway station or water supply'.[75]

Waller argued that inserting the qualifying terms of economic and geographic conditions was important in Upper Silesia's case 'as it would have been impossible to draw a coherent border based on plebiscite results, particularly in the centre of the disputed area which had very mixed results, with urban areas voting to be in Germany and rural areas in Poland'. Even though economic and geographic conditions were factored in, population came first and industry second in the boundary commission's considerations. Waller believed the case for the wishes of the inhabitants would be stronger in Ireland, where 'a plebiscite is unnecessary as the wishes of the inhabitants are already well known by the results of elections and other indications, and where unnecessary the expense and possible danger of a plebiscite are best avoided'.[76]

Based on Waller's research, O'Shiel wrote to the Free State Executive Council, claiming Waller's work altered their pre-conceived notions of boundary commission practices and procedures. He suggested that they must always insist on the international dimension of the Irish Boundary Commission, and, as 'would appear to be the case in every instance of what might be described as "wishes of the Inhabitants Commission" on the Continent, the terms of reference in Article 12 of the Treaty must suffice without further embellishment by either of the two plenary Governments'.[77] The commitment to self-determination demonstrated in the other post-First World War boundary commissions perhaps explains why the NEBB had so much faith in the Irish Boundary Commission to deliver for nationalists.

There was little dwelling on some of the key differences between the regions Waller looked at and the Irish case. Unlike the other European regions, Ireland was already partitioned before the Boundary Commission was due to convene, no time limit was specified for the setting up of the Commission and, most importantly, the chairman was not an independent appointee, being nominated instead by one of the contending parties, the British government.[78] While Waller highlighted that the latter could 'appoint a biased Chairman' under the terms of the Treaty, many in the Free State government seemed to take solace in Austen Chamberlain's commitment to 'appointing a thoroughly impartial Commissioner', probably a 'Dominion statesman or judge'.[79] Accordingly, the Free State's case was based on an assumption that the Irish Boundary Commission would be run along similar lines to the post-First World War commissions in Europe, another poor judgement call.

In the first half of 1923, Hugh A. MacCartan, responsible for the publicity division of the NEBB, visited Belfast and some border areas, such as Pettigo on the Donegal–Fermanagh border, Derry and South and East Down, including his home village of Aughlisnafin in Down, to assess local opinion on the Boundary Commission. He found most nationalists resigned and apathetic, frustrated by the delay in its convening, with many believing it would not actually make any difference. There was 'the feeling that the Free State was not troubling about the minority in the Six Counties'.[80]

The editor of *The Irish News*, Timothy McCarthy, told MacCartan in Belfast that by the time the Commission convened, through gerrymandering, 'the Partitionists will have achieved majorities in nearly every administrative unit and this would tell against us. He thinks that is the real object of the jerrymandering.' MacCartan argued that the 'delay in setting up the Commission had caused great confusion and divided councils in the nationalist ranks. One section based all its hopes on coming in to the Free State; the other, outside the affected areas, wanted to go into the "Northern" Parliament.'[81]

The *Irish Independent*, disagreeing with *The Irish News*'s scepticism over the Boundary Commission, in an editorial entitled 'Time for Action', wrote that 'Our Nationalist countrymen in the North not only resent the suggestion that Article 12 of the Treaty should become a dead letter, but they equally resent the delay in putting that clause into operation.'[82]

MacCartan, on his way to Castlewellan in Down in April 1923, met Joe Devlin at Amiens Street (now Connolly) station in Dublin – whether by accident or design is not clear. Echoing the views expressed by McCarthy, Devlin 'thought that the delay in the settlement of that question was seriously prejudicing the interests of the minority in the Six Counties by giving the Belfast Parliament time to "dig themselves in" and reduce the minority representation on public boards to vanishing point'. He 'did not think that the "Northern" Parliament would not [sic] come into an All-Ireland Parliament for an indefinite period. At first they thought they could not do without us, but they had altered that view and their present determination was to keep out as long as possible.' Although Devlin was correct in his assessment, MacCartan's visits north convinced him 'that the Unionists will "come in" as soon as it is a good business proposition to do so'.[83]

In May 1923, the month Civil War hostilities came to an end with the call by the anti-Treaty IRA's Chief of Staff, Frank Aiken, to dump arms, O'Shiel reported that 'the case of the Free State for submission to the Boundary Commission was now practically complete'. The Free State Executive Council decided to 'request the British Government to take the necessary steps for the setting up of the Boundary Commission in accordance with Article 12 of the Treaty'.[84] Kevin O'Higgins issued a statement to the press, stating that the Free State government was 'now rapidly approaching a condition of things that will enable us to take the necessary steps towards setting up the Commission'.[85] Some still favoured delaying, including directors of railway companies and the Governor General of the Free State, Tim Healy. Healy believed that former British Prime Minister Bonar Law was 'not favourably disposed towards the Boundary question', and even though he had retired, 'as long as he wields his present influence, quarters that might otherwise be friendly will not be inclined to assist us openly'.[86]

However, the Free State government felt it was important to make 'certain progress' on the Boundary Commission before the next general election, which subsequently occurred in late August 1923. No progress 'would be disastrous as their opponents would make great capital out of the assertion that the Government were taking no action in the matter'. Even government supporters were becoming anxious over the delay.[87] In a memorandum to the Executive Council in late May, O'Shiel claimed the Free State government should appoint 'on the eve of the Election, our Commissioner, and after this dynamic stroke go to the country. There is no doubt that such a stroke at such a time would enormously benefit the Government at the hustings.'[88] Cosgrave believed that 'the Government could not go to an election until the Irish representatives and the Chairman had both been appointed'.[89] In a meeting between Cosgrave and Tom Jones, representing the British government at the time, Cosgrave admitted that his silence on the boundary question had 'aroused serious suspicion in the minds of a large section of his own followers, particularly in the army'. He added that the 'Catholics in the North, moreover, resented it. It had hampered the efforts he had been making to get them to recognise the Northern Government. He repeated that he was now absolutely bound to press for the Boundary Commission.'[90]

O'Shiel offered some thoughts on who the Free State commissioner should be, declaring that they needed 'a man of great weight and sagacity, and one of irreproachable name'. Believing it irrelevant where he came from, Ireland or abroad, he should be 'a man without prejudice on the Northern Question, yet one who has a thorough mastery of the situation and with sufficient backbone to fight his corner hard and well, if necessary'. 'Above all,' O'Shiel added, 'he should be a person who is prepared to act on the Government's slightest suggestion – to go hard when the Government tells him to go hard, and to soften when the Government tells him to soften.' In O'Shiel's view, an 'ideal person ... would be Mr. James MacNeill, our High Commissioner in London ... I cannot, at the moment, imagine a more suitable person in every way.'[91] Geoffrey Hand, who was a distant cousin of the MacNeills,[92] believed that as 'an Antrim Catholic MacNeill was well aware of conditions in the north, even though his native glens could not hope to be affected by any mere boundary alteration. But he had also been a distinguished servant of the Crown in India, sure-footed in the corridors of power.'[93] However, it was his brother Eoin, and not James MacNeill, who was selected. According to Hand, 'Eoin MacNeill was a figure much better known and more acceptable to nationalist opinion than his brother (though James, it can be argued, might have proved a more skilled tactician in the event).'

Cosgrave wanted to appoint a commissioner who was a Cabinet minister, from the North, and a Catholic. Two Cabinet ministers were from the North, but Ernest Blythe was a Protestant, leaving Minister for Education Eoin MacNeill as the only option. Even though there were only seven Cabinet members, all under enormous strain due to the prevailing conditions in the Free State, Cosgrave felt it had to be someone from the Executive Council as it 'was too important to trust to anyone but a member of the innermost circle of government'.[94] Unwisely, he did not consider it an essential criterion that the commissioner should have a legal background.

Born in the Glens of Antrim in 1867, Eoin MacNeill was one of the founders of the Gaelic League in 1893 and the first editor of its newspaper *An Claidheamh Soluis*. In November 1913 his 'The North Began' article in the same newspaper became the catalyst for the formation of the Irish Volunteers weeks later, an organisation in which he played a prominent leadership role. MacNeill is arguably best known for his efforts to prevent the 1916 Easter Rising from taking place by issuing a countermanding order published in the *Sunday Independent* on Easter Sunday. Despite some considerable opposition due to his actions in 1916, he was actively involved in the reconstituted Sinn Féin, took the pro-Treaty side and became the Free State's first minister for education. Away from politics, he was considered one of the principal medieval Irish historians of his era and became the inaugural Professor of Early Irish History at University College Dublin (UCD).[95]

Dorothy Macardle, in her book *The Irish Republic*, claimed that MacNeill's appointment was affected by his impending general election contest with Éamon de Valera in Clare. Macardle wrote that once MacNeill was appointed as the government's representative on the Boundary

Commission, it 'thus constituted him the protagonist of Irish unity' and 'sent him to contest the elections against De Valera in Clare'. Hand dismissed this claim.[96] Macardle also claimed that during the election, 'Promises to insist upon the fulfilment of Article 12 of the Treaty and to see the Boundary issue through to a conclusion featured largely in the speeches of Government candidates.'[97] The Ulster unionist press also considered MacNeill's appointment as an election 'stunt'.[98] During the election campaign in Clare, where both MacNeill and de Valera were both elected, MacNeill claimed there 'will be no boundary; the boundary will be the sea and no other'.[99]

Privately, MacNeill had considerably more doubts. Speaking in 1927, he claimed he was well aware of the defects with Article 12 when he 'accepted the duty of acting on the Boundary Commission, and if I had consulted my personal interests I would not have accepted it ... the task imposed on me and undertaken under a sense of public duty and service was entirely repugnant to me'.[100] MacNeill revealed to Patrick McGilligan, a fellow Northerner and UCD scholar, after McGilligan was appointed to the Executive Council following the 1924 Free State Army Mutiny, that he had accepted the position 'because he did not believe that the commission would bring the benefits expected of it and would damage rather than assist the political career of the commissioner'. Declaring that the 'ripest fruit first falls', MacNeill said that he 'had stood too many blows to feel concern at the prospect of more, but it would be unfair to place such a burden on a young man at the beginning of his career'.[101]

The Executive Council ratified MacNeill's appointment on 12 July 1923. A week later, Tim Healy informed the British government, sending a letter to the Colonial Secretary, the Duke of Devonshire, of MacNeill's appointment and asking the British government to 'take the necessary steps on their part for constituting the said Commission'.[102] Cosgrave made MacNeill's appointment public the next day. Devonshire replied on 25 July, stating that once the general election in the Free State was over, it was 'the intention of His Majesty's Government at once to enter into communication with your Government and also with the Government of

Northern Ireland upon the further steps necessary to give effect to the provisions of Article 12 of the Treaty'.[103]

The path was then set for further delays with the holding of conferences instead of the convening of the Boundary Commission itself. By that point Devonshire and the rest of the British government were aware of Cosgrave's intentions. Cosgrave had told Jones he had no intention of appealing to the League of Nations if there were further delays and he was open to a conference between the British and Northern Irish governments on the boundary question, even though he believed it would 'cost me a good deal of support among my followers, but I will come, because that is the way in which it ought to be settled'.[104] Even if Cosgrave believed that a mutual settlement was the best solution, by showing his hand to the British government without seeking anything in return, he demonstrated his ineptitude as a negotiator, something that occurred again at crucial stages in the following years.

The Irish Free State government was committed to the Boundary Commission and to a united Ireland. The extent of the work completed by the NEBB, which was supported and funded by the Free State government, demonstrates this aptly.[105] Its commitment was probably based on a combination of internal pressure from Northern nationalists, republicans and its own supporters, as well as a genuine desire to pursue Irish unity. But it committed many errors based on preconceived assumptions which helped to fatally undermine the Free State's case before the Boundary Commission. Arguably, none was more consequential than the decision to erect customs barriers in April 1923.

Chapter Four

'... stereotyping the existing boundary'

WHEN HUGH MacCARTAN MET JOE Devlin in April 1923 on his way to County Down, Devlin told MacCartan that he was opposed to the introduction of customs barriers, which had been established at the start of that month by the Free State government, as he believed they 'would have the effect of stereotyping the existing boundary'.[1] A large dilemma for the Free State government was that attaining fiscal autonomy required the erection of a 'Customs ring' around its borders by sea and, crucially, by land. The government accepted Devlin's assertion that the creation of a land frontier 'may be regarded as stereotyping the present boundary line between the Free State and Northern Ireland and might, to that extent, prejudice our decision before the Boundary Commission'.[2] However, the Boundary Commission had not yet convened and the Free State felt it needed to pursue its own fiscal policies at the earliest possible opportunity. There could be no fiscal autonomy without customs barriers on the land border and if there was no fiscal autonomy then the British would still be dictating financial policy. Many in the Free State government also believed that the introduction of customs barriers should form part of its strategy to force Northern Ireland to end partition by first forcing it into economic union. However, like many of its strategies at the time, this idea was deeply flawed. It directly resulted in a harder and more permanent partition that existed for decades, acutely impacting on the daily lives of people on both sides of the border.

As nationalist Ireland's demands for greater independence became more entrenched after 1916, fiscal autonomy and control of customs and excise were seen as essential in any scheme of self-government that would be tolerable. Arthur Griffith argued that under the Government of Ireland Act 1920, 'the authority of the Irish parliament in College Green will not exceed the grocer at the corner'. He stated, 'The question of customs ... is a question of preventing Ireland from having her fiscal policy upset every time a new fiscal doctrine appeals to the English electors as good for England.'[3]

New solutions were needed to mollify Sinn Féin, with many in Britain accepting that fiscal autonomy for Southern Ireland would need to be granted. Ulster unionists were firmly opposed to such a move. In a hard-hitting editorial in January 1921, the *Belfast News-Letter* stated 'there are no moderate Sinn Feiners; there are only different sorts of extremists'. It claimed that the 'enemies of Ulster' want the Southern Parliament to have fiscal autonomy 'so that it can coerce Ulster by economic pressure, seeing that physical coercion is impracticable ... But they are mistaken. Irish unity will not be hastened by a Customs barrier between North and South, and if fiscal autonomy was granted this would be inevitable.'[4]

The Belfast Boycott provided evidence to Ulster unionists on the type of fiscal policies Sinn Féin would pursue if Southern Ireland was granted fiscal autonomy, protectionist policies that would do harm not only to the targeted victims, but also to the perpetrators. The boycott on blacklisted Belfast-based banks and firms was instigated by Dáil Éireann in August 1920 in response to what it saw as a pogrom against Catholics in Belfast from the summer of 1920, which resulted in thousands of Catholics suffering from violence, job losses and displacement from their homes.[5] While its economic efforts to hamper trade in Belfast met with mixed results, the boycott's aim to unify Ireland was an unmitigated disaster. Winston Churchill believed 'it recognised and established real partition, spiritual and voluntary partition, before physical partition had been established'.[6] While Sinn Féin members were earnest in their desire to help the Catholics of Belfast, the Belfast Boycott, in many ways, worsened the situation by adding a permanency and structure to partition that had not existed before.

Referring to negotiations that had just begun between Sinn Féin and the British government following the Truce in July 1921, the Northern Minister for Finance, Hugh Pollock, claimed that if fiscal autonomy was offered to Sinn Féin, that 'means an inevitable customs barrier between Ireland and England. As regards Ulster, we want no such barrier, knowing it impedes trade. If we must have some such barrier we would rather it would be with the south with its 4,000,000 people than England with its 40,000,000.'[7]

During the Treaty negotiations, when Lloyd George was trying to sell an all-Ireland Parliament to Craig, he claimed 'that Ulster would be led to economic ruin if she were separated from Southern Ireland'. Craig responded, 'You have apparently overlooked the fact that your proposal to break the fiscal unity of the United Kingdom would involve the fiscal separation of Ulster from Great Britain, with which 90 per cent of her trade is, directly or indirectly, conducted.'[8]

Thwarted by Craig in reaching an all-Ireland settlement, Lloyd George offered the Sinn Féin plenipotentiaries a Boundary Commission and then, shortly before the Treaty was signed in the early hours of 6 December 1921, full fiscal autonomy (see Chapter One). This allowed the Irish Free State to devise its own fiscal policies and tariffs separate from the United Kingdom, thus achieving a long-cherished goal of many Irish nationalists who believed autonomy without fiscal autonomy was not real autonomy.

While most of the Ulster unionists' attacks on the Treaty were focused on the Boundary Commission, there was also criticism of the fiscal powers to be transferred to the Free State. Lambasting the Treaty in an editorial, the *Belfast News-Letter* wrote that the Belfast Boycott 'is to continue, and it is to be intensified by all the legal powers of the Southern

Government. It is to insist on a rigid Customs barrier between North and South.'[9] Speaking about the Treaty to *The Northern Whig*, a 'leading businessman' from Belfast crystalised the fears shared by many unionists, stating:

> There is no direct coercion of Ulster in the arrangement ... but I fear there is every facility given for indirect coercion. If we don't come in under the Irish Free State it seems to be quite within the power of Sinn Fein to set up a customs barrier which would effectually kill our trade with Southern Ireland and cripple the port of Belfast as a distributing centre. It would, in fact, be tantamount to a tremendous tightening of the present boycott. We have not under the arrangement any power of retaliation or defence against such a policy. And we may rest fairly certain that the policy will be applied as a powerful means to constrain Ulster to come in.[10]

Reading such views would undoubtedly have convinced some in Sinn Féin that they had a powerful weapon at their disposal that could help to end partition. Collins, for one, believed customs barriers could do much harm to Northern trade. In the pact he signed with Craig in late January 1922, in agreeing to suspend the Belfast Boycott, he claimed 'the boycott was comparatively ineffective, and that if it became necessary to fight the Northern parliament they could set up an effective tariff-barrier in its stead'.[11] In addition to seeking fiscal independence from Britain, and to generate revenue for the exchequer, the fiscal policy of erecting customs barriers was also an attempt to apply economic pressure on the nascent Northern jurisdiction. As with the naive and destructive Belfast Boycott policy, many in the Free State were rooted to the belief that the economic pressure caused by customs barriers would force the North to end partition.

The Provisional Government, on the brink of civil war, felt it was not able to exert its fiscal autonomy immediately and asked the British government to act as agents of its revenue for the financial year 1922/23 before it pursued its own fiscal policies.[12] The Irish Free State was still determined to diverge from the British fiscal space at the earliest opportunity, and while it was clear that it would separate itself from the British financial system as a key symbol of independence, there remained some speculation in late 1922 on what the financial relationship would be between the Free State and Northern Ireland.

Writing a memorandum for the NEBB in November 1922, Joseph Johnston stated that a 'fiscal boundary ... is an automatic consequence of fiscal independence and, one might add, a necessity of good financial "housekeeping"'. He recognised, though, that a sea boundary was 'the most convenient and economical of all customs frontiers' and with Westminster responsible for the Northern frontier, both Free State and British governments had 'a common administrative interest, and the former a financial interest, in the customs frontier being as convenient as possible'.[13]

Johnston recognised some of the objections to a land customs frontier between the two Irish jurisdictions. A land frontier was more expensive, it 'tends to dislocate and divert trade from its natural channels', it is a 'fruitful source of political unrest', it 'tends to produce smuggling', and it 'causes inconvenience to travellers with a consequent diminution of traffic'. In Ireland's example, a land frontier would reduce the 'natural hinterland of towns such as Clones and Enniskillen, which at present serve large districts in both political areas'.[14] Johnston added, though, that the existing arrangement of being in a customs union was 'impossible as public opinion in Ireland requires the Free State to exercise its fiscal independence at the earliest possible moment'.[15] Refuting Hugh Pollock's suggestion of keeping the existing fiscal arrangement, Johnston claimed the 'Free State would have to follow slavishly every change in indirect taxation made by the British Chancellor of the Exchequer' if it were to remain in a customs union with the UK.[16]

In a letter to *The Irish Times* years later, in 1971, Johnston claimed that, much to his surprise, 'the Free State Government decided to control its own Customs and Excise even before the Boundary Commission sat to consider the general Boundary question', saying, that 'In doing so, they gave away the whole commercial and economic case for making a drastic alteration of the Boundary at all.' He stated that it was 'a pity' that the British government's suggestion at the time of a customs union with 'proceeds of indirect taxation assigned to the Free State area and the UK on the basis of a careful statistical estimate' was 'not seriously considered by our Government'.[17] Yet, judging by the memoranda and documents he wrote in 1922 and 1923 on customs barriers, it was apparent that a customs union encompassing the same duties and regulations with the UK was not seriously considered by Johnston either. Writing in February 1923, he claimed that the 'objective of current duties and restrictions' was 'frankly protectionist but the industries they seek to protect are confined exclusively to Great Britain' and the industries benefiting from the tariffs were 'not represented in the Free State or in Northern Ireland wither there is no earthly reason why these tariffs, devised exclusively in the supposed interests of certain cross channel industries, should be retained by the Free State'.[18]

The NEBB produced an anti-partition pamphlet, presumably with considerable input from Johnston, entitled 'If "Ulster" Contracts Out', before the North, as predicted, contracted itself out of the Irish Free State in December 1922. The pamphlet clearly inferred that the Free State would gain more finances by separating from the British fiscal system. It argued that Ireland's economic life 'has deteriorated continuously under the British fiscal system', that Ireland was too dependent on Great Britain. It contended that Ireland's place in British policy was to be 'the fruitful mother of flocks and herds'. Ireland 'commits the economic heresy of importing foodstuffs for her own use and exporting the small quantity she grows', 'buying the finished beef and selling the live animals ... Ireland exports at the point of lowest economic value and imports at the point of highest economic value'.[19]

In a series of articles on the fiscal consequences of the Treaty, *The Economist* claimed that if Northern Ireland opted out of the Free State, 'a land frontier there has got to be' and 'the resultant inconvenience and expense will be colossal'.[20] It advised Cosgrave to 'hold his hand as to the Boundary Commission' and postpone 'for a short while' the setting up of customs barriers between North and South. This, the newspaper contended, would facilitate 'an untying of knots and an unravelling of tangles which would be surprisingly profitable to Ireland, both South and North'.[21]

Although aware of the implications such a decision could have on the border between the Free State and Northern Ireland, the Free State government felt it had no choice, if Northern Ireland opted out of not only the Free State but also an Irish customs union, other than to erect customs barriers along the 300-mile-long land frontier from Carlingford Lough to Lough Foyle. Writing in *The Times* on 1 January 1923, Cosgrave stated:

> [Apart] from the Boundary Commission, the vexatious question of a Customs barrier will arise, out of which, no matter how friendly we may wish to be with the North, I can see no possible escape, if the North severs herself from the Irish fiscal unit and joins the fiscal unit of Great Britain. We cannot forgo our large fiscal independence in order to meet the North.[22]

Realising time was running out on the existing fiscal arrangements between the Free State and Great Britain, Charles Joseph (C.J.) Flynn, one of two revenue commissioners appointed after the Board of Revenue Commissioners was established in Dublin, wrote a letter to Cosgrave in early January 1923 advising that if it 'is the intention that the Free State should stand on its own fiscal legs from 1st April next [start of the financial year] it is of the utmost importance that a tentative scheme for the provision of a Customs frontier organisation should be completed at the earliest possible date'.[23] Cosgrave, who served as Minister for Finance as well as president of the Executive Council, subsequently instructed the Ministry of Finance to outline alternative arrangements, which it did (but all with drawbacks), to the setting up of a customs barrier, contending that if 'there were any probability that the Boundary Commission were likely to sit and complete its deliberations in the early future there would be a very strong case for postponing the frontier'. If, on the other hand, 'there is not, it may be difficult to justify postponement, with its consequences, to the Oireachtas'.[24] With time running out, at its meeting of 15 February, the Free State Executive Council decided to introduce customs barriers on 1 April 1923.[25]

Kevin O'Shiel acknowledged that trade would be affected by a customs border, but he contended that it would 'strike harder at Northern conditions'. He believed it was 'absurd' to suggest that erecting customs barriers would 'stereotype' the border and 'shows that those who use this argument know nothing whatever about international Customs conditions. There is nothing simpler than to alter a Land Customs frontier.' Referring to the occupation by French and Belgian troops of the Ruhr Valley in Germany that had taken place in January 1923, O'Shiel wrote, 'quite recently we have seen with what ease France as an invading power has been able to annex and put up new Customs Frontiers in overwhelmingly German and hostile territory'. O'Shiel asserted that after 'the findings of the Boundary Commission all we need to do is to advance our Customs lines from the present position to the edge of the new line of transferred territory'.[26]

Even though there was pressure from Ulster unionists, key business concerns in the Free State, and from people like C.J. Flynn from the Revenue Commissioners, to postpone the introduction of customs barriers for another year, the Free State government was determined to diverge from the British fiscal space as quickly as possible, partly due to its desperate need for finances at the time. Primarily because of the Civil War, the Irish Free State was economically impoverished at its inception. According to Michael Hopkinson, it is estimated that the 'material damage' arising from the Civil War 'amounted to more than £30 million and that it cost around £17 million to finance the war. Property damage easily exceeded that of the Anglo-Irish War.'[27] In 1923 there was an expenditure of £7,500,000 on the army and £1,250,000 in compensation.[28] The housing of over 12,000 republican prisoners and internees for most of 1923 was also a huge financial drain. By May 1923 there were 27,000 dependents' allowances granted. The Free State government also had difficulty collecting taxes and rates during and immediately after the Civil War, particularly in the most disturbed areas.[29]

Speaking shortly before the customs barriers were erected, Cosgrave stated that they would ensure that 'the Free State and Britain each get a fair share of the revenue on articles consumed in their own territory', something the Irish believed never happened when revenue was controlled by the British Treasury. He concluded by saying, 'After the first roughnesses in the system have been smoothed out, little difficulty is expected in the working of the system.'[30] Cosgrave's optimism proved ill-founded, as the introduction of customs barriers in April 1923 profoundly changed the lives of people for decades, particularly those who lived close to the border. It also altered the dynamic on partition, by adding a permanency and an infrastructure to it that had not existed before.

In the build-up to the introduction of customs barriers, many Ulster unionists expressed their disapproval of the move. However, some felt it would damage the Free State more than the North. The Northern government's Chief Whip, Herbert Dixon, suggested how the decision could impact on the Boundary Commission, saying, 'If they carried out their intention it would dispose of the boundary question, if it ever existed. They were going to set up their posts at certain places, thus creating a boundary and recognising it. What court of law could then proceed to say that it should be elsewhere?'[31]

James Craig claimed that the 'proposal to set up a Customs barrier on the Southern border would make the South, and not the North, responsible for partition'.[32] Agreeing with Craig's assertion that erecting customs barriers was 'a spiteful blunder', in an editorial entitled 'The Arch-Partitionists', *The Northern Whig* stressed that people in the Free State 'will be far heavier losers' than people in the North. On the idea that the new fiscal arrangements would 'provide a sure means of forcing Ulster to accept "unity"', the paper stated, 'Very little reflection should convince anyone that they will have the opposite effect.' Those in the Free State 'have shown that they are as ignorant of elementary economics as they are incapable of understanding the passionate loyalty of the Ulster people to the Throne'.[33]

Nationalists such as South Armagh MP John D. Nugent were also very critical of customs barriers, with Nugent seeing 'an altogether more sinister significance in the customs barrier. He interpreted its introduction on 1 April 1923 as an indication that the Free State Government was implicitly forfeiting any claims which its boundary bureau was preparing for the transfer of Tyrone, Fermanagh, Derry City, Newry and south Armagh.'[34]

Many of the arguments put forward by Johnston, O'Shiel and Hugh MacCartan from the NEBB emphasised the strong prospect of customs barriers being used as a weapon to force Northern Ireland into economic union and thus political union. Johnston did not accept the arguments made by some Northern nationalists that, by the Free State gaining large areas of Northern Ireland through the Boundary Commission and by using customs barriers to manipulate indirect taxation in the right way, all Belfast trade with the Free State would be brought 'to a complete stand still, that the Northern state will in consequence simply collapse and die of inaction in which case its surrender at discretion can be received'. He believed that no matter how generous the Boundary Commission was with territory, the most they could expect from numbers of people being transferred was around 260,000, and 'Belfast, free from the competition of Derry and Newry, might be able to exist with a population of about one million to cater for.' He did not envisage an optimistic Boundary Commission outcome bringing 'about the economic collapse of the Northern State'. He also believed a 'tariff war with Great Britain, like marriage, is not a thing to be entered upon lightly or without due forethought'. He felt that Belfast was more concerned with customs barriers than the Boundary Commission, and it seemed 'possible to strike a bargain in which we should guarantee freedom of trade to Belfast and they in turn should abandon large areas of their present territory to the Free State'. He added that, 'while the Customs barrier retains all the terrors of the unknown it might be worthwhile to barter some of their partly imaginary terrors for the sake of the liberation of large areas of the Northern territory'.[35]

Johnston also argued that as 'a considerably larger number of Free State citizens were in the habit of buying their domestic requirements in Derry, Strabane or Enniskillen than the number of Northern Ireland citizens who were in the habit of buying their domestic requirements in Clones', he believed that the injury over customs barriers 'would be felt by Northern Ireland much more seriously than by the Free State'. He estimated that 8,000 Free State citizens shopped in Derry, 10,000 in Strabane and at least 14,000 in Enniskillen. Conversely, less than 8,000 Northern Ireland citizens shopped in Clones.[36] He also contended that the negative consequences of fiscal separation were exaggerated. Despite fiscal separation, Canadian-grown wheat was exported from New York, and Brazilian coffee and Spanish ore were imported through Rotterdam before ending up in Germany.[37]

Johnston wrote at length about County Donegal, the county most affected by partition due to its geographic location. To mitigate against the 'shadow of an impending Customs Barrier' hanging 'over the present intimate and friendly commercial relations between Derry and Donegal', to escape 'the inconvenience of bringing their tea, sugar and other dutiable articles across the frontier Donegal people have lately been considering the feasibility of developing a new port of entry and commercial centre of their own'. What was once, as Johnston described, 'the slums of rural Ireland', where over two-thirds of the acreage of Donegal was 'scheduled as congested ... where poor law valuation per head of the population is less than 30/-', had seen big improvements since the 1890s 'through an extensive railway system in the county, congested districts boards relief help, and training of good agricultural practices, for example'. Co-operative movements like the Templecrone Co-operative Agricultural Society (the Cope) headquartered in Dungloe, managed by Paddy 'the Cope' Gallagher, had helped to break the 'gombeen' system, where, previously, local shopkeepers or 'gombeen' men were 'king of the area and where most of families' finances went to'. As well as enormously reducing the prices charged for a wide variety of goods throughout the Donegal highlands, Templecrone used Burtonport Port in Donegal frequently for corn, as opposed to being totally reliant on Derry. When the Specials prohibited the transport of goods from Donegal to Derry in 1922, 'Paddy Gallagher organised boats from Glasgow to Burtonport, Killybegs, and other Donegal ports ... Donegal people learned you could save one pound in ten by transporting directly to Donegal ports.' Johnston believed the 'arrival of a Customs Barrier provides an additional reason for Donegal people to develop their own commercial centre'. Donegal, 'and more especially Templecrone, has pointed the way to a worthy goal'.[38]

Regardless of what Johnston later wrote in 1971, in 1923, as a key economic adviser of the Free State, he believed that by the Free State using its fiscal powers to reduce customs and excise duties, for example, on products such as tea, alcoholic beverages, sugar and tobacco, it would soon dawn on the 'rapidly developing political intelligence' of the Northern businessman 'that so far as fiscal policy is concerned the Free State system is more in his interests than the British system'. With a porous land border, smuggling would thrive. The British custom authorities 'will have to abandon the attempt effectively to guard the land frontier and ... concentrate their attention on preventing such goods from finding their way into Great Britain from Northern Ireland'. Johnston believed that Northern Ireland would 'have the worst of both worlds for her trade with Great Britain will be watched just as closely as the trade of the Free State while she will not enjoy the legitimate advantages of Free State fiscal independence'. After such a fiscal squeeze on Northern Ireland, Johnston felt it then would be politically advisable

> to arrange a Customs Union for one year at the best political price the Free State can obtain for the first year. As a condition of renewal for a second year the political price should be raised, and so on from year to year until we all wake up suddenly to realise that

by slow degrees the Free State has in fact reabsorbed the Northern Territory.[39]

If anything, O'Shiel was even more optimistic on the power of the customs barrier to force Northern Ireland into economic union. In a memorandum to the Free State Executive Council in February 1923, he stated, 'Aiming, in the ultimate, for full National Union, political and economic ... we are convinced that the Customs Frontier if well used is one of the greatest cards in this policy'. He asserted that once the fiscal policy was in operation, in Northern Ireland, 'it will not take very long for a feeling to develop towards a Customs Union, and thence Political Union'.[40]

In a follow-up memorandum to the Executive Council two weeks later, O'Shiel claimed there was big consternation from merchants in Belfast and Newry over the proposed customs barrier and there was outright alarm in Derry, remarking, 'we have always regarded Derry City as the "Achilles heel" of the Northern Situation – a vulnerable spot in the apparently solid armour of Craig'. O'Shiel was

> convinced that not the Customs Barrier, but the exercise of our undoubted and hard-won right to collect and manage our own Customs and Excise, is good sound National policy in spite of all objections, and, further, that it would be ruinous for us to waive this right, particularly at this highly important juncture, with the Northern Question lying yet unsolved before us.[41]

From Hugh MacCartan's visits to border regions and to Belfast in early 1923, he also believed in the merits of customs barriers as an effective weapon to place pressure on Northern Ireland to accept economic unity. Even though he was warned by Tom and Michael Gallaher of Gallaher's tobacco factory in Belfast that customs barriers, as with the Belfast Boycott, would draw them closer to business in Great Britain, he was told by Belfast-based NEBB legal agent George Martin that wholesale spirit merchants in Belfast 'regarded the Customs barrier as worse than prohibition'. After visiting Derry, MacCartan believed 'the Customs barrier has brought the Unionist merchants up against the realities of Partition. I am convinced that when completely established conditions prevail in the South, the Derry merchants will take steps, not perhaps to bring Derry in alone, but to bring the whole Six Counties in with them.'[42]

This research, testimonies and advice was all relayed to members of the Free State Executive Council, who in many cases shared the views of Johnston, O'Shiel and MacCartan. Ernest Blythe, an Ulster Protestant, was considered by many to have a better understanding of the Ulster unionist mindset. Yet he, too, believed economic pressure could be put on the north-east through 'the cost and inconvenience of a customs barrier between the two territories and all its concomitants of armed frontier guards smuggling shooting [sic] and border lawlessness and transport difficulties'.[43] It is little wonder that the Free State government was so gung-ho about introducing customs barriers and unconcerned about the potential pitfalls for people's daily lives and also for the Free State's case before the Boundary Commission.

The significance of the creation of customs barriers on the border became apparent the moment their introduction was announced to the public in late February 1923, and they were enacted just weeks later, on 1 April, leaving very little time for people and businesses to prepare. In practical terms, the importing and exporting of merchandise across the border was now prohibited except through designated routes and at designated times. Customs stations were open for the clearance of merchandise between 9 a.m. and 5 p.m. daily, except on Sundays.[44] Farm produce was exempted, as was the removal of household furniture and small domestic supplies of non-dutiable goods.[45] Farmers were still expected to fill out 'several Customs forms', which left many of them in a 'disturbed state' according to Northern Minister for Agriculture Edward Archdale.[46] Cross-border roads were designated as 'authorized', 'concession' or 'unauthorized/unapproved'.[47] The British and Free State governments published the list of the 'authorized' or approved roads along with the relevant boundary posts and customs stations for each road. Every railway line crossing the border was approved for importation and exportation of merchandise. People wishing to move merchandise across the border had to submit a carrier's report to customs officials, where the actual goods were tracked against the documented amount, and the relevant fees were then gathered. Each report had to contain 'mark and numbers on the packages, the number of packages, description of the goods, net quantity of the goods, and value of the goods'.[48]

Although there was free movement of people across the border, those who crossed had their persons and personal effects examined to prevent smuggling. Goods carried 'by travellers for their personal consumption during a journey, or to privately-owned household effects, or to small private purchases of groceries' were not restricted.[49]

There was widespread disapproval of the decision, North and South, particularly from those closest to the border. Even though some Free State tobacco manufacturers were optimistic that their businesses would benefit as their competitors in the North and elsewhere would be burdened with increased costs, the Dundalk tobacco manufacturer P.J. Carroll objected to the erection of the barriers 'on the grounds that it would disrupt its access to the United Kingdom market' and 'they would have to drop their business outside the state altogether or set up a manufacturing plant outside the state. If they set up such a plant, numbers employed in Dundalk would be reduced by half.'[50] One Dundalk distillery put all its 150 employees on notice, their employment to be terminated on 1 April unless the proposed customs taxes were modified.[51] One Monaghan newspaper, the *Northern Sentinel*, deplored 'all the inconveniences of the present situation and the hampering effects on the commerce of the county that an artificial and entirely indefensible division has created'.[52] It was generally felt that the new customs barrier would lead to an increased cost of living for consumers, considerable confusion and lengthy delays in the handling of traffic.

As 1 April drew closer, the physical signs of the new measures began to appear. Declaration forms were issued at railway stations. Proclamations appeared in newspapers, signs and posters were displayed in prominent places. Construction began on customs huts and stations along the border, many of them temporary in nature, initially. The first customs post in Muff, County Donegal, was a tepee-like cloth construction.[53] A crude wooden structure surfaced in Clones in Monaghan.[54] One such hut near Emyvale, also in Monaghan, was burned by armed men.[55] Staff were brought in to operate the new stations. Railway companies hired extra staff to meet the extra demands. Many officials deployed north of the border were British and had previously held similar roles in the recently created demilitarised zone in the Rhineland.[56] The sheer scale of the preparation required and the infrastructure involved demonstrated that removing or even moving customs barriers to different locations should territory be transferred under the Boundary Commission would pose significant challenges and costs.

As well as being April Fool's Day, 1 April in 1923 was Easter Sunday, the day the new customs barriers came into operation. Traffic was light. Little disruption was caused by the new measures.[57] Once the Easter break was over, however, the real effects of customs barriers began to be realised. The new arrangement led to increased congestion at ports and border controls, with goods awaiting clearance, leading to heavy losses and disruption to businesses. It resulted in the closure of some border companies reliant on cross-border trade. The consequences of the new measures were most keenly felt by the border counties: Donegal economically cut off from Derry, Fermanagh from Monaghan.[58] Writing in July 1923, O'Shiel observed that 'Clones is badly hit by the Customs barrier and that all classes were hoping that it might soon be possible to raise it'. He added, though, it 'hits the Unionist traders even harder than the Nationalists'.[59] Months later, in October 1923, O'Shiel stated that the 'Free State citizens living on our side of the Border' were 'suffering inconvenience from the Customs Frontier' and were 'anxious that the Boundary Commission should move the Border north'.[60]

Although both jurisdictions opted for a relatively open border, with no barbed-wire entanglement to seal the frontier, it still severely curtailed the movements of residents along the border. The temporary roadblocks and closures people experienced along the border during the violence that engulfed the North in the first half of 1922 were replaced by more permanent roadblocks and obstructions that lasted for decades. Railway services suffered considerable disruptions – some train lines zigzagged the border several times, with customs examinations expected at each crossing. For instance, a train running from Clones to Cavan crossed the border six times in eight miles. Common sense soon prevailed and it was decided to curb the examinations to just the first point of entry beyond the border.[61]

In June 1923 the British government's Imperial Secretary for Northern Ireland, Stephen Tallents, invited the secretary of the Northern Cabinet, Wilfrid Spender, and his wife, Lillian, to tour the border with him. Lillian recalled their Crossley tender using a route that 'corkscrewed about in a most bewildering manner through innumerable by-roads in order to avoid crossing the Border', for they could be 'liable to be held up & searched & detained indefinitely, if nothing worse' if they did cross it. At Strabane she witnessed customs huts and sentries on both sides of the border. One of the two 'A' Specials officers accompanying them said 'that people come over freely from Lifford, the village on the Free State side to our side for business & amusement, but that it doesn't do for our folk to go their side'. Pettigo, divided by the Donegal and Fermanagh border, Spender said, had 'the unhappy condition of being cut-down in half by the Border which goes through the middle of the village, with our part one side & the Free State's the other, all complete with block houses, sandbags, barbed wire, Customs' huts'. Her husband, Wilfrid, noted that 'the whole of that part of the Country reminded him more than anything else of just behind the front-line in France'. Looking over at the other side at the 'beautiful blue mountains of Donegal' gave Lillian 'a strange feeling to see a country so unnaturally & ungeographically divided – like seeing a living creature cut in two'.[62]

The creation of the land border in 1923 undoubtedly added a high degree of permanency to partition – the physical machinery of the customs barriers helped to cement it. Up to this point, partition was seen by many as just an administrative burden hardly impacting on the daily lives of people. The introduction of the customs barrier made it tangible and real. This formalisation of the land border saw long-established economic and social ties drastically impeded. According to Catherine Nash, Lorraine Dennis and Brian Graham, the creation of the land border 'cut through complex local microgeographies of ethnic, political and religious difference, regional agricultural and economic networks, and senses of collective regional identity along its length'. The creation of the customs barrier in 1923 helped to 'establish the border's geography before it had been officially agreed at inter-state level' two years later in 1925.[63] In their book *Partitioned Lives: The Irish Borderlands*, Nash, Graham and Bryonie Reid observed:

> [D]espite the conventional conceptualization of the Irish border through the lens of the debate on the Boundary Commission and the politics and symbolism of partition, it was the imposition of new regulations and people's responses to them that constituted the border in this period. The political entered everyday life, not through the boundary commission or the ideological ramifications of partition, but through the ways in which the borderlanders came to terms on a mundane, daily basis with the existence of the customs barrier which impeded and constrained their established social and economic networks.[64]

It made perfect sense for Irish nationalists of all strains to achieve as much financial independence from Britain as possible, just as it did for Ulster unionists to desire as little financial independence from Britain as possible, given their yearning to remain fully integrated with the rest of the United Kingdom. Nationalists rightly contended that independence without financial independence was no real independence. Achieving financial independence was a key milestone for the Sinn Féin plenipotentiaries at the Treaty negotiations. Its symbolic significance as a crucial component of nationhood and independence cannot be overstated.

The nascent Free State government also wanted to take control of its own finances to generate more income for its badly needed coffers. This too was a justifiable reason, as the British Treasury had misdeclared Irish income and expenditure, generally to the detriment of Ireland, on many previous occasions. As Northern Irish governments subsequently discovered, British Exchequer interests lay with overall British concerns, often to the detriment of regions like Northern Ireland, something Arthur Griffith had often referred to.

However, the other main reason for seeking fiscal independence, to squeeze Northern Ireland economically, was not based on sound principles, just like the destructive and naive Belfast Boycott before it. While the Northern Ireland government did not want and was negatively impacted by the customs barrier, its effect was far less prohibitive on the North than many in the South believed it would be. Northern Ireland was more reliant on east–west trade than on north–south trade, and, as cited by Pollock, was willing to sacrifice trade with the Free State so long as it remained within the British customs union. The failure to grasp this by the Free State government, as well as those from the NEBB who advised it, was a critical error in a series of blunders made in the build-up to and during the Boundary Commission's existence.

Achieving financial independence from Britain, as all other dominions such as Canada and Australia had at the time, was clearly a huge objective for Sinn Féin; without it the independence gained by the Free State would have been very limited. However, there were consequences in demonstrating these newly acquired financial freedoms, particularly with the creation of a hard land border.

The impact the customs barrier had on people's lives dominated many of the representations to the Boundary Commission, which met for the first time eighteen months after its establishment. In its final report, the Boundary Commission stated that, 'Witnesses representing the rural population of the border districts impressed upon the Commission the inconvenience suffered owing to their being separated by a customs barrier from their market towns. Of 61 witnesses from East Donegal 54 laid primary stress on this point.'[65] The chairman, Justice Richard Feetham, describing it as 'the terrors of the Customs Barrier', continuously referred to it in his questioning and noted the damaging consequences it would cause if the boundary line underwent further changes.[66] Instead of the customs barrier having a positive effect on the Free State's case before the Boundary Commission, in many ways it had the opposite effect. By creating a whole infrastructure around the existing border, the Free State made it more secure and less likely to undergo major surgery. Unwittingly, the Free State government aided the Northern government in its quest to make the six counties boundary line permanent and stable.

Chapter Five

'Delay defeats Equity'

IN A MEMORANDUM DISTRIBUTED TO the Free State Executive Council in February 1924, Kevin O'Shiel informed the ministers that in Northern Ireland the new voting register 'has operated disastrously against Nationalist electors'. The 'old property qualifications have been restored, P.R. has been abolished, the electoral areas have been terribly gerrymandered and hundreds of Special Police from outside places have been put on the Tyrone and Fermanagh registers'. He warned that most of the nationalist-run local authorities were 'likely to go unionist' in the local elections, which had been postponed in 1923, to be held in 1924. Once they did so, 'it will give the Belfast Government's tenure of those lands infinitely greater security and will most gravely prejudice our case in the event of a Boundary Commission being set up'. Contradicting his previous stance from April 1923 of *Festina Lente*, O'Shiel believed, that they would 'be in the position of persons who have handed away the most telling part of their case and guilty of breaking the equity maxim that "Delay defeats Equity"'.[1]

The Northern Ireland government tried to prevent the Boundary Commission from convening at all but, failing that, tried to stall its establishment for as long as possible. Publicly, it vehemently opposed the Commission and vowed to have nothing to do with it, but it still assumed the Commission would convene, and before it did, the Northern government sought to paint as much of the six counties as possible, to use Michael Collins's words, 'with a deep Orange tint'.[2] It did this by diverting funds to infrastructure projects and by changing the electoral map of the areas that were being considered for transfer under the Boundary Commission. In the latter case it was helped by nationalists who, in many cases, relinquished their control of important local bodies by refusing to recognise the Northern jurisdiction before the Commission convened. Nationalists believed that Craig's government, during this time, was attempting to denote permanency to the six counties area as a compact unit. By the time the Commission sat for the first time in November 1924, Ulster unionists, according to Margaret O'Callaghan, had put 'in place a more integrated case, based upon fortifying an already existing boundary'.[3]

In May 1924 the Northern government proposed to provide a grant of £100,000 for the reconstruction of what was Carlisle Bridge over the River Foyle in Derry city, a contested area. This was opposed by many local authorities, including Derry Corporation, Derry and Tyrone County Councils, Strabane Urban and Rural Councils, and Limavady Council. Nationalists saw it as 'a political stunt not unconnected with the Boundary problem'.[4] The construction of the new bridge, Craigavon Bridge, was completed by 1933 and named after the Northern Ireland prime minister.

Derry was not the only city to see such political manoeuvres. Belfast had expanded rapidly throughout the nineteenth century, becoming a city in 1888. The population grew from 20,000 inhabitants in 1800 to just under 350,000 in 1901.[5] This put pressure on the Belfast City and District Water Commissioners to provide water to the ever-growing city. After investigations, the Silent Valley (previously known as the Happy Valley) in the Mourne Mountains in County Down was chosen as a site to supply water to the city. With its plentiful rain, it was envisaged the area could provide thirty million gallons of water a day. Although the land had been purchased in the 1890s and construction began in 1901, the building of a reservoir, delayed by the First World War, only started in the early 1920s.[6] To much fanfare, Lord Edward Carson arrived from England to lay the first sod of the new reservoir in October 1923.[7] Nationalists believed this was a cynical move by the Belfast government to show that an area which had a large nationalist majority in County Down was vital for Belfast to survive, let alone thrive, economically. Their concerns were well-placed, as the reservoir in the Silent Valley featured prominently in the Boundary Commission's deliberations.

Another reservoir in the Mourne Mountains, at Fofanny, which supplied water to the residents of Portadown and Banbridge, was also used as a reason for keeping the heavily nationalist-leaning area in Northern Ireland.[8] Likewise, Derry Corporation claimed to the Boundary Commission that it had commissioned a new water supply for the city of Derry to cost about £500,000 from a location near Dungiven in County Derry, approximately twenty miles from the city. One witness before the Commission, John Scott, claimed that 'if the City of Londonderry is to be dragged into the Free State it would be dependent upon this Water Supply situated in the heart of the County of Londonderry in Northern Ireland. The work in connection with this supply is now in progress, and a considerable sum has been expended to date.'[9] Nationalists, not without foundation, believed these works were sanctioned by unionists to show the economic interdependency of all areas within the six counties, including areas with large nationalist majorities. It is highly improbable that it was merely a coincidence that important and expensive infrastructure projects were sanctioned in areas of nationalist majorities while the boundary question was very much a live issue.

Far more disconcerting from a nationalist perspective were the attempts by the Northern government to manipulate the electoral profile of nationalist-dominated areas before the Boundary Commission was established. Nationalist witnesses to the Commission asserted that many nationalists were struck off the voting register 'by partisan collectors', while Specials had been added in great numbers. In the Lisnaskea Union in Fermanagh, Cahir Healy claimed that 'over 600 special police, who, obviously, as "birds of passage", paid servants of the state, who ought not to be there at all' were subsequently included on the voting register for the area, while nationalists were 'struck off'.[10] In addition, hundreds of nationalists, many of them leaders within their communities, remained interned without trial since 1922, something of which Healy had direct experience, with some remaining so until after the Boundary Commission collapsed. Hugh MacCartan, when visiting Castlewellan in County Down in April 1923, observed that large numbers of Catholics were emigrating from the area, while Protestants were not affected as they were either 'in the Specials' or held other public positions, options not available to Catholics.[11] In a memorandum entitled 'Disabilities of Northern Minorities', the NEBB described the 'B' Specials as 'terrorist in method and outlook and is not unlike the Black and Tan organisation whose methods and outlook it has tried to copy. Its object is to reduce the Catholic minority to a state of powerless subjection.' It claimed that the 'B' and 'C' Specials 'constitute a network of espionage and armed force which, even without overt action, tends to reduce the minority to helplessness. Practically every Protestant family in the Six Counties is represented in either the "B" or "C" Specials.'[12]

The Irish News claimed that 'under the cloak of industrial developments the Ulster Unionist leaders are carrying out a new plantation' after reports were received of new coalmines in Coalisland in Tyrone only hiring skilled miners from Cumberland and Scotland who were Protestants. When two miners from Lanarkshire in Scotland applied for jobs, they were asked 'What religion are you?' On answering that they were Catholics 'we were told that there was no work for us'. *The Irish News* contended that this was 'not an isolated instance, but was part of a considered policy to exclude Catholics, as far as it was possible to do so, from benefiting by the industrial development'.[13]

The NEBB also referred to the efforts of the Northern government to erode Gaelic culture, particularly the Irish language and Gaelic games dear to many nationalists. It believed that the 'attitude of Nationalist Ireland to the Gaelic culture is not at all understood by the people of the North', who think that 'the Gaelic movement is in some way directed against the non-Catholic minority, that its object is to provide a rigorous test by which in course of time the non-Catholic may be separated from the Catholics and excluded from every lucrative position in public life, that in fact it is a kind of disguised sectarianism'.[14]

The Ulster Unionists' removal of PR, which tended to provide more representation to minorities than the first-past-the-post electoral system, had been made to stifle nationalist representation, but also that of the labour movement. While its removal for the 1924 local elections negatively impacted both nationalists and labour, its subsequent removal for elections to the Northern Parliament affected the labour movement most severely. The January and June 1920 local elections under PR had been a chastening experience for Ulster Unionists. In the six-county area, nationalists won control of 'Derry City, Fermanagh and Tyrone County Councils, ten urban councils, including Armagh, Omagh, Enniskillen, Newry and Strabane, and thirteen rural councils'.[15] Unexpected nationalist and Labour Party victories in places such as Lurgan, Dungannon, Carrickfergus, Larne, Limavady, Cookstown and Lisburn were seen by nationalists as 'a rebuff to plans for partition'.[16] In Belfast Corporation, unionists went from having fifty-two to thirty-seven members, with Labour winning thirteen seats, and Sinn Féin and the Nationalist Party securing five seats each.[17] According to Michael Farrell, it was the 'first serious challenge to Unionist hegemony in the area'.[18] The result in Derry city was particularly galling for unionists. Of the forty seats, unionists won nineteen, Sinn Féin and the Nationalist Party won ten seats each, and Hugh C. O'Doherty, an independent nationalist, won the final seat.[19]

The removal of PR offered Ulster Unionists the chance to recover 'lost' local authorities, such as Derry Corporation and Tyrone and Fermanagh County Councils. According to Patrick Buckland, the grievance over the abolition of PR, 'which had been significant both as an actual safeguard and as a symbol of respect for minority views', was 'made the more real by the way in which boundaries of electoral areas were so drawn as to maximise Unionist strength at the expense of others'.[20] According to Cahir Healy, PR alone 'would not have delivered the [Fermanagh] County affairs into the hands of the minority; therefore, in addition, they had to bring forth this reshuffling of units, octopus shaped, which I hope, will be found to be unique in this sort of political warfare'.[21]

According to nationalists from Strabane in a statement to the Boundary Commission, Northern Parliament Unionist MP William T. Miller declared at an Orange demonstration on 12 July 1923 that when 'the Government of Northern Ireland decided to do away with Proportional Representation the chance we had been waiting for so long had arrived, AND WE took advantage of it'. He said unionists 'wanted among other things redistribution of District Electoral Divisions. In the end, we got, if not the whole, at least part of what we wanted.'[22]

A one-man commission under Judge John Leech was established by the Northern government in 1923 to redraw local government electoral boundaries. It held inquiries in contested areas 'where it appears that substantial inequalities exist in regard to populations and valuations'.[23] Unsurprisingly, 'the majority of these areas in question contained a Catholic and nationalist majority'.[24] Nationalists were sceptical, seeing the commission as 'purely and simply a proposed gerrymander of the area', a means to 'hand over control to the Ascendancy party'.[25] With a few exceptions, nationalists refused to meet the commission, resulting in unionists dictating 'the positioning of boundaries with meticulous care to their own complete satisfaction'.[26]

Some have questioned the wisdom of nationalists refusing to meet Leech's commission, with Brian M. Walker pointing out that in the two places where nationalists contributed to the commission, 'they were able to affect its findings'.[27] However, some of the outrageous decisions the commission made do raise questions about how effective nationalist representations would have been. For example, in the Clogher Rural District in Tyrone, the seat share went from almost an equal amount between unionists and nationalists to eleven for unionists and five for nationalists. Dungannon Urban Council, also in Tyrone, normally expected to return three nationalists. Under the new ward boundaries, however, it changed to a return of two unionists and one nationalist.[28] In

Enniskillen, the nationalist majority of 56 per cent obtained seven seats while unionists won fourteen seats.[29]

In 1920 'opposition parties won control of twenty-four local authorities out of twenty-seven, but by 1927 Unionists had a majority in all but twelve councils. Unionists recovered Londonderry Corporation and the county councils of Fermanagh and Tyrone.'[30] Unionists defended their actions by stating that boundaries were redrawn to take account of rateable value as well as population: 'those who paid the most rates were entitled to the biggest say in the conduct of local government'. This dubious defence of the rich being entitled to stronger representation than the poor benefitted unionists, who were on average richer than nationalists.[31] The NEBB claimed that this 'course was dictated by the fact that the Unionists, having been planted on the good lands, have holdings of much greater average valuation than their opponents'.[32]

The electoral changes in Northern Ireland were scathingly attacked by the NEBB, which claimed that the 'ultimate aim is the practical disenfranchisement of minorities generally and particularly of the great Nationalist minority of 34 per cent'.[33] According to Brendan O'Leary, the 'changed electoral system and "Leeching"' also 'had their consequences magnified by nationalists' and republicans' decisions to engage in electoral boycotts. After the 1924 local elections, nationalists held just two councils. When the Boundary Commission was eventually seated, a false impression of unionist electoral dominance prevailed throughout the new entity.'[34] Cahir Healy explained that, having won eleven of the twenty seats in Fermanagh County Council in 1920, had nationalists contested the elections in 1924, 27,096 Protestants would have elected thirteen unionists, and 34,740 Catholics would have elected seven nationalists. He believed this justified the boycott of the 1924 elections, as 'decency demanded that we leave public affairs to those who for the time being had managed to seize control'.[35]

Before the local elections, and cognisant of the perception that would be created at the Boundary Commission once unionists took over previously nationalist-controlled local authorities, in February 1924 Kevin

O'Shiel advised that the Free State government, before it engaged in any more conferences with the Northern government, should demand that the upcoming local elections be postponed for twelve months. Otherwise, 'AFTER these elections no argument of ours will prevail against the GREAT FACT that these districts, once in favour of a Dublin Parliament, have all gone in favour of a Belfast Parliament'.[36] The editor of *The Irish News*, Timothy McCarthy, shared similar sentiments, saying that 'the wholescale jerrymandering was an example of the evils of delay'.[37]

Nationalist representation was also diminished by public representatives who refused to give an oath of allegiance to the king and the Belfast Parliament (see Chapter Two). For example, Father Felix Canon McNally, chaplain of the Newry Union Workhouse, stated he had 'no objection whatever to give an Oath of Allegiance to His Majesty, but ... refused to make the Declaration of Allegiance to that [Northern] Parliament'.[38] According to J.H. Collins, as well as there being an antagonistic paid commissioner in the Newry district, 'Armed Bodies of Belfast Constabulary seized the Public Buildings in the District and held them by force'.[39] Unionists justified this by arguing that the non-compliant local authorities were rightly suspended for 'their refusal to perform the duties imposed on them in pursuance of the Local Government (Ireland) Acts'.[40]

The boycotting of elections and public bodies did not enjoy universal support within Northern nationalism, particularly amongst those living in east Ulster who had no prospect of being transferred to the Free State. Joe Devlin told Hugh MacCartan in April 1923 that he had decided not to go into the Northern Parliament 'until the Boundary Commission had finished its work, but that great pressure was being brought on him to go in now to protect educational and other interests'.[41] Daniel McCartan, clerk of the Crown and peace for County Down, told MacCartan that he 'was strongly against the non-recognition attitude of some of the Councils which ... merely played into the hands of the Belfast Parliament'. He believed that the 'besetting sin of the Nationalist minority was that it always based its politics on a desire to "spite the other fellows" rather than keep itself or the country as a whole, and that a change of mentality was needed'. MacCartan described Daniel McCartan as a 'recogniser'.[42]

In contrast, NEBB legal agent for Belfast George Martin believed those urging nationalists to take their seats in the Belfast Parliament were 'compromisers', only 'interested in the hope of honours, positions, social intercourse with the "great" and defending the threatened liquor interest'.[43]

The ability of the Northern government to make the existing boundary more permanent and seemingly secure with these electoral and practical measures was due to the lengthy delay in the convening of the Boundary Commission. While that delay was partially caused by martial turmoil in the Free State and political volatility in Great Britain, the Northern government's refusal to appoint its commissioner was the primary factor.

The conference on the boundary question suggested by the British Colonial Secretary, the Duke of Devonshire, in July 1923 was initially delayed by the Free State general election at the end of August that year. O'Shiel saw an opportunity created by republicans doing far better than expected in the election, winning forty-four seats and increasing their vote share by 5.6 per cent from the previous election in June 1922. He believed that the '44 Irregular TDs are, at the present juncture, almost a blessing in disguise, as they will enable us to fight a much harder fight in this great matter of the future North–South relationship, and (possibly) drive a harder bargain than we could have done, say before the last Election', adding that they could 'blame everything on to them and the British cannot say anything in reply'.[44] Just as Craig used the 'extreme' elements in his ranks to pursue his case, Cosgrave could do likewise with republicans.

Northern nationalists, who were already frustrated by the fact that the Free State government had agreed to participate in a boundary conference without insisting on the immediate convening of the Boundary Commission, were now further angered by continual delays to the holding of this conference. The Duke of Devonshire was unable to host it in October 1923 as he was too busy with sittings of the Imperial Conference in London, so the conference was tentatively scheduled for 16 November.[45] Eoin MacNeill, who was in London at the Imperial Conference, sensed there was no urgency on the British government's part to convene the conference and wrote to Kevin O'Higgins that 'a big political fight is coming on in Great Britain over the Protection issue and they are unable to think of anything else'.[46] Much to the surprise of most, Stanley Baldwin called an election on the issue of tariff reform while the Imperial Conference was in session. Naturally, the boundary conference planned for mid-November was cancelled, not to be taken up again until the start of 1924 and under a new British government.

Touring border areas in October 1923, James Craig gave the impression that he was sticking to his 'not an inch' strategy. In Lisnaskea in Fermanagh on 13 October, he declared that their 'enemies and those who threatened them would have to trample over his grave before they stole a yard of the territory that belonged to Northern Ireland'. On the same tour, at Brookeborough, he left the door open for some border rectification when he stated that no 'loyalist within the boundary of those Six Counties would be transferred into the Free State without his will, unless the loyalists themselves insisted on it'.[47]

Craig accepted the invitation to the Duke of Devonshire-proposed conference with W.T. Cosgrave on the boundary question. He consistently maintained that he would never recognise the Boundary Commission but was open, as he claimed was agreed with Michael Collins in January 1922, to rectification of the border by mutual agreement. In a memorandum to the British Home Office in October 1923, the Northern government contended that the agreement between Collins and Craig then was 'at least as binding upon the Imperial Government as the Treaty itself'. In the memorandum, the Northern government also falsely claimed that during negotiations in 1919 on the Government of Ireland Bill, in 'the interests of peace, the people of Ulster in order to meet the representations made by the then British Government reluctantly agreed to surrender the three Counties – Cavan, Monaghan and Donegal', when in reality, it was the UUC who objected to the inclusion of nine counties in Northern Ireland suggested by the British government. As it had not been consulted about the Boundary Commission clause of the Treaty after Craig was told by Lloyd George on 25 November 1921 that 'the rights of Ulster will be in no way sacrificed or compromised', the Northern government stated that 'the provisions as to the Boundary Commission are in conflict with ethical justice and public right – with ethical justice because they destroy an agreement without the consent of one of the parties to it; with public right because they override the constitution of a body which had received legal existence before the agreement was made'.[48]

Without any evidence, in the same memorandum, the Belfast government contended that in 1919 there was a small unionist majority in Counties Fermanagh and Tyrone.[49] The 1911 census and elections held in Fermanagh and Tyrone suggested that this was not true, with Catholics and nationalists holding a small but still significant majority in both counties. In the 1922 Westminster general election in Fermanagh–Tyrone, both nationalist candidates, T.J. Harbison and Cahir Healy, defeated their unionist rivals, James Pringle and William Allen respectively. Harbison and Healy repeated the feat in the Westminster general election a year later, with slightly reduced majorities.[50] When providing evidence to the Boundary Commission, Healy (who was interned at the time of his election victories) claimed, 'With every disadvantage facing us – an inflated and hostile police force, a hostile Government in charge of all election matters, with hundreds of our best workers in prison or banished across the border,' both Harbison and he won 'by majorities of 6,596 and 6,228 on the first occasion and by 6,270 and 5,986 on the second. It was thus that the electors decided, as late as 15 months ago, the very issue that your Commission is now trying.'[51]

The 1923 Westminster general election was an historic one that saw the Conservatives removed from office and replaced by the Labour Party, taking office for the first time. As no party secured a majority, though, there was much uncertainty that Labour would form a government going into 1924. The Conservative Party remained the largest party after the election. The NEBB believed that while it was probable some government would be formed, under such fragile circumstances it 'must be weak and anxious to avoid trouble'. It believed a 'Labour or Liberal Government would probably give the strongest support to our claims, but there is no doubt that any pressure brought to bear on Ulster by such a Government would consolidate the Conservatives in opposition.' Overall, the bureau felt a conference should not be postponed on the boundary question, as local elections were to be held in gerrymandered areas in May 1924, the next general election would be 'on the new Register which is more favourable to Partitionists in Tyrone and Fermanagh', and the more time that passed, the more it would be used by 'the Belfast Government to capture jobs and dig themselves in in the disputed areas'. The plight of Northern Catholics and of prisoners in the North, who had been interned since 1922, also made 'an early settlement imperative', and the bureau believed it was better 'to push on' while English politics was in disarray and any government was weak. A 'strong government could come at any time'.[52]

The NEBB also felt many Northern nationalists from the border regions were unrealistic in their expectations of what could be achieved. Any attempt to show border nationalists 'that the whole matter is surrounded with difficulties will tend to arrest the feeling, which is widespread in the North, that the Government have deserted the Northern Catholics'. The Free State government was a trustee of border nationalists but also 'a trustee for the whole country, both for the people of the South and for the Nationalists in the six counties who could not be affected by the Boundary Commission' and had to take their views into consideration too.[53]

Despite Northern nationalist opposition to participation in a conference, the NEBB felt it was the Free State government's 'duty to accept the invitation'. It felt the Boundary Commission itself was 'not an ideal solution because it does not necessarily lead to national union and might easily lead in the opposite direction'. Its enforcement 'as a purely hostile measure against the North might quite conceivably lead to renewed bloodshed in the country, in which event the chief sufferers would be the Nationalists resident in the Six Counties'. In typically optimistic fashion, the bureau, writing in December 1923, believed that the delay in setting up the Boundary Commission was in the Free State's favour. Peace 'has been established, the Loan has been floated, the hunger strike broken, a civil Police Force established, while the last election has altered the composition of the British House of Commons in our favour, and has left the Conservatives too weak to give much support to the Belfast Government'.[54]

Before assuming power, the British Labour Party had tended to be anti-partition and pro-united Ireland, although this stance waned the closer it came to power. By 1924 'Labour was weary of the Irish question and loath to provoke it to new life'.[55] Despite this, Ulster unionists still feared that the Labour Party's policies on Ireland would reflect those it had in opposition. As Labour was on the verge of forming a government in January 1924, the Northern government's Chief Whip, Herbert Dixon, claimed that if the fears they had were to transpire, and 'the Labour Government attempted to do something on the people of Ulster, then, not for the first time, they would show that Ulster could take care of itself'.[56]

While some of the new British Cabinet had strong Irish connections – the Minister of Health, John Wheatley, was born in Waterford and the Lord Privy Seal and deputy party leader, John Clynes, was the son of an Irish labourer – Prime Minister Ramsay MacDonald and Colonial Secretary John Henry (J.H.) Thomas were not known for their Irish nationalist sympathies. According to Paul Murray, MacDonald 'exhibited a sympathetic attitude to Unionists, combined with a distaste for both Irish Nationalism and Catholicism as well as for southern Irish people in general, some of whom he seems to have regarded as less than fully human'.[57] O'Shiel noted that Thomas had 'never shown himself conspicuously friendly' to Ireland.[58]

Reliant on Herbert Asquith's Liberal Party to keep his minority government afloat, it was always improbable that Ramsay MacDonald would diverge radically from previous British governments' policies on Ireland since the 1921 Anglo-Irish Treaty, a Treaty the Labour Party supported. The Labour Party's main objective was to show that it could govern responsibly, and this, coupled with the arithmetic constraints of the administration, prevented it from doing anything deemed too radical about Ireland. MacDonald was also acutely aware of the Irish question's capacity to derail political fortunes in the UK, as it had done for much of the previous forty years.

While eager to avoid bringing the Irish question back into Westminster politics, the Labour government still had to deal with the Boundary Commission, which remained in cold storage. Both MacDonald and Thomas tried to kick the can down the road by either stalling the convening of the Boundary Commission or, through their preferred option of facilitating conferences between the two main Irish protagonists, Craig and Cosgrave, to induce them to reach an agreement without the need for the Commission to convene at all. Days after taking office, Thomas wrote to Tim Healy, and the British Home Secretary, Arthur Henderson, wrote to the Governor General of Northern Ireland, the Duke of Abercorn, inviting both Irish governments to a conference in London. In Thomas's letter to Healy, he claimed the government's opinions on the boundary question 'do not differ from those of their predecessors'.[59] Both Irish governments accepted the invitation, with the conference scheduled to begin on 1 February 1924.

Beforehand, Cosgrave contemplated with the Executive Council the possible offers that could emanate from the conference. He predicted that Craig would insist the 'two Parliaments [are] to remain as they are and the two Cabinets to function as the Council of Ireland; Northern Parliament constituencies to return members to English Parliament'. Cosgrave wrote that he would only consider such a proposition if 'We preside', 'That majority rule prevails' and 'That the chairman has a casting vote'. He also believed that 'the North-East will demand the same fiscal policy as Great Britain. Any such proposition, however, is a derogation of status and, of course, cannot be entertained if the North-East insists.' Cosgrave contended that 'these proposals without corresponding accommodation towards the minority in the North-East are more than we could stand for and that we would not have any justification in agreeing to them'.[60] While the Free State government ultimately sought Irish unity, it is important to note that Cosgrave and others would only consider such unity if the Free State did not lose any of the powers it had attained in 1921, thus closing the door to many options for unity. 'Having won international recognition,' as Kevin Matthews has asserted, 'they were not about to allow the British to engage in a "whittling down" of their status even if that was the price to be paid for ending partition.'[61]

On the issue of the Specials, Cosgrave would only agree to a 'Local Militia and liability for their own Constabulary' if the Northern government withdrew all penal acts against the minority; there was a reconstruction of constituencies in the north-east 'on a par basis'; PR was retained for ten years; people were disqualified if they did not take their seats; customs barriers were retained; the boundary was rectified 'to make it a more suitable line'; and the British withdrew their war debt claims. He concluded, 'This may mark the division more strikingly, but as that is likely in any case, we get a fairer deal for our people in the North. We cut away entirely from England. We have full control in the major part of the country and North-East is left without its reserves and may possibly look more to us than across.'[62]

E.M. Stephens from the NEBB believed it would be difficult to achieve the political union Cosgrave contemplated without 'taking away from the power of the Dail'. He also questioned how political union could be possible while the North retained representation at Westminster, as well as the wisdom of retaining customs barriers, writing that 'if the fiscal system, in force in the North and in the Free State, once diverge, and new vested interests spring up, political union will become daily more difficult'.[63]

At a conference of Free State Executive Council members, NEBB representatives and senior civil servants on 28 January 1924, Eoin MacNeill argued that 'a hard and fast stand should be made on the plebiscite system with the smallest possible area as unit'.[64] Geoffrey Hand believed that, at the time, MacNeill was 'in much closer touch with legal and political realities than was Cosgrave'.[65] To counter Craig's argument of using the Government of Ireland Act 1920 to claim 'what we have we hold', Attorney General Hugh Kennedy and others 'pointed out that the 1920 Act was an arbitrary division of Ireland without the consent of either population … The boundary provided by that Act disposed of large areas against the will of the population. Tyrone and Fermanagh had in two elections rejected the division.' The Treaty 'provided machinery for revision of this injustice, and it was the duty of the British Government who had created the injustice to see that this machinery was availed of'.[66]

At the boundary conference, which was held in London, J.H. Thomas offered a Council of Ireland-type solution, with the 'two Irish cabinets acting in its place for a provisional period of one year'. Dáil Éireann and the Northern Ireland House of Commons would hold joint sittings, but legislation would only become law when passed by both houses. The Free State would postpone its demand for the Boundary Commission to convene during the provisional period, and the Northern government would delay its plans to enforce its abolition of PR for local elections.[67]

British Cabinet Secretary Tom Jones was pessimistic about this proposal's chance of success, writing, 'an All-Ireland Council would come into being, with very limited powers at first, but which would grow with growing confidence. The snag is to provide Ulster with what she would consider adequate representation on such a Council. She will want a "fifty-fifty" basis.' Jones and his colleagues did not think 'that Ulster would yield a fraction of an inch. [Lord] Londonderry is the only reasonable negotiator, and he is too weak to bring along the rest of his party.'[68]

The Free State government was unanimous in its rejection of Thomas's suggestion while the Northern government gave lukewarm support. Cosgrave stated, 'We are not asked in these proposals to share our independence with the Parliament of Northern Ireland, but to limit our independence and to give the Northern Parliament a veto on our legislation and a share in our administration of services withheld from it.' Ernest Blythe said that 'to set up a joint parliamentary body to deal with Fisheries, Railways and Diseases of Animals would be to invite complete failure'. The desire 'for National unity would certainly induce the Free State members to offer accommodation at every point, but there is little to give hope that their advances would be reciprocated by the Northern representatives'. Kevin O'Higgins believed the services were too limited and the 'only important matter is Railways – a deadlock in that seems certain. The two other matters are negligible.' 'The most fatal criticism of the proposals', O'Higgins felt, was 'that the country would not touch them'. If they did not propose Irish unity, 'we look rather like self-confessed lepers'.[69] Eoin MacNeill said that the 'bare reading of it is enough to arouse indignation, but indignation by itself gets us nowhere'.[70] The Executive Council agreed that 'proposals could not be accepted by the Government of Saorstat Eireann' and desired 'that the Conference should be resumed without delay'.[71]

The conference did not resume, mainly due to Craig becoming seriously ill. Lady Ruby Carson had observed at the beginning of February that Craig was not 'well & is being inoculated again with those bugs he had in the war'.[72] Writing to Cosgrave in mid-February, the Free State High Commissioner in London, James MacNeill, said, 'it appears that Sir James Craig is not merely ill, but very ill. Thomas says this and Lady Lavery confirms it ... Lady Lavery says that Craig's condition is thought to be dangerous as he has some heart complications.'[73]

Craig was advised to take a long rest and to go on a Mediterranean cruise. With his doctor suggesting he should ease himself back into work, the Northern Cabinet believed the conference should not be held for another three months, as 'whatever the result of the Conference the Prime Minister would be involved in a very critical situation which would make it essential for him to take a very active part'. Craig accepted that the Free State government would not accept the proposals from early February as it 'transferred very little real power to the proposed joint Parliament' and would want an all-Ireland parliament instead. He appeared to show that there was some flexibility to participating in some form of all-Ireland parliament, admitting that if the Northern government rejected the Free State's proposals, 'the negotiations would break down and that we should be face to face with a very grave crisis', but, on the other hand, 'if the Northern Government decided to accept the suggestion of some form of joint meeting of Parliaments he felt that it would be necessary for the Prime Minister to make it very plain to the people of Ulster why the Government had adopted this course'.[74]

At the same time, an article written by Craig was published in the English Conservative magazine *The Spectator*. Claiming that 'Ulster is British and is as much an integral part of the United Kingdom as Yorkshire or Lancashire', Craig stated that all of Northern Ireland 'should be retained under the Union Jack and not transferred under any other emblem, which some day may represent Republicanism and complete severance from the Mother Country'. It was important, not just for Northern Ireland, but for the whole United Kingdom to 'keep this part of the Empire inviolate'.[75]

In the intervening period between the February and April conferences in London, the Free State government faced a crisis that threatened to seriously destabilise the country once again so soon after the Civil War had ended. Senior officers of the National Army, led by Liam Tobin and Charlie Dalton, mutinied in March over the planned demobilisation of the army, their fears over the government's interpretation of the Treaty, and the dwindling influence of IRA veterans from the War of Independence in the army.[76] The mutiny resulted in the resignation of two Executive Council ministers, Richard Mulcahy and Joseph McGrath.

According to the NEBB, it did not take long for the 'Orange Press' to take advantage of the mutiny, with a suggestion made 'that the real reason for the mutiny was that a movement was on foot to declare a Republic and attack "Ulster", and the Government's failure to assent to this programme precipitated a mutiny'. 'The reasons for these alarmist reports are obvious,' wrote the NEBB; they were 'calculated to strengthen the "Northern" position in regard to the Boundary Commission and to justify the continuation of the subsidies towards the maintenance of the Special Constabulary'.[77] The NEBB's assessment was correct. The Northern government wrote Home Secretary Henderson a letter saying that the mutiny had strengthened those calling for a republic, who were 'notorious for their hostility to Northern Ireland', which 'causes the Northern Government very grave concern, and we therefore feel it essential to maintain all our Constabulary Forces at their present strength until the position is clearer'.[78] Also stoking fears from the Free State Army mutiny, Craig told his Cabinet that he would seek a meeting with Ramsay MacDonald to tell him that 'in his opinion a Republic was almost inevitable in the Free State, and that therefore it was only a question of the area to be included in that Republic. An attempt to force the Northern Government under this Republic would undoubtedly lead to bloodshed and disaster.'[79] Demonstrating the deep-rooted paranoia that existed in Northern Ireland at the time, in November 1922 the military adviser to the Northern government, Arthur Solly-Flood, had warned Craig, without any evidence, of division within the Free State Army, with some of its senior figures maintaining 'that the prospect of dealing drastically with Ulster at some future date as the only thing which keeps the National Army together'.[80]

Despite using the mutiny to plead for the maintenance of the Specials at their existing strength, in a visit to London the Northern Minister for Finance, Hugh Pollock, and the head of the civil service, Ernest Clark, received a frosty reception from the British Chancellor of the Exchequer, Philip Snowden, who found it hard to justify providing a grant of one million pounds for the Specials again, due to the 'peaceful condition' of Northern Ireland. Craig had already been spurned by Labour's Secretary of State for War, Stephen Walsh, who was of Irish descent himself, to retain the 'C1' Specials to be 'prepared for their formation as a Territorial division'.[81]

At the meeting with Snowden, Pollock said the peaceful conditions were caused by the 'Police organisation' but the 'omens at present were not favourable, and the recent military emeute clearly showed that the [Free State] Government had little control over the extremists'. J.H. Thomas then joined them and 'asked the Chancellor not to reach a decision on the subject of the grant but to keep an open mind on the question until the outcome of the coming conference was seen'. Clark claimed that both Snowden and Thomas intimated that 'some action must be taken towards conciliation and agreement with the South on the subject of the boundary, or that it would be impossible to carry any financial measure for the benefit of Northern Ireland in the future'. His impression was 'that the [British] Government intend, as I have always thought they did intend, to deal with these two questions together'.[82] The diehard *Morning Post* wrote that the withholding of the grant for the Specials was proof that 'the Socialist Government is using this as a lever to force the hands of Ulster and compel her to abandon her legal and constitutional rights'.[83]

Thomas took Pollock aside after the meeting and 'attacked' the Northern government's action 'in respect of PR and suggested', as Pollock recalled, 'that if we would agree to its suspension in the meantime he would endeavour to get Cosgrave to meet our PM privately and would try and force him into conceding a simple rectification of the Boundary, leaving Tyrone and Fermanagh out of the discussion'.[84] Tom Jones wrote in his diary that Thomas claimed, 'he had put upon' Pollock 'the fear of the Treasury stopping our money grants for the payment of "Specials"'. Jones remarked that Thomas was 'very proud of himself as a negotiator, but I fancy knowledge of his methods must be spreading. Cope ventured to suggest that Craig might be placated with a peerage. Thomas replied: "He can have a b...dy Dukedom if it will do the trick; I made a Peer and two Knights yesterday."'[85]

Jones himself was asked to go to Ireland by Thomas (through Lionel Curtis) 'to spy out the land'. Despite Jones's protests of not wanting to put his 'foot into the Irish bog again', he did go. The British government had noticed a hardening of attitudes within the Free State government, partly caused, as Jones believed, by its weak handling of the Army Mutiny, resulting in its members being 'determined to show themselves strong on the Boundary issue, and have sent a stiff letter to us asking that the Commission shall be set up forthwith'.[86] It may also have been caused by heeding the advice of the Free State Governor General, Tim Healy, who recommended that the government 'preserve a very stiff and unbending attitude, being careful never to yield an inch'. For an example of effectiveness, the government need look no further than Craig: 'He is like a piece of iron. He never yields, for he knows that should he yield he would be torn to pieces in Belfast within twenty-four hours afterwards.'[87] Cosgrave had previously stated to Curtis that the Northern government was unbending; 'the pinpricks were all on one side and the forbearance all on the other'.[88] He confided in Norman Gerald (N.G.) Loughnane, the Colonial Office representative in the Free State, that Ulster Protestants were the 'spoiled children of politics' who were 'quite incapable of making concessions'.[89]

The Free State government was getting increasingly frustrated with the constant delays. Due to the mistreatment of Catholics and nationalists in the North, it felt 'that the effect of further postponement would be to deprive of the benefits of the Treaty those persons whose interests Clause 12, without which the Treaty would never have been accepted, was specially designed to protect'. Healy, therefore, requested that the British government 'take the necessary steps to complete the constitution of the Boundary Commission without further delay', while adding that his government was still open to a settlement with Northern Ireland 'on the basis of the reunion of Ireland'.[90]

Thomas replied to Healy, asking that the Free State government delay its request for the Northern government to appoint its commissioner, but Healy wrote back that there should be no further delay, stating that it 'cannot agree to the continued postponement of the settlement of this problem, and they consider that the personnel of the Boundary Commission should be completed, not later than the 1st May next'.[91]

On visiting Dublin, Tom Jones recognised the dangers for the Free State government of the ongoing delays in the convening of the Boundary Commission, writing that the 'fear of the growing opposition to the Government, and of it rallying around the failure to operate Article 12, is having more and more weight in their minds'. He proposed that 'we must absolutely stop growing suspicion here that they are in league with us to delay Article 12 indefinitely, while allowing Ulster to gerrymander constituencies in anticipation of any Commission that may come along'.[92] The republican newspaper *Éire* wrote at the time that the boundary conferences and their postponements were 'a mere device for throwing dust in the eyes of the Irish people', that the stalling of the Boundary Commission sitting, with the Free State government acting as willing accomplices, showed that the entire Treaty 'from its inception' was 'a fraud, a delusion and a snare'.[93]

The Free State government only agreed to participate in the conference in London on 24 April if, in the likely event of it breaking down, the British government would exercise its powers under Article 12 and appoint a chairman of the Commission. According to Jones, the morning session of the conference went 'rather well, on the lines of a voluntary Commission to be set up by Craig and Cosgrave, and to consist of local experts'. However, in the afternoon 'it became clear that, as the price of agreeing to a voluntary Commission, Craig would demand from Cosgrave the surrender of his legal right to a Commission under Clause 12 of the Treaty'. The conference soon ended without agreement. On meeting with Cosgrave afterwards, both Jones and Curtis agreed with Cosgrave that if he had surrendered Article 12, 'it would be open to the North, unobtrusively but effectively, to block any agreement by the voluntary Commission'.[94]

Ramsay MacDonald coaxed Craig and Cosgrave to meet one more time, which they did at the end of May, where, predictably, no agreement was reached. Much to the disconsolation of MacDonald and his colleagues, they were forced to take the course they had no desire to take: to arrange for the Boundary Commission to function by appointing a chairman and to have the Northern Ireland representative appointed, with or without Craig's help. The controversy surrounding the appointment of the Northern Ireland representative threatened to bring the Irish question back to the centre of British party politics yet again.

In preparing for the first conference in February 1924 with the Northern and British governments, the NEBB had written a memorandum for the Free State government entitled 'Possible basis for union', which looked at options that could bring about Irish unity. The crux of the dilemma facing the Free State government, the memorandum argued, was whether the Irish unity options 'if accepted by us, tend to detach the North more and more in sentiment and political circumstances from Great Britain or, contrariwise, will it tend to attach us more and more to the orbit of British public life thereby undermining secretly but effectively our present political, financial and fiscal independence?' The NEBB felt the Free State must 'guard against methods of unification which would unite us, not so much with the north, as with Great Britain at the expense of our national independence'.[95]

The Free State government had fought too hard for and cherished too dearly the measures of independence it had achieved to sacrifice any of them for the sake of Irish unity. It was hoping, despite all the signs to the contrary over the previous decade and more, that Ulster unionists would forgo parts of their relationship with Britain to develop closer ties with the rest of Ireland. It continuously failed to grasp that Ulster unionism's hatred for Dublin was stronger than its love for the Empire, which often was conditional. On the prospect of joining an all-Ireland parliament, *The Northern Whig* editorialised that it 'would as soon consider a proposal for accepting the suzerainty of Turkey or Soviet Russia', sentiments undoubtedly shared by many unionists in Northern Ireland.[96] 'It is clear', writes Clare O'Halloran, 'that the Free State government formulated its northern policy in isolation, without any reference to, or specialist knowledge of, unionist opinion.'[97]

With both Irish governments unwilling to accept an offer from the other that both could stomach, the conferences were always unlikely to succeed. The choice, as Kevin O'Higgins stated, 'lay between political unity and secession, but attached to the privilege of secession' was the Boundary Commission.[98] For the Free State government, and particularly for Northern nationalists close to the border, it remained the only avenue left to achieve something from the partition morass.

Chapter Six

'... the Government will nominate a proper representative'

IN 1924 A CRISIS IN British party politics was brewing again over the Irish question on the issue of the Boundary Commission. Determined that Ulster would not bring new controversy to the body politic in Britain, the Conservative Party leader Stanley Baldwin wrote to party colleague Edward Wood (later Lord Halifax), 'If the Commission should give away counties, then of course Ulster couldn't accept it and we should back her. But the Government will nominate a proper representative and we hope that he and Feetham [Richard, Irish Boundary Commission chairman] will do what is right.'[1] Baldwin's commitment to support the Ulster unionist cause on the Boundary Commission issue was a reflection of the overwhelming views of most British politicians, to meet Ulster unionist demands as far as possible, thus thwarting those of nationalist Ireland. In the period from the quest to appoint a chairman from the end of April 1924 to the appointment of Joseph R. Fisher as the Northern Ireland representative at the end of October that year, British politicians from the Conservative and Labour parties were extremely duplicitous in their dealings with the Free State government, aided and abetted by much of the British press.

Once the conference in London on 24 April broke down, the Labour government had to appoint a chairman of the Boundary Commission and then overcome the subsequent impasse caused by the Northern government not appointing its representative. Its first choice as chairman, Sir Robert Borden, turned down the offer precisely because of the difficulties that arose over the Northern Ireland nominee.

Lionel Curtis had suggested to Winston Churchill as far back as September 1922 that Borden, the former Canadian prime minister, would be an ideal candidate.[2] According to Geoffrey Hand, although 'Borden had been in legal practice for most of his life[,] his celebrity and importance were as prime minister of Canada from 1911 to 1920, and his selection strongly suggests that the British government still had hopes of a political solution by conciliation rather than a quasi-judicial one by arbitration'.[3] Through the Canadian government, both MacDonald and Thomas invited Borden to be chairman on 1 May. He turned them down 'unless both the Free State and Northern Ireland agreed to appoint representatives'.[4] The Northern government stated Borden's 'appointment would have been welcomed ... had she been able to recognise the Boundary Commission'.[5] In a letter to Cosgrave, James MacNeill wrote, 'I'm told Borden is a stupid man. I wonder if a Colonial is safer than an Englishman who is intelligent, straight and judicially minded.'[6] Despite his intelligence being questioned, he was still able, as Nicholas Mansergh contends, 'to retreat honourably from an unwelcome assignment'.[7] Borden admitted to the press baron Lord Beaverbrook that he '"was not sorry that the North persisted in its refusal", taking him off the hook'.[8]

The appointment of the chairman was the sole preserve of the British government, yet the Free State government was aware of the vital importance of the role. Even before the Treaty was signed, 'MacNeill had warned de Valera against accepting a chairman nominated by the British government'.[9] While the Free State had rejected a proposal to lobby Bonar Law to appoint an impartial chairman in late 1922, there is a note in one of the Taoiseach's files in the National Archives of Ireland from an unknown source, undated, suggesting that every effort should be made 'to have Hon. Thos. Givens (President Australian Senate) selected as chairman of the Commission. He is a good Irishman (though 40 years left Tipperary) and safe.' The note also states: 'Any other possibility risky. The other party do not know the real views of Givens and should not be enlightened.'[10] Tipperary-born Thomas Givens had left Ireland for Queensland in Australia at the age of eighteen, becoming a newspaper editor and politician. He served as president of the Australian senate from 1913 to 1926.[11] It is unknown if the Free State government approached the British government about Givens, or anyone else for that matter.

On 26 May the British government approached Justice Richard Feetham, through the South African government, as its next choice, after Borden's refusal, for chairman. Feetham accepted.

Richard Feetham was born in 1874 in Penrhos, Monmouthshire, in Wales. His father, William, was the Anglican vicar of Penrhos. Two of Richard's brothers followed in their father's footsteps, with William Crawley becoming a vicar in South Africa and John Oliver becoming the Anglican Bishop of Queensland in Australia. After studying at Oxford University, Richard was called to the Bar in 1899. He volunteered to serve in the Second Boer War and was appointed deputy town clerk of Johannesburg in 1902.[12] He served under Lionel Curtis, a friend from his Oxford days. Along with Curtis, he became a member of Lord Alfred Milner's so-called 'kindergarten', a group of civil servants who served under Milner's 'South African imperial reformulation projects' while Milner was High Commissioner of South Africa.[13] On the relationship between Curtis and Feetham, a correspondent in Johannesburg informed the Northern government that these 'two hunt in couples, and are politically sympathetic'.[14] He was also a member of the Round Table movement that originated from Milner and Curtis and sought to promote closer union between Britain and its dominions.

Feetham became a judge on the South African Supreme Court a year before he was appointed chairman of the Irish Boundary Commission. He also chaired other international commissions in India, Kenya and China.

As chancellor of the University of Witwatersrand in Johannesburg, he 'staunchly upheld the principle of academic autonomy and opposed legislation prohibiting the admission of "Non-White" students to White tertiary institutions'.[15] Demonstrating this opposition to apartheid, in 1961, as chancellor, he unveiled a plaque at the university that contained the wording, 'it is our duty to uphold the principle that a university is a place where men and women, without regard to race and colour, are welcome to join in the acquisition and advancement of knowledge'.[16]

Writing in 1969, Hand said of Feetham:

> His earlier career, his contribution to the Boundary Commission and its Report and his later opposition to the apartheid regime in South Africa (he died as recently as 1965) suggest a conscientious lawyer with a keen analytical mind, courageous in standing for Christian and liberal ideas. He could, however, leave on those who knew him – and respected him – the impression of a somewhat humourless and unimaginative man. An obituarist wrote of 'his extraordinary industry and conscientiousness', and no one who has seriously studied his approach to the Irish Boundary Commission is likely to question that tribute.[17]

Curtis and Feetham had remained in touch through the Round Table and Curtis had tried, unsuccessfully, to get Feetham to draft the final version of the Treaty in 1921.[18] He was more successful in 1924 when he suggested offering the chairmanship of the Boundary Commission to his friend. Writing to Craig and Cosgrave just after Feetham was approached, Ramsay MacDonald stated, 'that, as in our view the Chairman of the Commission should be someone not connected with any of the three Governments concerned, we are sparing no pains to find a qualified person from one of the self-governing Dominions'.[19]

While Feetham was based in the dominion of South Africa, he was still British and a close intimate of some key figures in Whitehall. Writing to Churchill in August 1924, Curtis said that 'Feetham is a chairman exactly of the kind you contemplated. F.E. [Lord Birkenhead] says he is the ablest of the South African Judges which is probably the ablest of all the Dominion benches.' Curtis believed 'him to be the justest and most fearless man I have ever met, and also a man constitutionally of conservative temperament'.[20] On his appointment as chairman, Curtis sent Feetham a short cryptic telegram: 'England expects.'[21] While it can be dangerous to read too much into some passages of writing, undoubtedly the British felt they had a man as chairman who would be sympathetic to their understanding of Article 12 of the Treaty.

Craig was not overly perturbed by Feetham's appointment, telling his Cabinet that the representations he had received about him 'were favourable on the whole'.[22] Carson was less impressed, sneering, 'I feel not sore, but a little disappointed that you could not get anybody in the United Kingdom to settle these matters, and you have to go, I forget where it is to – Timbuctoo [sic] or somewhere or other – to find somebody who can solve this knotty question.'[23]

Craig had been further reassured by J.H. Thomas's belief 'that the Boundary Commission is merely concerned with an adjustment of the actual boundary'.[24] James MacNeill had also got wind from talking with an old journalist friend of his that Thomas 'thought only line or adjustment of boundary was to be considered'.[25]

Ramsay MacDonald shared that view also. He corresponded extensively with Lady Edith Londonderry, wife of the Northern Minister of Education. In one letter, he complained to her that the 'burden of Atlas was nothing to mine. His was the world; mine is the follies of the world.' He explained that the 'difficulty about our expressing a view that Clause 12 was meant to be a rectification of boundary is that apparently the South people had a different pledge from Mr Lloyd George'. He believed that 'the wording of the Clause shows that it contemplates a rectification only, & I cannot believe that any arbitrator would take a different view. I understand that that is Feetham's view, but that may be mere gossip.' He pleaded with her 'to help like a dear good woman to give us peace' by asking her Ulster unionist friends to be reasonable.[26]

The reply from Lady Londonderry was not encouraging, saying that MacDonald 'must be reasonable too and keep the faith with Ulster'. She mercilessly mocked the Irish, saying they 'can be very charming but they certainly are an inconsequent race – in fact, very like children and when given too much latitude, they get out of hand'. She did not understand why MacDonald's government made such an effort to meet the Free State government's needs, writing, 'Too much attention is bad for the young and causes them to show off.'[27]

Carson expressed similar sentiments on what he believed was the British government's placating of the Free State government, saying that Ulster was 'being attacked in an endeavour to save the fortunes of a Government in the Free State which in every detail of its government and administration has abandoned all pretence of any loyalty to the Crown'.[28]

To many in Britain, as Hugh MacCartan observed, the 'Ulstermen' were seen 'as their kin'.[29] On the other hand, as Carson alluded to, the Free State government was making great strides to exert its independence and drift further from the Empire. Unlike some of his Labour Party colleagues, but like most of his Labour Cabinet colleagues, J.H. Thomas was a firm believer in the British Empire. At the British Empire Exhibition at Wembley in May 1924, he toasted 'the Empire', saying that his government 'intended above all to hand to their successors one thing when they give up the seals of office, and that was the general recognition of the fact that they were proud and jealous of, and were prepared to maintain, the Empire'.[30]

While Northern Ireland fully embraced the British Empire Exhibition, with many displays at its 'Ulster' pavilion, the Free State did not participate. In a letter to the Minister for Foreign Affairs, Desmond FitzGerald, James MacNeill strongly suggested that the Free State be represented at the opening of the exhibition to be presided over by the king, as absence 'would be regarded as wilful discourtesy'. He added that if Cosgrave was in London at the time, 'I think he must attend.'[31] Cosgrave curtly replied to FitzGerald that he had 'no patience with their semi social events. If in the future when an opportunity for Ministers of this State to devote time to such affairs our proximity to England must not presuppose our absorption in these festivities & events. We have our own.'[32]

Apparent to British observers was the importance the Free State attached to its membership and involvement in the League of Nations, which allowed it to develop an Irish foreign policy that did not stem solely from Anglo-Irish relations. According to Michael Kennedy, 'Ireland's natural tendency was towards a European-centred foreign policy. Thus, France, Britain, Spain, Germany, Italy and especially the small European states were Ireland's natural constituency in the international environment.'[33] By joining the League of Nations in September 1923, the Free State government was able to avail of a new avenue to press its case over the boundary question. It allowed the Free State government to strengthen its claims that it was an international agreement more so than an intra-empirical one.[34] British government circles were concerned that the Free State would bring the delay in the convening of the Boundary Commission before the League of Nations, particularly after it registered the Treaty with the League on 11 July 1924.[35] Tom Jones noted in March that he would 'not be surprised to see the Free State take the matter to the League of Nations. It would be the sort of spectacular play which would appeal to them.'[36] *The Morning Post* claimed the registering of the Treaty with the League was 'another move in the quiet game of turning a Dominion in name into a Republic in practice'.[37]

The British did not share the Free State's enthusiasm for the League of Nations' potential involvement in resolving issues relating to the boundary question in Ireland. Later, in November 1924, a dispatch from the British government claimed that 'any Convention concluded under the auspices of the League' is not 'intended to govern the relations inter se of the various parts of the British Commonwealth', concluding 'that the terms of Article 18 of the Covenant are not applicable to the Articles of Agreement of 6th December, 1921, and are informing the Secretary-General of the League accordingly'.[38] The Free State government drafted an angry response to be sent by Tim Healy:

My Ministers find it impossible to accept a view which interprets in a distorted and restricted sense the rights and obligations of the Members of the League of Nations. They can see no clause in the Covenant which in any way purports to differentiate as between the various States Members of the League. There is nothing, in their view, to justify any one Member in withholding or attempting to withhold from any other Member or group of Members any of the rights conferred by the Covenant on all Members of the League without exception.[39]

In a letter to *The Scotsman* in August 1924, Patrick J. Ford picked up on remarks made by Lord Londonderry days earlier questioning the Free State's loyalty to the Empire. Londonderry had said that the 'Union Jack in Dublin is conspicuous by its absence. Any reference to the Sovereign is carefully omitted, and in the speeches and newspaper articles the doctrine of separation is preached throughout the whole of Southern Ireland.'[40] Ford disputed Londonderry's claims, stating that at the Tailteann Games, which had been hosted by the Free State government in the summer of 1924 and were 'regarded by Free Staters as a sort of apotheosis of the revival of purely Irish self-government in the South', and where 'on such occasion a little over-concentration on the purely national emblem might have been excused', an eyewitness counted 'no less than 28 Union Jacks' in 'the short distance between the Horse Show [in Ballsbridge] and Croke Park'. The 'absence of this symbol of Imperial unity was not, therefore, peculiarly conspicuous'.[41]

Arthur Hyslop, in turn, responded to Ford's letter saying the 'short distance between the Horse Show and Croke Park' is 'over four miles long, and through the busiest and best streets in Dublin' and that he was in Dublin on 2 August, the day of the Tailteann Games opening ceremony, and of the hundreds of flags flying, he 'only saw four Union Jacks. One of the Union Jacks, over a bank in College Green, was being hauled down as I passed.'[42]

For his part, Cahir Healy disputed the loyalism of Northern Ireland that Lord Londonderry had spoken about, saying 'it was a loyalty to itself.

It would be loyal only so long as it suited it. He was reminded of the nursery rhyme, "Love Mammy, love Daddy, but love myself best of any".' While there were 'plenty of Union Jacks flying – because it pleased the English', you 'could not find one ounce of practical loyalty' and when 'it no longer suited her Northern Ireland would adopt the attitude she exhibited in 1914, when a cargo of arms was imported from Germany, defying all the King's horses and all the King's men'.[43]

The Tailteann Games was not just a sporting event, but also had cultural and industrial displays on show. Described by Mike Cronin as 'a central act in state projection and self-promotion', the central aim of the games 'was to put the new Irish state on display, to invite in outsiders and to demonstrate what Ireland might achieve now that her destiny was in her own hands'.[44] An industrial pageant was held through the streets of Dublin on the opening day of the games, 'which allowed Irish firms to demonstrate their traditionalism and nationalism, as well as their adherence to modern industrial methods'.[45] It is unclear if this display of industrial independence annoyed the *Daily Mail*, but another industrial-related decision of the Free State government was sharply criticised by the newspaper. The involvement of the German company Siemens-Schuckert in the construction of the Ardnacrusha power plant as part of the Free State's Shannon hydroelectric scheme was seen by the *Daily Mail* (anti-German in outlook at the time) as a strategy by the 'German syndicate to obtain a monopoly in the development of electrical power to be produced from the Shannon and other rivers, and so gain economic control of the whole country'. The paper added that it was 'unlikely that the Government of Northern Ireland will fall a victim to this ambitious notion' but contended that 'the Free State Government and its most influential officers are supporting these German schemes to the utmost. Consequently the indications are that partition in Ireland will be confirmed and made permanent in this way.'[46]

The perception, often with good reason, that the Free State was moving away from the Empire in its outlook, worried many in Britain and the Empire, including those from the Round Table who wanted to pull the Free State back towards the gravity of the Empire. Writing in the organisation's periodical, *Round Table*, in April 1924, editor John Dove believed Britain and Ireland at the time were 'on the horns of a dilemma'. No matter what decision the Boundary Commission arrived at would lead to problems. Giving 'the Free State what it asks or anything like it would not be accepted in Ulster'. On the other hand, 'a mere adjustment of the boundary, which seems to me far more likely ... would have much the same effect in the South as a refusal on our part to set up the Commission'. The Free State would regard it 'as a fake, a gerrymandering of the same type as Craig's alteration of the constituencies. It would bring Free Staters and Republicans together and revive all the old hatred of England.' He believed the only way of reaching a satisfactory solution was through a mutual agreement.[47] In an editorial in the *Round Table* shortly before Feetham's appointment, Dove wrote that if 'Ulster is still part of Great Britain, it is the duty of the British Government to see that her word is honoured and her law obeyed'.[48]

Feetham's role, as he saw it, was to judge the merits of the case in front of him as impartially as possible. Yet he was from the same background and ideology as people like John Dove and Lionel Curtis, people who believed passionately in the British Empire and its role in the changing world of the 1920s. In August 1924 Curtis claimed to Churchill that 'the Free State has advanced most preposterous and extravagant claims as to the meaning of Article 12 in response to pressure from their own supporters and still more from their domestic foes in Ireland'.[49] Curtis was referring to claims for the transfer of substantial portions of Northern Ireland to the Free State. That this was 'in response to pressure' was, in itself, a preposterous claim from Curtis, who, if he knew as much about Ireland as he claimed he did, would have known of the consensus in the Free State that it was entitled to claim large parts of Northern Irish territory. Curtis also believed that the Boundary Commission should deliberate on conditions as they were then, not as they were in 1921, a stance adopted by Feetham that had a significantly negative impact on the nationalist case.[50] Feetham remained in regular contact with his fellow travellers in the Round Table and was accompanied by Dove on his journey from Britain to Ireland almost immediately after he had arrived from South Africa to take up his role as Boundary Commission chairman.[51] His world view did not bode well for the Free State case.

While Cosgrave wanted to steer the boundary issue along an international route, Ramsay MacDonald focused on the intra-Empire dimension instead, as evidenced by his options for chairman of the Boundary Commission. For all the British, regardless of political affiliation, the issues that arose from the Boundary Commission were structured around Empire rules, not international ones. This was not just evident in the British government's dismissal of the League of Nations having any role in intra-Empire disputes and in how the chairman was chosen, but also the power the British government believed was vested in the Privy Council to interpret and make rules for all the contesting parties, including the Free State.

With the Free State commissioner and chairman appointed, it only remained for the Northern government to choose its representative. After the breakdown of the 24 April conference in London, Arthur Henderson had invited the Northern government to 'take the necessary steps with a view to the selection of the members [sic] of the Commission to be appointed in accordance with the provisions of Article 12 by the Government of Northern Ireland'.[52] The Duke of Abercorn, responding on behalf of the Northern government, declined to do so.[53]

The 'loose draughtsmanship' of the Treaty became a problem yet again, as there was no provision in the agreement for the scenario of one of the three contending parties refusing to appoint its commissioner.[54] Lionel Curtis drew up a memorandum for the British Cabinet proposing to refer the difficulty to the Judicial Committee of the Privy Council, under an Act of 1833.[55] Introduced during King William IV's reign, the Act 'ordained that it shall be lawful for His Majesty to refer to the Judicial Committee for hearing or consideration and such other matters whatsoever as His Majesty shall think fit'.[56]

Demonstrating a total disregard for the Free State's sovereignty, Curtis and J.H. Thomas wanted the Cabinet to refer the actual interpretation of Article 12 to the Privy Council.[57] Thomas had told Craig in May that the 'Imperial Government would be quite prepared to recommend that this clause should be referred to the Privy Council in order that the meaning of the term "boundary" should be elucidated'. Craig told his Cabinet that if the Privy Council decided 'in restricting the latitude of the Boundary Commission, he thought it not unlikely that the Free State would refuse to take part in it'. On the other hand, 'if the Privy Council gave a ruling which was satisfactory from our point of view, the British Government might send out a further invitation to the Northern Government to appoint its representative', which suggests he would accede to this request.[58]

Tom Jones was opposed to the Privy Council interpreting Article 12 as it was 'certain to arouse suspicion of bad faith in the Free State, and in any case they were matters which could be raised by the Commission itself when the necessity arose'.[59] On 'British Law Officers' advising the British government that the Boundary Commission was unable to sit without a Northern Ireland representative, *The Freeman's Journal* highlighted something ignored by most British stakeholders – that 'the British Law Officers, whatever they may have advised, are not the interpreters of the Treaty. On the English side this duty rests with Parliament, as on Ireland's side it rests with the Oireachtas.'[60]

Jones noted in his diary days later that Curtis was considering resigning from the Colonial Office at the time as he did not believe the Labour government was 'making an honest effort to put the Treaty through'. He was particularly disturbed by Thomas, whom he felt was 'under Craig's thumb, and that, as usual, it is Craig's word which carries most weight in Whitehall'. Jones added that 'Craig knows how to play up to Thomas's vanity, and with all the Wembley [British Empire Exhibition] limelight there is real danger of Thomas not giving his whole mind properly to the Irish business … He is playing Craig's game of delay.'[61]

The Judicial Committee of the Privy Council was not tasked with interpreting Article 12 in the end. Instead, its main remit was to look at what options were possible after the Northern government refused to appoint its commissioner.[62] Ramsay MacDonald, maintaining his stance of the boundary question being an Empire-wide affair, in the summer of 1924 selected two members for the Judicial Committee from the UK, Lord Dunedin (Andrew Murray) and Lord Blanesburgh (Robert Younger), as well as Sir Lawrence Hugh Jenkins, formerly Chief Justice of the High Court of Bengal, Lyman P. Duff, Judge of the Supreme Court of Canada, and Sir Adrian Knox, Chief Justice of Australia.[63] It took Knox a month to arrive from Australia, adding yet another delay to the protracted process.

The two Irish governments were invited to have legal representation at the Judicial Committee. The Northern government accepted, with lawyer and Conservative MP Douglas Hogg and the Northern Attorney General, Richard Best, acting as its representatives.[64] Asserting its independence, the Free State government refused to have anything to do with the Privy Council, with Tim Healy informing Thomas that 'my Ministers cannot be regarded as being parties to the reference to the Judicial Committee or as being in any way committed to the acceptance of the opinions which may be obtained'. By the further delay while waiting for Knox to arrive from Australia, Healy said his ministers were 'gravely concerned ... with the prospect of a further delay in the operation of the Boundary Commission' and in the meantime:

> The requirement of the Treaty that the Boundary should be determined in accordance with the wishes of the inhabitants should first be ascertained, and there is no reason why this matter should not be undertaken forthwith by the Chairman of the Commission immediately on his appointment in conjunction with the representative of the Irish Free State (Dr. Eoin McNeill [sic]). It merely involves the organisation of the requisite machinery and the collection of statistical information and raises no question of policy.[65]

Cosgrave followed up with a letter to MacDonald, saying the delay over Knox would be proof to many people in Ireland 'that the British Government must have known all along that Sir James Craig would decline to appoint its representative, and that the reference to the Judicial Committee is a device to cause further delay, and if possible to shelve the whole matter'. He wrote that 'a census of the wishes of the inhabitants must be taken before the Commission can settle down to consider the problems which they will finally have to determine. This is purely a matter of machinery for the ascertaining of facts and statistics, so that they may be available for the Commission to work upon.'[66]

MacDonald replied that all the delays were unavoidable on his part and his decision to refer to the Judicial Committee of the Privy Council was important so that the public could see that 'the Commission is legally appointed. We are dealing with the terms of a Statute. As executive Governments, our opinions as to whether the Commission is constituted when two members are appointed are of no legal value.' For MacDonald, the 'Treaty is but the dry bones of a settlement. In the last two years you have clothed it with flesh, but we have yet to breath into its frame the living spirit of reconciliation.' He wanted to 'enlist you, your Government and all Ireland, including the North, in the cause of bringing back peace to the world'.[67] Cosgrave responded that he felt it was 'essential for the maintenance of harmony between nations that the wishes of the inhabitants should be a primary consideration in any system of government'.[68]

There was no agreement on what preliminary work Feetham and MacNeill could do if a Northern Ireland representative was not appointed. Almost immediately after his arrival from South Africa in early July, Feetham travelled to Ireland, where he met both Irish governments, including Eoin MacNeill in Dublin. In a statement to the press, Feetham stated that he had agreed to 'informal discussions' with Cosgrave and Craig 'to see if an agreed settlement could be reached'. He was also offered co-operation from them for a tour of the border so that he could study for himself 'economic and geographic conditions'.[69] The *Belfast*

News-Letter took comfort from Feetham's statement that he had 'come to the conclusion that the Commission, in any modifications which it may make, must keep close to the border'.[70]

In Craig's first meeting with Feetham, he said he would facilitate bringing 'into the Irish Free State Roman Catholics who were anxious to be transferred', but he 'could never be a party to the compulsory transfer of any loyalists or of any Roman Catholics against their wish'. Craig also said that 'if any referendum of inhabitants took place he would not insult loyalists by asking their wishes, since he had no doubt what the replies would be', but that his 'information showed that the vast majority of Roman Catholics had no wish for transfer, though owing to fear of intimidation they would doubtless vote for it in case of a referendum on the subject'.[71] The same claim was later made by many unionist representations to the Boundary Commission – that many Catholics wanted to stay in Northern Ireland – while some nationalists claimed that many Protestants wanted to be transferred to the Free State; most of these were ignored by Feetham.

At their initial meeting in July 1924, Feetham suggested to Craig that J.H. Thomas should summon a meeting of Craig and Best from Northern Ireland and Cosgrave and newly appointed Attorney General John O'Byrne from the Free State, as well as Feetham, to see if an agreement could be reached on 'the areas of each side of the Frontier where the inhabitants could be consulted as to their views'.[72] This clearly shows Feetham's interpretation that both sides of the border could gain and lose territory, but also that he was open to and pursued the use of plebiscites. Craig stated that the 'transfer of loyalists from Northern Ireland on any large scale would not be tolerated' but added that 'in the event of one or two loyalists being resident in an area overwhelmingly Roman Catholic arrangements should be made to offer such Protestants very full compensation to transfer to Northern territory'.[73] Using Imperial structures to resolve queries, Feetham subsequently asked for the Judicial Committee of the Privy Council to deliberate on whether the Boundary Commission could 'conduct a plebiscite in the affected areas and, if so, how could it enforce the ordinary provisions of the electoral law?' He also asked about majority or unanimous rules for Commission decisions and if the Commission would 'be able to enforce the attendance of witnesses and to examine them under oath?' He was advised that 'other than administrating oaths, legislation would be needed for other areas to apply'. There is, as Geoffrey Hand has claimed, no evidence that these 'decisions' were reported to the Free State government.[74]

Lionel Curtis believed Feetham and the Boundary Commission should not ask Westminster for powers to hold a plebiscite, firstly, due to the complex and awkward amendments 'to specify limits of deviation', which 'would occupy pages' of the legislation, but mainly because of the potential of deploying the British Army in areas where a plebiscite was held. He wrote that the 'contingency that the Commission may report that they are unable to discharge their task without taking plebiscites and are unable to take plebiscites unless equipped with statutory powers, ought to be faced'. It was, in his judgement, 'a serious mistake to suppose that, if the Commission asked for and were refused such powers, the Free State would acquiesce ... I have no doubt whatever if the Commission ask for these powers and are refused by H.M. Government, the Free State will say that the Treaty has been broken.'[75]

Curtis wrote a memorandum to the British government, expressing similar sentiments, focusing more on the messy military implications of the boundary crisis than on the political ramifications. Curtis claimed that if the Boundary Commission believed a plebiscite was necessary, it was 'almost certain to meet with the armed resistance of the Protestant majority throughout Northern Ireland'. On the other hand, if the Commission restricted itself to mere border rectifications or did not function at all, 'Curtis thought it likely that a republic would be declared in Dublin.' In that scenario, Curtis thought there would need to be a blockade of the Free State.[76] The prospect of Ulster resistance to the British Army spooked many within its ranks, as it was all too reminiscent of the crisis from ten years previously when the Curragh Mutiny occurred. The general staff of the British Army believed 'three divisions and a cavalry brigade would be needed to control an organized Ulster Unionist opposition'.[77]

In the febrile atmosphere that was developing over the boundary issue in the summer of 1924, the Northern Minister of Home Affairs, Richard Dawson Bates, submitted a memorandum to the Northern Cabinet in August entitled 'The Resources at Present at the Disposal of the Northern Government for Dealing with Disorder'. In it, he claimed the Northern government had 'enough resources to deal with current threats' but it had 'not, however, attempted to prepare for organised warfare on a wholesale scale. This could only be adequately dealt with by properly organised mobile Forces.' He contended that if 'manual attacks are made from Southern Ireland by the use of the Free State Army, the superiority will, prima facie, rest with the Force possessing artillery and aeroplanes. Even a single Bombing Aeroplane can do a great amount of damage, which we have no means of preventing.'[78] He claimed that the Free State Army at the time was in possession of six 18-pounder guns, eleven trench mortar batteries, six Hotchkiss guns and eleven aeroplanes (one Handley-Page bomber, six Bristol fighters, two Bristol Scouts and two instructional planes). Including officers, Dawson Bates believed the Free State Army's strength was 18,743 and although its exact number of rifles was unknown, 50,000 had been taken over from the British and he estimated 'that 20,000 men could be armed in addition to the present army strength'.[79]

Conversely, by August 1924, even with the reduction of 'the Special Constabulary Forces by the expedient of not replacing wastage', Northern Ireland had 3,945 'A' Specials, 20,171 'B' Specials and 8,299 'C1' Specials at its disposal, with access to 37,000 rifles and 387 machine guns, as well as 600 motor vehicles, which included 200 Crossley tenders and 166 Lancia lorries.[80]

Dawson Bates wanted to know from the Cabinet what precautions needed to be taken 'in the event of Ulster being left to defend itself'. If the decision of the Boundary Commission was 'found to be unsatisfactory to the people of Northern Ireland, what is to be the policy of the Northern

Government towards the British Government; and the Free State Government?' Was 'force to be used? The Border Counties are clamouring for a statement on this point, especially in view of the declaration "What we have, we hold".' He concluded by stating they would be 'hampered by the limitation on our powers involved by our inability to have an Army, and by having to obtain this warlike material from Great Britain'.[81]

Incredibly, as with the Specials, the Northern government was contemplating asking the British government for more military funding and weapons so that it could feasibly use them against British forces. And, as in 1914, Ulster unionists had sympathetic ears in the British Army, including the commander of British forces in Northern Ireland, A.R. Cameron, who maintained that the Free State and its army had to be considered 'a possible and really a probable enemy'. Despite many having grave objections to the Specials, Cameron believed their 'value in an emergency is clear'.[82]

Rumours were swirling of the Free State Army amassing troops on the border for much of 1924, disseminated by disgruntled unionists and elements of the diehard press, mainly in Britain. Speaking at the Sir Robert Peel Loyal Orange Lodge, controversial Royal Ulster Constabulary (RUC) District Inspector John Nixon claimed in January 1924 that although the six counties were still intact, 'the border was surrounded by the ENEMY, who had armoured cars, artillery, and aeroplanes, and indeed every kind of engine of war supplied to them by the Imperial Government'.[83] In October the *Daily Mail* reported that farmers who arrived in Derry from the Free State noticed 'unusual activity on the part of Free State troops near the Derry–Donegal border. It is stated that military huts similar to those used by special constabulary on the border are being hurriedly erected about 400 yards from the boundary.'[84]

One Conservative MP, William Pomeroy Crawford Greene, speaking at a unionist demonstration in Enniskillen, claimed 'there will be many Englishmen whose arms and bodies will be at your [Ulster unionists] service, and who will help you financially as well as in the field over the boundary question'.[85] At a unionist meeting at Ballyclare Orange Hall in

Antrim, Reverend S.T. Nesbitt threatened that if an attempt was made to impose a Northern Ireland commissioner, 'tens of thousands of Ulstermen would rise in their might against any Act that would take from them Tyrone, Fermanagh, South Down and the City of Londonderry. Thousands of men would come from England and Scotland to defend the Ulster boundary.'[86]

Regardless of the threat, imaginary or not, the Tory Party came out strongly in favour of 'Ulster' in 1924, insisting that no one would coerce Northern Ireland physically or politically. Craig gained the support of many in the party, some who were very close to him and Carson. Craig had a meeting with the Conservative Shadow Cabinet at the beginning of May 1924, where he told them that 'he got more time and more interest from the present Government on the Ulster question than he did from his own associates'. The Shadow Cabinet were convinced to do more and 'appointed three of their members, Lord Carson, Lord Birkenhead and Sir Douglas Hogg to act as a special committee' on the Ulster question.[87] This committee reported back that the Boundary Commission could not function unless Northern Ireland had a representative but 'there was no certainty that it would limit itself to making minor changes to the Irish frontier'.[88] Birkenhead suggested appointing the Northern representative 'who should retire if not satisfied', but Craig dismissed this idea as something that would be 'fatal, for not only would Ulster have been accused of sulking should she do so, but that the two other members of the Commission might still have proceeded to give a decision which might have been binding'.[89] This was the scenario the Free State would face in November 1925, after MacNeill resigned from the Commission.

After meeting with the Conservative leader Stanley Baldwin and Winston Churchill in June, Craig was hopeful that the Conservative Party would make a statement that 'would bind the party to uphold Ulster's cause, though owing to the part played by the Conservatives in negotiating the Irish Treaty, they would not be able to repudiate its provisions'.[90] Although most Tories felt they could not repudiate the Treaty, they collectively distorted what had been agreed in December 1921 in a relentless campaign in 1924, aided by much of the British press, which dismissed all Free State Boundary Commission claims as extravagant and ridiculous, insisting on the primacy of the Government of Ireland Act 1920 and that, at most, there could only be slight rectification of the boundary.

The British signatories all claimed in 1924 that their clear intention when signing the Treaty in 1921 was for miniscule border rectification only. Speaking in April in Liverpool, Lord Birkenhead insisted that the Treaty was written in 'plain language' that it could only mean minor border rectification.[91] One of the Irish signatories, Eamonn Duggan, took exception to Lord Birkenhead's claim that 'neither Mr. Collins nor Mr. Griffith ever took the slightest exception to the construction which, speaking officially and with high legal authority, I placed upon this Article of the Treaty', emphatically denying it to be true, when 'Mr. Griffith and Mr. Collins had on several occasions given it as their view that the Commission would bring about considerable transfers of territory.'[92]

Other British signatories who, like Birkenhead, were trying to rehabilitate themselves within the Conservative Party, and Churchill, who was looking to rejoin the party after a hiatus in the Liberal Party for over two decades, were more strident in their views on the meaning of Article 12 by 1924. Austen Chamberlain claimed that he had agreed only to 'the rectification of the existing boundary, it was not the creation of a new boundary'.[93] Laming Worthington-Evans said likewise, 'It was not intended that there should be large transfers of territory.'[94]

As Churchill sought his re-entry into the Conservative fold, he became more vociferous in insisting that a small boundary rectification was only ever envisaged by the British government when the Treaty was signed in 1921.[95] He was keen to avoid 'potentially embarrassing issues such as the border question in Ireland' surfacing again, particularly for it to become a domestic British political issue, as it would 'raise the question of the meaning to be attached to Article 12', something that could be very embarrassing for Churchill. Local Conservatives did not consider Churchill as a candidate for them in the West Toxteth by-election in the spring of 1924 'because of his past attitude to Ulster'.[96] Conservatives in Epping only recommended his candidature in the constituency if he pledged to 'back no change of the Irish boundary that did not have Northern Ireland's approval', something Churchill was willing to do.[97] At a speech in Epping in October 1924, he stated that it was perfectly clear that the Boundary Commission 'was not intended that Ulster should be mutilated and destroyed'.[98]

To bolster his stance, Churchill also arranged for a letter from Lord Birkenhead to Arthur Balfour, written in March 1922, to be published in the press in 1924, which appeared to support mere rectification of the boundary in Ireland. Churchill, aligning himself closer with the diehard wing of the Conservative Party, met with Balfour at Edward Carson's house to discuss the publication of the letter. Lady Carson noted that 'at present he [Churchill] is on the side of Ulster'.[99]

In Birkenhead's letter to Balfour, he wrote that Article 12 of the Treaty 'contemplates the maintenance of Northern Ireland as an entity already existing – not as a new State to be brought into existence upon the ratification of the Articles of Agreement'. The Article just provides 'for the modification of those boundaries'. On Collins's claims at the time that the Article implied large-scale transfers from Northern Ireland to the Free State, Birkenhead wrote, 'The real truth is that Collins, very likely pressed by his own people and anxious to appraise at their highest value the benefits which he had brought to them, in a moment of excitement committed himself unguardedly to this doctrine, and that it has no foundation whatever except in his overheated imagination.'[100] When sending the letter to the *Northern Whig* editor and Ulster Unionist MP Robert Lynn, Balfour explained that he was in Washington when the Treaty was signed, 'and on my return in the middle of February, 1922, I felt some anxiety lest it should have inadvertently done an injustice to Northern Ireland in respect of its boundary. Lord Birkenhead's letter was intended to allay my doubts, and did so effectively.'[101]

Birkenhead subsequently claimed to Churchill that the published letter was doctored from the original 1922 one, as it omitted Michael

Collins's 'honest if hot-headed' belief that the Boundary Commission would substantially reduce Northern Ireland's territory. 'The plain truth,' Birkenhead told Austen Chamberlain, was that the Treaty would never have been signed without the promise of the Commission.[102] While the correspondence Birkenhead had with Churchill and Chamberlain remained private, the original altered letter entered the public domain, confirming to many that it was only Collins's 'overheated imagination' behind the extravagant claims of major surgery on the border. Churchill insisted that Birkenhead's subsequent clarifications to him and Chamberlain should remain private, saying to Birkenhead that the publication of the 1922 letter would only 'do you good among the Die-Hards and Ulstermen'.[103]

By the time of the publication of Birkenhead's letter, the Judicial Committee of the Privy Council had ruled on 30 July 1924 that the Boundary Commission needed to consist of the three appointees and legislation would be needed to overcome Northern Ireland's refusal to appoint its representative. Tom Jones, who shared the British consensus that the Treaty 'meant a rectification of the boundary, not two counties', described the Privy Council's decision as 'beastly awkward'. He saw Stanley Baldwin but was met with 'a diehard reaction, more so than I ever remember having before from him. I urged immediate legislation in the House and begged him to cooperate ... "But it is difficult to forgive assassination and to forget their behaviour in the war."'[104] Baldwin and his Conservative Party were more interested in appeasing Craig and the Northern government than working with the Labour government. As Geoffrey Hand has contended, while 'the British government negotiated with Dublin, the British opposition negotiated with Belfast'.[105]

MacDonald and his colleagues were in a quandary after the Privy Council's decision. Fresh legislation was needed for the British government to appoint the Northern Ireland representative on the Boundary Commission. However, as Tom Jones pointed out, if the British unilaterally introduced legislation relating to an international treaty, 'Cosgrave's opponents would say that if the British Parliament could alter the Treaty, so could the Irish Free State'. Jones believed that if 'there is no course other than legislation then we must send to Southern Ireland a proper document legally drawn and only altering the Treaty by consent'.[106]

The British government organised another conference in London on 2 August 1924 involving Thomas, Henderson and MacDonald on the British side, Cosgrave and John O'Byrne on the Free State side, and Hugh Pollock and Lord Londonderry on the Northern Ireland side. Craig was ill again, with Lady Carson remarking that same day, 'I think there will be an awful row in the end over the boundary, it's a great drawback that James Craig is so ill & can't take part.'[107] Craig embarked on another cruise shortly after, this time to the Baltic Sea. He was, according to Lady Carson, also struggling financially to maintain his role as Northern Ireland prime minister, telling Lord Carson that 'he really can't afford it & he is encroaching on his capital all the time'.[108]

Before the meeting began, Thomas told Cosgrave that legislation needed to be introduced if Northern Ireland persisted in refusing to appoint its commissioner. Cosgrave 'pointed out the necessity for having the proposed legislation enacted before the British Parliamentary recess, indicated the distrust which would be occasioned by delay, and foreshadowed the possibility of an Irish Government coming into power which would denounce the Treaty'.[109]

When all the representatives were present, the British suggested that Craig and Cosgrave should 'endeavour to work out an agreed boundary and that any matter on which they could not agree should be referred to (a) Mr. Justice Feetham, or (b) the Colonial Office, or (c) the Boundary Commission'. This was turned down by Londonderry, who 'pointed out that such a proposition was out of the question, and enlarged upon the difficulties facing us by any suggestion of the possibility of a transfer of Ulster territory to the Free State'.[110]

Ramsay MacDonald made a 'strong appeal upon the grounds of empire stability for the agreed boundary proposal'. There also was a 'suggestion that the Commission might be constituted of the two

Commissioners already appointed'. Incredibly, this was dismissed by Cosgrave, who claimed it would make Feetham 'open to criticism on the grounds of partiality'.[111] Surely it would have been better for the Free State's sake to have two commissioners instead of three, with two of those three appointed by the British? Once again, Cosgrave showed his naivety and lack of foresight at the negotiation table. Pollock was not impressed with Cosgrave or O'Byrne, saying Cosgrave 'took very little part in the proceedings, except to say his position was a very difficult one, as the Southern people were pressing his Government to insist upon the carrying out of the treaty' and O'Byrne 'hardly spoke during the whole course of the conference'.[112]

Making little progress, MacDonald eventually proposed, for the 'honour of the British people', that his government would introduce legislation to enable the British government to appoint the Northern Ireland commissioner. He received lukewarm, non-committal responses from Londonderry and Pollock. MacDonald also informed the attendees that the British government would provide 'funds to migrate persons who were unwilling to remain in the jurisdiction within which their places of residence were located following the operation of the Boundary Commission'.[113]

At a Free State Executive Council meeting the following day, there was strong opposition to MacDonald's plan to introduce legislation that week and then allow the House of Commons to adjourn until October. It 'decided that the delay entailed thereby could not be entertained, and that the immediate passage of the Bill through the British Parliament before adjournment should be insisted on'.[114] Thomas and Henderson were sent on a hurried visit to Dublin where it was agreed to call back Parliament in September instead of October. An agreement was then reached and signed by Cosgrave and MacDonald that the Westminster and Dublin Parliaments would pass legislation allowing for the British government to appoint the Northern representative.[115]

Thomas introduced the legislation to the House of Commons days later, saying the Bill's passage would be completed by 30 September if the Northern government did not appoint its commissioner before then. There was a real danger that the minority Labour government could fall over the boundary question, resulting in another general election, the third in less than two years. But this issue was more of a dilemma for the Conservative Party than the Labour Party. It did not want to fight another election, potentially because its members sought to breach the Treaty. If the British breached the Treaty, instigated by the Tories, the Irish could do likewise and declare a republic, a set of circumstances that could be considered reckless by the British electorate. On the other hand, Stanley Baldwin argued 'that a pledge of honour was implicit in the 1920 Act, a pledge as binding as any of the promises explicitly made in the Treaty', vowing 'that Conservative MPs would fight any legislation to "alter the Treaty by changing the Character" of the Boundary Commission'.[116] Baldwin faced a potential split in his party between the diehards, who would continue to support Craig, and those who saw no reason to risk 'electoral oblivion just because Craig was unwilling to compromise'.[117]

Tom Jones thought it doubtful that Baldwin could carry his party in supporting the legislation introduced by the Labour government. He attacked 'Ulster' for holding up the Treaty, despite 'all the cash she has had out of the British Exchequer', which 'weighs not at all with her'. Jones saw three ways out: 'persuade Ulster to appoint a third member to the Commission; compel her to approve a person appointed by us; do nothing'.[118]

Baldwin reluctantly made a visit to Belfast where he tried to convince Craig and his colleagues to allow Labour's Bill to go through Parliament without a fight. He also offered a veto to Northern Ireland by saying he would back 'Ulster' if 'the Commission should give away counties'. Although Craig stated he wanted the Tories to fight Labour on the Bill, Baldwin was satisfied that neither Craig nor Carson favoured fighting an election over the issue. If the Bill was thrown out by the Tory-heavy House of Lords, the election 'would be fought on whether the Commons or the hereditary peers were to prevail'.[119]

The claims from different British politicians that the Boundary Commission could only make minor rectifications and the pledge to Ulster over the Government of Ireland Act 1920 being honoured continued relentlessly as the crisis over the boundary deepened. Tom Jones commented in his diary that he was preparing the case for border rectification, but it was 'ruinous to define'.[120] As well as Birkenhead's 1922 letter to Balfour being published, Lord Walter Long, the main architect of the Government of Ireland Act 1920, on his deathbed in September 1924, claimed that when he was framing the Government of Ireland Bill, he resolved that Ulster members

> should receive a definite pledge from me, on behalf of the Cabinet, to the effect that, if they agreed to accept the Bill and to try and work it when passed, it would be on the clear understanding that the Six Counties, as settled after the negotiations, should be theirs for good and all, and there should be no interference with the boundaries or anything else, excepting such slight adjustments as might be necessary to get rid of projecting bits, &c.[121]

Long, who was a rabid unionist to the end, claimed he was unanimously backed to make the pledge by Lloyd George's Cabinet at the time. This claim was refuted by Lloyd George, who stated that 'no pledge with reference to boundaries was ever given, even of a private character' and, in fact, it was the Ulster unionists themselves who made the suggestion of a Boundary Commission and 'we had that in our mind a year later when negotiating the Treaty'.[122]

Weeks earlier, Lloyd George supported the contents of Lord Birkenhead's 1922 letter to Balfour, saying it contained 'the only responsible interpretation of that important Clause'. With Feetham being a man 'whose ability, integrity and impartiality is above challenge', Lloyd George could not 'imagine he will come to wild and unreasonable decisions which would tear up the territory of Ulster and leave it as a province with nothing but an unconsidered remnant of its land and population'. While he felt the present crisis was 'merely the uncombed fringe' of the Irish question, he warned that the 'Irish banshee has once again appeared in our midst as it always does in every moment of difficulty in the history of this island', claiming that the crisis over Home Rule in 1914 was one of the causes of the outbreak of the First World War, emboldening the aggression of Germany, which felt the British were too distracted and divided over Ireland at the time to mount a military challenge.[123]

The central unionist figure during the 1914 Home Rule crisis, Edward Carson, wrote a letter in September 1924 to the *Daily Mail* saying that before Bonar Law approved the Treaty, Carson had had a long meeting with him, 'in which he stated that he had the most explicit assurances from the Government that Article 12 could only be construed as relating to a rectification of the frontier as determined by the Act of 1920'.[124] Carson followed up his *Daily Mail* letter with an article in *The Morning Post* describing 'the motives that prompted Ulster's attitude from 1916 onwards, and the sacrifices that Ulster made in the interests of the Empire and in the belief that the Act of 1920 was a final settlement'.[125]

A group of over thirty MPs from the Conservative, Labour and Liberal parties, led by Lord Curzon, embarked on a tour of the border that same month, meeting unionists and some nationalists from both sides of the border. Curzon had also led an earlier tour of Tory MPs who visited the border in June 1924, 'to study the Irish Boundary question at close quarters'.[126] *The Irish News* advised nationalists to stay away from the touring party, as it might attach a 'degree of importance' to a group of 'nonentities to their bootlaces', a group who had no interest in changing their minds but would, no doubt, at the end of the tour remain 'profoundly convinced of Sir James Craig's wisdom and of the justice of his cause'.[127] In a statement delivered after the tour, Lord Curzon declared that the 'people in the South could go a long way to secure a settlement if they only showed that they were loyal and that they were not going to make impossible demands'.[128]

The framing of the Boundary Commission to merely rectify the border by British politicians was aided and abetted by most of the Tory-controlled British media throughout 1924. One weekly bulletin of the NEBB described the efforts the Tory press was making to support Craig, writing that on 'the Tory side a pro-Ulster campaign is being started in the Press reminiscent of the Ulster Volunteer days'. The *Daily Mail*, the bureau claimed, 'in which it has been stated a controlling interest has been secured by the Tory Party, returns again and again to the support of Craig'. The *Daily Telegraph* writes that 'coercion, we may say at once, will never be sanctioned by the public opinion of Great Britain, which holds most strongly that we have gone to the utmost limit in imposing undesired conditions upon the only part of Ireland that is well-disposed towards us'.[129] The same paper published a map showing the 'extreme Free State claim' in August, and in September said that the 'Six Counties are the irreducible minimum'.[130]

In requesting that Bolton C. Waller come to London to assist him, Hugh A. MacCartan complained about 'reckless propaganda' from the British press, saying it 'would require one man and one typist working full speed to reply to all the misstatements in the provincial press alone'. He intended to publish 'a weekly summary of misstatements entitled "Fallacies of the Week" giving the misstatement and the reply in each case'. He believed that 'Belfast has started the biggest, most expensive and most intelligent campaign I have seen yet,' comprising the weekly 'Letter from Ulster' speeches by Conservative members and leaders, leading articles in the big provincial unionist newspapers, special articles by skilled journalists, statements by the Ulster Association, and letters to provincial papers from local residents in the six counties. MacCartan recognised the 'great advantage' Belfast had with the Conservative papers 'definitely committed to the "Ulster" attitude and are very influential'. He thought that 'the Liberal papers incline towards the "rectifying" view. I doubt very much whether any party in England will enthusiastically adopt our larger view.'[131] W.T. Cosgrave railed against the English press for treating the Free State government as unreasonable and Craig as 'the white-haired boy, the Hyacinth Halvey, the good young man of all the testimonials'.[132]

To combat the press onslaught from unionists, MacCartan believed there needed to be

> a weekly letter from Dublin continually restating our case; to get in touch with sympathetic Labour and Liberal members (also Conservative) to promote our case; to get leading Liberal papers to take up our case; special article from people like [former IPP MP] Henry Harrison on constitutional, J.W. [James Winder] Good [political journalist and writer] on general, [Joseph] Johnston on economics, [Trinity College Professor Edward] Culverwell on legal, etc.; regular statements from [Eamonn] Duggan and NEBB; leaflets sent to increasingly wider area; and dinners to [sic] leading journalists in London.[133]

The NEBB recognised that one person in England (MacCartan) was insufficient 'to cope with the work in London' and there needed to be one more member of the NEBB staff there, as well as chartering 'articles and a press agency to distribute articles, etc.', while James MacNeill, whose High Commission office MacCartan worked from, believed 'lunches and dinners should be offered to journalists to tell our side of the story'.[134]

MacCartan and others in the NEBB submitted articles and letters to newspapers refuting some of the claims made on the British side. In a letter to *The Manchester Guardian*, MacCartan dismissed the March 1922 Birkenhead letter to Balfour, showing previous statements from Birkenhead which contradicted the views he expressed to Balfour.[135] The NEBB also responded in *The Times* and *The Scotsman* to the Birkenhead letter in a similar fashion.[136]

While most of the British signatories were available to (and did) give their views on Article 12 in 1924, there was a paucity of Irish signatories who could or would. With Collins and Griffith dead, and Robert Barton and George Gavan Duffy personae non gratae of the Free State government, it was left to Eamonn Duggan to counter the claims of the British signatories. He claimed that during the Treaty negotiations the Sinn Féin plenipotentiaries 'made the situation plain to the British negotiators', that Article 12's 'purpose as we clearly understood, was not merely to rectify an inconvenient frontier, useful as that might be – but to prevent an avoidable injustice which would otherwise be inflicted on people who desired to be with us'. He claimed the 'whole of Article 12 was in fact based on the principle of self-determination' and that similar interpretations were given by Birkenhead and Lloyd George immediately after the Treaty was signed.[137]

Cosgrave declared that statements made in the British press about Free State 'demands and counter-demands are quite untrue'. He adhered 'to the principles of the Treaty (by whatever machinery worked out) that the wishes of the inhabitants of the borderlands shall prevail'. He claimed the Free State government's 'patience has been grossly abused', not by the British government, but by other British politicians and the press, 'who have poisoned the atmosphere against us and made every effort to prejudice the Tribunal to whose decision this matter has been entrusted, even by trying to impose a particular construction of the terms of reference to the Boundary Commission contained in the Treaty'.[138]

There was internal debate within the Free State government on the ambiguous wording of Article 12, an issue that had become quite apparent from the British interpretations being totally at variance with those of the Free State. Kevin O'Shiel suggested that the government 'ought not to leave this alleged ambiguity to be decided by the British nominee on the Boundary Commission'.[139] Kevin O'Higgins agreed with O'Shiel, writing to Cosgrave, 'we cannot allow ourselves to be manoeuvred into a position in which an alleged ambiguity in Article 12 of the Treaty is to be left to the decision of the Boundary Commission which, in effect, means to the decision of a Chairman appointed by the British Government'. He also stated that 'some form of arbitration must be agreed upon, and such arbitration must take place before the Commission is set up. There must be no ambiguity or alleged ambiguity in the terms of reference of the Commission.'[140]

However, Hugh Kennedy, the attorney general at the time, stated that the Free State government should 'not admit any ambiguity exists or that any question of interpretation can arise'. He believed:

> [If] any question of interpretation arises at all, it will arise at an early stage of the proceedings of the Boundary Commission. If disagreement as to the meaning of the Terms of Reference should then appear, the question will be how that disagreement is to be solved. It would be open for the Commission in my opinion to refer back the Terms of Reference to the Governments concerned for further instructions on the matter in dispute.[141]

Kennedy's advice was adopted and no effort was made to address the ambiguity of the wording of Article 12 before the Boundary Commission was established, arguably another critical error by the Free State government. The Irish, as Kevin Matthews has said, 'averted their eyes from this specific question hoping, it seems, that it might go away on its own'.[142]

As the legislation was on track to allow the British government to appoint the Northern Ireland commissioner, Kevin O'Higgins believed an offer should be made on the boundary question 'after the Bill has become law and the Commission stands ready to function'. He asked a member of the NEBB (possibly Bolton C. Waller) to draw up a proposal, which O'Higgins presented to the Executive Council on 25 September 1924. The proposal suggested minor alterations to the border; the restoration of PR, a reversal of gerrymandering, disbandment of the Specials and a release of prisoners; nationalists to enter the Northern Parliament to participate in local government; Article 5 of the Treaty, which outlined financial commitments to be paid by the Free State to Britain, to be waived; a customs arrangement 'obviating some or all of the present difficulties'; and some 'system of joint Government, giving an opportunity of advance to fuller Union later'.[143]

Further proposals followed, resulting in a committee being appointed by the Executive Council on 1 October 'to make recommendations to the Government as to the nature of an offer which could reasonably be made to the North East after the completion of the constitution of the Boundary Commission'.[144] The prospect of making an offer to Northern Ireland was still being discussed right up to the appointment of Joseph R. Fisher as the final commissioner in late October, but it is unclear if any offer was actually made to Craig. If it was, it was not accepted, nor did it form the basis of further talks. The Boundary Commission was going to be constituted after all.

Labour's Bill to appoint the Northern Ireland commissioner was passed in the House of Commons and, although there were fears the House of Lords would block the Bill, it was passed in the Lords on 11 October without amendment but 'with a resolution declaring that nothing more than an adjustment of boundaries by the Commission would be acceptable or could be enforced'. O'Higgins was outraged by the resolution, calling it a 'very deliberate attempt to influence the Commission on an international question, such as they would not attempt on the lowliest Petty Sessions Court in their own country'.[145]

The Free State and Northern nationalist case was dealt a significant propaganda blow in the general election that followed the collapse of the Labour government in late 1924, when nationalists lost their two Westminster seats in Fermanagh and Tyrone. Most blamed Éamon de Valera for the losses. Since his release from internment in July 1924, de Valera had focused much of his attention on partition. He believed that republicans would be justified in opposing the Treaty in the long run, partly over the boundary question, saying 'the Ulster problem will remain for us and it will be a very difficult problem'.[146] Accusing the Free State government of recognising partition, de Valera claimed that at 'no time did he ever put forward any proposal under which any part of Ireland would be free to set up a separate Parliament independent of the rest of Ireland'. This was refuted by the Free State government, who published his Document No. 2, issued during the Treaty Dáil debates (see Chapter Two), to show there was no difference between his document and the Treaty on Ulster.[147] Another senior republican, Maurice 'Moss' Twomey, while acknowledging in August 1924 that Northern nationalists were 'keeping quiet – satisfied that they are allowed to live' with most of them looking 'upon the satisfactory solution of the Boundary Question as the most that could possibly be achieved' and viewing 'Republicans as attempting the impossible and as a menace to their peace', believed the majority of them were 'behind the Republic' and 'some effort should be made at the next election to nominate Republican candidates'.[148]

In the October 1924 Westminster election, de Valera sanctioned the running of republican candidates in the North, including in Fermanagh and Tyrone, which at the time were held by nationalists Harbison and Healy. Fearing a split vote, both incumbents decided not to run. Harbison described the republican intervention as 'one of the greatest political crimes in the annals of the two Counties', while Healy claimed that Northern nationalists were being used 'as a pawn in the Southern game'.[149]

As expected, with most nationalists boycotting the election, the two republican candidates in Fermanagh and Tyrone, Michael McCartan and Thomas Corrigan, who secured just over 6.5 per cent each, lost out to Ulster Unionists Charles Falls and James Pringle, who both secured over 43 per cent of the vote each.[150] It was a devastating blow for nationalists so close to the convening of the Boundary Commission and prompted a review of de Valera's policy towards the North. According to John Bowman, de Valera was chastened by the experience and 'was hereafter wary of attempting to determine from Dublin any detailed strategy for northern nationalists'.[151] For the Ulster Unionists it was a triumph, holding all thirteen Westminster seats in Northern Ireland after the election, including the symbolically important ones of Fermanagh and Tyrone, with the Boundary Commission looming. Lady Carson wrote in her diary, 'Tyrone & Fermanagh we have won by 23,000. It's too thrilling. Now no one will dare touch those counties.'[152]

Joseph R. Fisher was publicly announced as the Northern Ireland representative of the Boundary Commission in October 1924 during the general election campaign, a position for which Lady Carson's husband had earlier been considered. According to Lady Carson, in late September

1924 Sir Henry Mallaby-Deeley, a Conservative politician, was sent by Ramsay MacDonald to their house to sound out Edward Carson 'as to whether he would sit as the representative of Ulster on the Commission if he was appointed'. While Carson 'felt he had to say he would', Lady Carson was 'not sure he feels very happy about it. Anyhow he said he couldn't decide without talking it over with James Craig as James has said he would appoint one. It seems poor Ulster can never get settled.'[153]

The Northern Cabinet discussed the prospect of Carson as its commissioner on 30 September. In handwritten notes marked 'very secret & confidential', Craig said there was a 'Movement on to inform [British] Govt. to appt. EC [Edward Carson] as their nominee ... He would [be] full[y] bound to accept in Ulster's interests. This would mollify N Govt. While EC remains on Comm'n we should be satisfied no harm, for if real harm he would resign & we should then [also resign from the Commission].' Craig also said that 'loyalists will be comforted with 20% compulsory distribution allowance', something MacDonald had agreed to provide for people who were transferred to the Free State.

While it is not clear exactly who initiated the move to appoint Carson as commissioner, the suggestion appears to have come from Ramsay MacDonald and was clearly supported by Craig, who, however, only had lukewarm support from his Cabinet colleagues, if at all. MacDonald had been pressing Craig to 'name a man' to be the Northern Ireland representative, with Craig saying, 'is it not better to get a man of such outstanding ability on the Comm'n to look after Ulster's interests'.[154] But others saw dangers in Carson being appointed, with Lord Londonderry saying, 'If Lord C appointed difficult for us to fight [boundary] bill' and 'it will look like a put-up job'. Edward Archdale, Minister for Agriculture and Commerce, questioned the fairness to Carson, as how would loyalists feel about him if they were transferred to the Free State? Minister for Labour John M. Andrews saw in the 'dangerous question of Newry a very difficult one for Carson especially if we get Inishowen'. Craig declared that 'Carson would not give up Newry'.[155] According to Kevin Matthews, some leading Ulster Unionists attacked Carson for 'losing' Cavan,

Donegal and Monaghan in 1920. Carson subsequently turned down the appointment, after being told by Craig 'that it would cause a "crisis" in the six counties'.[156]

Geoffrey Hand claims that, despite the delays and problems caused over the issue of appointing a commissioner, Craig still played a major part in the appointment of the eventual Northern Ireland representative, Joseph R. Fisher, one of the last acts of Ramsay MacDonald's first government. According to Hand, 'It is not quite certain that MacDonald permitted Craig to nominate privately where he had caused so much trouble by refusing to nominate publicly, but it seems likely that this is what happened.' On 10 October Thomas wrote to Fisher, 'asking him to take the appointment, and Fisher's appointment was made public a fortnight later'.[157] While Northern nationalists were punished for boycotting and obstructing Northern institutions, the Northern government was rewarded for boycotting and obstructing the Boundary Commission and Fisher turned out to be an ideal appointment for Ulster unionists.

Joseph Robert Fisher was born in Raffrey, County Down, in 1855. His father was the Presbyterian minister there. He studied at Queen's College before being called to the English Bar but was more interested in journalism and political history than the law. He became editor and managing director of *The Northern Whig* in 1901, staying in the post until 1913, a time of great upheaval in Ulster. According to Fisher's obituary in *The Northern Whig* after his death in 1939, 'in opposing to the death Dublin Rule for the North, Mr. Fisher did a man's part with both voice and pen'.[158]

Fisher was also an historian, whose books included *Finland and the Tsars* and *The End of the Irish Parliament*.[159] In his introduction to a history of the Ulster Liberal Unionist Association in 1913, he claimed, 'Ulster is once more showing itself to be the key of the Imperial position in Ireland' and welcomed the body's support for the 'maintenance of the Union at all hazards and the refusal to submit to any "second-class citizenship"'.[160] Fisher was an early advocate of partition as an end in itself instead of as a means to end Home Rule for Ireland.[161]

An illustration of British government and Sinn Féin delegates in session during the Treaty negotiations in London in late 1921. The Sinn Féin delegates devoted much time to the 'Ulster Question' during negotiations, but agreed to an ambiguously worded Boundary Commission that was at the root of the many subsequent problems faced by Irish nationalists. (*Illustrated London News*)

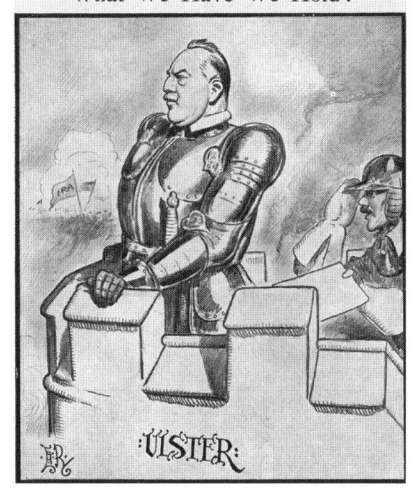

Almost from the moment of the signing of the Anglo-Irish Treaty in December 1921, Northern Ireland's Prime Minister James Craig adopted a 'not an inch' strategy that ultimately prevailed. (*Bystander*)

Michael Collins beside Richard Mulcahy at the funeral of Arthur Griffith in August 1922, just days before his own death at Béal na mBláth. (*Illustrated London News*)

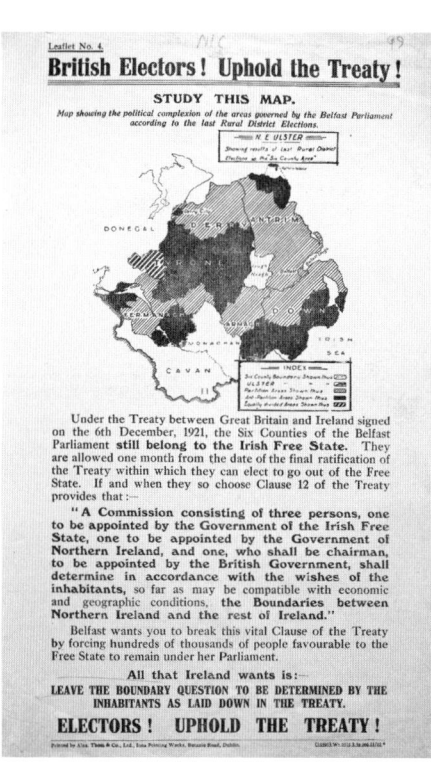

The North Eastern Boundary Bureau (NEBB) was established in October 1922 by the Provisional Government of the Irish Free State to collect and compile data, and to prepare the government's case before the Boundary Commission. It undertook a huge volume of work throughout its existence, including publishing and distributing leaflets, pamphlets and a book. Here is one leaflet distributed to British audiences. (Courtesy of the National Library of Ireland)

The delegation to the League of Nations when the Irish Free State was admitted in September 1923. Kevin O'Shiel, NEBB Director, is standing fourth from the left. Becoming a member of the League of Nations allowed the Free State to avail of a new avenue to press its case over the Boundary Commission. (Courtesy of University College Dublin Archives)

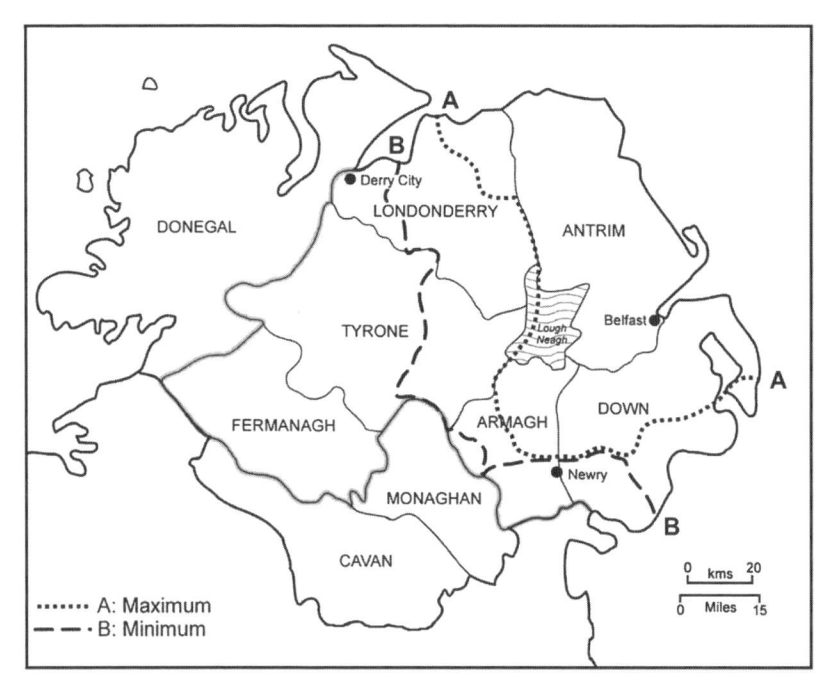

The NEBB recommendations on 'maximum' and 'minimum' territorial claims to be made to the Irish Boundary Commission. Both projections were significantly more generous to the Free State than the award actually proposed by the Boundary Commission. (Courtesy of Kieran Rankin)

RUC and customs officers at a border customs post in Killeen near Newry around 1930. (Courtesy of the Museum of the Police Service of Northern Ireland)

Construction began in the early 1920s of a reservoir to supply water to Belfast residents in the Silent Valley in the Mourne Mountains, which was used as an argument by Ulster unionists to retain all of County Down in Northern Ireland. (Courtesy of the Deputy Keeper of the Records, Public Record Office of Northern Ireland, D1403_2~062~A)

President of the Irish Free State Executive Council W.T. Cosgrave, British Prime Minister Ramsay MacDonald and Northern Ireland Prime Minister James Craig at Chequers, the country residence of the British prime minister, in May 1924. Several conferences between the two Irish governments were hosted by the British government in 1924. All failed to reached an agreement. (*Sphere*)

Political cartoon by 'Fionnbarr' mocking the African connections of the Irish Boundary Commission chairman, Justice Richard Feetham, who was a member of the South African supreme court. Others, such as Edward Carson, also mocked Feetham for the same reason, sneering, 'I feel not sore, but a little disappointed that you could not get anybody in the United Kingdom to settle these matters, and you have to go, I forget where it is to – Timbuctoo [*sic*] or somewhere or other – to find somebody who can solve this knotty question'. (Courtesy of the National Library of Ireland)

THE BOUNDARY COMMISSION MEETS.
RAMSAY MACDONALD : " *This is our friend Eoin. He thinks Antrim and Derry City are in Ireland, so we brought you over here to put him right!* "

Richard Feetham and Lionel Curtis are seated second and third from left respectively in the middle row. Both Feetham and Curtis, who were friends since they studied in Oxford University, were members of Lord Alfred Milner's 'Kindergarten', a group of civil servants who served under Milner's 'South African imperial reformulation projects' while he was High Commissioner of South Africa. (*Illustrated London News*)

The Conservative Party leader from May 1923, Stanley Baldwin, while serving as British prime minister or as leader of the opposition, sought to get the best possible outcome for Ulster unionists throughout the Irish Boundary Commission saga. (*Illustrated London News*)

Reflecting much of the British media's stance as the impasse over the Irish Boundary Commission threatened to bring the Irish question back to the centre of British party politics in the summer of 1924, *Punch* magazine portrays the native Irish as rough and dirty while Ulster unionists are portrayed as stoical and resolute.

AN INTERVAL FOR REFLECTION.

F.B. Bourdillon, Joseph R. Fisher, Justice Richard Feetham, Eoin MacNeill and C. Beerstecher in Armagh in December 1924. The Irish Boundary Commission undertook a preliminary tour of Ireland shortly after its establishment. (Courtesy of the National Library of Ireland)

The town of Pettigo is divided by the Donegal and Fermanagh border. Towns like Pettigo and Clones in Monaghan were singled out by the Irish Boundary Commission as being most adversely affected by the border. (Courtesy of the National Library of Ireland)

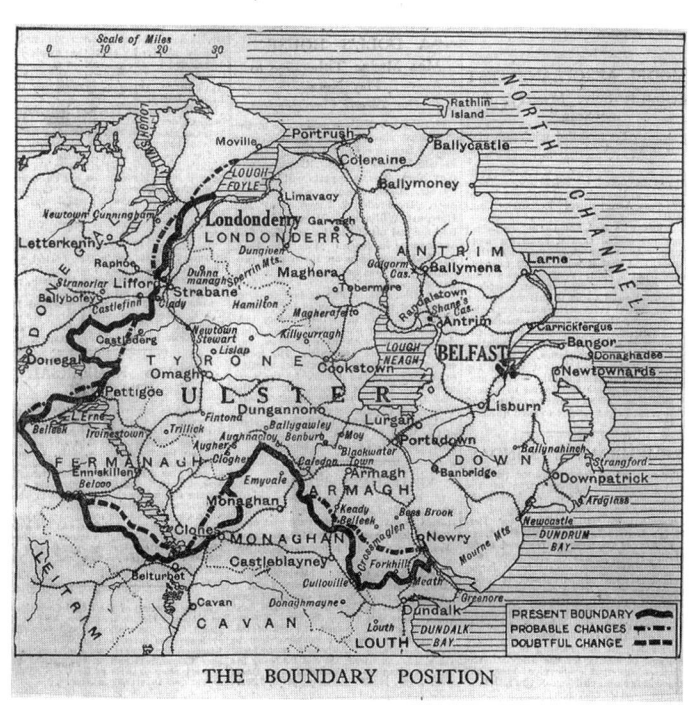

The projected Irish Boundary Commission award published by the Conservative-leaning *Morning Post* newspaper on 7 November 1925 was very close to the actual proposed award of the Boundary Commission. It was the catalyst that led to the resignation of Eoin MacNeill and the breakdown of the Commission.

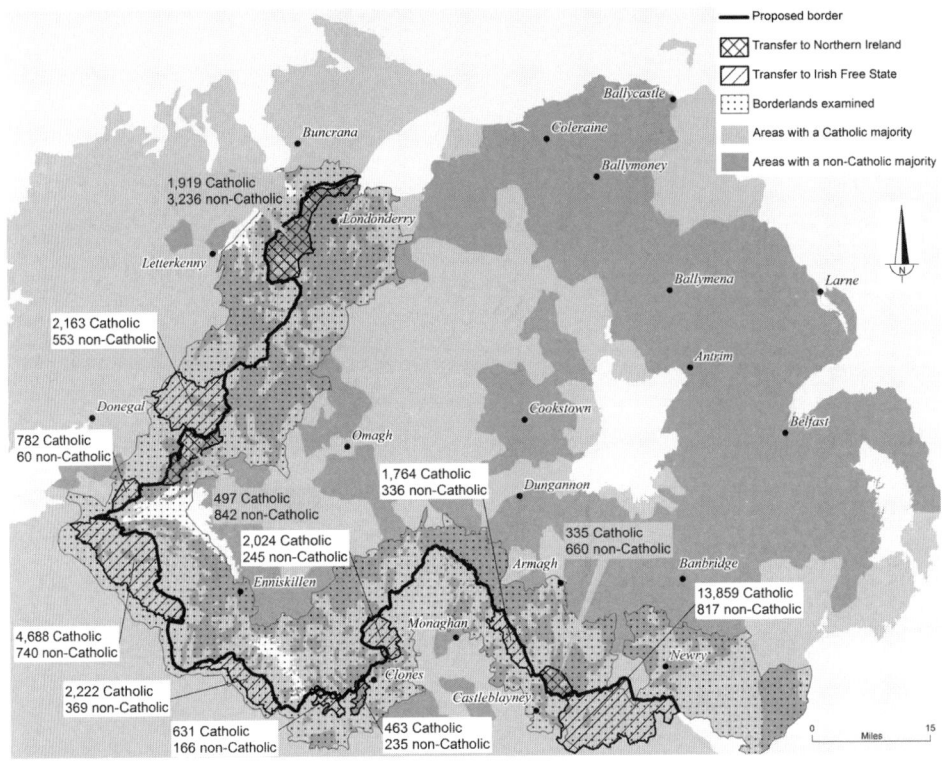

Map of the proposed award of the Irish Boundary Commmission. Falling far short of Irish nationalist expectations, the proposed award recommended that 183,290 acres and 31,319 (27,843 Catholic and 3,476 non-Catholic) people were to be transferred from Northern Ireland to the Free State, and 49,242 acres and 7,594 (2,764 Catholic and 4,830 non-Catholic) people were to be transferred from the Free State to Northern Ireland. These figures are based on the report that Feetham and Fisher drew up, the figures on the map above differ slightly. (Courtesy of National Archives of the United Kingdom)

Signatories to the Tripartite or London Agreement of 3 December 1925 between the British, Irish Free State and Northern Ireland governments, which left the border unchanged and defined as it was under the Government of Ireland Act 1920. (*Illustrated London News*)

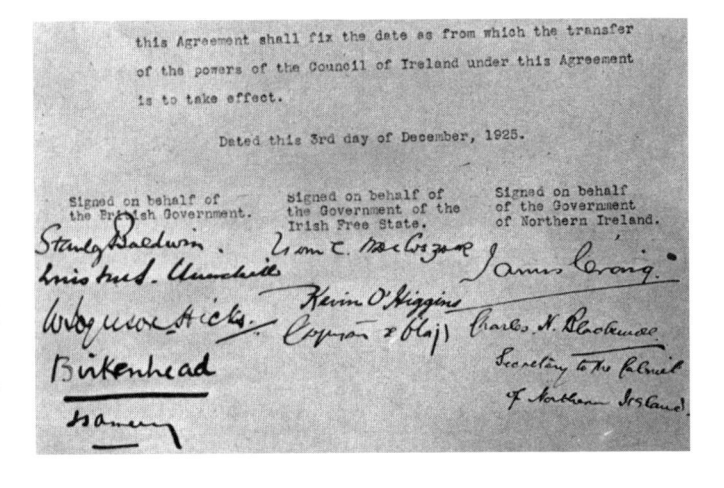

Whether he was trying to or not, his canvassing for the role of commissioner was in situ in the letter pages of The Times long before his appointment, where he strongly defended Northern Ireland's stance over the Boundary Commission. In one letter, on 4 February 1924, Fisher claimed the Government of Ireland Act 1920 was the 'Principal Act', more so than the 1921 Anglo-Irish Treaty.[162] In another letter he wrote that the boundary could be delimited, which 'can be accomplished by mutual agreement in the course of a week, with the aid of a couple of surveyors', but what 'cannot be accomplished by such means is the dismemberment of Northern Ireland. That State is constituted by Act of Parliament and ... can only be destroyed or dismembered by the same authority.'[163]

Fisher had also remained close to Craig and Carson after his time at The Northern Whig. Writing to Craig in late 1922, he thought Northern Ireland could benefit from rectification of the border. He stated, 'We ought to bear our share of the burden of congestion and misery, and Ulster can never be complete without Donegal. Donegal belongs to Derry, and Derry to Donegal.' He also wanted 'North Monaghan *in* Ulster and South Armagh *out*', writing, 'we should have a solid ethnographic and strategic frontier to the South, and a hostile "Afghanistan" on our northwest frontier would be placed in safe-keeping'. The border he envisaged 'would take in a fair share of the people we want and leave out those we don't want. There are no more passionately Northern people than in North Monaghan and East Donegal.'[164]

There was little doubt that Fisher would do what was right for Ulster unionist interests. Both Fisher and Feetham were from legal backgrounds and for the duration of the Boundary Commission were devoted to it full-time. Fisher was paid £1,200 per annum.[165] Eoin MacNeill was not from a legal background and had to balance his Boundary Commission duties with his role as Free State Minister for Education.

Fisher's appointment as the third commissioner allowed for the Boundary Commission to be established, which it was just days later. It may have been a relief to the Free State government and border nationalists that, after lengthy delays, the Boundary Commission, promised under the Treaty was finally in place. It is probable, though, the optimism felt towards the Commission at the start of 1924 had been drained away by the events of that year. The tactics used by British political parties, wilfully assisted by the British press, were duplicitous and underhand, projecting a narrative on what was agreed in December 1921 that would not have been acceptable to the Sinn Féin plenipotentiaries at the time. Both the Conservative and Labour parties tried their utmost to evade their responsibilities over the Treaty, and failing that, the Conservative Party in particular tricked people into thinking that the Boundary Commission involved, as Kevin O'Higgins put it, 'just a dinge here and a bulge there along the existing line'.[166]

So powerful and successful was the effort, that by the time the Boundary Commission was set up, most people believed that the only acceptable and logical interpretation of Article 12 was for only slight rectifications to the border, and they also believed in the primacy of the Government of Ireland Act 1920 in honouring the 'pledge' made to 'Ulster'. Feetham, as a judge, was well able to form his own views, but given his world view, the people he was close to, and the invented narrative around Article 12, it was always unlikely he would divert from the British and Northern Ireland viewpoints, which, much to the disappointment of nationalists in 1925, he did not.

Chapter Seven

'... the primary but not the paramount consideration'

IN THE UNPUBLISHED BOUNDARY COMMISSION report written by Justice Feetham and Joseph R. Fisher following the resignation of Eoin MacNeill in late 1925, they posed the question, 'What is the relation between the three different factors mentioned as affecting the determination of boundaries – wishes of inhabitants and economic and geographic conditions?' They also asked, 'In what sense is the reference to economic and geographic conditions to be understood, and what are the areas in relation to which such conditions are to be taken into account?'[1] They attempted to answer the questions in their report, writing, 'Under the terms of the Article the wishes of the inhabitants are made the primary but not the paramount consideration.' They added to this somewhat ambiguous answer by stating:

> The first point for the Commission to consider in dealing with a particular area is the question of the wishes of the inhabitants of that area, but such wishes are only to prevail 'so far as may be compatible with economic and geographic conditions'. The intention of the Article as indicated by its reference to such conditions is that the Commission should take into account the

economic and geographic relations between different areas, and should avoid drawing a boundary line which, by its defiance of economic or geographic conditions, would involve, as the result of its adoption, serious economic detriment, or geographic isolation, to communities on either side of it.[2]

The difference between the words 'primary' and 'paramount' is subtle. Primary could be interpreted as first in a group, whereas paramount could be construed as supreme. While the 'wishes of the inhabitants' was the first factor to consider, it did not necessarily follow that it was the factor of supreme importance for a particular area. Thus, in many areas, the Boundary Commission was able to override the wishes of the inhabitants based on perceived economic or geographic concerns. This, according to Eoin MacNeill subsequently, 'did not allow the inhabitants to be judges of their own economic advantage, and made it possible to hold that some undefined economic condition could override the wishes of the inhabitants'.[3] It is unclear whether MacNeill expressed those concerns while the Boundary Commission was sitting, as there is no evidence that he did. Crucially, as the Boundary Commission began its job of determining the border by inviting people and groups to present their cases, the strength of the nationalists' case resting on the most part on the 'wishes of inhabitants' was not the trump card they expected or hoped it would be. It became apparent to many nationalists quickly after the Commission was formed that Feetham did not share many of their views.

The Boundary Commission met for the first time shortly after Fisher was appointed, on 6 November 1924, at its office for its duration, No. 6 Clement's Inn in London. F.B. Bourdillon was appointed secretary of the Boundary Commission. Bourdillon was an Oxford don who had 'already acquired relevant experience on the Upper Silesian commission. The British government had engaged him on preliminary work at an early stage.'[4] He played a crucial role while the Boundary Commission operated, and while the influence he had on the Commission's decision-making is unknown, it is noteworthy, as Kevin Matthews has pointed out, 'that Bourdillon's interpretation of Article 12 bears a striking resemblance to the one later outlined by Feetham'.[5]

At that first meeting on 6 November documents, such as the Government of Ireland Act 1920, the Irish Free State Constitution Act 1922, and the Report of the Judicial Committee of the Privy Council from earlier in 1924 amongst others, were presented to the Boundary Commission. Interestingly, the 1911 census returns for all nine Ulster counties were presented, as were those from Leitrim and Louth.[6]

The commissioners 'resolved that no statement should be made for publication as to the work or proceedings of the Commission except with the authority of the Commission' and it 'was further understood that no Commissioner would consult any of the Governments concerned as to the work of the Commission, or would make any statement as to such work either to any Government or any individual without first consulting his colleagues'.[7] While Feetham and MacNeill stuck scrupulously to the commitment, with MacNeill keeping his Executive Council colleagues in the dark, much to their frustration at times, Fisher did not.

Almost immediately after agreeing to keep Commission matters confidential, Fisher was writing to then editor of *The Northern Whig*, Robert Lynn, in November and December, 'revealing details of the Commission's work'.[8] After his appointment in October, Fisher had proposed to Northern Cabinet Secretary Wilfrid Spender the setting up of a 'back channel of communication so that the Belfast Government could provide "the necessary statistical, economic, and topographical information" he would need to counter Free State claims'.[9] He subsequently wrote many letters to Florence Reid (*née* Stiebel), wife of the Ulster Unionist MP at Westminster for Down, David Reid, informing her of the Commission's proceedings, information which undoubtedly filtered through to Ulster Unionist ranks.[10]

The first meeting of the Boundary Commission also saw the commissioners resolve to ask the British, Irish Free State and Northern Ireland governments 'whether they wished to submit to the Commission statements of their cases or to appear before it'.[11] Both the British and Northern Ireland governments declined.[12]

For Craig and the Northern Cabinet, they had to balance their policy of not recognising the Boundary Commission with ensuring that Ulster unionists were not negatively impacted by its award. Speaking in early December, Craig stated that the Northern government refused 'to acknowledge the powers of any Commission to alter the boundary, as defined by the Act of 1920, and declines to tender evidence, or be represented'. He believed 'to do so would prejudice its claim to repudiate any finding that may be reached'. On the other hand, Craig wanted to make it clear 'that local authorities, business men, or private individuals may give evidence if they wish' and 'the Government will not feel embarrassed, nor will their position be in any way prejudiced' if people and groups did so.[13]

Although the Northern government did not publicly recognise the Boundary Commission, behind the scenes it was centrally involved, through the UUC, in co-ordinating the submissions and evidence of unionist representations to the Commission. Its Chief Whip, Herbert Dixon, liaised with the UUC secretary, A.W. Hungerford, while the Commission was operating to deliver a consistent and coherent message in cases put forward by unionists.[14]

At the second meeting of the Boundary Commission, on 7 November, the appointment of an assistant secretary was discussed, specifically 'who should be nominated by Dr MacNeill. It was understood that Dr MacNeill would consider the question and perhaps bring forward a definitive suggestion at the next Meeting.'[15] J.J. Hearne was nominated by the Free State Executive Council, but at the Boundary Commission meeting of 28 November, when the 'question was discussed whether one or two assistant Secretaries, if any, should be appointed', MacNeill 'said that he would not proceed with his nomination until the matter had been further considered'. MacNeill informed the Executive Council on 4 December that Feetham 'had objected to the appointment of an Irish representative on the staff' and MacNeill proposed to send a letter of protest to Feetham, but there is no evidence that he did. The matter was dropped and Hearne was not appointed.[16]

Crucially, there was no preliminary discussion at the outset of the Commission on how Article 12 should be interpreted. Instead, Feetham was allowed to take the lead and offer his own interpretations as the Commission continued along its path. One such occasion was the meeting with counsel from the Free State.

The Free State government, the only one of the three governments to present its case, had submitted a statement to the Boundary Commission and asked to meet. The government stated the 'wishes of the inhabitants of the area were recognised to be the dominant factor', insisting that the Commission's work only 'consists in ascertaining the wishes of the inhabitants of "Northern Ireland"'.[17] The Free State's counsel, who met the Boundary Commission on 4 and 5 December, was led by Attorney General John O'Byrne and included Sergeant Henry Hanna, Patrick Lynch and Cecil Lavery. Solicitor George Murnaghan and NEBB secretary E.M. Stephens accompanied them. Travelling by train from Holyhead to London, Stephens recalled that the party wanted to focus on preparing for their meeting with the Commission – all except Eoin MacNeill, who was with them on the journey. According to Stephens, MacNeill 'as frequently happened drifted off his own subject on which he was always interesting. He told me that he had been working at photographs ... He then passed on to discussing the origins of townlands.' MacNeill's travel bag went missing when they arrived at Euston Station but was later retrieved.[18] All this gives the impression that MacNeill was distracted and potentially distracting in preparations for what were crucial meetings for the Free State government.

These hearings were an opportunity for the Free State to present its case, and the questions and responses from Feetham were part of robust exchanges to tease out more information from the Free State counsel. At them, O'Byrne put forward the claim that Article 12 only applied to the inhabitants of Northern Ireland and territory could not be taken from the Free State. The 'unquestioned and unquestionable fact that the problem which Article 12 was designed to solve was the problem existing in the six counties of North Eastern Ireland'.[19] The difficulty Feetham had with this assertion was 'that the terms of the Article do not say "exclude" from Northern Ireland. It says "determine the boundaries" – which might mean either exclusion or inclusion.'[20] Feetham also stated that the 'new territory is to be "Northern Ireland" for the purpose of the Government of Ireland Act, 1920, and should be capable of maintaining a Parliament and Government', a strong hint that he believed the North's territorial integrity should remain, suggesting only slight rectifications to the border would be considered.[21]

O'Byrne stated, 'it would be necessary for this Commission to take a plebiscite so as to ascertain directly from the people concerned under which jurisdiction they are anxious to be'. Feetham replied, 'The Articles of Agreement do not refer to a plebiscite, and do not provide for conferring on the Commission, or on anyone, powers to take a plebiscite.'[22] Fisher also interjected to say that if there was to be a plebiscite, 'we should want an Act of Parliament. I do not see anyone in a disturbed district opening a polling post; the police might simply move them on.'[23] In November 1924 the Northern Attorney General, Richard Best, had advised his government that neither the 'Northern Government nor the Imperial Government can, except by Act of Parliament, authorise the Boundary Commission to institute a plebiscite of the inhabitants of any area.' To give effect to an award made by the Boundary Commission, Best believed subsequent legislation would be necessary.[24]

Another contention of O'Byrne's was that it was 'the conditions applicable when the Treaty was entered into that must be taken into account'. The 'delay [in constituting the Commission] should not be allowed to prejudice the position'. For Feetham, the wording of Article 12 'did not fix any time limit'.[25] The objections raised by him at these meetings were based on the interpretations he ultimately drew from Article 12 and were all detrimental to the Free State's case.

As well as inviting the three governments to make representations, the Boundary Commission invited written submissions from public bodies, associations and individuals to be sent by 31 December 1924. Its members also undertook a preliminary visit to Ireland in December, 'for the purpose of seeing portions of the country, acquainting itself with economic and geographic conditions, and ascertaining what sources of information are likely to be available for the purposes of its work'. No formal sittings were scheduled for the tour, just informal conversations with different people and groups.[26]

According to Geoffrey Hand, Craig made several attempts to obstruct the Commission. He 'alleged that MacNeill might be the object of hostile demonstrations or worse and sought to prevent commissioners taking any evidence in Northern Ireland'. Craig claimed he was under pressure from the Church of Ireland Primate, Archbishop Charles Frederick D'Arcy, who was reputed to have said that 'if any of the Commission visited him, he would take steps to have them removed from his house'. Stanley Baldwin, by then returned as British prime minister, and the new Home Secretary, Sir William Joynson-Hicks, were sceptical of Craig's concerns, as was the Imperial Secretary in Northern Ireland, Stephen Tallents, who found out that people like Basil Brooke 'regarded the prospect of such a visit with equanimity' and so the archbishop's remark 'disturbed Craig more than … the report of it disturbs me'.[27] As it transpired, when the Commission members were beginning their tour, the Northern Ministry of Home Affairs offered them 'any protection that may be found necessary'.[28]

The three commissioners were accompanied by Commission Secretary Bourdillon, Feetham's private secretary C. Beerstecher and the shorthand writer Alfred Marshall on the tour, which began in Armagh on 9 December, with three nights spent at each of the four stops: Armagh, Enniskillen, Newtownstewart and Derry.[29] The 'luxurious Crossley', previously the official car of the lord lieutenant of Ireland that Feetham travelled in, and a 'great yellow touring car' that MacNeill travelled in, became a 'familiar sight in many of the border areas' as the commissioners travelled hundreds of miles in the two weeks spent in Ireland.[30] A 'dogged band of pressmen "shadowed the Commissioners like sleuths of the law" every step of the way'.[31] After the commissioners visited Strabane, one local nationalist told *The Irish Times* that he did not 'care a pin what Government I live under, as long as I am given equal rights and opportunities with my neighbours' and 'that all of us here want to see that intolerable nuisance of a Customs barrier abolished as soon as possible'.[32]

In Armagh, the commissioners visited the Catholic and Church of Ireland primates. Archbishop D'Arcy did not take steps to have them removed from his house.[33] From their base in Armagh, the commissioners visited Newry, the Carlingford Lough area and the Armagh–Louth and Armagh–Monaghan border. They also visited the Silent Valley reservoir in the Mourne Mountains. After viewing the Silent Valley works, they drove through the Mournes to the Banbridge–Portadown Waterworks in Fofanny.[34]

E.M. Stephens from the NEBB visited Armagh and Newry in December 1924, shortly after the Boundary Commission party had left. The nationalists he met in Armagh town 'were nervous of any boundary, and were for this reason probably more interested in the idea of ultimate union than the people of towns lying near the border which could conveniently be included in the Free State with their entire hinterlands'. They were particularly 'nervous of a boundary alteration which might include Keady in the Free State and leave Armagh in Northern Ireland'.[35]

In Newry, he found the political situation 'more difficult than in other parts'. Given the influence of leading republican Frank Aiken, who was based in Newry, 'a very large number of the Sinn Feiners in that district seem to be republican in their tendencies. This leads to many of them standing aloof from the Boundary Commission.'[36] The RUC Inspector General's office received reports on nationalist meetings held in border areas about the Boundary Commission, which were subsequently sent to the Northern government. At a meeting attended by Stephens, the RUC reported that 'some members of the old Nationalist Party were present and took the matter light heartedly but will give no assistance'.[37]

The meeting Stephens attended in Newry was what 'might be described as a bad-tempered meeting', where one speaker said 'that the Free State Government had done absolutely nothing to assist the neighbourhood in preparing its case'. Stephens 'took particular exception' to those remarks, pointing 'out that legal agents had been employed by the North Eastern Boundary Bureau in each district charged with the duty of preparing the case for their area in brief form', as well as his office publishing 'in book form the information it had collected in this and other ways, all of which was now available for those who wished to prepare a case for their district'. A republican leaflet from 18 May 1923 was circulating in Newry at the time entitled 'Ulster Betrayed, The Startling Admission of Eoin MacNeill' by Father Isidore B. Mooney. Father Mooney claimed he was informed by MacNeill in April 1922 that Fermanagh, Tyrone, South Armagh and South and East Down would remain in Northern Ireland. Overall, Stephens noticed considerable apathy and scepticism in Armagh and Newry about the effectiveness of the Boundary Commission.[38]

After Armagh, the commissioners moved to Enniskillen on 13 December, where they visited the Fermanagh–Monaghan border around Roslea and Clones. They also visited Fermanagh's borders with Cavan and Leitrim.[39] Afterwards, they moved to Newtownstewart, where they viewed Donegal's border with Fermanagh and Tyrone. A nationalist representation who met the commissioners in Omagh on 17 December was not happy with their meeting, with one claiming it was 'all bosh', while another claimed that the group came out of the interview 'just about as wise as they went in'.[40]

Worryingly for the nationalist case, the viewings of the Boundary Commissioners were mainly happening close to the existing boundary, suggesting only small rectifications were likely. Some unionists were not satisfied either. Egbert Trimble, a member of Enniskillen Urban Council, asked Feetham 'to state the terms of reference to the Commission and the interpretation the Commission placed upon them before the council should give any evidence'. When Feetham asked Trimble to submit the council's case, Trimble replied that Feetham was asking him to 'finesse my King and Jack, with you sitting over me with the Ace and Queen, in dummy'. Demonstrating that he had no intention of giving anything away, Feetham replied, 'I am sorry I do not understand you ... I know nothing about cards.'[41]

A similar encounter happened with members of Fermanagh County Council in Enniskillen, by then a unionist-controlled body. The deputation consisting of, amongst others, MPs James Cooper and Charles Falls, and future Northern Ireland prime minister Sir Basil Brooke, told Feetham they were uncertain about participating in the Boundary Commission 'as they did not know what the terms of reference to the Commission were, whether they were dealing with the whole of the Co. Fermanagh, or merely a slight Border rectification'. Feetham replied that 'these were questions he could not answer'.[42]

Following the visit to Derry, a made-up story developed about MacNeill that was persistently told in Dublin for years afterwards to demonstrate his scholarly detachment. It was recalled that he left his fellow commissioners on one occasion in Derry to visit by himself one of Ireland's most significant ancient monuments, the Grianán of Aileach in Inishowen in County Donegal. But in fact, instead of it being 'an archaeological frolic of MacNeill's own, it was a Sunday excursion by the commissioners and their staff, organized by the mayor [of Derry]'.[43]

At Derry, just as the commissioners were concluding their tour, the *Derry Journal* published a bombshell piece of news for nationalists. Feetham had informed a nationalist deputation in Derry that 'historic considerations are not to be taken into account in determining the border' and 'that the Commission are not endowed with powers to take a plebiscite for the purpose of ascertaining the wishes of the inhabitants'. Those calling for a plebiscite were, according to the *Derry Journal*, 'merely beating the air'.[44] Even though the Treaty was an international agreement, a point the Free State government was trying unsuccessfully to emphasise, it was clear that Feetham, in his decision-making, was only concerned with the opinions of British bodies, such as the Colonial Office, the Privy Council and Westminster. He adjudged a plebiscite could not be held by only consulting with British bodies and not Free State ones on the feasibility or not of holding one. The Boundary Commission issued a statement refuting the claim that 'the Commission would not have any regard to historical considerations', but did not refute the claim that there would be no plebiscite.[45]

From their brief interactions with the Boundary Commission in December 1924, there was a deep sense of foreboding amongst Northern nationalists that the Commission would not deliver what they were hoping it would. People and groups prepared written submissions in December 1924 while the commissioners were visiting border areas. By the start of 1925 the Commission had received 130 separate representations, of which twenty-three were submitted by local authorities, thirteen by other public bodies, forty-four by local political groups, and fifty by private individuals and businesses.[46] Additional submissions were made in January and February 1925, and even during the course of the hearings from March. Where submissions for the same regions conflicted with each other, the Boundary Commission sent each side the counter-submission to facilitate the interview process.

In the time between the receipt of written submissions in late December 1924 and the commencement of the formal interviews in March 1925, Feetham sought to augment the staff of the Boundary Commission. Major Robert Albany Boger from the Royal Engineers was hired as a chief technical assistant. He had been mentioned in dispatches during the First World War. While serving with the Royal Flying Corps, he was taken prisoner and interned in Germany for most of the war's duration. He served for over three years from 1920 to 1923 as the British Commissioner on the Upper Silesia Boundary Commission.[47] Feetham was unable to secure the appointment of a statistical assistant, so an assistant secretary, Dr C.J. MacPherson, was hired instead. As Hand has contended, it is 'puzzling that MacNeill does not seem to have exerted himself to find Irish or dominions candidates for any of these posts'.[48]

E.M. Stephens undertook a taxing schedule during the Boundary Commission, travelling to the key locations being considered for transfer from December 1924 to July 1925. He was assisted by Hugh A. MacCartan, who also visited different areas. Both men noted that there was little interest in the Commission in areas with little prospect of inclusion in the Free State, with nationalists in places such as Limavady and Dungiven in South Derry not submitting many claims. According to Stephens, the reluctance was caused 'as traders, and others, who would be in a position to speak on the economic situation, do not wish to create a feeling against themselves in the neighbourhood'. MacCartan encountered the same issue in Magherafelt, where residents felt 'it would be unwise to provoke the hostility of the powers that be without any hope of escaping their authority'. In early 1925 there was relative peace 'and the people are so glad of the change that they do not want to give any excuse for reprisals'. The apathy in Magherafelt was not helped by the local parish priest, Canon Quinn, 'an old supporter of the Irish Party', who 'keeps out of politics, and, as usual in the North, his indifference is reflected in the attitude of the Catholics generally'.[49]

In East Tyrone MacCartan visited Cookstown, Dungannon and Clogher. Clogher was the district least prepared, again due in part to the local parish priest not being enthusiastic, as well as a 'few laymen of standing not taking any interest in the matter'. In Dungannon, as was replicated with many nationalist cases, there was an emphasis on the wishes of the inhabitants based on 1911 census figures, the last census taken in Ireland before the Boundary Commission convened. At a meeting of Dungannon residents, it 'was also agreed that "economic and geographic" conditions should not be put forward in the direct evidence'.[50] A Tyrone-based local registration agent (Mr McConnell) claimed that Aughnacloy and Ballygawley wanted to be linked to Monaghan for economic reasons 'but that otherwise these districts were rather apathetic about the Boundary question'.

On receiving feedback about the discontent among farmers in the North, who felt the Free State 1923 Land Act terms were 'much more favourable than those proposed for Northern Ireland', Stephens directed the Free State publicity department to publish a comparative outline of both land purchase terms in local Omagh-based papers.[51]

Stephens believed 'that on account of its economic relations with Donegal, Derry is the weakest spot in the Northern Government's party system. I intend, if possible, to obtain more accurate details as to the Protestant opinion in Derry, and particularly to find out what cleavage, if any, exists.' However, he was warned by businessman and former deputy lieutenant of the county, Charles O'Neill, that while 'partition was ruining Derry, and that Protestant wholesalers had suffered, and were suffering, very heavily in their business', he still did not think they would look for inclusion in the Free State as they 'were so long accustomed to vote by party, that they could not get away from it now'.[52] In his own submission to the Boundary Commission, O'Neill recommended the transferring of Derry city to the Free State. Otherwise, the 'tendency of the Belfast Government is to reduce it to the status of a mere village'. On the other hand, 'as the leading Port in the North West of the Free State it would have a new lease of prosperity, so by inclusion therein, the City has everything to gain and nothing to lose'.[53]

Throughout this process, the Free State government maintained its contact with the Boundary Commission. Bourdillon told the Executive Council's Cabinet Secretary, Diarmuid O'Hegarty, that the Commission was willing to hear all claims, including ones from the Free State wanting to be transferred to Northern Ireland, but would not publicly disclose its interpretations.[54] Cosgrave, who was paranoid about losing Free State territory more than anything else, subsequently claimed 'that the Commission has no authority under the Treaty – which is the basis of its authority so far as Saorstat Eireann is concerned – to transfer any part of our territory to Northern Ireland'.[55] In a case of the Free State government trying to convince itself that none of its territory could be transferred, O'Hegarty then sent a letter to Bourdillon saying:

> [The] decision of the Commission to hear arguments and evidence in support of claims which involve the inclusion in Northern Ireland of territory situate on the Free State side of the existing border is not to be taken as implying that they have come to a decision adverse to the contention of the Government of the Irish Free State that Article 12 of the Treaty cannot be interpreted as

giving authority to the Commission to transfer to Northern Ireland any of the territory of the Irish Free State – a contention which has already been argued at length before the Commission by Counsel on their behalf.[56]

Meanwhile, the Northern government publicly maintained the illusion that it was not recognising the Boundary Commission, while, privately, it was. Spender wrote to A.W. Hungerford in February 1925 that, to combat nationalist representations from Derry, Craig believed in the 'importance of meeting the arguments adduced by the other side, which the Boundary Commission, if no reply is made, may think to be an unanswerable case, instead of being, as it is, very special pleading'. Spender stressed the importance of 'loyalists stating their case' in Tyrone and Fermanagh.[57] Craig intervened again to request that Hungerford work with Henry Vance, chairman of the Aughnacloy Town Commissioners, for the sake of unionist unity in County Tyrone, stating that 'unless the case is carefully presented, one of the arguments might be held as a good reason for the inclusion of Aughnacloy in the Free State'.[58]

The RUC assisted the Northern government in combating nationalist cases before the Boundary Commission by spying at nationalist gatherings and obtaining submissions and documents from nationalists. One RUC report dealt with nationalist meetings in Down. At one, in Glasdrumman, that was seeking delegates to give evidence, the Commission was 'treated as a joke' and 'nobody anticipates that South Down will be included in the Free State'. At Castlewellan, the RUC claimed there was very little interest in such meetings, with most Catholic farmers there stating 'quite frankly that they prefer to remain in Northern Ireland'. At another meeting in Ballynahinch to select delegates, Michael O'Reilly from Dromora was selected. However, he said he knew nothing about it and was selected without being consulted. The RUC claimed he was 'a loyal man, and he stated that he would not act as delegate nor attend the meeting, as he had no grievance against the Northern Government and did not wish for inclusion in the Free State'.[59]

The RUC was not always successful in obtaining information. After a meeting of the 'Nationalists of Fermanagh' in Enniskillen approved a draft document of evidence, the RUC stated it had 'not been possible to obtain a copy of the evidence to be submitted to the Commission'.[60]

The Boundary Commission arrived back in Northern Ireland in early March 1925 to begin formal hearings. It met first at the Judges' Lodgings in Armagh from 3 to 7 March. It held its sittings for Down at the Great Northern Hotel in Rostrevor from 9 March, with one sitting for East Down at the Slieve Donard Hotel in Newcastle on 18 March, before going back to Armagh on 19 March. The hearing of evidence was then interrupted by the general election for the Northern Ireland Parliament and resumed after Easter, from 22 April. It met at Killyhevlin in Enniskillen from 22 April to 6 May, at the Irish Society's House at St Columb's Court in Derry from 14 May to 5 June, and finally at Knock-na-Moe in Omagh from 6 June to 2 July. There were morning and afternoon sittings most days, with time allowed for the Commission to visit places when the need arose. Overall, 575 witnesses representing fifty-eight groups and public bodies were heard, as well as ten individuals who had also submitted representations.[61] The evidence suggests that, while some women attended preliminary meetings, often held at town halls, all the witnesses who gave evidence to the Commission were men.[62] As Peter Leary has written, witnesses 'usually had property and status, many were well advanced in years, and few could be described as young. They were of the sort who made up the Nationalist and Unionist activist cadre of the border region: clergy, solicitors, merchants, and strong farmers; often former or incumbent elected representatives and their agents'. Neither republicans nor 'the much talked about labouring and small farming classes' took part.[63]

Throughout the sittings, the main argument used by nationalists looking to be transferred to the Irish Free State was that the wishes of the inhabitants should override economic and geographic factors, and, as Catholics made up the majority in most of those areas, the areas should be transferred to the Irish Free State. They 'assumed that the wishes of the inhabitants would be the overriding concern of any boundary commission'.[64] However, as Paul Murray convincingly reasons, it made 'little sense for nationalists to base their main arguments on the wishes of inhabitants as these figures, by and large, were already known'.[65]

As no plebiscite was carried out, the Boundary Commission relied on the 1911 census figures, election results and evidence provided by witnesses to determine the wishes of the inhabitants. Feetham generally supported the assumption that all Catholics tended to be nationalists who sought inclusion in the Free State and all Protestants tended to be unionists who sought inclusion in Northern Ireland.[66] Based on submissions to the Boundary Commission, in most cases, this rule held true. Submitting evidence on behalf of the Newry Urban District Council, spirit merchant Robert O'Rorke claimed, 'It is nearly entirely on the religious division. The entire Protestant population want to be included in the Northern Government, and I might say 999 Catholics out of every 1,000 are easily in favour of inclusion in the Free State.'[67] George Bennett was an exception, a Protestant who supported the inclusion of South Down and South Armagh in the Irish Free State, stating, 'I am myself a Protestant in religion but I am an Irishman and share the political opinions of the majority of my Countrymen. I desire inclusion in the Irish Free State.'[68]

The primary reason cited for inclusion in the Free State by most nationalists who submitted evidence was that most people living in the areas they represented sought as much. Many of the submissions from nationalists provided the Boundary Commission with the 1911 census returns it already had to prove their areas had 'an unanswerable case' for inclusion in the Free State. The wishes of these inhabitants must override all other considerations according to nationalist representations from Tyrone, Magherafelt, Armagh Urban District, electoral divisions of Middleton and Keady in Armagh, and the Poor Law unions of Newry, including Crossmaglen and Kilkeel.[69] According to the 1911 census figures, 74.6 per cent of the population of Newry was Catholic and was therefore overwhelmingly in favour of being included in the Free State.[70] Likewise, Father Felix Canon McNally, parish priest in Upper Kilevey and Catholic Chaplain to the Newry Union Workhouse, claimed the district electoral division of Kilevey in South Armagh had a total population of 2,305 in 1911 made up of 2,283 Catholics and just 22 from all other denominations.[71]

Nationalist ex-servicemen from Omagh claimed that 'the vast majority of the people of this District and of the whole county of Tyrone are Nationalist and Catholic and it is their desire that they should be incorporated with the Nation to which they belong and which has been set up as the Irish Free State'.[72] A committee representing the nationalists of County Fermanagh stated that, based on the 1911 census and on local and national election results in 1918, 1920, 1922 and 1923, the 'claim of Fermanagh for inclusion in the Free State ... is grounded upon the democratic principle of the peoples' will'.[73]

Many nationalists believed they could only be retained in Northern Ireland through coercion, and they referred to their political rights being removed by the Northern government, highlighting the suspension of nationalist-controlled local authorities by April 1922 and the decision not to contest the local elections of 1924, when those taking their seats were obliged to take an oath of allegiance to the Crown and the Northern government. As a result, bodies such as Fermanagh County Council, Derry City Corporation, Newry Rural District Councils 1 and 2, and Kilkeel Rural District Council, which had been controlled by nationalists, were taken over by unionists 'without any Authority from the majority of the Inhabitants' according to Patrick Connolly, an ex-Poor Law Guardian and ex-Rural District Councillor from Newry.[74] Unionists countered that the non-compliant local authorities were rightly suspended for 'their refusal to perform the duties imposed on them in pursuance of the Local Government (Ireland) Acts' and, in any event, they would still have won their seats in a contested election.[75]

In addition, moves made by the Northern government to undermine their civic rights within Northern Ireland through the abolition of PR and the gerrymandering of electoral districts were highlighted by many nationalists seeking transfer. The Derry Nationalist Registration Association claimed that after a readjustment of ward boundaries in Derry city, 'Catholics being 56.21 per cent of the population get 40 per cent of the representation, and all others (Protestants), 43.79 per cent of the population get 60 per cent of the representation'.[76] In his submission, Cahir Healy referred to a report in the *Fermanagh Herald* of distressed farmers from Eshnadarragh in Fermanagh looking for relief help being asked by a committee of Lisnaskea Rural Council whether they 'would prefer to stay within the six counties, or be attached to the Free State', intimating that their answers 'will be our guide what we may, or may not do'.[77]

Fr M. McGuire, parish priest of Kilskeery in Tyrone, in asking for his community to be released from 'further Northern tyranny' and to be included in the Free State, highlighted how the Catholic population in his parish had been mistreated by the Northern government over the previous three years, which included claims of murder, death threats, physical assaults, imprisonment without trial, raiding and plundering, malicious burning of Catholic schools and homes, confiscation of property, all perpetrated 'by the armed officials of Specials of the Northern Government with the connivance of that Government or without any serious attempt to bring the perpetrators to justice'.[78] The Boundary Commission replied 'that the work of the Commission is set out in its terms of reference and that it would thus be outside the scope of the Commission to enquire into charges such as those set forth in your letter'.[79]

The many testimonies of nationalists highlighting their mistreatment under the Northern jurisdiction appeared to make little impression on Feetham and Fisher. In their final report, just a few lines were devoted to nationalist complaints about the Specials, the abolition of PR and 'the recent redivision of constituencies for the purpose of Local Government elections'. Of some nationalists' desire to end partition and have Ireland unified, 'the Commission pointed out that its duty under its terms of reference was to determine a boundary, and not to decide the question whether there should be a boundary or not'.[80]

Nationalists were not the only ones to present cases of mistreatment to the Commission. Unionists also cited their treatment by nationalists as reasons not to transfer them to the Free State. Sir Basil Brooke, in his capacity as a county councillor in Fermanagh, listed the Specials who had been killed, wounded or kidnapped in Fermanagh since 1921. Based on what happened in the past, 'it would be most unjust now to hand over any portion of Fermanagh to the Free State where it would entail at the same time the handing over of one single inhabitant who has carried out his duties to his country and to the Empire'. Based on the Civil War and the (perceived) continued violence in the South, Brooke asked that, if the Free State government appeared 'not to have the power to protect even their own adherents, how much less will they be in a position to secure the lives of their quondam enemies?'[81]

Most unionist submissions to the Boundary Commission did not focus on the wishes of the inhabitants, but some points were raised on the levels of unity within the Catholic community. J. Moore Boyle, a solicitor representing the Newry Chamber of Commerce, claimed that Catholics were divided between those who sought a republic and those who favoured inclusion in the Free State.[82] Robert Forsythe, chairman of Kilkeel Rural District Council, also asserted that the Catholics of the Kilkeel Union were 'divided in their political outlook as a large section of them are republican and the leaders of the republican party are against the fixing of a boundary line in Ireland'.[83] Some unionists tried to deny nationalist electoral success in Tyrone and Fermanagh, with one, solicitor Edmund Orr, claiming, in his submission, that there was a majority against the Irish Free State in both counties in the election to the Northern Parliament that year, as unionists and republicans secured 46,603 votes versus 36,090 for the Nationalist Party, an anti-Free State majority of 10,513. Orr failed to mention, of course, that unionists and republicans had very differing views on practically everything else, including on partition.[84]

When unionists referred to the wishes of the inhabitants, many believed differences should be accounted for between permanent residents and those who crossed the border temporarily for seasonal work (all mainly Catholics), and those who paid the most rates (mainly Protestants). This case was made by some unionists in Warrenpoint and Newry, who claimed that people should be differentiated based on the rates and taxes they contributed, and that those who paid the most were in favour of retention in Northern Ireland.[85] Another example was Drummully, a locality in Monaghan almost completely cut off from the rest of the county by the Fermanagh districts of Clonkeelan and Derrysteaton, 'almost certainly a ballybetagh – a nearly vanished pre-colonial sept land resurrected as an international boundary', according to Peter Leary.[86] Even though, according to the 1911 census, there were 264 Catholics and 184 Protestants living in Drummully, the Protestant inhabitants claimed to the Boundary Commission that they owned thirty-eight of the sixty-three farms in the area and paid seven-eighths of the taxes. They believed 'it was their right that their wishes should be consulted as to the government under which they were to live'.[87]

The Raphoe Presbytery in East Donegal claimed it represented over 900 Presbyterian families and, 'in view of the fact that the Protestant population owns a preponderating proportion of the land and pays – correspondently – a much larger proportion of the rates', petitioned 'the Boundary Commission for the inclusion of the eastern part of the county in the six-county area'.[88] The Donegal Protestant Registration Association, representing unionists of Donegal, claimed that in many parts of the area 'the only really permanent element in the population were the landowners and the prosperous farmers. The servants employed by them – mostly Catholics – were hired on a Six Months Contract and generally left at the end of their time for some other district'. Nationalists in Donegal disagreed, claiming 'that these considerations were partly unfounded, as in many cases labourers often remained on the same farm for years or, at most, moved to another farm in the same district'. One witness pointed out that as there were many marriages in this class, 'this would of itself necessitate a certain permanence of abode'.[89] The Cliff district electoral division in Donegal, close to Belleek in Fermanagh across the border, comprised 169 Catholics and ten non-Catholics in 1911. However, the loyalists insisted that 'the Unionists are the largest property owners in the area, and consequently pay the greatest proportion of the rates' and therefore should be included in Northern Ireland.[90]

While admitting there was a Catholic majority of between 4,000 and 5,000 in Derry city, John Scott claimed the 'Roman Catholic majority is composed principally of men engaged in unskilled labour such as Dock labourers and ordinary labourers and women who are employed in Shirt Factories. These people are almost exclusively employed and paid by Protestant employers.' In a statement demonstrating breathtaking superiority, he also stated, the 'unskilled labour in the City is largely performed by labourers from Donegal who drift in and generally bring their wives and families. These are the people who are huddled together in the West and South Wards, almost every house being occupied by three and sometimes four families, and each family occupying only one room.' He believed if 'the life of the City was dependent upon these people, then in short time the streets would be deserted and the works idle … "that the grass would soon be growing on the streets of Derry" would become an accomplished fact'.[91] He also stated that four-fifths of Derry's capital was owned by and three-quarters of the city's taxation came from Protestants. By 'Tradition, Association, Situation, Connection, Race, Religion and every other tie, Derry City forms an integral part of Northern Ireland, and you might as well cut off a man's head and expect him to live as to separate Derry City from the Six Counties.' Scott concluded with a flourish, writing that should it be 'decreed that Derry City be placed under the domination of the Free State Government', a government that 'prides itself upon its disloyalty, which has erased the King's name from every official document, and eliminated the Crown from its emblem', then 'Derry will only be taken over the dead bodies of loyal men and women who will not sell their birthright'.[92]

In one submission from Lieutenant Colonel F.T. Warburton, who was based in Portarlington in County Laois, in an extraordinary jibe at the Irish language, he claimed no one from the North should be forced to come into the impoverished Free State, who over-tax people just to squander the money 'in the attempt to revise a barbarous guttered language without poetry, literature, commercial words, sounding in many cases like something between coughing and spitting'.[93]

Countering the unionist argument that those who occupy the 'greater part of the land and pay the major portion of the rates' should have a disproportionate say on where they lived, Fermanagh nationalists stated, 'the poor are members of the national community equally with the rich'.[94] Cahir Healy stated that unionists 'have based their claim to Fermanagh rather on the possession of bullocks and grass than the goodwill of human beings'.[95] Strabane residents John Devine and John O'Doherty also condemned the treatment of people as bartering tools by the unionists of Strabane, writing, 'As to the suggestion of exchanging a portion of Tyrone for a portion of Donegal, it seems most unreasonable to ask that the wishes of the inhabitants should be disregarded, and that they should be bartered as chattels to suit the whims of any political party.'[96]

A representation from a group called the 'Inhabitants of the City of Londonderry and the North West Liberties' also condemned the treatment of people as more important based on their wealth and political power, stating, 'according to all recognized principles of modern civilized society, the humble labourer, the struggling artisan, the small dealer, to mention only a few, are each and all entitled to be considered "inhabitants" on equal footing so far as Political rights and freedom of conscience are concerned, with the wealthy manufacturer, the wholesale merchant, or the absentee landlord'.[97] Such demands were still being called for decades later in the North during the 1960s civil rights campaign, one of the main goals of which was 'one man, one vote'.

However, much to the dismay of nationalists, Feetham believed, 'a distinction may, I think, fairly be drawn between different classes of the population, on the principle that the more permanent elements of the population of a particular area have a greater interest in the destiny of that area, and that their wishes are therefore entitled to greater weight'.[98]

Unionists mainly focused their cases for inclusion in Northern Ireland on economic factors, with almost all submissions claiming their regions were intrinsically linked economically with Northern Ireland, although it is important to note, as Terence Dooley has, that 'some of the evidence submitted on economic grounds was used merely as a pretext. The real motivation for transfer to Northern Ireland (or to stay in Northern Ireland) may have been based on political factors.'[99]

Writing to A.W. Hungerford in February 1925 about the case for Derry city, solicitor T.C. Wylie stated there was 'no doubt the figures as to Population are against us'. It was, therefore, important 'to show how Derry has prospered for the past thirty years both in Population and wealth'.[100] While both nationalists and unionists in Donegal agreed on the importance of Derry city to Donegal, nationalists insisted Derry should be in the Free State while unionists insisted that Donegal, at least the parts of the county with large unionist numbers, should be transferred to Northern Ireland. For nationalists, an illustration of Donegal's economic importance to Derry was the Londonderry and Lough Swilly Railway Company. While the headquarters of the company was in the six-county area, almost the full mileage of its railway lines, except for a couple of miles, was in the Free State. To nationalists, 'inasmuch as Derry has been the shop for Donegal, the latter as Customer has a legitimate claim upon it'.[101]

Unionists also insisted that the main distributing centre for Donegal was Derry, stating:

> [T]he economic importance of Derry to Donegal cannot be sufficiently emphasised ... Such towns as Letterkenny, and to a lesser extent, Stranorlar, may serve as local retail centres, but the fact remains that the whole district, and it is not going too far to say the whole county, appears to be economically dependent on Derry. Derry is the natural port of Co. Donegal.[102]

The case of Middletown District Electoral Division in County Armagh demonstrates how economic arguments were closely aligned with political wishes. While nationalists claimed that, economically, Keady, Monaghan and Glaslough were Middletown's principal market towns and Armagh city was only a market for flax, unionist inhabitants refuted such claims, stating Middletown was not economically connected with County Monaghan, that the principal cattle fair was Killylea, and that the great bulk of the district's farm produce was marketed in Armagh. It even obtained its bread from Armagh. They asserted that Armagh was an economic unit entirely bound up with the North and that 'those Catholics who have a stake in the district are opposed to inclusion in the Irish Free State'.[103]

William Johnson, a solicitor based in Newry, claimed 'it could materially interfere for a considerable length of time with our tourist trade that we enjoy here from Northern Ireland' if Warrenpoint was transferred to the Free State.[104] Martin Hamilton, general manager of the linen firm Bessbrook Spinning Company, asserted they had no economic links with the Free State.[105] Coal importer and ship owner Frank Fisher believed Newry would lose its coal and linen trade if it was transferred to the Free State. He also mentioned the higher cost of living there compared to Northern Ireland, stating, 'A £1 note can at present buy more in Newry than in Dundalk and this fact has a bearing on local wages.'[106] A special committee established by the Newry Urban District Council countered that the linen industry was in steep decline, claiming:

> [I]t is well known that the linen Industry in Northern Ireland instead of making progress is retrogressing for at the time we prepare this statement out of the three Spinning Mills in the town of Newry one has been entirely closed down for two or three years and the other two are working half-time while the Mills of Bessbrook Spinning Co. Ltd. in spite of the fact that they are at present situated in Northern Ireland are not working full-time and are not working to capacity.[107]

Feetham looked at economic conditions as they prevailed in 1924/25 and not how they were interpreted by the Treaty signatories in 1921. In fact, he refused to hear any evidence on how the Treaty signatories interpreted Article 12, despite its obvious ambiguities.[108] This proved highly damaging for the Free State cause. Unionists either looking to be transferred to or remain within Northern Ireland were quick to point out the higher taxation and generally higher cost of living in the Free State, partly caused by the crippling Civil War.[109] The use of the Silent Valley reservoir to supply Belfast residents with water was used as an argument to retain all of County Down in Northern Ireland. The Belfast City and District Water Commissioners objected to any part of South Down being included in the Free State as it 'would expose the Commissioner's Works to easier attack and necessitate continuous protection'; and placing 'the Commissioners Works under a jurisdiction different from that under which the Area served' would lead to 'interference with the undertaking', 'Restrictions in the use of the water' and 'increased taxation'.[110]

Arguably more damaging for the nationalist case was the customs barrier introduced by the Free State government in April 1923 along the existing border (see Chapter Four). Feetham regularly referred to the damaging consequences of the customs barrier in his questioning. He told the Free State Inspector of Customs & Excise, P. O'Golain, that it was obvious the customs barrier had made 'the position much more irritating for people along the border'.[111] Both unionists and nationalists went into some detail on the effects the customs barrier had on their daily lives and livelihoods. Major R.L. Moore, who owned land in Cliff in Donegal, claimed that since the barrier was erected, his tenants looking to make the one-mile-long journey to Belleek in Fermanagh via motor car were no longer able to use the 'unapproved' road where he lived and instead had to make a 'round-about' journey through Ballyshannon, nine miles away, to get to Belleek.[112] Similarly, Thomas Johnston from Pettigo claimed that in order to get to Kesh from the Donegal side of Pettigo, a distance of four miles, since the customs barrier was introduced, 'we must first go to Belleek, 12 miles, and then on to Enniskillen, 20 miles, and back on that journey 20 miles to Kesh'.[113] Border towns like Pettigo and Clones in County Monaghan were 'singled out by the Boundary Commission as being most likely to suffer from the adverse social and economic effects of the border it now found on its very doorstep'.[114] John Scott, on behalf of a group called the 'Loyalists of Londonderry City', stated that if 'any attempt was made to bring Derry City into the Southern area', the leading shirt and collar factories that employed between 8,000 and 10,000 in the city, 'would undoubtedly close down rather than submit to the nuisance, trouble, worry and expense of sending their goods through the Customs Barrier'.[115]

Strabane nationalists felt that the 'setting up of the Customs Barrier has to a very large extent shut off business transactions between Donegal and Strabane'. The obstruction the barrier caused removed Strabane 'from its status as a first class business town. The cattle market which was one of the best has gone down considerably and the same is true of its other markets.' Towns in Donegal, such as Donegal town, Raphoe, Castlefin and Letterkenny, benefitted from Strabane's loss of trade.[116]

While unionists in the more southerly counties of the North believed the placing of a customs barrier north of where they lived would lead to large financial losses and considerable inconvenience, nationalists claimed they were already suffering from the effects of the existing customs barrier by losing customers from their hinterland in the Free State. Asserting that their economic prosperity lay with the Free State, nationalists sought for the boundary line to be drawn northwards.[117]

Nationalists in Aughnacloy claimed that turnover in trade had decreased by 75 per cent because of the customs barrier. Even though farmers were exempt from paying duties on their goods, Monaghan-based farmers avoided the creamery near Aughnacloy they used to frequent as they were unable to purchase groceries or provisions there without paying duties. From a geographic and economic point of view, they claimed, 'Aughnacloy has an extremely strong claim for inclusion in the Free State in order that the markets and business of the Town may be revived and brought back to the standard of 1916.'[118]

Due to the customs barrier, Patrick McConville, a baker from Crossmaglen, was unable to take products with sugar in them across the border. He was 'cut off from the vast majority of his Customers in the Counties of Monaghan and Louth and the Bakery is since closed down'.[119] Matthew H.

McCann, a baker based in Newry, faced the same problems, stating that output from his bakeries had 'been considerably reduced owing to the fact that the confectionery made by my firm cannot now be carried by my carts over the Customs barrier'.[120] John Foster, a draper also based in Newry, claimed, 'Since the Customs Boundary was put up a lot of people come to Newry to buy boots and wear them home and do not pay duty on them.' He believed 'a barrier north of Newry would very seriously affect the shipping trade. Anything that affects the prosperity of the town affects the retailer. There is no doubt that farmers north of Newry, if the barrier were between them and Newry, would not cross it.'[121] Charles O'Hare, vice chairman of Newry Urban District Council and a partner in a wholesale retail chemist firm O'Hagan & O'Hare, demonstrated the devastating impact customs barriers had on his businesses, claiming the 'wholesale trade with customers in the existing area of the Free State is practically destroyed since the establishment of the existing temporary border'. The goods of his firm were 'variable and breakable, requiring very careful packing; cases are opened on the border for examination, goods are disturbed, and repacked badly so that leakages are abnormal, causing great difficulty with carriers, who, when claims are made, state that they were badly packed'. The firm's expenses had increased by 14 per cent since the imposition of customs barriers and the threat of further tariffs prohibited the expansion of the business.[122]

In one of the few instances showing support for customs barriers and tariffs, Francis O'Hanlon, secretary of Mullan Mills in Emyvale in Monaghan claimed, 'a Woollen factory and a little village attached had been lying idle and derelict for many years until the Irish Free State's tariff of 15 per cent on imported foot-wear'. This encouraged local businesspeople 'to avail of the opportunity to start a Boot & Shoe Factory, thus encouraging Irish industry and help to give much-needed employment to many of the young people in the district'.[123]

Nationalists in border areas stated there were no economic conditions incompatible with those areas being transferred to the Free State. In Keady in County Armagh, they claimed the town was cut off from a considerable area in County Monaghan that had previously formed part of its economic sphere. One witness claimed that if 'free communication were established with the port of Dundalk which is much nearer to Keady than Belfast, Keady would benefit considerably'. Industries such as linen, baking and tailoring in Keady, which had suffered considerably because of the customs barrier, would survive and flourish if it was included in the Irish Free State.[124] Edward A. Lamb, secretary of Newry Port & Harbour Trust claimed 'the interests of the port of Belfast will always be paramount and receive preferential treatment from every authority in Belfast including the Government of Northern Ireland to the detriment of the port of Newry'.[125]

The NEBB's Joseph Johnston, who provided evidence at several hearings of the Boundary Commission, believed 'overwhelming economic considerations would have to be proved before the Commission would be justified in going against the wishes of the inhabitants'. He further contended that 'the commercial hinterland which is the background of Newry's activities, is, even under present conditions, to a greater extent in the present Free State area than in Northern Ireland', claiming the bulk of Newry's grain and flour trade was with Monaghan and Cavan in the Free State.[126]

The third factor to be considered in any revision of the border was geographic, and this took on added significance, with Feetham deciding that smaller units such as district electoral divisions, instead of large units such as entire counties or Poor Law unions, should form the basis of areas to be considered for transfer. When Patrick O'Neill MP claimed all of east Down should be transferred to the Free State, Feetham contended that the town of Newcastle, with a Protestant majority, was not a small area and this would have to be considered.[127] In Tyrone, with the Catholic population more or less concentrated in the centre of the county, the decision not to consider whole counties was detrimental to the nationalist case for inclusion for many districts there.[128]

Unionist inhabitants of Mullyash district electoral division in County Monaghan based some of their claims for inclusion in Northern Ireland on geographic considerations, claiming if Mullyash was 'added to the present county (Armagh) area, the boundary of the County towards the Free State would be considerably shortened and straightened'.[129] Likewise, three farmers, Maxwell Boyle, Joseph Henry and Samuel Cargill, who had land in Monaghan and Armagh, felt that, due to the introduction of customs barriers, which caused a significant burden to them, and for geographic reasons, if 'the line was shifted and this pocket [in Monaghan] included in the North it would shorten the boundary line & leave convenient access from both sides of the Main Rd'.[130] Henry, who had forty-four acres in Armagh and ninety in Monaghan, claimed, 'I am sitting on the border.'

Others in North Monaghan, such as Dr William Johnson Smyth, wanted to be transferred from 'a lower civilisation'. Smyth claimed that 'Swarms of Roman Catholic labourers have joined the local population during and since the Great War – replacing loyal protestants who left – wore his majesty's uniform in the Great War – and never returned.' While most loyalists wanted to be transferred to the North, few would 'dare make known their wishes to be placed in the Ulster area: To do so would be their ruin – sooner or later – their death'.[131]

The submissions by unionists in Mullyash, Glaslough and Drummully to be transferred to Northern Ireland alarmed Monaghan County Council, with one member claiming 'that the Boundary Commission had no right to interfere with any Free State territory'.[132] The council asked to see the submissions from the three areas and was told by the Commission that it needed to send a submission first.[133]

Unionists also contended that Carlingford Lough was a natural geographic boundary, with William Johnson stating that to transfer Warrenpoint 'into the 26 County area would not only be incompatible with the existing Geographical conditions but would be substituting for the present natural so well defined boundary of Carlingford Lough an unnatural and ill defined line of demarcation'.[134] According to E.M. Stephens, and worryingly for nationalists from South Down, Feetham himself had suggested that 'Carlingford Lough might be regarded as a good natural boundary'.[135] This argument was refuted by the Newry

Urban District Council, which claimed that South Down 'will be bounded both on the west and on the South by territory at present under Irish Free State jurisdiction and on the east by the sea ... There is therefore no geographic condition which can be adduced to prevent the area from being retained in the Irish Free State.'[136]

Cahir Healy noted that, geographically, Fermanagh was 'surrounded by the Free State for an area of perhaps sixty miles', and a 'great deal of our trading is done with the Free State counties and buyers from the midlands take the greater part of our cattle', but argued that these were 'minor considerations in Article Twelve beside the wishes of the inhabitants' and 'other considerations must give way before the paramount one of the desires of the people'.[137] In replying to Alexander E. Donnelly's case for County Tyrone to be included in the Free State, Edmund Orr, secretary of the County of Tyrone Boundary Defence Association, countered that 'Tyrone has not the same relationship, geographically or economically, with any of the Free State counties, as it has with Co. Armagh on its eastern side, and Co. Derry on its northern side.' Orr claimed 'the contour of the County between Tyrone and these counties is so alike that it is difficult in dozens of places to determine the actual boundary line. The mountain range referred to in our opponents' case only stretches a comparatively short distance between Tyrone and South Derry.'[138]

The county most affected geographically by partition was Donegal, almost completely isolated from the rest of the Free State. Most nationalist submissions from Donegal and Derry stressed the social, economic as well as geographic bonds between these two places, with one witness, Reverend John O'Doherty, arguing 'that Donegal people viewed Derry as part of Inishowen and, as such, a part of Donegal'.[139] One group representing nationalists from Donegal claimed that the River Foyle offered 'a very natural geographic boundary; and this geographical consideration helps to confirm us in the hope that at least the Port and city west of the river will be transferred to the Free State'.[140] Unionists saw it differently, with submissions for Inishowen to be attached to Derry city, and others looking for the transfer of the eastern part of Donegal, and in some cases the entire county, to Northern Ireland.[141] Cahir Healy derided the fact that unionists in Donegal 'would generously leave the Pilgrimage of Lough Derg to the Free State, and at the same time include the only road leading to it in Northern Ireland. I suppose the pilgrims might be expected to get in and out by aeroplane.'[142]

Throughout the hearings, E.M. Stephens prepared nationalist witnesses for their interviews with the Boundary Commission. He held public meetings, conducted mock interviews with witnesses and provided feedback from previous sittings. In some instances, he had to motivate witnesses who were downbeat about their prospects of receiving a favourable outcome from the Commission. In some areas, nationalists were 'splendidly organised', such as Newry, where they were helped by J.H. Collins. Even though nationalists there held 'very different political views', they were 'unanimous in saying that whatever their different views might be they were all anxious for association with the rest of Ireland, and anxious to be relieved of the necessity of living under the authority of the Belfast Government'.[143]

Stephens felt there was less unity in other areas, particularly Derry. He wrote that he 'had more difficulty in carrying on my work in Derry than in any other Nationalist centre in the North. I had no opportunity, as I had elsewhere, of addressing a general meeting of witnesses, and working up enthusiasm in the presentation of the case.' He claimed the 'people in Derry seemed unaccustomed to working together. I met witnesses either separately or in groups of two or three.' Whereas in other areas, all the nationalist witnesses attended together to follow the proceedings closely, the nationalist witnesses in Derry only turned up when it was their turn to be interviewed.[144] Some did not turn up at all. Derry businessman J.J. Madden failed to attend, which 'was generally attributed to the fact that newspaper reporters had succeeded in obtaining the names of the witnesses and had published them in the press, thereby creating the obvious danger of losing customers'.[145] Farmers' Party TD John White, despite being interviewed by the Boundary Commission, believed 'it did not matter what evidence was given, that the boundary would be fixed by backstairs methods, if it was changed at all, it would be changed in favour of Northern Ireland, and denounced the Free State Government's policy'.[146]

The mood among nationalists in the Magherafelt district was even gloomier, with the NEBB's legal agent there, P.J. Agnew, claiming 'that the whole district was apathetic on the boundary question, as there was no chance of the area being included in the Free State'. So pessimistic was Agnew that he failed to turn up for his own hearing with the Commission.[147]

Stephens found that nationalists in East Tyrone held similar views. He believed, as 'East Tyrone is situated a long way from the existing border, and has many economic associations with Belfast, it was an area which I was afraid might not produce a substantial body of evidence'. For Stephens, there 'was a natural difficulty in organising such a district where apathy about the Boundary Commission was naturally more marked than in areas more easily included in the Free State'.[148]

In Fermanagh, some felt that Joe Devlin's decision to enter the Northern Ireland Parliament following the April 1925 election was 'an indication that no good result is expected from the Commission and that an effort may be expected to form a Nationalist party in the Belfast Parliament under the leadership of Mr. Devlin'.[149]

The second election for the Northern Ireland Parliament was called by James Craig at the beginning of March, while the Boundary Commission was sitting in Armagh and Down. It was held on 3 April. Craig called the election to save 'Derry, Tyrone and Fermanagh, and the Border'.[150] He used the election to mobilise unionist support while the Commission was sitting. It was the last election of the Stormont era held under PR, and a disappointing one for Craig, with the Ulster Unionist Party reduced from forty to thirty-two seats. Other than republicans who ran separately, the rest of nationalism in the North amalgamated and won ten seats, an increase of four, all taken from what was a united Sinn Féin party in 1921. Republicans won two, with the Northern Ireland Labour Party winning three, independent unionists winning four, and a single-issue candidate, Gerry Henderson, for unbought tenants on land, winning a seat in County Antrim.[151] The *Irish Independent* wrote of the blow to Craig, who 'had made an announcement a month ago which was tantamount to an assertion that this election was to be a display to intimidate the Boundary Commission. He has failed ignominiously to achieve the result at which he aimed, and he leaves the arena politically weakened and battered.'[152] On the other hand, *The Times* claimed that Craig's losses mainly took place in Belfast and County Antrim. In the border counties, where the 'existing boundary was the predominant issue', there was an increase in the unionist poll. Adding 'together official and independent Unionists on the one hand and Nationalists and Republicans on the other there is the following result: Total Unionist vote 245,650; Total Anti-partition vote 112,359; Doubtful 25,659'.[153]

After the 1925 election, nationalist witnesses in places like Derry and Fermanagh remained downbeat about their prospects with the Boundary Commission. This was partly explained by their interactions with Feetham during their interviews. He asked the newly elected nationalist MP Basil McGuckin 'whether he did not think that the transference of Derry to the Free State would be a serious surgical operation'. McGuckin interpreted this 'as indicating a reluctance to make any change'.[154] Archdeacon John Tierney from Enniskillen was asked about 'the effect of transferring the Catholic districts in the south of Fermanagh into the Free State and assigning the rest of the County, which would then be predominantly Protestant, to Northern Ireland', with Feetham enquiring 'whether the Catholics in the Southern area would prefer inclusion in the Free State under these conditions to remaining in Northern Ireland with the rest of the County'. Others in Fermanagh were asked similar questions, leading 'them to believe that the Chairman was bent on rectification and intended to use the gerrymandered District Electoral Divisions to their disadvantage'.[155] Stephens tried to improve morale by pointing out that Feetham 'was bound to ask the most difficult questions he could devise, and particularly questions suggested by the Unionist case, in order to elicit the facts'.[156]

In contrast to their neighbours, nationalists in South Armagh, and South and East Down were satisfied with Feetham, who 'made a remarkable impression on the witnesses who have given evidence'. They told Stephens, 'His questions have been courteous, but searching, and that they display a very remarkable knowledge of the district.' They also believed 'the findings of the Commission will be in accordance with the evidence'.[157] Ironically, it was the nationalists from Down who could have the strongest claim to feel most aggrieved by Feetham's findings, with no part of the county recommended for transfer to the Free State.

Witnesses made few comments about Eoin MacNeill and Joseph R. Fisher, partly because both took such peripheral roles during the sittings. In Hand's opinion, the two men may have thought 'that interventions by them might seem provocative or leading, according to whether the witness was hostile or friendly'.[158] All the interviews were dominated by Feetham, who asked the vast bulk of the questions, with the other two commissioners rarely intervening. After resigning from the Boundary Commission, MacNeill claimed that Fisher had 'all through the proceedings of the Commission ... been impassive and had left all to Feetham'.[159] The same could have been said of MacNeill, whose input was infrequent and often irrelevant. In one interview with H.D. Green, managing director of an oatmeal and Indian meal mill in Omagh, MacNeill asked Green whether 'anybody in Ireland experimented with those flaked forms of wheat they manufacture in America?' He continued a pointless meandering exchange with Green that bore no relevance to the Boundary Commission proceedings.[160]

Fisher's focus seemed more on filtering the Boundary Commission proceedings through Ulster Unionist ranks than on the proceedings themselves. Craig's biographer St John Ervine was sent the correspondence between Lady Florence Reid and Fisher while the Boundary Commission was convening. Writing from Enniskillen, Fisher told her in April that there was no likelihood of a report being issued before September. In May he wrote 'that since Devlin went into the Belfast Parliament, there are signs of a drying up of the enthusiasm for the I.F.S. It seems as if, before we are through, we may be putting Nationalists out of Northern Ireland into the Irish Free State against their will.'[161] And from Omagh, in late June, Fisher told Lady Reid:

> All is going smoothly, and the more extravagant claims have been practically wiped out. It will now be a matter of border townlands for the most part, and no great mischief will be done if it is worked out on 'fair give and take' lines, even if the 'religious' figures involve rather more give than take. The outer fringe of Fermanagh, the Clones region, Aughnacloy and South Armagh, have all been perambulated from end to end, and although we may have to go pretty deep in some places, the result will, I think, be a stronger and more compact territory, with not inconsiderable bits added.[162]

Ulster Unionist politicians made several statements in the summer of 1925, boasting that the Boundary Commission would deliver for them. The veil of paranoia and uncertainty of four years over the Commission seemed to have shifted from the unionist psyche by then, undoubtedly aided by Fisher's leaks. At a Twelfth of July event, James Cooper MP declared he 'would nearly guarantee that practically the whole of Fermanagh would remain in the Six Counties'. A month later, he said, when 'the report of the Border Commission came it would be found that Sir J. Craig had not let them down'. At the same time, speaking in Limavady, another Ulster Unionist MP, Sir Malcolm Macnaghten, stated, 'Derry was safer – the results of the last election made it so. Enniskillen was safe; Newry was safe, as it was vital to the economic existence of Ulster.'[163]

The Free State government did not have the luxury of a commissioner providing regular reports on the progress of the Commission. It remained in the dark. It also continued with the illusion that no Free State territory could be transferred to Northern Ireland. Cosgrave declared in February 1925 that as far as the Free State government was aware, 'no demand has been made from our side of the Boundary for inclusion in Northern Ireland'.[164] Once this proved not to be the case, the Free State government requested from the Commission the 'representations made in respect to claims of inclusion in Northern Ireland by persons and associations at present within the jurisdiction of the Irish Free State'. Bourdillon subsequently sent submissions from Glaslough, Mullyash, Drummully and a portion of the parish of Clough in Monaghan, and submissions from Pettigo and other parts of Donegal, mainly from parts of the county adjacent to Derry, Tyrone and Fermanagh. Other submissions for transfer to Northern Ireland from the Free State included that of Castle Saunderson in Cavan, with Somerset Saunderson famously having said, 'Now I have no country' when he found himself on the wrong side of the border after partition.[165] The Free State government also received representations made by the Belfast Waterworks, Portadown and Banbridge Waterworks and one relating to the Bann reservoir.[166]

Free State Attorney General John O'Byrne responded to the Belfast Waterworks submission by arguing that supplying water to Belfast, an area not part of the boundary dispute, in no way could be used as an economic argument for keeping the parts of Down where the Silent Valley reservoir was located in Northern Ireland. He contended that the economic conditions provision in Article 12 was 'confined to economic conditions affecting the particular area in question and in which it is being applied as a corrective, and that it does not entitle the Commission to consider possible economic inconveniences which may be suffered by persons in another area whose exclusion from the Free State is not in dispute'.[167] The same argument applied in respect of the Portadown and Banbridge Waterworks submission.

O'Byrne led another deputation of counsel for the Free State government to London to meet the Boundary Commission in August 1925. If it had not dawned on the Free State government beforehand, it must have dawned on it after this meeting that it was becoming increasingly likely that the Commission would not deliver a favourable award to nationalists. At the meeting, O'Byrne claimed that economic and geographic factors were only put into Article 12 'to prevent absurdities and anomalies', and said, 'the wording itself was qualifying, giving supremacy to the wishes of the inhabitants'. Feetham replied, 'Though the wishes of the inhabitants are put first, I am not sure that they can rightly be described as the governing factor … I doubt whether, as Article XII stands, you can correctly say it makes the wishes the governing factor because it puts in another factor which may over-ride them.' On the issue of the Belfast Waterworks, he said, 'But you say in looking at it we are to shut our eyes, when it is a question of what is to be done with this portion of South Down, to the fact that the interests of Belfast may suffer.' O'Byrne replied that it would not be unreasonable for Belfast Waterworks to have to deal with the Free State if the waterworks were in Free State territory, claiming many other corporations operated in that way already.

O'Byrne also claimed that Articles 12 and 14 of the Treaty implied that the Boundary Commission could only relate to Northern Ireland and not to the Free State. Feetham countered by asking if the Treaty did not give powers to the Boundary Commission to shift the boundary either way. Patrick Lynch, also in attendance for the Free State counsel, claimed that the intentions of the Treaty signatories should be ascertained, saying, 'you must interpret the language as you find it having regard to the facts that you have ascertained and the parties you were dealing with at the time you signed the contract'.[168]

John O'Byrne's predecessor as attorney general, Hugh Kennedy, by then Chief Justice of Ireland, wrote a memorandum after the Free State counsel's meeting with the Boundary Commission, criticising Feetham's rigid use of English law. Not only did Kennedy think Feetham's interpretation of English private contract law was incorrect, he also believed Feetham should not apply 'narrow and rigid principles governing the interpretation of English private contracts' in 'dealing with an international instrument' such as the Treaty. He strongly argued that the 'intention in fact was that the Commission set up under the proviso to Article XII was to deal only with the disputed area then included in Northern Ireland'.[169]

Kennedy sent his opinion to Cosgrave, who in turn sent it to MacNeill. MacNeill refused to send it to Feetham, pointing out the personal nature of the criticism of Feetham as the main reason for not doing so. He wrote to Cosgrave, 'You know that I have recognised from the beginning the commanding position held by the Chairman ... Nothing is to be gained by antagonising him on the personal ground, but a great deal may be gained by a sturdy impersonal argument.' MacNeill believed if he submitted Kennedy's memorandum it 'would have to be circulated to all three commissioners and might provoke the other two into an irrevocable decision against it', adding, 'Considering the finality and importance of the proceeding, though I am not a lawyer, I must in the last resort act on my own judgement and use so much only of the document as I consider proper for the purpose.' He suggested alterations to make the memorandum more acceptable, but as Hand has claimed, the 'evidence is not clear that these were effected and the opinion circulated'.[170] It was clear, though, that MacNeill was acting independently of the Free State government of which he was a member, being resolute in his commitment to the independence of the Boundary Commission. This factor came starkly into focus weeks later.

Feetham wrote to his mother in July 1925 after completing the long and undoubtedly exhausting Boundary Commission sittings, saying, 'I am not expecting to return to Ireland for some time to come – if at all.'[171] It is unknown if he ever did return at any stage in the future, but he never returned in his capacity as chairman of the Commission. While he may have been welcome in unionist quarters, he would not have been in many nationalist communities, particularly those close to the border. Despite all the evidence nationalists and the Free State government had painstakingly produced, and the clear advantage nationalists possessed on what they believed was the most important criterium, 'the wishes of the inhabitants', in most of the disputed areas, Feetham's interpretation stunned nationalists and led to a political crisis in the Free State.

Chapter Eight

'... inertia, incapacity, and appalling ineptitude'

PREPARATIONS WERE AFOOT TO MITIGATE against complications arising from territory being transferred from one Irish jurisdiction to another even before the Boundary Commission announced its results. In June 1925 F.B. Bourdillon sent letters to the British and Free State governments, stating that under Article 12, 'the boundaries as determined by the Commission become ipso facto the boundaries for the purpose of the Government of Ireland Act, 1920, and of the Articles of Agreement for a Treaty, without further action on the part of the Governments or Parliaments concerned'. He said that the article, in yet another example of 'loose draughtsmanship', made 'no provision expressly enabling the Commission to delay the effect of its determination, once that determination has been duly made', but the Commission believed it was 'essential in the public interest that a reasonable interval should be secured between the announcement of any decision of the Commission determining the boundaries and the actual taking effect of that determination'.[1]

Fearing the dangers that could occur with the border being changed without any prior notice, the British and Free State governments met in London in July 1925 to discuss the arrangements they could collectively make for the required changes needed across multiple departments for the transfer of territory, and the need for a transitional period from announcement to enforcement. At the meeting, it was proposed that the 'first essential was the preservation of law and order, and the administration of summary jurisdiction; next the postal services; then the fiscal services; and finally the principles on which officials were to be dealt with'. Kevin O'Higgins saw no difficulty in gardaí replacing the RUC in transferred barracks, but 'B' and 'C' Specials resident in areas transferred to the Free State would have to abide by the Free State law on possession of firearms. He recommended that those 'B' and 'C' Specials be disarmed by either the Northern Irish or British governments during the transition period.[2]

W.T. Cosgrave directed government departments to produce memoranda highlighting the main implications for their departments of territory potentially being transferred from Northern Ireland to the Free State. Free State Army Chief of Staff Peadar MacMahon insisted that the army must be prepared for three eventualities: a peaceful transition without any disturbances; acceptance by the Northern government but armed conflict with inhabitants of transferred territory; or the refusal of the Northern government to accept the Boundary Commission's findings. MacMahon declared, 'Should the third eventuality materialise, unless the British step in and force the Commission's findings then war must be the inevitable result.'[3]

Most departments who replied to Cosgrave's request for memoranda were less apocalyptic in their answers than MacMahon, with some, such as the Department of External Affairs, claiming that no changes were required at all on its part. The Department of Agriculture envisaged that little change was required for legislation enacted before partition, but for 1924 Acts such as the Agricultural Produce (Eggs) Act and the Dairy Produce Act, 'some legal instrument would appear to be necessary before they could be made to relate to added areas'.[4]

Eoin MacNeill's Department of Education did not envisage any serious difficulty in assuming control of transferred educational services but wanted to know beforehand if the Northern government would facilitate the transfer of records and documents of the schools affected. In the likely probability of the Northern government not cooperating, experienced inspectors would have to visit the schools and procure the pertinent facts, such as salary information. Transferred teachers were expected to be subjected to the 10 per cent salary reduction in operation at the time in the Free State. Initially, teachers' word on what they earned would suffice 'subject to adjustment when the necessary verification had been obtained'.[5]

For the Department of Finance, customs barriers posed the biggest challenge regarding the transfer of territory. Customs stations and boundary posts would have to be uprooted, if possible, and moved to the new boundary line. Arrangements with railways and on approved roads would have to be changed, as would all the supplementary notifications. The changes imposed on staff (all public sector employees), including their housing, needed to be considered as well as the disposal or examining of goods in transit.[6]

Individual residents would also face some changes. The rates for old-age pensioners would require adjustment in accordance with the provisions of the Free State Old Age Pensions Act, 1924. As with teachers, if the Northern government did not help with the transfer, 'it would be necessary to obtain fresh claims from pensioners and to investigate each case de novo'.[7] Unemployment insurance at the time was paid as an uncovenanted benefit in Northern Ireland, while in the Free State the unemployed only received benefits covered by contributions. A danger was envisaged by E.M. Stephens that some people who were receiving unemployment benefit in Northern Ireland would immediately become penniless once transferred to the Free State, unless some special provision was made, such as relief grants or employment schemes.[8]

Ernest Clark, who retired as head of the Northern Ireland civil service in 1925, submitted his thoughts to the Northern government's Attorney General, Richard Best, on the steps required for any transfer of territory. He believed that a date of operation was needed to be laid down and envisaged that 'Customs Stations will probably all need to be changed'. Issues such as outstanding death duties and lawsuits, county court circuits, and existing decrees by government judges and local officers, would all need to be adjusted once territories were transferred.[9] While ultimately none of these changes were required, as the border remained unaltered, they demonstrate how much the two Irish jurisdictions had diverged just four years after Ireland was partitioned.

While the Free State was preparing for change, the Northern government was considering steps to take in preparation for a legal case against the Boundary Commission if any of the 'unit' of 'Ulster' was transferred to the Free State. This included the appointment of three men from Newry (showing there remained some fears within Ulster unionism that Newry could be lost) to 'put forward a legal protest against their transfer to the Free State if the Northern Government indemnifies them for all costs' and for those proceedings to start on 'the actual date of the Boundary Commission's Report'. The Northern government would try to 'place a temporary embargo on the transfer from their jurisdiction of any area until a final decision is given' on the legal cases, and an appeal would be made by the Ulster Association aimed at the people of the Overseas Dominions 'suggesting that the British Government might hand over a portion of their territories without their consent if this precedent is allowed to pass unchallenged' and to the people of Britain that 'the proposed transfer means to Northern Ireland a transfer of, say, Kent to Germany, pointing out that it is a transfer of individuals who were loyal during the war, in a large measure, to placate those who were hostile to us'.[10] The Northern government even considered 'that the Imperial Government take over the management of Northern Ireland for two years and run it themselves' if there was 'great opposition' to the Boundary Commission proposals.[11]

As speculation mounted over the areas to be transferred, the Boundary Commission, having gathered a substantial body of evidence through written submissions, interviews, meetings, maps and statistics, set about redrawing the border. A series of meetings were held from late

September 1925, culminating in one on 17 October when the Commission was able 'to record a decision approving in its general features a line showing the whole of the new boundary to be adopted, and instructions were given for the preparation of a full detailed description of this line with the necessary maps'.[12]

Feetham prepared a memorandum, which he submitted to MacNeill and Fisher on 11 September. The main draft conclusions he reached included:

- The existing boundary holds good 'where no sufficient reason, based on considerations of which the Commission can properly take account, is showing for altering it'.
- The Boundary Commission 'has power to shift the existing boundary line in either direction'.
- 'the Commission is not to reconstitute the two territories, but to settle boundaries between them. Northern Ireland must, when the boundaries have been determined, still be recognisable as the same provincial entity.'
- 'where the case rests solely on the wishes of the inhabitants, it will not regard the case as made unless the majority in favour of the change is a substantial majority'.
- 'the wishes of the inhabitants taken alone should not be regarded as sufficient to justify a change in mixed communities or districts where the evidence points to only a small percentage of advantage on one side or the other' and, also, 'the greater the importance of the change demanded in its effect on territory and population, the higher the percentage of inhabitants who support the change which should be required to justify it'.
- 'the wishes of the inhabitants are made the primary but not the paramount consideration. It may be the duty of the Commission in some case to override the wishes of the inhabitants, whether for or against transfer, by reason of economic or geographic considerations.'

- The Commission 'should seek to avoid drawing a boundary line which, by its defiance of economic or geographic conditions, would involve, as the result of its adoption, serious economic detriment, or geographic isolation, to communities on either side of it'.
- Inhabitants 'means persons having a permanent connection with the area concerned. Temporary or casual residence within an area cannot be regarded as qualifying a person to have his wishes considered.'
- The 'absence from the Article of any provision enabling the Commission to conduct a plebiscite affords ground [*sic*] for inferring' as 'it was not the intention of the parties to the Treaty that the Commission should ascertain the wishes of the inhabitants in that manner' and 'in seeking to give effect to the wishes of the inhabitants, rely on the verdicts of bare majorities'.
- The Commission relies on the 1911 census returns 'as affording an indication of the wishes of the inhabitants, the members of Protestant denominations being reckoned as wishing to be in Northern Ireland and Roman Catholics as wishing to be in the Irish Free State'.
- The Commission should be 'prepared to take as a unit of area in relation to which the wishes of the inhabitants are to be ascertained the smallest area which fairly be entitled [*sic*] ... to be considered separately', and not large areas such as counties or Poor Law unions.[13]

Practically all of Feetham's conclusions favoured the unionist over the nationalist case. As Paul Murray has ascertained, his 'interpretation of all the major issues to which Article 12 gave rise was uniformly unfavourable to the Nationalist point of view'.[14] By disregarding the views of the negotiators of the Treaty, he misread their intentions, certainly those of the Sinn Féin negotiators. While most people considered the Boundary Commission clause a penalty on Ulster unionists for not joining an all-Ireland parliament, Feetham did not.[15]

Eoin MacNeill responded to the potential publication of Feetham's memorandum by recording that Feetham had requested that its contents 'should be dealt with by verbal discussion' rather than by written comments. MacNeill wanted to circulate, at a later stage, also informally, 'an Opinion, stated to have been obtained from a high legal authority', probably Hugh Kennedy's memorandum from 19 September that MacNeill had amended to remove personal criticisms of Feetham (see Chapter Seven).[16] MacNeill's first request was presumably, as Ted Hallett has contended, 'to justify not presenting a formal challenge to Feetham's memorandum'.[17] While no record remains of MacNeill's disapproval of Feetham's memorandum, he subsequently claimed at an Executive Council meeting that he 'stated his objections to it in detail, having summarised the various points by way of brief outspoken marginal notes'.[18]

In a demonstration of his total dominance over the Boundary Commission, its award reflected Feetham's interpretations. At its meeting of 17 October, the changes to the boundary were substantively agreed upon, and with some tweaks, were:[19]

Section A: Area in East Tirconaill adjacent to the Liberties of Londonderry. (Transferred to Northern Ireland)			
Acreage	Population	Catholic	Non-Catholic
30,295	5,149	1,919	3,230
Section B (i): Area in Tirconaill forming part of the District Electoral Division of West Urney. (Transferred to Northern Ireland)			
819	60	-	60
Section B (ii): Area in County Tyrone forming part of the Rural District of Castlederg. (Transferred to Irish Free State)			
34,228	2,716	2,163	553
Section C (i): Area in Tirconaill including towns of Pettigo and District Electoral Division of Grousehall. (Transferred to Northern Ireland)			
11,510	1,339	497	842

Section C (ii): Area Western portion of County Fermanagh including Belleek, Garrison and Belcoo. (Transferred to Irish Free State)			
51,650	5,428	4,688	740
Section C (iii): Area in Tirconaill comprising Belleek Island. (Transferred to Northern Ireland)			
3 (Sluice-gates and gate-keeper's lodge			
Section C (iv): Area in Southern part of County Fermanagh. (Transferred to Irish Free State)			
16,167	2,591	2,222	369
Section C (v): Areas in Eastern part of County Fermanagh. (Transferred to Irish Free State)			
18,628	3,808	3,147	661
Section C (vi): Area in County Monaghan forming part of District Electoral Division of Drummully. (Transferred to Northern Ireland)			
336	51	13	38
Section D: Nil			
Section E (i): Area in County Armagh comprising parts of District Electoral Divisions of Tynan, Middletown, and Derrynoose (Transferred to Irish Free State)			
8,928	2,100	1,764	336
Section E (ii): Area in County Monaghan comprising parts of District Electoral Division of Mullyash, Church Hill and Carrickaslane. (Transferred to Northern Ireland)			
6,279	995	335	660
Section E (iii): Area in Southern part of County Armagh including greater part of former Rural District of Crossmaglen and adjoining portion of that of Newry No. 2. (Transferred to Irish Free State)			
53,694	14,676	13,859	817

In total, 183,290 acres and 31,319 (27,843 Catholic and 3,476 non-Catholic) people were to be transferred from Northern Ireland to the Free State and 49,242 acres and 7,594 (2,764 Catholic and 4,830 non-Catholic) people were to be transferred from the Free State to Northern Ireland.[20] From looking at the areas and numbers of people involved, it is striking that areas suggested for transfer to the Free State from Northern Ireland had overwhelming numbers of Catholics compared to non-Catholics while areas suggested for transfer to Northern Ireland from the Free State had non-Catholic majorities too, but nowhere near as substantial as those recommended for transfer the other way. Protestants 'transferred to Northern Ireland were to bring half as many Catholics with them, whereas Catholics going the other way would only bring one-tenth of their number of Protestants'.[21] It was clear that Catholics and nationalists had to jump more hurdles to be considered for transfer. In essence, in most disputed areas, minorities, even very small ones, held a veto over the majority population. In the words of Murray, 'Feetham's explicit abandonment of the majoritarian principle became an essential means of restricting the scope for change.'[22]

The Boundary Commission recommended that Derry city and Newry remain in Northern Ireland. It reasoned that Derry should remain 'under the same jurisdiction as the areas in the counties of Londonderry, Tyrone and Fermanagh, which it serves as a wholesale centre and port'.[23] Newry (with an almost 75 per cent Catholic population) and its surrounding areas should remain in the North, according to the Boundary Commission, as it 'leaves the town in the same jurisdiction as both the area north of the town which it serves as principal market centre and source of retail supplies, and the area, limited in the south-east by the Mourne mountains, in which Newry shares these functions with Warrenpoint, Rostrevor and Hilltown'.[24] Derry city's economic connections with Donegal and Newry's with many areas within the Free State, both substantial, were not deemed important enough to recommend transfer. The omission of Newry from the Free State was unquestionably the most egregious decision of Feetham's and made little sense even considering the convoluted rules he had concocted.

What is most surprising about the recommended award, is not that such an award was made (the writing had been on the wall for some time after all), but that MacNeill appears to have consented to it or, at the very least, made no substantial objection to it. According to Hand, in the meetings between 13 and 17 October, 'when the shape of the award was formed, MacNeill seems to have argued somewhat with his colleagues'.[25] However, the award appeared to be agreed by all three commissioners on 17 October. Feetham and Fisher clearly thought they had MacNeill's support and Bourdillon received his backing to seek permission from the Irish registrar-general 'to publish detailed figures of religious affiliation in support of the award'. He also went to London for further meetings 'held on 4 and 5 November and on 5 November the commissioners provisionally approved a draft of the actual terms of the award'.[26]

Meanwhile, Fisher was revealing all to Ulster Unionists. David Reid informed Craig on 18 October, based on his wife's correspondence with Fisher, that 'Newry and the whole of Co. Down is safe ... We lose no town of any importance. I hope it will represent a line which can be accepted.'[27] Fisher wrote to Carson on the same day, 'No centre of even secondary importance goes over, and with Derry, Strabane, Enniskillen, Newtown Butler, Keady and Newry in safe keeping, your handiwork will survive.' He concluded by writing, 'If anybody had suggested twelve months ago that we could have kept so much I would have laughed at him, and I must add that the Chairman and John MacNeill have been throughout models of fair play and friendly courtesy.'[28] According to Stephen Tallents, Craig, by then roughly aware of the boundary changes, held a meeting of Ulster Unionist MPs for border constituencies to the Northern Parliament on 29 October, where he recommended they all stand together, 'none going off half-cock when the Report came'. If the 'Report was in the nature of a trimming [as he knew by then it would be] and not of a ruthless shearing, it was up to them to do all in their power to get their people to accept it peaceably and without disorder'.[29]

It appears that the British government was, like the Free State government, in the dark on the details of the Boundary Commission award by late October. Tom Jones advised British Prime Minister Stanley Baldwin on 28 October that the 'Report ought to be applied automatically whatever it is ... Once you begin to discuss, and negotiate and adjust you are in the Irish bog again.' Baldwin conceded he was finding it difficult to control his Cabinet on the boundary issue, saying the 'moment the subject was mentioned at the Cabinet they all got excited; [Lord] Salisbury and Jix [Joynson-Hicks, Home Secretary] were bursting their buttons with eagerness to talk so I am going to see Feetham'. Baldwin told Jones he would tell Feetham

> that, while I do not want to know the details of the Boundary Report, what I want is his opinion on the chances of bloodshed on the border when the Report comes out. If I can be assured of that, then I can come back to the Cabinet and tell them that I think the Report ought to go through automatically, after any precautions have been taken.[30]

As it transpired, no meeting took place between Baldwin and Feetham at that point.

At its meeting of 5 November, the Boundary Commission decided to arrange a meeting for 19 November with both the British and Free State governments to confer with them on the Commission's award.[31] This meeting never took place, though, mainly due to a report in *The Morning Post* on 7 November which revealed a largely accurate outline of the Commission's planned award.

While the Commission was deliberating there had been much speculation in the press on the potential new boundary line. On 24 August the *Sunday Express* predicted that 'Considerable territory will probably be handed over to Free State. Three Reports likely', and on 1 September *The Irish News* predicted that parts of Donegal and Monaghan would be transferred to Northern Ireland, while the 'best part of South Down', including Newry, and large parts of Fermanagh would be transferred to the Free State.[32] Similarly, the *Sunday Independent* anticipated the Free State would gain practically 'the whole of South Armagh' and the town of Newry, but some Donegal districts close to Derry 'will be lopped off the Free State'.[33] According to Kevin Matthews, the *Sunday Express* article 'sparked two months of fevered, and often contradictory, speculation in newspapers on both sides of the Irish Sea'.[34] Writing from Biarritz in

October, the Free State Governor General, Tim Healy, said, although he hoped there was no 'ground for the fears about Innishowen [sic], yet it is possible Feetham might join with Fisher to effect such an amputation'.[35] On 6 November the *Daily Mail* reported that while the Boundary Commission 'will be unable to present a report unanimous on every point, substantial agreement has been reached on findings by no means unfavourable to Ulster'.[36]

It was the projected award published in *The Morning Post* on 7 November that went beyond a mere prediction. Publishing a map alongside its forecast, it reported that 'no important territory will go to the Free State. The changes proposed will consist of adjustments only. Ulster will lose neither Enniskillen nor Newry.'[37] In its editorial, the newspaper stated that Feetham and 'his fellow Commissioners' had 'planned and whittled the line to make it a little straighter and a little smoother than it was left by our panic-stricken politicians in search of a settlement'.[38] The *Morning Post* forecast was so close to the actual award that most people have assumed since that Fisher leaked it to the newspaper, something to which he never admitted.[39] Culpability still probably lies with him, as it is likely the award details were leaked by someone who had received the details from Fisher either directly or indirectly.

The *Morning Post* forecast did not seem to perturb the Free State Executive Council or MacNeill initially, but once border nationalists started to protest and express their anger at the abysmal forecast, it soon dawned on the Free State government that it was facing a political crisis of high magnitude. Still hopeful that the *Morning Post* forecast was inaccurate, the *Derry People and Donegal News* was still worried about 'the traditional axiom of Irish politics – to never place confidence in British politicians or their agents in dealing with this country'. It advised that 'should Mr. Justice Feetham adopt a partisan role it would be the duty of the Free State Government to withdraw their representative from the Commission and devise such line of action as the situation may then demand'.[40]

Protest meetings were held in border places. At the Strabane meeting, it was concluded 'that Strabane had a clear case from every point of view, according to the terms of the Treaty, for inclusion in the Free State, and a demand was made at the meeting, which was held in the Barrack Street Hall, that the Treaty be carried out in its entirety'. A deputation went to Dublin to meet with the Free State Executive Council to press the matter.[41] The Dublin correspondent of the *Strabane Chronicle* stated that if Eoin MacNeill had agreed to the award as reported in *The Morning Post*, he had been 'hypnotised by Mr. Justice Feetham and Mr. Fisher' and 'he will never again be heard of in Irish politics, and he will go down to history as the man who helped to make the partitioning of Ireland permanent'. MacNeill 'can sign no such report unless he wishes to commit political hari-khari'.[42]

Cosgrave and Blythe received deputations from Donegal and Monaghan respectively, and government ministers met rank-and-file members of their party, Cumann na nGaedheal, to discuss the boundary question.[43] The *Irish Independent*, in commenting on a growing intense 'feeling of anxiety in Free State border circles' reported on 'considerable shooting in the Camlough district' of Armagh 'regarded by the people as jubilation consequent on Unionist anticipation of the Boundary Report'.[44] The *Daily Mail* wrote of an Irish republican plot in London to steal the Boundary Commission papers at its office on Clement's Inn, claiming that twenty-seven members of the Special Branch of Scotland Yard were guarding the building 'day and night' against the plotters, whose aim was to 'raid the offices and ransack them of their contents by a lightning dash of armed men'.[45] Tom Jones later wrote of Feetham and Fisher being 'under police protection' after MacNeill's resignation.[46] Speaking in the Dáil on 11 November, Cosgrave was still sticking to his stance that no territory from the Free State could be transferred to Northern Ireland, saying, 'the contention of the Executive Council is that the provisions of Article 12 of the Treaty cannot be construed as empowering the Commission to transfer to Northern Ireland any of that territory'.[47]

There is no indication that MacNeill informed Cosgrave at this juncture that the *Morning Post* prediction was largely accurate and that the Free State was scheduled to lose as well as gain territory. Admittedly, he was busy with the education estimates in the Dáil from 11 to 18 November.[48] However, his continued silence only made matters worse. On a boat journey to Dublin with Executive Council colleague Patrick McGilligan on 6 November, the day before the *Morning Post* forecast was published, MacNeill told McGilligan he 'was appalled at the political prospect thus opened and felt it his duty to communicate his discovery to Cosgrave when he reached Dublin'.[49] There is no evidence, though, that Cosgrave was made aware of the details of the award until two weeks later, 20 November, the day MacNeill resigned from the Boundary Commission.

The official minutes of the Boundary Commission recorded at its meeting of 20 November, 'Dr. MacNeill informed the Commission that he had decided that morning to withdraw from the Commission and to place his resignation as a member of the Commission in the hands of his Government.' Feetham tried unsuccessfully to convince him to change his mind, with MacNeill saying before leaving, 'notwithstanding his withdrawal the Commission should continue its work'.[50]

In recalling the Commission meeting the previous day, MacNeill told the Executive Council on 21 November that he had informed the other commissioners 'that a situation of extreme gravity had arisen in Ireland consequent on the *Morning Post* Revelations'. Feetham replied 'that the *Morning Post* statement was not accurate, but admitted in response to a question from Dr. MacNeill that it was substantially correct'. After being in touch 'with representative persons of all kinds in Ireland', the 'unanimous opinion of all classes was that the fixing of a boundary line such as that indicated in the *Morning Post* would be a violation of the Treaty'. MacNeill said that 'under the circumstances he had come to the conclusion that it was his duty to withdraw from the Commission and to place his resignation immediately in the hands of his Government'. He concluded his statement with a rambling, mainly pointless, account of a conversation between Feetham, Bourdillon and him over retrieving his copy of Feetham's memorandum from 11 September.[51]

Ted Hallett has rightly pointed out, based on MacNeill's recollection of his resignation to the Boundary Commission, that he 'misled his

Executive Council colleagues in implying that he was surprised by the *Morning Post*'s description of the Award and in not revealing that he had been party to it', when he clearly had.[52]

MacNeill's resignation appeared to have come like a bolt from the blue for Feetham. He had hoped to spend his birthday with his mother at Penrhos that weekend but wrote to her on 20 November cancelling, as 'extra work has suddenly been thrown on me which I can't avoid'.[53] Days later he wrote to her, 'as you will understand kept tremendously busy as the result of recent events – & I am afraid I can't leave London now until my troubles are over'.[54]

The shock to the Free State government was undoubtedly far greater, with James MacNeill telling Leo Amery, the Colonial Secretary of the British government, 'the proposed award, which I understand differed only slightly from the "Morning Post" account, surprised my Government utterly'.[55] Cosgrave made an unscheduled trip to Emyvale in Monaghan, close to the border on 22 November, where he gave an unplanned speech. Speaking about the *Morning Post* forecast, Cosgrave said 'it was sufficiently detailed and sufficiently unjust to give rise to a feeling of disquiet which has manifested itself in the various deputations which I have received since its publication'.[56] He claimed:

> This lamentable result can only be explained by the persistent and unscrupulous use of threats of violence and political pressure. From the moment the Boundary Commission was in course of formation threats have been circulated, emphasised, and encouraged by an influential section of the British Press. British politicians lent their influence to the unscrupulous movement. Public men in the highest positions lent themselves without hesitation to the campaign of whittling away by misrepresentation the rights which a large number of Irishmen had acquired by treaty and statute to be returned to the Government of their choice. This campaign had the express purpose of prejudicing the Commission in their interpretation of their terms of reference.[57]

Describing MacNeill as 'an honourable man', Cosgrave announced he left the Commission 'and has proved that so far as he was concerned our confidence in him was not displaced'. Cosgrave had 'lost faith in the other members of the Commission, and [is] forced to the conclusion that they have allowed themselves to be swayed in the discharge of their judicial duty by the threats and political influences which have been brought to bear upon them'. He contended that MacNeill left 'because justice was not being done, because the rights of our people in the North that were enshrined in Article XII were being shamefully flouted and their destinies being made the plaything of hostile prejudice'.[58]

Also speaking in Emyvale, which formed part of his constituency, Ernest Blythe stated that if Feetham and Fisher continued with the Boundary Commission's work, 'it will be turning a ridiculous farce into a great tragedy'.[59] Commenting on the Emyvale speeches, *The Northern Whig* editorialised that the 'playboys of the Free State', instead of 'taking the beating they now apparently regard as inevitable like good sportsmen, they declare that they "won't play any more", and incontinently leave the field'.[60]

A day after his speech, Cosgrave received another bombshell from the remaining two Boundary Commissioners. In their statement to the press, Feetham and Fisher claimed their relations with MacNeill up to 20 November had 'been relations of the closest mutual confidence' and his resignation came as a 'complete surprise' to them. Up to then, MacNeill 'had made perfectly clear his intention of joining with us in signing the Commission's Award embodying a boundary line the general features of which were approved and recorded in our Minutes as long ago as Saturday 17th October'. Since that date, 'the whole work of the Commission has proceeded on the basis of the definitive understanding between us that our Award embodying the line agreed upon was to be unanimous, and a full detailed description of the line with the necessary maps had been in course of preparation'.[61]

The statement made Cosgrave's defence of MacNeill in Emyvale very misplaced, but it is hard to see how Feetham and Fisher could have viewed

MacNeill's behaviour any differently. Whether he jumped or was pushed is unclear, but MacNeill was forced to take the only other action now left to him and resign from the Executive Council. In his resignation speech to the Dáil, he claimed that in his capacity as a commissioner he 'was not purely and simply the representative of a Government nor was I an advocate for a particular point of view. I was and I undertook to be a representative of a trust created by the Treaty, by Article 12 of the Treaty ...' He refuted Feetham and Fisher's statement, not on the 'bare facts', but 'in the colouring, the very decided colouring, which it gives to the statement of fact, I do most distinctly controvert it'.[62] He admitted that 'the members of the Commission had arrived at an agreement as to the high desirability of having an award signed by all three Commissioners'. But:

> The ground of that agreement has not been stated. The ground for it was not that the Commissioners were unanimous as to principles of interpretation upon which the award was to be based, or consequently that they were unanimous as to the manner in which the principle should be applied in detail. The ground for that agreement was purely and simply this: that the form of the award, when it appeared, should provide the least possible fuel for renewed, perhaps embittered, controversy.[63]

MacNeill also claimed there were 'profound differences, not merely differences of opinion, between us – I shall say between the Chairman and myself – as to the fundamental principles upon which an award ought to proceed', with those differences 'known to the Chairman at the time when we were engaged upon the consideration of the details of the award'. He said one such difference was that he believed Article 12 'was to enable the exercise of a franchise to take place which had been denied and withheld in the case of the Act of 1920', while Feetham 'held that the Act of 1920, and the time which had elapsed, had created a *status quo* which should only be departed from when every element and every factor would compel us to depart from it'. MacNeill also believed that Feetham introduced 'a new governing and dominant condition into Article 12, a political condition, a political consideration which was made a dominant consideration', one that was not part of Article 12, but which Feetham allowed to overrule the wishes of the inhabitants if the Northern government would suffer politically by a transfer that could jeopardise its position under the Government of Ireland Act 1920. While, for MacNeill, the 'wishes of the inhabitants' was always the dominant consideration, for Feetham sometimes economic considerations were dominant; at other times it was the wishes of the inhabitants.[64]

He argued that what he agreed to was on the 'ground of avoiding renewed and, perhaps, deepened controversy – was not to pronounce unanimity where there was no unanimity, but, purely and simply, to sign the award, in common with the other Commissioners'. He found the deliberations placed him in a 'position of exceptional difficulty' and at no time was there any debate on 'the principles of interpretation'. He conceded that he may be at fault for not demanding, requiring and challenging, 'at the earliest convenient stage, a discussion of the general principles of interpretation and a decision upon those principles'. He felt it was 'probably true that a better politician and a better diplomatist, if you like, a better strategist, than I am would not have allowed himself to be brought into that position or difficulty'.[65]

The *Derry Journal* did not mince its words in its withering editorial the next day, saying nationalists on both sides of the border had found 'themselves the victims of unchanging guile and craftiness on the one hand, and the most hopeless incompetence and botchery on the other'. It found it hard to understand how MacNeill 'allowed the Commission to drift on the rocks of such utter debacle without one word of warning to the Government that appointed him', writing that his 'conduct all through seems to have been marked by inertia, incapacity, and appalling ineptitude'. No man 'was ever entrusted with a heavier responsibility, and no man ever collapsed so abjectly under his burden'. Ultimately, 'no worse selection for the Boundary Commission could have been made'.[66] A priest from Jonesborough near Newry, Fr McDonnell, wrote in a letter to Tim Healy, 'What a disaster it was to have selected McNeill [sic] ... to think such a simpleton ... was entrusted with such a task.'⁶⁷ E.M. Stephens' wife, Lily, wrote in her diary on the night of MacNeill's Dáil speech: 'Bombshell. Commission statement. Resignation from Cabinet of McNeill [sic]. Speech in Dail. Let the country down shamefully. Our work & splendid case betrayed.'⁶⁸ Even his brother James felt Eoin was right to resign, writing, 'I have just heard of my brother John's resignation from the Executive Council. I think that was unavoidable, and I hope it will be helpful.'⁶⁹

St John Ervine said the 'vaporous and vacillating' MacNeill was a 'wambling professor' who 'should have restricted all his activities to the solution of problems in Gaelic grammar. Here he could do no harm, even if he could do no good.'⁷⁰ Kieran Rankin has described MacNeill as 'pathetically out of his depth'.⁷¹ In a kinder evaluation, Michael Tierney claimed MacNeill 'was blamed because he could not put right what others had already put wrong'.⁷² The Boundary Commission brought 'an abrupt and painful end to his adventurous and fruitful public career'.⁷³

Geoffrey Hand, in assessing MacNeill's performance as a commissioner, suggested the best word to describe it was 'ambiguity'.⁷⁴ While that might be a good word to describe Article 12 of the Treaty, a better word to describe MacNeill's performance is 'bizarre'. His actions and behaviour throughout the time he was involved in the Commission were bizarre. There was no compunction on him to act as a plenipotentiary and ignore his Executive Council colleagues, to put the needs of the Commission over the government of which he was a member. He belatedly claimed that he objected to many of Feetham's interpretations, but clearly not forcefully. He could have strenuously objected (threatening to resign even) to the Commission's trajectory on several occasions, including on 11 September when Feetham submitted his memorandum and on 17 October when the Commission agreed the bulk of the award. It makes no sense for MacNeill to have thought a unanimous decision with such a cataclysmic award for nationalists was less likely to cause controversy than him resigning or issuing a minority report. He was also, as Hallett has pointed out, misleading in the information he provided to the Executive Council from the time of the *Morning Post* forecast on 7 November to his resignation from the government on 24 November.[75]

It is important to acknowledge that MacNeill's position was incredibly difficult, and no matter who the Free State commissioner was, it was unlikely that the aspirations of the Free State government and particularly of border nationalists would have come close to being met. However, his performance throughout the Boundary Commission, and even after the *Morning Post* report, made what was a difficult position infinitely more so. When the Free State government tried to negotiate its way out of the mess it found itself in, the blunders of MacNeill weakened Cosgrave's and O'Higgins's hands from the off.

Chapter Nine

Craig 'had won all down the line'

THE DEBACLE THAT TRANSPIRED IN late 1925 following Eoin MacNeill's resignation resulted in the collapse of the Boundary Commission and was a political disaster for Cosgrave and the Free State government, as well as a political triumph for Craig and the Northern government. Most of all, it dashed the dreams of thousands of Northern nationalists to be free from Northern governance.

With the Boundary Commission considering MacNeill's resignation as 'not a valid or effectual resignation', and eager to deliver its award 'at an early date', Cosgrave rushed over to London to have it buried instead.[1] He was coming under increasing pressure from multiple fronts. The leader of the official opposition in Dáil Éireann, the Labour Party's Thomas Johnson, said there should be two resignations, Cosgrave's as well as MacNeill's.[2] Sinn Féin leader Éamon de Valera stated, 'Stripped of its stage setting, what the present position clearly reveals is the intention to leave the Boundary as it is. In other words, the people of South Down, South Armagh, Derry City, as well as of the Counties of Tyrone and Fermanagh, are to be sacrificed.' The 'revelations of the Boundary Commission have torpedoed' the pretence that it could end partition, and he warned that supporters of the Treaty were in for another shock 'when that other Commission provided for in the Treaty – the Financial Commission – is set up and comes to deliver its award. As a warning in advance, I inform all those concerned that the demand of the British at the time of negotiations was for a yearly sum of over £19,000,000.'[3]

De Valera was referring to Article 5 of the Treaty, which set out the Free State's 'liability for the service of the Public Debt of the United Kingdom' as well as 'payment of War Pensions', the sums to be determined by 'arbitration of one or more independent persons being citizens of the British Empire'.[4] It soon came into focus as a way for the Free State government to save some face from the disarray in which it found itself. *The Irish Times* reported on 25 November of an effort by 'responsible and influential persons in London' to bring about an 'agreed solution', which involved the 'cancellation of Articles XII and V of the Treaty'.[5]

The first of multiple meetings in a week of intense negotiations between the Free State, British and Northern Irish governments took place on 26 November 1925. Cosgrave asked for a conference with Stanley Baldwin due to the 'difficult and very anxious situation' his government faced. He sought a settlement over the boundary issue that would make it 'less likely to afford grounds for serious discontent and possible disorder'.[6]

Cosgrave argued for a conference to reach a solution, claiming there was an 'acute situation in Donegal where it is understood a rich portion is to be taken away and transferred to Ulster', saying the *Morning Post* article had 'created a furore in Donegal and disquiet in Tyrone and Fermanagh; feeling was much the same in Monaghan'.[7] He felt 'that the proposed line went against the spirit of the undertaking embodied in the Treaty. It was not satisfactory from any point of view as it left the minority in no better position.' Cosgrave contended that 'Article 12 had been drawn up to solve the situation and if the lines now proposed were adopted, it would have been better never to have suggested Article 12.' He sought a 'saner and better solution' and 'strongly urged that the Boundary Commission should not issue their award either now or at any time'.[8]

The Colonial Secretary, Leo Amery, claimed the Boundary Commission could only be prevented from issuing its award through fresh legislation, with Cosgrave replying, 'there was justice above the law. Why should not the bargain be reconsidered if it were now found to suit neither party?' Cosgrave 'was concerned with the position which would arise if the line were drawn, and the Northern "Specials" were put in the transferred areas ... this armed force was regarded by many in the South as a political force'.[9]

Demonstrating the difficulty MacNeill had left the Free State government in, Cosgrave 'admitted that the fact of Mr. MacNeill's agreement on the 17th October was a difficult point. Had Mr. MacNeill been in touch with border or Free State feeling, he could scarcely have been a party to that agreement. He had resigned; it was a deplorable situation.' He also pointed out that the Boundary Commission had 'been held three or four years after the signing of the Treaty, and the situation which had developed since the signing of the Treaty was in their minds. That was not fair. Had the Commission been held immediately after the Treaty, there would have been a different orientation.'[10] Cosgrave replied to the claims of Austen Chamberlain and Leo Amery that only small changes to the border were ever envisaged at the time of the signing of the Treaty, saying, 'Had it been mere rectification, they would not have asked for a Boundary Commission with all the trouble and delay involved.'[11]

Cosgrave was asked to leave while the British representatives consulted with each other. Upon his return, Baldwin stated, 'we imposed this Commission on an extremely reluctant Ulster. If this unhappy disclosure had not been made, and had the report been favourable to you, you would have expected us to impose it on Ulster.' Cosgrave agreed with the point. Baldwin claimed he could not 'compel Ulster in any direction. We have no means of doing so,' but he was prepared to meet Craig and 'urge him to meet you on this matter. I would be willing to ask the Commissioners to hold up their promulgation in the hope that in the short interval, some agreement could be reached. We shall have to find some way of holding up the award.' While Cosgrave's preference was for a conference between the British and Free State governments, the British attendees insisted Northern Ireland's consent was needed for any agreement to be reached. Cosgrave then agreed to meet with Craig, if such a meeting could be arranged.[12]

Lord Birkenhead did not hold out much hope for a meeting of minds between Cosgrave and Craig, writing, 'the differences which sunder Moslems from Hindus are not as bitter or as unbridgeable as those which divide Orangemen from the rest of Ireland'.[13]

Cosgrave was desperate and he came across as such. He was negotiating from a position of extreme weakness, something the British and Craig were acutely aware of. According to Tom Jones, Cosgrave said they had 'one safeguard – De Valera's lack of political foresight'. If de Valera had actually sat in the Dáil with his forty-plus TDs, 'he could put Cosgrave in a tight corner'.[14]

At a meeting of the British Cabinet attended by Craig on the same day as the meeting with Cosgrave, Chamberlain claimed that Cosgrave had given him the impression 'of a man very puzzled to know how to deal with the situation, but a man anxious for peace'. Craig 'said that he was anxious to find a way out of the present difficulty but the Committee should rule out of their minds any idea that Ulster would be prepared to sacrifice territory to save Mr. Cosgrave's face'.[15] He had told his wife, who was ill at the time, that he had 'a feeling in my bones that the present boundary will be allowed to stand, and Article 5 washed out ... It is a delicate, tedious, and nervy job, but if I can bring off "Not an Inch", I will be very pleased.'[16] In the meeting with the British Cabinet:

> [Craig] suggested that as the Free State were apparently chiefly concerned with the case of Catholics, who under the settlement would be barred from entry to the Free State, an agreement might be reached whereby Northern Irish Roman Catholics might be exchanged for a corresponding number of protestants living in areas in the Free State. The Northern Irish Government would make arrangements to plant exchanged protestants in areas vacated by Catholics under such an arrangement. If agreement could be reached on the practical basis of mutual exchange he

had no particular views on the question whether the existing boundary should be maintained, or whether that proposed by the Commission should be adopted.[17]

Lord Birkenhead and Chamberlain were open to Craig's suggested population exchange, but Winston Churchill, by then chancellor of exchequer, objected, saying Craig's proposal would mean 'in effect £4,000,000 from the British Exchequer. He could not accept such a proposal and even if he did parliament certainly would not entertain it.' He also objected on the grounds 'that it tended to accentuate and perpetuate differences between Northern and Southern Ireland which he hoped in time would otherwise grow less acute'. He suggested two alternatives: grant the award or 'agree to leave the Boundary question as it was for a term of say 25 years and in the meanwhile to endeavour to build up either in the Senate or on the Council of Ireland some plan for joint action between the North and South where common interests were affected'. Amery, on the other hand, believed the 'present opportunity might ... be taken to eliminate the obligation that would exist after 1927 of bringing into existence the Council of Ireland which he regarded as unworkable'.[18]

Typically, and as Churchill had anticipated, Craig then asked for 'further financial assistance'. He claimed his 'financial difficulties had been greatly increased owing to unrest on the border. He could have made large economies by disbanding the Special Constabulary had it not been for this position. As it was, if he had done so the demobilised Specials might have formed independent armed bands impossible to control.' He referred to two areas due to be transferred to the Free State – Garrison and Roslea – saying 'evacuation of the inhabitants' was 'essential as there would certainly be murder if they were allowed to remain. They were all marked men owing to the way they had defended themselves from a previous raid from the Free State.'[19] A *Belfast Telegraph* reporter was told by loyalists in the Roslea area of Fermanagh 'that they were determined to fight to the last man before they would go into the

Free State'.[20] Craig had suggested to the British Home Secretary, William Joynson-Hicks, earlier in the month that a tribunal be created, with Fisher as the chairman, 'to adjudicate claims for financial "compensation to Protestants" arising out of the Commission's award or for damages caused by its implementation'.[21] Joynson-Hicks told Craig the British Cabinet felt compensation was 'out of the question', with it being noted in the Cabinet that Southern loyalists in the Free State, 'who have been crying out for compensation now for four years' would react angrily.[22]

To Churchill's mind, the 'proposal for a remission of £4,000,000 clearly showed that the real aim was a general easement of Ulster finance. To this he was unwilling to assent, any more than he would be prepared to agree to give up the financial advantages of Article 5 of the Treaty, though he had no doubt that he would be invited to do so.' Craig thought that a meeting with Cosgrave 'would be useless unless the question of funds for compensation in Northern Ireland had first been settled'. Once Baldwin intervened, suggesting it would make sense for Craig to meet Cosgrave that afternoon, with him also attending along with Churchill to deal with any financial issues as they arose, Craig agreed to meet with Cosgrave.[23]

At the meeting between the two Irish leaders, in return for leaving the existing boundary in place, Craig offered to release thirty nationalist prisoners held since 1922, something to which Cosgrave did not agree.[24] Cosgrave returned to Dublin, where the Executive Council decided to send its Vice President and Home Affairs Minister Kevin O'Higgins to London to see if he could fare better.

O'Higgins travelled to Chequers, the official country residence of the British prime minister, with Patrick McGilligan and John O'Byrne on the weekend of 28–29 November, where they met Baldwin initially. In a far more robust performance than Cosgrave's two days previously, O'Higgins claimed 'that no party but ourselves is ready or able to carry on against those who oppose the Treaty'. The crisis could 'lead, if not directly then eventually, to a break-up of the State based on the Treaty. If we face the Dail on the basis of the old line with a few concessions from Craig (e.g. prisoners) our own Party would scout us.' He added that the Free State government would be politically extinct and the British government would have to pick up the pieces.[25]

Baldwin said there were 'three courses open and trouble, in the nature of the case, attends any of them'. They were: let the Boundary Commission award stand; keep the existing boundary; or a new boundary to be agreed between the two governments. Baldwin, as an outsider, 'could not see how even an angel could devise a boundary which would be agreed, so we are thrown back on one or two'.[26]

O'Higgins offered a less critical and more appropriate defence of MacNeill than Cosgrave had in front of the British, saying that at 'an early stage MacNeill agreed in the abstract with his colleagues that if the award was not going to make matters worse it should be signed by all three but that this should not imply that there was no disagreement on details. Sector by sector they worked their way down the line, MacNeill fighting all the way.' O'Higgins was particularly bemused by 'how the award could leave Newry out. The same arguments for leaving Newry out of the Free State were used against putting Eastern Donegal into Northern Ireland and applied in full – or fuller – force.'[27]

O'Higgins claimed the award as outlined in the *Morning Post* forecast would not be accepted in the Free State. It would only lead to 'hate and the starting of the old fires which the Treaty had laid'. On every platform, they would have to face the cries, 'We have been tricked again: see how your Treaty works when it comes to hard facts.' O'Higgins said his government could not 'stand up to these statements and say that they are not true because we believe that they are true and that the award does not fulfil the intention of the Treaty'. The people, he said, 'might have to consider whether Ireland's membership of the League of Nations opened up any course for them to take'.[28]

O'Higgins then asked for 'some substantial alleviation for the Nationalists of the North-East. If we could say that these Nationalists are not getting all that we expected in the Treaty but the Special Police are to go and other restrictions, political and local, are to be abandoned, there might be a chance for us to carry the Dail with us.' He said that Northern nationalists were 'politically impotent and are kept down by an army of Special Constables paid and maintained by the British Government'. O'Higgins suggested that the Commission felt threatened by the Specials, taking 'the line of least resistance; where the special police were thick in the North the Commission sheered away'. Free State government supporters believed, O'Higgins asserted, that 'the Commission has been influenced by "specials" standing with their finger on the trigger'. He did 'not know whether there is anything to be hoped from a tripartite conference and asking Craig to give "Catholic emancipation" in the North-East'.[29] He also believed the 'men who could never have got out under a boundary award from living too far North to be affected, would feel happier, and the satisfaction of those people would be some set-off against the disappointment of people who had been hoping that the award would get them out'.[30]

The following day, having received details of the actual award proposed by the Boundary Commission from Bourdillon, Baldwin told the Free State representatives 'that the line in the Award is not the same as that given in the *Morning Post* map' and if the 'discussion was to be of practical value, it would be much better to base it on the real Award and not on the *Morning Post*'s representation'. O'Higgins, not interested in seeing the full award, replied 'that trifling inaccuracies in the *Morning Post*'s indication of the Award did not affect them. An Award leaving Newry and its economic hinterland within Northern jurisdiction could not be an award based on the evidence before the Commission. Newry is the acid test.'[31]

Craig then arrived and said that if their 'discussions were to be of any value all the cards must be on the table, and each must say exactly what was in his mind'. O'Higgins then delivered what Tom Jones described as 'a brilliant and eloquent statement of the Free State case'.[32] He said the Free State had 'never shared the view which had emerged in England under Parliamentary pressure ... that this Boundary was a small and innocent thing, just a dinge here and a bulge there along the existing line'.[33] He was more critical of MacNeill then, saying MacNeill's 'attitude of giving agreement in the abstract and yet fighting his colleagues sector by sector was incomprehensible to his colleagues on the Executive Council'.[34] 'The position of the Catholics in the North', he said, 'is not equal to that of Catholics elsewhere: if the Free State Government could say that the Catholics' lot would be improved and they would cease to be "hewers of wood and drawers of water" then they might survive.'[35]

Craig wished 'to exonerate himself and his colleagues from the charge of ever having done anything else but emphasise to the Free State that they were living in a fool's paradise as to what the outcome of the Commission would be'.[36] He reiterated his agreement with Collins from January 1922 (see Chapter Two) and 'had told Ramsay MacDonald at the time of the setting up of the Commission that great harm was been done in the South by the people there being brought up to believe that they would get great advantages from the Commission'.[37] He was unwilling to budge on the safeguards for Northern nationalists O'Higgins wanted.

With tension in the air, Baldwin's wife, Lucy, sat uneasily as 'the boundary' between Craig and O'Higgins during lunchtime, and tried to lighten the mood by saying, 'I am not the bone of contention – I am too plump.'[38] After lunch, from 2.30 to 3.50 p.m., Craig and O'Higgins 'closeted together alone'. Craig then met Baldwin, John Anderson and Tom Jones and told them it 'all hangs on Clause 5'. According to Craig, they both agreed to the release of prisoners to be settled by the British prime minister; Clause 5 to go; the boundary to remain as it was; and Specials not to be mentioned, with O'Higgins accepting Craig's assurances on them. Craig said he also wanted the Council of Ireland dropped. O'Higgins told Craig he would talk to his colleagues.[39]

Craig informed Baldwin 'that as between the old and the new boundary he had no deep convictions. It was the toss of a penny.' He also warned the British prime minister, 'You'll never get a bob under Clause 5.'[40] Speaking in the House of Lords days later, Edward Carson also suggested the British government would get no money under Article 5, which was roughly calculated, pending an arbitration, that the Free State owed over £150 million. Carson asked, 'Were you going to send a gunboat up the Liffey? Why, you had been beaten out of the country already.

Were you going to blow up the Custom House – which had already been blown up by the Free Staters? The whole thing was ridiculous.'[41]

Craig claimed that O'Higgins said, 'they must sweeten their supporters either with concessions to Catholics by Craig, which he won't give, or by Article 5. Latter will act faster.' O'Higgins also referred to de Valera's remarks about the Free State having to pay £19 million per annum under Article 5.[42] It appears that O'Higgins's trenchant performance earlier on had melted away after talking alone to Craig.

With most points agreed by the representatives at Chequers, Cosgrave was invited to come back to London on 1 December to reach an agreement with Churchill on Article 5. Baldwin said, 'he would do what he could do with the Cabinet to bury the Commission'.[43] According to his biographers, Baldwin afterwards related with pleasure the words one of the Irish representatives (probably O'Higgins) said to him as they were leaving Chequers: 'We had better travel separately, Prime Minister. To be seen arriving in London together would not be good for either of us.'[44]

At a meeting in the British Treasury on 1 December, led by Cosgrave on the Free State side and Churchill on the British side, Cosgrave revealed the stark financial position the Free State was in compared to 1922. He said he would prefer to keep the existing border rather than accept the Commission's award, due in part to him receiving 'something in the nature of an Ultimatum from the tail of the party which normally supported the Government in the Dail'.[45]

O'Higgins believed the Free State government could survive the existing boundary remaining 'if they got compensation in one of two directions': 'either to secure an amelioration of the conditions under which the Nationalists were at present living in North-East Ireland or to obtain some form of concession by which they would be able to deaden in the 26 counties the echo of the outcry of the Catholics in North-East Ireland'. He would 'personally greatly prefer to secure the first of these alternatives' but had 'succeeded in making no headway on these lines in his discussions with Sir James Craig'. Craig told O'Higgins 'that he could not re-enact what he had repealed, nor repeal what he had enacted'. If 'it was impossible to secure any form of alleviation for the Nationalists in the six counties, would it be possible for the Free State Government to obtain compensation in some other form?'[46]

On Article 5, O'Higgins said he had spoken to the Free State's finance minister, Ernest Blythe, who 'maintained that financially there was nothing in that Article from the point of view of Great Britain. The Free State Treasury held ... the result would be that the contribution, if any, would be negligible.'[47]

Churchill claimed that, under Article 5, an arbitrator 'might reasonably be expected to award Great Britain the sum of 155¾ million and if that sum were paid over a period of 60 years it would mean an annual annuity of £8¼ millions at 5%'. If, however, 'the rate of interest were reduced to 3½%, the annuity for the same period would be 6¼ millions'. It would be difficult for the British government to renounce on behalf of the taxpayer such a large claim, especially in the time of economic constraint they were in. Northern Ireland would undoubtedly look for a reduction or abolition of its contribution, as would the Dominions. Southern loyalists would also 'object to any waiving of British rights while the damages they had sustained had, in their view, only been met to an inconsiderate extent'.[48]

Cosgrave claimed there was no possibility of the Free State meeting payments, even at the more generous figure of £6 million. The British government 'surely did not wish to see the Free State bankrupt'.[49]

The Lord Privy Seal, Lord Salisbury, said the Free State government would have great difficulty in correlating its desire for better conditions for Catholics in Northern Ireland with the desire for relief under Article 5. He thought 'it a dangerous position to occupy'. O'Higgins 'admitted that the Free State Government would be open to the taunt of having sold the Roman Catholics in Northern Ireland, but such an argument would only be a half truth'. Having failed to get any concessions from Craig, there 'would no doubt be an outcry from the Roman Catholics who would get no relief, but could not the Free State Government get some form of concession to prevent that outcry finding an echo in every one of the twenty-six counties in the Free State'? The 'position would no doubt be invidious, but the Roman Catholics in the North would it seemed, be let down in any case'.[50]

Churchill asked if a combination of the British government going some distance on Article 5 and Craig also going some distance in ameliorating the lot of Catholics in the North would be of interest to the Free State. He was aware of some objections to PR, to which O'Higgins replied that PR was the cause of the 'sharpest conflict of opinion between the majority and the minority' and the 'best evidence of goodwill that Sir James Craig could give towards his minorities would be to restore proportional representation'. Churchill understood that the Specials were to be disbanded 'as soon as the boundary question was disposed of', whereas O'Higgins felt Craig was non-committal on that point during their conversation days earlier. The Specials survived for another forty-five years.[51]

In an example of the British government pretending it was an impartial arbitrator between two squabbling factions, Salisbury 'enquired whether there was any actual oppression of Roman Catholics as such in Northern Ireland to-day'. Both O'Higgins and Cosgrave pointed out how Catholics were discriminated against 'in the administrative life of the country', in terms of public jobs and within the policing services, and how the electoral changes had negatively affected them.[52]

Cosgrave claimed his aim 'was by surrendering some immediate advantage to obtain something of far greater value in, say, 20 years, and that was a better feeling between the North and South, by eliminating the dispute and distrusts that existed to-day'. He hoped this would make it possible 'in the future of their becoming one country with the same political outlook'. Churchill replied, 'that was his hope, and it had, he believed, been that of all those who had signed the Treaty'. Cosgrave 'would much prefer to secure improved conditions for the Roman Catholics in Northern Ireland, but failing this he looked for more than a moratorium of the provisions of Article 5'.[53]

After taking a break, the conference resumed at 6.15 p.m., with Craig and C.H. Blackmore, assistant secretary to the Northern Cabinet, joining the meeting. Salisbury 'said he felt it his duty to say at once that the British Government could not entertain a proposal for writing off Article 5' but was 'prepared to consider proposals for postponing payment under the Article'. He also said:

> [F]air treatment of all members of the community was essential and indeed it was a fundamental consideration of British policy. He and his colleagues had accordingly asked Sir James Craig whether any steps could be taken to improve the position of Catholics in Northern Ireland. They were anxious not only to eliminate injustice, which was not, of course, admitted, but to destroy the feeling that injustice existed.[54]

Craig defended his government's record in its treatment of Catholics, saying many of the criticisms were unfounded. One-third of the RUC was to be comprised of Catholics (which never happened). Relief for the unemployed was strictly allocated based on population, with Catholics receiving one-third of the relief. If 'only those in Northern Ireland were left alone by mischief-makers they would win through successfully. If any practical suggestions were made to him he would do his best to meet it [sic].'[55]

Craig then suggested 'that the two Governments of Ireland should meet together for joint consideration at an early date. If charges were made against either Government let those who made them substantiate their case before the joint Cabinet meeting.' Churchill said the proposal of joint meetings 'was of enormous importance'. Cosgrave 'enquired what business would be transacted by a joint meeting of the two Irish Cabinets. He foresaw great difficulties if it were to act by (say) a majority vote' and 'if they were brought forward at this stage as a contribution to the present discussion they would certainly be regarded as a piece of eyewash'.[56] Salisbury then, as Tom Jones said, 'flew a kite'.[57] He suggested

> the appointment of an official liaison officer, appointed (say) by the Roman Catholics and Nationalists in North-East Ireland?

Would they feel increased confidence if they had their own official representative to put forward their grievances? Such a representative would, he contemplated, be on close terms of confidence with Sir James Craig and would have direct access to the Northern Irish Cabinet. The appointment of such an officer would form part of the terms of arrangement whereby the Free State definitely abandoned their hopes of assisting the Catholics on the boundary. It would, in fact, be a substitute for their former ambitions.[58]

Tom Jones claimed Salisbury even suggested appointing Joe Devlin as the liaison officer.[59]

It was Cosgrave who appeared most lukewarm on a suggestion that had much merit to it, believing 'it would be a mistake to define a proposal to this and in the form of a definite agreement. It would be better to allow it to be the natural outcome of a growing improvement of natural understanding.'[60] Instead of looking to obtain something tangible, Cosgrave suggested something worthless and intangible. His eyes were clearly fixed on waiving Article 5 at that point.

Churchill believed the Free State could make the following agreement work: Article 12 abrogated; moratorium of Article 5 commitments for X amount of years; a responsible liaison officer for Northern Catholics; and periodic joint consultation between both Irish governments. 'All were agreed that unity in Ireland was the goal to be aimed at and that the results of partition were bad. A definite declaration on the part of the Irish Governments that they would meet in joint Council from time to time might do good to the cause of unity.' Interestingly, Craig did not object to Churchill's statement but said he 'feared that such a proposal might in the present circumstances be a source of embarrassment to Mr. Cosgrave'.[61]

O'Higgins again suggested that PR be restored in the North as it 'was designed to provide adequate parliamentary representation for minorities'. Craig claimed PR was 'proving a failure all over the world. Broken down in Australia and New Zealand. You'll probably be driven to abolish it. I can't stick P.R. Does not seem to be British. Too Continental.' Incredibly, Cosgrave sided with Craig, saying, 'For my part I'd like it out of the way.'[62] Cosgrave also 'foresaw great difficulties' with Craig's willingness to consider joint Free State–Northern Irish Cabinet meetings being a formal part of the agreement.[63] His behaviour is hard to reconcile with someone truly desiring Irish unity or wishing to help Northern nationalists.

In a conference in the Treasury again the following day, Cosgrave closed the door further on any agreement with Craig, saying, 'Politically an agreement with Sir James Craig would not be of value to the Free State Government.' He did not believe Craig would 'deliver the goods ... a paper agreement with Northern Ireland would under existing conditions be useless to the Free State'.[64] It appeared that Cosgrave was attempting to sabotage efforts to ameliorate the plight of Northern nationalists so that the negotiations stayed focused on waiving Article 5.

With the 'grievances of Northern Nationalists ... disposed of once and for all' the 'only question remaining to be discussed was that of finance'.[65] After consulting alone, Churchill and Cosgrave suggested two alternative proposals: 'The debt of the Free State should be fixed at £6 millions, the payment spread over an agreed period'; or 'Article 5 should be waived and the Free State should repay the British Government moneys paid for compensation since 1921 plus 10 per cent on the awards made by the Courts under the Damage to Property Act 1923.' The British Cabinet preferred the second option, much to the relief of Cosgrave, who said the 'arrangement now proposed showed a spirit of neighbourly comradeship which had never before been revealed. The active cooperation of Sir James Craig in promoting this spirit was also most welcome.'[66] Regardless of whether it was going to be paid or not, the waiving of Article 5 resulted in a debt write-down of 80 per cent of the Gross National Product of the Free State, 'the largest relief settlement of the twentieth century', as John FitzGerald and Seán Kenny have ascertained.[67]

The agreement was finalised the following day, 3 December 1925. The three government leaders agreed to meet with Feetham and Fisher and ask them to suppress the award. Churchill said, 'It could be published later as a matter of historical interest.' They also resolved to introduce legislation immediately for their agreement to take effect.[68] Under the agreement Article 12 of the Treaty was revoked, and Northern Ireland's boundary remained as it was defined under the Government of Ireland Act 1920; Article 5 was waived for the Irish Free State; the Free State became liable for malicious damage incurred during the War of Independence and agreed to repay the British government moneys already paid in respect of such damage, with the Free State government committing to increase by 10 per cent its payments for malicious property damage experienced from the start of the Truce to the end the Civil War; and the Council of Ireland was scrapped. Instead, 'the Governments of the Irish Free State and of Northern Ireland shall meet together as and when necessary for the purpose of considering matters of common interest arising out of or connected with the exercises and administration of the said powers'.[69]

A clause was subsequently added 'that the cases of prisoners convicted in Northern Ireland in respect of offences during the period of disturbance shall be reviewed by the British Government whose decision in each case shall be accepted by the Government of Northern Ireland'.[70] Amongst the prisoners were a Cumann na nGaedheal TD, Seán MacCurtain, and several Free State Army officers.[71] At 8 p.m. that night, the agreement was signed in triplicate by representatives of the three governments. Cosgrave said to Craig at one stage, 'One of us no doubt will hear from the other?'[72] They never met again.

Cosgrave and O'Higgins issued a statement to the press, saying they had 'sown the seeds of peace. The problem with which we were confronted is not new. It has baffled two generations.' They claimed the agreement 'provides a sane and constructive solution. Born of a generous desire for peace and friendship, this agreement, accepted in the spirit in which it was negotiated and signed provides the basis of a sure and lasting peace. We confidently recommend it to the Irish people.'[73] Despite Cosgrave describing what became known as the London Agreement as a 'damn good bargain', it is highly unlikely either had any confidence in the agreement at all.[74] Indeed, Cosgrave was fooling few people. Wilfred Spender, by then head of the Northern Ireland civil service, later claimed that Cosgrave did not believe it was a good bargain and during a meeting with Craig 'burst into tears and said that Lord Craigavon had won all down the line and begged and entreated him not to make things more difficult for him'.[75]

The agreement was welcomed by some. *The Irish Times*, in its editorial on 4 December, considered that the 'great work of appeasement must be regarded not as an end, but as a beginning'.[76] In more muted terms, the *Irish Independent* contended the Free State government had 'made the best bargain possible in the circumstances' while acknowledging 'that there will be much disappointment in the Nationalist areas on the Border'.[77] Kevin O'Shiel, by then working in the Irish Land Commission, praised Cosgrave for his 'courage and vision' on what he described as a 'great event'. For someone who had done more than almost anyone to prepare for the best outcome from the Boundary Commission, surprisingly, O'Shiel stated in a letter to Cosgrave, 'We must not forget that had we got our maximum demands nearly 400,000 Catholic Nats. wd. be left behind & under such circumstances, we may be sure they wd. be treated with scant courtesy.' Were the Boundary Commission to give 'us everything we demanded there wd. still be in Belfast hands, at least one entire County (Antrim) & enormous chunks of the other five counties "permanently partitioned for ever" by the Treaty itself'.[78] He also said he could not understand Thomas Johnson's attacks on losing the Council of Ireland.

Johnson was scathing in his condemnation of the London Agreement, saying the nationalists of the North had been 'sold for less than nothing'. He said the waiving of Article 5 was substituted by 'an entirely one-sided indebtedness of considerable amount' by taking responsibility for the 'whole cost of the Anglo-Irish war', a 'tacit admission that Ireland was not entitled to wage that war' and 'by implication also the Government of the Free State has given a certificate of good character to the "Black and Tans"'. Always a supporter of the Council of Ireland, he condemned its abolishment, which destroyed 'every link between the Northern

Parliament and the Free State Parliament, leaving no impediment whatever to the unlimited extension of the powers of the Northern Parliament, and making partition complete and final'.[79]

While the Council of Ireland was considered an 'irritant' to the Northern Ireland government even though it never once met, the Free State government readily abandoned it. Due to the enhanced and independent nature of the Free State's political status, the remit of the Council had changed from being tasked with dealing with all-island issues to ones just affecting Northern Ireland. The Free State government ascertained this would not have helped towards unity, with Ernest Blythe claiming it was 'a body which would have done no good and might have done harm'.[80] Kevin O'Higgins had previously mocked Johnson's 'obsession' with the Council as a means to bring about Irish unity, describing it as a trivial body that would only deliberate over 'thistle cutting' and 'sheep dipping'.[81]

Johnson and the other Labour Party TDs met with the absentee Sinn Féin TDs led by de Valera in Dublin's Shelbourne Hotel on 8 December to protest the London Agreement. Sinn Féin had held a public meeting condemning the agreement on O'Connell Street in Dublin two days previously.[82] Independent and Farmers' Party TDs also attended the Shelbourne meeting, as did a deputation from the North, which included Cahir Healy and T.J. Harbison. Strong opposition to partition was expressed at the meeting. Of the republicans' hopes for a united Ireland, *The Times* wrote, 'The delusion that the Irish are at present potentially one nation dies hard among these enthusiasts, who still kick against the pricks of fact.'[83] At the meeting, de Valera was urged to enter the Dáil to vote against the ratification of the London Agreement, but he refused to do so. The *Irish Independent* reported that 'the question of entering the Dail had been exercising the minds of the Republicans' for some time.[84] Instead, de Valera appealed for a referendum to be held on the boundary question, an appeal naturally ignored by the Free State government.[85]

In private, though, de Valera 'commented that while Sinn Féin could not, he felt, renege on its mandate from the last election to absent itself from the Free State institutions, at the next election it should offer the electorate a policy of taking its seats if the requirement of the oath was removed'.[86] According to Noel Whelan, the issue of Sinn Féin TDs taking their seats in the Dáil 'was given new impetus by the fiasco over the report of the Boundary Commission'.[87] The government bill to ratify the London Agreement that was passed easily could have been defeated had de Valera, with his forty-eight TDs, sat in the Dáil. Shortly afterwards, at an extraordinary Sinn Féin Ard-Fheis, when his resolution for Sinn Féin TDs to enter the Dáil once the oath of allegiance was removed was defeated, he resigned as president of the party and founded Fianna Fáil the following month.[88] Shortly after gaining power in the Free State in 1932, de Valera told J.H. Thomas that the 1925 agreement 'has meant the consummation of the outrage of partition and the alienation of the most sacred part of our national territory with all the cultural and material loss that this unnatural separation entails'.[89]

Cosgrave, knowing it was not a 'damn good bargain', nevertheless tried to spin the London Agreement as best he could. In justifying the agreement to the Dáil, he claimed, 'It stabilises our financial position. It secures that we are deprived of none of our citizens.'[90] When talking of 'our citizens', he was of course only referring to citizens of the Free State. When a delegation of Northern nationalists asked to address the Dáil that December, Cosgrave said he 'certainly was not in favour'.[91]

Cosgrave's talk of the agreement facilitating Irish unity through goodwill and closer co-operation came to nothing either. While there were some ministerial and civil service meetings between North and South subsequently, and there was co-operation over policing and postal services members being allowed to cross the border for practical reasons to avoid long journeys, these meetings and agreements were not advertised.[92] Cosgrave's government was fearful of being identified as 'partitionist' by its political opponents in the Free State for engaging with the Northern government.

The loose agreement suggested by Craig as a replacement for the Council of Ireland, of joint meetings of both Irish governments 'at an early date', never materialised, with Cosgrave and Craig never meeting each other again. The next meeting between the heads of the two Irish governments occurred forty years later when Seán Lemass met Terence O'Neill in 1965. Labour Party TD from Clare Patrick Hogan asked Cosgrave in the Dáil in February 1928, 'on how many occasions since the signing of the Agreement amending the Treaty, dated 3rd December, 1925, and in respect of what subjects the Governments of the Irish Free State and Northern Ireland have met to consider matters of common interest'. Cosgrave responded, 'No meetings of the nature referred to have taken place.'[93] Even the suggestion by E.M. Stephens, when he was winding down the operations of the NEBB, for the Free State government to appoint a Northern policy co-ordinator (preferably him) to facilitate closer co-operation between North and South, which in turn would assist in bringing about Irish unity, was dismissed by the Free State government, with each government department allowed to continue their own separate policies (if they had any) towards the North.[94] Cosgrave may have publicly espoused a united Ireland, but his actions and lethargic approach in bringing it about suggests his only real concern was for the territory under his control, the Irish Free State.

The London Agreement was arguably the most significant victory of James Craig's political career. Not only had he 'permanently' secured Northern Ireland's borders, but the Council of Ireland was also jettisoned. When he arrived back from London, a large crowd greeted him in Belfast. Later that December, 'the members of the Northern Senate and House of Commons presented him with a silver Celtic cup on which their signatures, in facsimile, were engraved. The words "Not an Inch" were inscribed on the plinth.'[95] Edward Carson said he felt quite satisfied 'that the Ulster people were in safe hands in having Sir James Craig as their representative at the conferences. His whole heart and soul have, as I so well know, been always centred on doing what he could for the benefit of the Ulster people that he and I love so well.'[96] The *Belfast News-Letter* described Craig as 'a faithful guardian' of Ulster unionists' interests and 'that from the first day that the Boundary Question was raised he has maintained a consistent and determined attitude'.[97]

Speaking in the Northern House of Commons, Craig stated they had 'vindicated our position, discharged our every obligation, and kept faith with the loyalists of Ulster'. He also claimed that Cosgrave and his colleagues had shown 'a fresh feeling, showed a new aspect towards the problems that lie before Ireland ... I was greatly struck by the readiness with which they met me with regard to the question of the Council of Ireland', adding:

> [W]e earnestly pray that at long last, when we and they are in equal positions in regard to the services that are affected, we shall be able to meet when necessary from time to time to discuss in a friendly way, not only what would benefit particularly North or South, but all Ireland, and I trust, too, Great Britain and the Empire.[98]

Craig subsequently said 'the sign of the times were [sic] favourable to the removal of the Customs boundary between North and South Ireland. That would be worth all the pacts and treaties ever signed.'[99] There was much speculation, after the signing of the London Agreement, that the customs barrier would go, with Craig leading the calls for its disbandment. Representing the minority in East Donegal who were 'sold out' and not transferred to Northern Ireland, independent TD Major James Sproule Myles said he welcomed the 'spirit of comradeship' between the two Irish governments, and 'that in pursuance of his policy in that direction one of the first steps he should take should be towards removing entirely that unholy Customs barrier that accentuates more than anything else the division between North and South'.[100] Many East Donegal unionists desiring transfer to Northern Ireland in 1925 signed a petition in 1934 requesting the transfer of their region to the North, but it had no effect.[101] Likewise, despite the calls by Myles and others, the customs barrier remained, only rescinded with the establishment of the European Union Single Market in 1993.

Although Craig had won a decisive political victory, and notwithstanding his talks of goodwill in the immediate aftermath, he made no effort to be conciliatory towards the substantial Catholic minority in the North. At a time when his political capital was soaring, he squandered the chance to reach out to Northern nationalists. 'Instead of making a sustained attempt to win over the minority by assuaging their fears and suspicions,' as Patrick Buckland has written, 'he preferred to concentrate on maximising his party's support and sustaining Unionist control in the North. In fact, Craig could never rise above his position as leader of the Ulster Unionists.'[102]

For Northern nationalists, particularly for those close to the border, the London Agreement was the ultimate betrayal meted out to them by the Free State government. To this date, many Northern nationalists still feel this sense of betrayal acutely. An incredulous Cahir Healy said the agreement was 'a betrayal of the Nationalists of the North and a denial of every statement put forward by the Free State in their alleged support of our case since 1921'. 'For what have the Nationalists been sold?' he asked. 'Is it for the cancellation of Article 5?' John Redmond 'was driven from public life for even suggesting partition for a period of five years. The new leaders agree to partition for ever.'[103]

The Irish News, in its 4 December 1925 editorial entitled 'Money decided the great "Boundary Question" at last', said it 'shed no tears over the grave of that Commission'. In 'the Six Northern Counties our Nationalist and Catholic peoples are left altogether and absolutely to their own devices: now they must begin the task of organising themselves in self-defence'. The paper found 'consolation in the terms of the ninth Beatitude: "Blessed are they that expect nothing, for they shall not be disappointed"', concluding that 'the Nationalists of the Six Counties must look ahead ... and realise, once and for all, that their fate in Ulster rests with themselves'.[104] *The Irish News* also mentioned that the Commission's 'precious Report, its masses of evidence, its elaborate maps, its vast array of "secret" documents under police protection, are to vanish forever at the stroke of a pen'.[105]

Richard Feetham was very disappointed by the shelving of his Boundary Commission report and award. He believed 'the new Boundary as proposed would produce great improvement on both sides'.[106] As Ivan Gibbons has pointed out, 'its stifled recommendations in 1925 certainly more effectively, in at least most cases, reflected the wishes of local inhabitants than the six-county boundary belatedly reconfirmed' and 'it could be argued that more than two hundred lives might have been saved between 1969 and the mid-1990s if the Boundary Commission's recommendation that south Armagh be transferred to the Free State had been enacted'.[107] With Cosgrave calling for the report to 'be burned or buried as a bigger settlement had been reached beyond any that the Award could achieve', Feetham had to agree not to publish the award. He was, instead, offered an audience with King George V in Buckingham Palace and was able to send an open letter to Baldwin, published in *The Times*, justifying his actions and decisions as Boundary Commission chairman.[108] He met the king, who 'talked rather freely of the peculiarities of his Irish subjects', before embarking on his long journey back to South Africa over the Christmas period.[109]

James MacNeill was informed in late December 1925 that the Boundary Commission papers were 'stored under seal in our Strong-Room where they will remain buried as long as their sepulchre on the other side continues'.[110] Twenty 'copies of the Report, with full plans, one copy signed by Feetham and Fisher, were deposited at the Cabinet Office. All others, with plates from which the maps had been made, were destroyed.'[111] The report remained sealed for over forty years. The British government opened the files to the public on 1 January 1968, with Geoffrey Hand publishing his edition of the report the following year.[112] The contents of the buried Boundary Commission report were revealed to the public just as the problem it failed to resolve flared up again with the start of the Troubles.

Conclusion

EOIN MacNEILL TRIED TO REHABILITATE his political career somewhat when he unsuccessfully ran for TD in June 1927 in the National University of Ireland constituency, where he had once held a seat. Seeking to mitigate the 'adverse factor' of his performance on the Boundary Commission to his candidature, he attempted to justify his performance. He claimed:

> [The] thing that mainly made the Boundary Commission fruitless was the defective character of Article 12 of the Treaty. The adoption of this article admitted by implication that the Boundary fixed in the Act of 1920 was indefensible and unconstitutional. In the whole question at issue, the British Govt was from first to last one of the principals. But by Article 12, the British Govt, itself responsible for the Act of 1920 and a principal in the controversy, was made the umpire and practically the deciding judge.[1]

He considered the wording of Article 12 to be a 'great defect', with 'the wishes of the inhabitants' to prevail so far as they were 'compatible with economic conditions'. This, he believed, 'did not allow the inhabitants to be judges of their own economic advantage, and made it possible to hold that some undefined economic condition could override the wishes of the inhabitants'.[2]

There are some merits to MacNeill's arguments. He was faced with a thankless task. No matter who was chosen as the Free State representative on the Boundary Commission, they were always likely to face an uphill battle to achieve even a minimum of the demands of Irish nationalists. The ambiguous wording of Article 12 of the Treaty, whether by fault or design, was at the heart of most of the problems nationalists subsequently encountered over the following long four years. The Sinn Féin plenipotentiaries were at fault for agreeing to such vague wording, while the British negotiators probably designed the clause in such a way to offer them manoeuvrability options on which they readily capitalised.

Article 12 was a poorly drafted, hastily written clause. There was no alternative option offered if one of the parties refused to appoint its commissioner. The decision of the Northern government not to do so almost prevented the Boundary Commission from convening at all and was responsible for the longest delay in its establishment. Also, no time of preparation was offered from the time of the Commission's award to its implementation. The British and Free State governments had to meet to overcome this potential obstacle.

Regardless of the sizeable obstacles MacNeill faced, it is hard to disagree with the *Derry Journal*'s assessment that his performance was marked by 'inertia, incapacity, and appalling ineptitude'.[3] For much of the Commission's proceedings, he embodied the caricature of the absent-minded professor, seemingly uninterested in what was happening around him. By not strenuously objecting or issuing a minority report to the proposed Boundary Commission award, and the manner of his resignation from the Commission, and then the Executive Council, turned what could at least have been a propaganda win for the Free State into one of containment of a potentially terminal crisis for his government.

From a nationalist perspective, arguably a bigger problem than the ambiguous wording of Article 12 was the British government getting to choose the chairman of the Boundary Commission. While the wording of the clause was similar to the wording of other boundary commissions in Europe at the time, all of those were convened by independent chairmen. Geoffrey Hand suggested the nationalist gibe 'Feetham-cheat 'em' attributed to Tim Healy was unfair to Richard Feetham, and no one produced any piece of evidence to back up their claims that he lacked integrity as the Commission's chairman.[4] Yet it is hard to escape the unfairness of his proposed award and how all his interpretations favoured the unionist over the nationalist cause. While his honour perhaps may not be questioned, his bias certainly should be. This bias may have been because of his background and world view, a world view that embraced the important global role of the British Empire, which was always unlikely to favour those who sought to distance themselves from it. MacNeill remarked that throughout the Boundary Commission sittings, Joseph R. Fisher was very 'impassive and had left all to Feetham'.[5] With Feetham sharing most of Fisher's interpretations, there was no need for Fisher to be more assertive.

Fisher's persistent breaching of the confidentiality agreement approved by the commissioners at their first meeting was unquestionably valuable to Ulster unionists during the Boundary Commission sittings. In statements and interviews, nationalists tended to focus on the 'wishes of the inhabitants', even though the 1911 census returns and details on elections were readily available. Many also spent some time describing how they were mistreated in Northern Ireland, despite their complaints being outside the scope of the Commission. Given his correspondence with Spender, Lynn and Florence Reid, it is probable that Fisher assisted the UUC and the Northern government in steering unionist representations towards issues he believed were important to Feetham, such as economic factors.

The long delays in the convening of the Boundary Commission lessened the prospects of a favourable outcome for Irish nationalists. From the moment the clause was triggered in December 1922, the Boundary Commission was delayed by civil war, elections, change of governments, an Imperial Conference, boundary conferences among the parties involved, illnesses, obstructions, judicial reviews, and even some cases of lengthy travel. It is important to note that the Civil War did untold damage to the Free State's case, crippling it financially and reputationally before the Commission convened. The two-year delay was compounded by Feetham's decision to consider conditions as they were in 1925 and not in 1921. Aided by the Northern government's efforts to paint its territory with a 'deep Orange tint', as Michael Collins put it, Northern Ireland had attained a permanency by 1925 it did not have in 1921.

W.T. Cosgrave's Cumann na nGaedheal government took seriously the Boundary Commission, as well as its pursuit of a united Ireland, certainly up to the tripartite agreement negotiations in late 1925. This stance may have been motivated by looking over its shoulder or ahead to the future, or perhaps, and most likely, it was a combination of both. The dedication of the staff and the scale of the work completed by the North Eastern Boundary Bureau was laudatory. The work, however, was often directionless, based on assumptions that did not hold true. It made many wild assumptions and based much of its extensive output on those assumptions.

The NEBB can be allowed some latitude for making assumptions on how Article 12 was going to be interpreted, as its members were, like everyone else, grasping in the dark. NEBB representatives shared the same poor understanding of the mindset of Ulster unionists that bedevilled senior Sinn Féin members ever since the party became the leading nationalist party in Ireland from 1918. The Free State government and the NEBB failed to understand that Ulster unionists hated Dublin more than they loved the British Empire, resulting in many critical errors. Kevin O'Shiel was convinced in May 1923 that Irish unity was close to being realised. They continuously misjudged Ulster unionists, overemphasising the importance of the hard-headed Ulster businessman trope in decisions made by the Northern government.

The Free State government's most significant error was arguably the decision to erect customs barriers in April 1923. While this decision was made to assert the Free State's financial independence and to improve its dire financial position, it was also made to financially pressurise Northern Ireland into an all-Ireland parliament. The Free State protagonists failed to see what Northern nationalists, such as Joe Devlin, did – that it stereotyped the border before the Boundary Commission had even convened. Its consequences were amongst the main complaints made by people who submitted evidence to the Commission. Feetham placed a large emphasis on the effects of customs barriers in his questioning and decision-making, arguing, for example, that Newry should remain in Northern Ireland partly because of the negative impact the placing of customs barriers north of the town would have.[6]

The role of W.T. Cosgrave throughout the Boundary Commission saga needs assessment. He pushed for, financed and supported the NEBB. He devoted a considerable amount of time and resources to get the best possible solution through the Commission. Up until late 1925, he consistently showed empathy for Northern nationalists and condemned the coercion they experienced in the North. However, his appointment of MacNeill as the Free State commissioner was a dreadfully poor decision, not only because of MacNeill's unsuitability for the role, but also because MacNeill, as an Executive Council member, did not have the time to devote fully to the Commission that was badly needed. Cosgrave put too much faith in the fairness he expected from the Boundary Commission and failed to heed the internal warnings over the ambiguity in interpretations of Article 12.

Cosgrave was also a terrible negotiator, constantly telegraphing his thoughts to British and Northern Irish stakeholders. Baldwin and Craig undoubtedly could see the panic in his eyes when he rushed over to London to have the Boundary Commission report shelved. He contradicted O'Higgins, siding with Craig on the abolition of PR. His behaviour leading up to the signing of the London Agreement was in ways contemptible, where he attempted to sabotage, on more than one occasion, attempts to ease the plight of Northern nationalists, focusing his efforts instead on the waiving of Article 5. He demonstrated that he had abandoned Northern nationalists over money. After readily discarding the Council of Ireland, he talked up the prospect of a warm relationship and regular meetings with Craig, but they never met again and all his utterances on achieving Irish unity vanished after 1925. While some of the rhetoric remained, 'policy and political contact' with the North was jettisoned.[7] His stance from 1925 reflected all Southern government approaches towards the North for decades – strong on rhetoric, devoid of policy – including those of his successor, de Valera.

The Cumann na nGaedheal government survived the crisis created by the breakdown of the Boundary Commission but it was severely damaged. Somes of its TDs, including, William Magennis, Denis McCullough, Pádraic Ó Máille and Christopher Byrne, resigned from the party in protest over the Commission fiasco, with some going on to found a new political party, Clann Éireann.[8] They subsequently joined Fianna Fáil, the party de Valera formed in 1926, after the ineffectiveness of the Sinn Féin abstentionist policy was brought home to him as the crisis over the Commission unfolded and he left Sinn Féin. His new party went on to dominate politics in the twenty-six counties for decades.

British governments, from David Lloyd George's coalition government in 1921 to Stanley Baldwin's Conservative government in 1925, including Ramsay MacDonald's first Labour government in between, acted to deceive nationalists and to ensure the outcome of the Boundary Commission would favour unionists by only recommending cosmetic changes to the border. They did this by ensnaring Sinn Féin into agreeing to a vague clause in the Treaty, by stalling on the convening of the Commission, by promising unionists that no substantial changes would be made to the border regardless of the Commission's recommendations, and by appointing Conservative and unionist commissioners who were never going to agree to an extensive rectification of the border. For the British government, the highest point of danger was in 1924 due to the political crisis that ensued over its appointment of Northern Ireland's commissioner. By late 1925, with the Free State in such a vulnerable position over the MacNeill fiasco, both the British and Northern Irish governments held all the cards.

A parallel feature to the Boundary Commission saga were attempts by the Free State government to move away from the Empire and assert its newly gained independence, while the British government tried to pull it back into the Empire's orbit. On the one hand, this manifested itself by the Free State ignoring the proceedings of the Judicial Committee of the Privy Council and, on the other hand, by the British government diminishing the role of the League of Nations in resolving intra-Empire disputes. The Free State sought unsuccessfully for the Treaty's international credentials to be prioritised in how the boundary question was settled, whereas the different British governments in power at the time ensured it remained an Imperial issue. The Free State government's quest for Irish unity was severely compromised by its stance that no offer of Irish unity should be accepted if it jeopardised any of the independence it had attained since 1921. This was never likely to impress Ulster unionists.

The 1925 London Agreement was a triumph for James Craig more than anyone else. Under enormous pressure, both internal and external, he steadfastly stuck to his 'not an inch' strategy and refused to recognise the Boundary Commission, publicly at any rate. Not only did the tripartite agreement secure Northern Ireland's existing borders, the 'irritating' Council of Ireland was disbanded also. In his and his government's opposition to the Commission there was considerable hypocrisy at play. He thought it outrageous that unionists were expected to adhere to an agreement, the Treaty, they took no part in, while expecting nationalists to accept the Government of Ireland Act 1920 that they were not consulted on. Craig also went to great pains to express the importance of the Government of Ireland Act, it being considered a sacrosanct agreement, yet he had no problem in 'swooping away' parts of the Act he did not like, such as the Council of Ireland.[9] He also wilfully ignored his commitments to Imperial contributions and protecting minority rights that were embodied in the Act. His government severely punished nationalist bodies for boycotting Northern institutions, while it benefitted by boycotting the Boundary Commission. Craig, with his popularity soaring after the London Agreement, had a perfect opportunity to be magnanimous towards the nationalist minority. He chose not to, governing solely for Ulster unionists instead, leaving Northern society to remain bitterly divided. While the border issue was 'settled' by late 1925, divisions remained as malignant as ever.

For almost everyone, the Boundary Commission was an unsatisfactory solution, but for border nationalists on the Northern side, it had offered real tangible hope. The slow and steady sapping of their rights and influence in the early years of partition had a devastating effect on their morale and confidence, and they clung desperately to the hope of being released from their burdens. There were though, inherent weaknesses in some of the Northern nationalist arguments and many were overly expectant of what was not in the gift of the Free State government to deliver. Some expected that the entire counties of Tyrone and Fermanagh as well as Derry city, Newry and other places in South and East Down, and South Armagh would be transferred to the Free State. However, if the Commission decided to use the county as the unit to be considered, only Tyrone and Fermanagh would have been transferred. If the Boundary Commission chose smaller units, parts of Tyrone and Fermanagh would have remained in Northern Ireland.

It was not just the Free State government that felt Northern nationalists were overly expectant. Some republicans did too, with a 'Northern Republican' claiming in *An Phoblacht* in 1934 that, instead of Northern nationalists being 'betrayed' and 'let down', the North 'let itself down', noting that the number of 'active Volunteers in the North-East was infinitismal [sic]' before the sectarian riots in 1920 and condemning its 'hopeless, slavish dependence on the "Free State" government'.[10]

After 1925, Northern nationalists had to accept, 'whether they liked it or not, that they were citizens of Northern Ireland'.[11] Joe Devlin and Thomas McAllister, MP for County Antrim, decided to enter the Northern Parliament following the April 1925 election. They were followed by three more nationalists in 1926. By 1928 there were ten. Cardinal Patrick O'Donnell, the Catholic primate of all-Ireland, remarked, 'The area of the Six Counties is now fixed as the area of Northern Ireland, and everyone within it has to make account of that fact.'[12]

The fallout from the Boundary Commission has left a bitter taste in the mouths of Northern nationalists ever since. Their trust in British governments (always threadbare) evaporated completely, but perhaps, more importantly, their trust in the South suffered an irrevocable blow, due to the Free State government's abandonment of the North for financial benefits. The mistrust still resonates today. Many Northern nationalists believe there is a partitionist mindset in the South and that the 'establishment' political parties there – Fianna Fáil and Fine Gael – are not interested in Irish unity, despite rhetoric to the contrary. There is contempt for the geo-blocking of programmes in the North, particularly sporting ones, by RTÉ, the provision of weather information from Met Éireann for just the twenty-six counties, the naming of the twenty-six-county state as Ireland under the Constitution, and the prohibition of citizens in the North from voting in Irish presidential elections. As prospects of a border poll have entered public discourse since the acceptance of the Good Friday Agreement of 1998, focus has shifted to an ambiguous clause in that agreement: Schedule 1 (2), which states that the British Secretary of State for Northern Ireland 'shall exercise the power' to call a border poll 'if at any time it appears likely to him that a majority of those voting would express a wish that Northern Ireland should cease to be part of the United Kingdom and form part of a united Ireland'.[13] As with the original Boundary Commission, many Northern nationalists believe this clause leaves the power in the hands of the British government, with some fearing that this could prevent a border poll from occurring at all, with, to quote Cahir Healy, 'the liberties and rights guaranteed to the nationalists ... scrapped, and the people sold into political servitude for all time'.[14]

ENDNOTES

INTRODUCTION

1. R. Fanning, M. Kennedy, D. Keogh and E. O'Halpin, *Documents on Irish Foreign Policy: Volume 1* (Dublin: Royal Irish Academy, 1998): Final text of the Articles of Agreement for a Treaty between Great Britain and Ireland as signed, 6 December 1921.
2. K.J. Rankin, 'The role of the Irish boundary commission in the entrenchment of the Irish border: from tactical panacea to political liability', *Journal of Historical Geography*, vol. 34 (2008), p. 422.

CHAPTER 1

1. R. Fanning, *Fatal Path: British Government and Irish Revolution 1910–1922* (London: Faber & Faber, 2013), p. 269.
2. K. Middlemas (ed.), *Thomas Jones: Whitehall Diary: Volume III: Ireland 1918–1925* (London: Oxford University Press, 1971), p. 111.
3. Ibid., p. 110.
4. J. Anderson and L. O'Dowd, 'Imperialism and nationalism: The Home Rule struggle and border creation in Ireland, 1885–1925', *Political Geography*, vol. 26 (2007), p. 944.
5. House of Commons Debate, 11 June 1912, vol. 39 col. 771, available from http://hansard.millbanksystems.com, accessed 1 September 2024.
6. Bodleian Archives and Manuscripts (hereafter Bodleian Archives), Archive of Henry Herbert Asquith (hereafter Asquith Archive), MS. Asquith 39: Miscellaneous letters and memoranda on the Irish Question, 1913-1914, undated memorandum.
7. Other than the exclusion of four, six or nine counties, three senior civil servants in Dublin Castle (Sir James Docherty, Sir H.A. Robinson and W.F. Bailey) devised schemes that attempted to shape the exclusion zone demarcation lines. See, C. Mulvagh, 'Ulster Exclusion and Irish Nationalism: Consenting to the Principle of Partition, 1912–1916', *Revue Française de Civilisation Britannique*, vol. 24, no. 2 (2019).
8. Bodleian Archives, Asquith Archive, MS. Asquith 39, Letter from King George V to Asquith on 3 May 1914.
9. Ibid., Letter from King George V to Asquith on 11 August 1913.
10. Bodleian Archives, Archive of Lionel George Curtis (hereafter Curtis Archive), MS. Curtis 90: Ireland, 1924–1946, 1950.
11. Bodleian Archives, Asquith Archive, MS. Asquith 39, Letter from John Redmond to Asquith on 5 May 1914.

12 Ibid., Memorandum 'Population of Four Counties and Two Boroughs', undated.
13 1911 Census of Ireland, available at https://www.cso.ie/en/statistics/historicalreports/census1911/, accessed on 4 January 2025.
14 E. Phoenix, *Northern Nationalism: Nationalist Politics, Partition and the Catholic Minority in Northern Ireland 1890–1940* (Belfast: Ulster Historical Foundation, 1994), p. 17.
15 Ibid., p. 35.
16 A. Jackson, *Judging Redmond and Carson* (Dublin: Royal Irish Academy, 2018), pp. 228–9.
17 D. Gwynn, *The History of Partition (1912–1925)* (Dublin: The Richview Press, 1950), p. 190.
18 M. Laffan, *The Partition of Ireland 1911–1925* (Dundalk: Dundalgan Press, 2004), p. 66.
19 N. Mansergh, *The Unresolved Question: The Anglo-Irish Settlement and Its Undoing 1912–72* (Yale: Yale University Press, 1991), p. 130.
20 Public Record Office of Northern Ireland (hereafter PRONI), D640/7, Letters between Colonel Crawford and James Craig and Edward Carson, 16 February 1920.
21 Ibid., 4 May 1920.
22 Mansergh, *The Unresolved Question*, p. 131.
23 C. Moore, *Birth of the Border: The Impact of Partition in Ireland* (Dublin: Merrion Press, 2019), p. 21.
24 M. O'Callaghan, '"Old Parchment and Water"; the Boundary Commission of 1925 and the Copperfastening of the Irish Border', *Bullan; An Irish Studies Journal*, vol. 5, no. 2 (2000), p. 34.
25 C.K. Matthews, 'The Irish Boundary Crisis and the Reshaping of British Politics: 1920–1925', PhD thesis, London School of Economics and Political Science (2000), p. 57.
26 Fanning, *Fatal Path*, p. 265.
27 Ibid., p. 264.
28 B. O'Leary, '"Cold House": The Unionist Counter-Revolution and the Invention of Northern Ireland', in J. Crowley, D. Ó Drisceoil and M. Murphy (eds), *Atlas of the Irish Revolution* (Cork: Cork University Press, 2017), p. 818.
29 J. Bowman, *De Valera and the Ulster Question 1917–1973* (Oxford: Oxford University Press, 1989), p. 51.
30 PRONI, Cabinet Papers of Stormont Administration (hereafter CAB) 4/10, 22 July 1921.
31 See, for example, *The Times*, 7 May 1924, p. 14.
32 University College Dublin (hereafter UCD) Archives, Ernest Blythe Papers, P24/22, Office Correspondence Relating to the Peace Negotiations, June–September 1921, 10 August 1921.
33 Dáil Éireann Debates, vol. S, no. 4, 22 August 1921, available from www.oireachtasdebates.gov.ie, accessed on 2 September 2024.
34 Bowman, *De Valera and the Ulster Question*, p. 56.
35 Ibid. pp. 56–7.
36 A. Grant, *The Irish Revolution 1912–23: Derry* (Dublin: Four Courts Press, 2018), p. 126.
37 Lord Longford (Frank Pakenham), *Peace by Ordeal: The Negotiation of the Anglo-Irish Treaty, 1921* (London: Sidgwick & Jackson, 1935), p. 93.
38 Fanning et al., *Documents on Irish Foreign Policy: Volume 1*, Memorandum by the Irish Delegation in reply to British memorandum of 27 October, p. 297.
39 Matthews, 'The Irish Boundary Crisis and the Reshaping of British Politics', p. 68.

40. UCD Archives, Richard Mulcahy Papers, P7/A/72, Fourth Session of Irish Peace Conference in Downing Street on 14 October 1921.
41. Ibid., Fifth Session of Irish Peace Conference in Downing Street on 17 October 1921.
42. Fanning et al., *Documents on Irish Foreign Policy: Volume 1*, Memorandum of the proposals of the Irish delegates to the British representative, 24 October 1921, pp. 288–90 and Arthur Griffith to Éamon de Valera (Dublin), 24 October 1921, pp. 290–1.
43. UCD Archives, Richard Mulcahy Papers, P7/A/72, Memorandum of meeting at Winston Churchill's house between Arthur Griffith & Michael Collins and David Lloyd George, Winston Churchill and Lord Birkenhead on 30 October 1921.
44. Ibid., Minutes of Sub-Conference held at House of Lords between Arthur Griffith & Michael Collins and Lord Birkenhead on 3 November 1921.
45. Fanning et al., *Documents on Irish Foreign Policy: Volume 1*, Arthur Griffith to Éamon de Valera (Dublin), 9 November 1921, pp. 305–6.
46. Fanning, *Fatal Path*, p. 282.
47. Mansergh, *The Unresolved Question*, p. 119.
48. Fanning, *Fatal Path*, p. 272.
49. K. Matthews, *Fatal Influence: The Impact of Ireland on British Politics, 1920–1925* (Dublin: University College Dublin Press, 2004), p. 41.
50. House of Commons Debate, 7 November 1921, vol. 148 col. 21, available from http://hansard.millbanksystems.com, accessed 3 September 2024.
51. Matthews, 'The Irish Boundary Crisis and the Reshaping of British Politics', p. 70.
52. Press clippings of *Morning Post* articles, PRONI, D3015/3/B/2, Volume of press cuttings [Irish 2], including the *Morning Post* leak on the Boundary Commission, 31 October 1921.
53. Matthews, 'The Irish Boundary Crisis and the Reshaping of British Politics', p. 70.
54. Ibid., p. 74.
55. For details of the correspondence between Lloyd George and Craig in November 1921, see, for example, *The Times*, 14 December 1921, p. 15 and North Eastern Boundary Bureau, *Handbook of the Ulster Question* (Dublin: The Stationery Office, 1923), pp. 31–3.
56. *The Times*, 14 December 1921, p. 15.
57. Fanning, *Fatal Path*, p. 294.
58. *The Times*, 14 December 1921, p. 15.
59. Matthews, 'The Irish Boundary Crisis and the Reshaping of British Politics', p. 81.
60. PRONI, D640/7, Letters between Colonel Crawford and James Craig and Edward Carson, 7 November 1921.
61. J. McColgan, *British Policy and the Irish Administration 1920–22* (London: George Allen & Unwin, 1983), p. 69.
62. R. Lynch, *Revolutionary Ireland, 1912–25* (London: Bloomsbury, 2015), p. 101.
63. T. Bowman, *Carson's Army: The Ulster Volunteer Force, 1910–22* (Manchester: Manchester University Press, 2007), p. 199.
64. Matthews, 'The Irish Boundary Crisis and the Reshaping of British Politics', p. 103.
65. McColgan, *British Policy and the Irish Administration*, p. 69.
66. Middlemas (ed.), *Thomas Jones: Whitehall Diary: Volume III*, pp. 156–7.
67. Bowman, *De Valera and the Ulster Question*, p. 63.

68 UCD Archives, Richard Mulcahy Papers, P7/A/72, Letter from Griffith to de Valera on 8 November 1921.
69 Matthews, 'The Irish Boundary Crisis and the Reshaping of British Politics', p. 77.
70 Fanning et al., *Documents on Irish Foreign Policy: Volume 1*, Arthur Griffith to Éamon de Valera (Dublin) on 12 November 1921, pp. 307–8.
71 Middlemas (ed.), *Thomas Jones: Whitehall Diary: Volume III*, p. 161.
72 Ibid., 164.
73 Longford, *Peace by Ordeal*, pp. 177–8.
74 Ibid., p. 180.
75 C. Kenny, *Midnight in London: The Anglo-Irish Treaty Crisis 1921* (Dublin: Eastwood Books, 2021), p. 103.
76 Fanning et al., *Documents on Irish Foreign Policy: Volume 1*, 'Tentative suggestions for a Treaty presented by Thomas Jones to Arthur Griffith', 16 November 1921, p. 310.
77 P. Murray, *The Irish Boundary Commission and its Origins 1886–1925* (Dublin: University College Dublin Press, 2011), pp. 86–7.
78 NAI, TSCH/3/S1801 E, Boundary Commission: general matters, Copy of Letter sent by John Chartres to General Mulcahy, 5 February 1924.
79 Bureau of Military History, Witness Statement 979, p. 44, available from www.bureauofmilitaryhistory.ie/, accessed 4 September 2024.
80 UCD Archives, Richard Mulcahy Papers, P7/A/72, Memorandum from Irish Representatives, 22 November 1921.
81 Fanning, *Fatal Path*, p. 300.
82 Fanning et al., *Documents on Irish Foreign Policy: Volume 1*, Arthur Griffith to Éamon de Valera (Dublin), 23 November 1921, p. 316.
83 Ibid., Facsimile reproduction of draft treaty, David Lloyd George to Arthur Griffith, 30 November 1921, p. 325.
84 Ibid.
85 Murray, *The Irish Boundary Commission and its Origins*, p. 243.
86 Fanning et al., *Documents on Irish Foreign Policy: Volume 1*, Manuscript notes by Michael Collins on the second revise of the British treaty proposals, 2 December 1921, p. 336 and p. 342.
87 Ibid., Copy of secretary's notes of meeting of the cabinet and delegation held 3 December 1921, p. 344.
88 J.A. Gaughan, *Austin Stack: Portrait of a Separatist* (Dublin: Kingdom Books, 1977), p. 168.
89 Fanning et al., *Documents on Irish Foreign Policy: Volume 1*, Copy of secretary's notes of meeting of the cabinet and delegation held 3 December 1921, p. 345.
90 Bowman, *De Valera and the Ulster Question*, p. 68.
91 Murray, *The Irish Boundary Commission and its Origins*, pp. 105–6.
92 Matthews, 'The Irish Boundary Crisis and the Reshaping of British Politics', pp. 88–9.
93 Ibid., p. 89.
94 Middlemas (ed.), *Thomas Jones: Whitehall Diary: Volume III*, p. 183.
95 C. Moore, 'Reinforcing partition through fiscal policy', *Irish Political Studies*, vol. 39, no. 2 (2024), p. 346.

Endnotes

96 UK National Archives (hereafter NAUK), Press clipping of *Evening Standard* article, CUST 118/134, Ireland – land barrier and boundary commission (1923–1925), 5 March 1923, p. 6.
97 Fanning, *Fatal Path*, p. 309.
98 W. Churchill, *The World Crisis Volume 4: The Aftermath (1923)* (London: Rosetta Books, 2013, electronic version), p. 230.
99 Ibid., p. 336.
100 R. Lynch, 'The Boundary Commission', in Crowley, Ó Drisceoil and Murphy (eds), *Atlas of the Irish Revolution*, p. 828.
101 Middlemas (ed.), *Thomas Jones: Whitehall Diary: Volume III*, p. 234.
102 Mansergh, *The Unresolved Question*, p. 220.
103 *The Irish News*, 31 July 1924, p. 4.
104 Fanning, *Fatal Path*, pp. 310–11.

CHAPTER 2

1 R. Lynch, *The Partition of Ireland, 1918–1925* (Cambridge: Cambridge University Press, 2019), p. 198.
2 Ibid., p. 143.
3 House of Lords Debate, 14 December 1921, vol. 48 cols. 39–53, available from http://hansard.millbanksystems.com, accessed 6 September 2024.
4 Middlemas (ed.), *Thomas Jones: Whitehall Diary: Volume III*, p. 189.
5 *Belfast News-Letter*, 7 December 1921, p. 6.
6 *The Northern Whig and Belfast Post*, 7 December 1921, p. 4.
7 *Belfast Telegraph*, 8 December 1921, p. 4.
8 PRONI, D1633/2/25, Diary of Lady Lilian Spender, 16 December 1921.
9 *The Northern Standard*, 21 October 1921, p. 3.
10 Matthews, 'The Irish Boundary Crisis and the Reshaping of British Politics', pp. 95–6.
11 Middlemas (ed.), *Thomas Jones: Whitehall Diary: Volume III*, pp. 189–90.
12 PRONI, CAB 4/29, 10 January 1922.
13 Ibid.
14 Gwynn, *The History of Partition*, p. 203.
15 A.C. Hepburn, *Catholic Belfast and Nationalist Ireland in the Era of Joe Devlin 1871–1934* (Oxford: Oxford University Press, 2008), pp. 230–1.
16 M. Ó Fathartaigh and L. Weeks, *Birth of a State: The Anglo-Irish Treaty* (Dublin: Merrion Press, 2021), pp. 146–7.
17 Dáil Éireann Debates, vol. T, no. 9, 22 December 1921, available from www.oireachtasdebates.gov.ie, accessed on 8 September 2024.
18 Ibid.
19 Fanning et al., *Documents on Irish Foreign Policy: Volume 1*, Proposed Treaty of Association between Ireland and the British Commonwealth presented by Éamon de Valera to Dáil Éireann in January 1922, p. 370.
20 Quoted in J.A. Cousins, *Without a Dog's Chance: The Nationalists of Northern Ireland and the Irish Boundary Commission, 1920–25* (Dublin: Merrion Press, 2020), p. 88.

21 P. Buckland, *The Factory of Grievance: Devolved Government in Northern Ireland 1921–1929* (Dublin: Gill and Macmillan, 1979), p. 73.
22 Phoenix, *Northern Nationalism*, pp. 156–7.
23 R. Lynch, *The Northern IRA and the Early Years of Partition, 1920–1922* (Dublin: Irish Academic Press, 2006), p. 95.
24 Phoenix, *Northern Nationalism*, p. 155.
25 Ibid., p. 209.
26 Ibid., p. 212.
27 J. Bardon, *A History of Ulster* (Belfast: The Blackstaff Press, 2001), p. 499.
28 *The Manchester Guardian*, 7 December 1921, p. 10.
29 House of Commons Debate, 14 December 1921, vol. 149 cols 40–42, available from http://hansard.millbanksystems.com, accessed 8 September 2024.
30 Matthews, 'The Irish Boundary Crisis and the Reshaping of British Politics', p. 97.
31 House of Commons Debate, 16 December 1921, vol. 149 col. 315, available from http://hansard.millbanksystems.com, accessed 8 September 2024.
32 Matthews, *Fatal Influence*, p. 240.
33 For Churchill's involvement with the Irish Boundary Commission, see C. Moore, '"I See All Your Difficulties": Winston Churchill and the Irish Boundary Commission', *Finest Hour: The Journal of Winston Churchill and His Times*, no. 197 (2022).
34 House of Commons Debate, 16 February 1922, vol. 150 col. 1272, available from http://hansard.millbanksystems.com, accessed on 8 September 2024, and Matthews, *Fatal Influence*, p. 71.
35 Matthews, 'The Irish Boundary Crisis and the Reshaping of British Politics', p. 132.
36 NAI, TSCH/3/S1801 A, Boundary Commission: general matters, including correspondence between Michael Collins and Sir James Craig, Provisional Government Minutes on 20 January 1922.
37 PRONI, D1507C/7, Lady Carson Non-Irish Papers, Diary entry, 20 January 1922.
38 B. Barton, 'The Dáil cabinet's mission to Belfast', in C. Nic Dháibhéid, M. Coleman and P. Bew (eds), *Northern Ireland 1921–2021: Centenary Historical Perspectives* (Newtownards: Ulster Historical Foundation, 2022), pp. 37–43.
39 M. Hopkinson, 'The Craig-Collins Pacts of 1922: Two Attempted Reforms of the Northern Ireland Government', *Irish Historical Studies*, vol. 27, no. 106 (November 1990), p. 147.
40 K. Glennon, *From Pogrom to Civil War: Tom Glennon and the Belfast IRA* (Cork: Mercier Press, 2013), p. 100.
41 Hopkinson, 'The Craig-Collins Pacts of 1922', p. 147.
42 PRONI, CAB 4/30, 26 January 1922.
43 Hopkinson, 'The Craig-Collins Pacts of 1922', p. 147.
44 *The Cork Examiner*, 27 January 1922, p. 5.
45 Cousins, *Without a Dog's Chance*, pp. 122–3.
46 NAI, TSCH/3/S1801 A, Boundary Commission: general matters, including correspondence between Michael Collins and Sir James Craig, Provisional Government Minutes on 30 January 1922.
47 Mansergh, *The Unresolved Question*, p. 224.
48 NAI, TSCH/3/S1801 A, Boundary Commission: general matters, including correspondence

between Michael Collins and Sir James Craig, Provisional Government Minutes on 2 February 1922.
49 *The Freeman's Journal*, 3 February 1922, p. 5.
50 NAI, TSCH/3/S1801 A, Boundary Commission: general matters, including correspondence between Michael Collins and Sir James Craig, Provisional Government Minutes on 6 February 1922.
51 See, for example, *Belfast News-Letter*, 16 May 1924, p. 7.
52 Mansergh, *The Unresolved Question*, p. 187.
53 NAI, NEBB/1/4/5, Six Counties boundary controversy, Statement by Captain Chas Craig MP in Press on 4 February 1922.
54 K. Glennon, 'The Dead of the Belfast Progrom', 18 May 1924, available at https://thebelfastpogrom.com/2023/04/22/the-dead-of-the-belfast-pogrom-updated/, accessed on 9 September 2024.
55 S.B. Newman, 'For God, Ulster and the "B"-men': the Ulsterian revolution, the foundation of Northern Ireland and the creation of the Ulster Special Constabulary, 1910-1927', PhD Thesis, Birbeck, University of London (2020), p. 240.
56 Laffan, *The Partition of Ireland*, p. 94.
57 NAI, TSCH/3/S1801 A, Boundary Commission: general matters, including correspondence between Michael Collins and Sir James Craig, Provisional Government Minutes on 30 January 1922.
58 See Moore, *Birth of the Border*, pp. 75–6.
59 See, for example, NAUK, HO 267/13, Land Registry Transfer of Documents, 16 March 1923.
60 PRONI, CAB 4/37, 8 February 1922.
61 Matthews, 'The Irish Boundary Crisis and the Reshaping of British Politics', p. 119.
62 *The Times*, 15 February 1922, p. 10.
63 Bodleian Archives, Curtis Archive, MS. Curtis 89: Ireland, 1916–1924, Letter from Curtis to Churchill on 19 August 1924.
64 A. Hezlet, *The 'B' Specials: A History of The Ulster Special Constabulary* (London: Tom Stacey Ltd, 1972) p. 61.
65 NAUK, HO 45/24812, Miscellaneous matters arising from the Partition of Ireland, 9 May 1922.
66 Lynch, *The Partition of Ireland*, p. 144.
67 Ibid.
68 Matthews, *Fatal Influence*, pp. 72–3.
69 NAI, TSCH/3/S1801 A, Boundary Commission: general matters, including correspondence between Michael Collins and Sir James Craig, Letter from Collins to Craig.
70 Ibid., Provisional Government minutes on 9 June 1922.
71 Fanning et al., *Documents on Irish Foreign Policy: Volume 1*, Extract from a letter from George Gavan Duffy to Ormonde Grattan Esmonde (Madrid) on 22 May 1922.
72 NAI, TSCH/3/S1801 A, Boundary Commission: general matters, including correspondence between Michael Collins and Sir James Craig, Provisional Government meeting minutes on 25 May 1922.
73 *The Times*, 21 March 1922, p. 13 and 24 March 1922, p. 14.
74 For accounts of the 'McMahon Murders', see E. Burke, *Ghosts of a Family: Ireland's Most*

Infamous Unsolved Murder, the Outbreak of the Civil War and the Origins of the Modern Troubles (Dublin: Merrion Press, 2024), and T. Wilson, '"The most terrible assassination that has yet stained the name of Belfast": the McMahon murders in context', *Irish Historical Studies*, vol. 37, no. 145 (May 2010).

75 M. Farrell, *Arming the Protestants: The Formation of the Ulster Special Constabulary and the Royal Ulster Constabulary, 1920–7* (London: Pluto Press, 1983), p. 100.
76 NAI, TSCH/3/S1801 A, Boundary Commission: general matters, including correspondence between Michael Collins and Sir James Craig.
77 Ibid.
78 Bardon, *A History of Ulster*, p. 500.
79 Buckland, *The Factory of Grievance*, p. 228.
80 Bardon, *A History of Ulster* p. 500.
81 Bodleian Archives, Curtis Archive, MS. Curtis 89, Letter from Curtis to Churchill on 19 August 1924.
82 A. Dolan and W. Murphy, *Michael Collins: The Man and the Revolution* (Cork: The Collins Press, 2015), p. 196.
83 Matthews, 'The Irish Boundary Crisis and the Reshaping of British Politics', p. 133.
84 Churchill, *The World Crisis Volume 4*, p. 253.
85 Ibid., p. 254.
86 Ibid., pp. 266–7.
87 Matthews, *Fatal Influence*, p. 90.
88 Roy Jenkins, *Churchill: A Biography* (London: Pan Books, 2001), p. 376.
89 UCD Archives, Papers of Kevin O'Higgins, P197/110, Letter from Kevin O'Higgins to Patrick McCartan, 12 September 1924.

CHAPTER 3

1 NAI, TSCH/3/S2027, Northern Ireland Boundary: Secret Document, 1922–1924, Memorandum from Kevin O'Shiel to each member of the Executive Council on 21 April 1923.
2 NAI, TSCH/3/S1801 A, Boundary Commission: Provisional Government Meeting Minutes on 2 October 1922.
3 R. Fanning, M. Kennedy, D. Keogh and E. O'Halpin, *Documents on Irish Foreign Policy: Volume 2: 1923–1926* (Dublin: Royal Irish Academy, 2000), Memorandum by Kevin O'Shiel to William T. Cosgrave on 25 September 1922.
4 E. Sagarra, *Kevin O'Shiel: Tyrone Nationalist and Irish State-Builder* (Dublin: Irish Academic Press, 2013), p. 201.
5 NAI, TSCH/3/S4743, Boundary Bureau: formation and winding up, Memorandum on The Boundary Commission Organization, etc., 14 October 1922.
6 L.W. White and A. Carpenter, *Dictionary of Irish Biography*, available from http://dib.cambridge.org/, accessed on 11 September 2024.
7 See G. McElroy, *Dictionary of Irish Biography*, available from http://dib.cambridge.org/, accessed on 11 September 2024, and obituary in *The Irish Press*, 29 August 1972, p. 4.
8 NAI, TSCH/3/S4743, Boundary Bureau: formation and winding up, Letter from Kevin O'Shiel to W.T. Cosgrave, 22 October 1922.

Endnotes

9   Obituary in *The Irish Press*, 2 October 1943, p. 3.
10   NAI, TSCH/3/S4743, Boundary Bureau: formation and winding up, North Eastern Boundary Bureau, Final Report on 26 February 1926.
11   See C. Morrissey, *Dictionary of Irish Biography*, available from http://dib.cambridge.org/, accessed on 11 September 2024, and obituary in *The Irish Times*, 29 July 1936, p. 8.
12   NAI, TSCH/3/S4743, Boundary Bureau: formation and winding up, North Eastern Boundary Bureau, Final Report on 26 February 1926.
13   Ibid.
14   NAI, TSCH/3/S11209, Northern Ireland: deputation to Provisional Government, verbatim report of meeting relating to Boundary Commission, Official report of Deputation to the Government from the Six County Border in reference to the Boundary Commission on 11 October 1922.
15   Ibid.
16   Ibid.
17   UCD Archives, Ernest Blythe Papers, P24/70, Memorandum by Ernest Blythe on Policy in Regard to the North East, 9 August 1922.
18   Ibid.
19   NAI, TSCH/3/S11209, Northern Ireland: deputation to Provisional Government, verbatim report of meeting relating to Boundary Commission, Official report of Deputation to the Government from the Six County Border in reference to the Boundary Commission on 11 October 1922.
20   Ibid.
21   J.A. Cousins, 'Without a "Dog's Chance": The Devlinite *Irish News*, Northern Ireland's "Trapped" Nationalist Minority, and the Irish Boundary Question, 1921–1925', PhD thesis, Simon Fraser University (2008), p. 208.
22   NAI, TSCH/3/S4743, Boundary Bureau: formation and winding up, Letter from Kevin O'Shiel to W.T. Cosgrave on 22 October 1922.
23   Ibid., The Boundary Commission Organization, etc. on 14 October 1922.
24   *Evening Herald*, 7 December 1922, p. 4.
25   R. Lynch, '7 December 1922: Ulster opts out of the Irish Free State – Partition and Power: Unionist Political Culture in Northern Ireland', in D. Gannon and F. McGarry (eds), *Ireland 1922: Independence, Partition, Civil War* (Dublin: Royal Irish Academy, 2022), p. 305.
26   *Irish Independent*, 6 December 1922, p. 9.
27   *The Freeman's Journal*, 8 December 1922, p. 5.
28   NAI, TSCH/3/S1801 E, Boundary Commission: general matters, Statement Proposed to be Presented on Behalf of the Government of Saorstat Eireann on the Re-Assembly of the Conference in London, 19 February 1924.
29   PRONI, CAB 4/67, 12 January 1923.
30   *Irish Independent*, 8 December 1922, p. 5.
31   *Fermanagh Herald*, 9 December 1922, p. 3.
32   See, for example, *The Northern Whig and Belfast Post*, 25 January 1923, p. 7 and *The Irish Times*, 23 January 1923, p. 4.
33   NAI, TSCH/3/S2027, Northern Ireland Boundary: Secret Document, 1922–1924, Memorandum from Kevin O'Shiel, undated.

34 Ibid.
35 Cousins, 'Without a "Dog's Chance"', pp. 222–3.
36 *Belfast News-Letter*, 8 December 1922, p. 8.
37 *Belfast Telegraph*, 24 October 1922, p. 4.
38 NAI, TSCH/3/S2027, Northern Ireland Boundary: Secret Document, 1922–1924, Letter sent by Sean Milroy to O'Shiel on 8 December 1922.
39 Ibid., Memorandum from O'Shiel with details of reports from Bolton Waller on 10 January 1923.
40 Ibid., Memorandum from Kevin O'Shiel to each member of the Executive Council on 10 February 1923.
41 *Belfast Telegraph*, 26 January 1923, p. 6.
42 Ibid.
43 M. Hopkinson, *Green Against Green: The Irish Civil War* (Dublin: Gill & Macmillan, 2004), p. 251.
44 NAI, TSCH/3/S2027, Northern Ireland Boundary: Secret Document, 1922–1924, Memorandum from Kevin O'Shiel on 7 February 1923.
45 NAI, NEBB/1/3/1, Reports to North Eastern Boundary Bureau, Pamphlet F, North-East Ulster: The Boundary Position Explained.
46 Matthews, 'The Irish Boundary Crisis and the Reshaping of British Politics', p. 193.
47 NAI, TSCH/3/S2027, Northern Ireland Boundary: Secret Document, 1922–1924, Report from Kevin O'Shiel to each member of the Executive Council on 30 May 1923.
48 NAI, NEBB/1/3/4, Reports to the North Eastern Boundary Bureau Chairman, Memorandum on English Attitude regarding Boundary Commission, B.C. Waller, undated.
49 NAI, TSCH/3/S2027, Northern Ireland Boundary: Secret Document, 1922–1924, Memorandum from Kevin O'Shiel to each member of the Executive Council on 10 February 1923.
50 NAI, TSCH/3/S4743, Boundary Bureau: formation and winding up, North Eastern Boundary Bureau, Final Report, 26 February 1926.
51 See, for example, North Eastern Boundary Bureau article, 'Customs Barrier on the Border: What "Northern" Ireland Stands to Lose', in *Fermanagh Herald*, 23 December 1922, 3 and *Ulster Herald*, 23 December 1922, p. 7.
52 NAI, NEBB/1/3/1, Reports to North Eastern Boundary Bureau.
53 NAI, TSCH/3/S3342, North East Boundary Bureau: weekly bulletin.
54 North Eastern Boundary Bureau, Handbook of the Ulster Question.
55 NAI, Department of Agriculture (92/2/2305), Ordnance Survey Office, Preparation of Northern Ireland Population Map for North Eastern Boundary Bureau.
56 NAI, TSCH/3/S4743, Boundary Bureau: formation and winding up, North Eastern Boundary Bureau, Final Report on 26 February 1926.
57 PRONI, CAB 4/67, Letter from Wilfrid Spender to A.W. Hungerford, 11 January 1923.
58 PRONI D1327/24/3, Bundle of Documents Relating to the Co-ordination by Unionist Headquarters of the Efforts of Local Unionist Associations to Gather and Submit Evidence to the Irish Boundary Commission.
59 NAI, TSCH/3/S2027, Northern Ireland Boundary, Secret Document, 1922–1924, Report from Kevin O'Shiel to each member of the Executive Council on 30 May 1923.

60 *The Irish Statesman*, 18 December 1926, p. 354.
61 *The Observer*, 19 June 1921, p. 15.
62 NAI, TSCH/3/S2027, Northern Ireland Boundary, Secret Document, 1922–1924, Report of Possible Boundary Lines.
63 NAI, TSCH/3/S1801 C, Boundary Commission: general, including appointment of Eoin MacNeill and request for completion of Commission, Minutes of Executive Council Meeting on 5 June 1923.
64 See NAI, NEBB/1/3/4, Reports to the North Eastern Boundary Bureau Chairman.
65 NAI, TSCH/3/S2027, Northern Ireland Boundary, Secret Document, 1922–1924, Memorandum from Kevin O'Shiel to each member of the Executive Council on 2 March 1923.
66 See NAI, NEBB/1/3/3, Reports to the North Eastern Boundary Bureau Chairman.
67 NAI, NEBB/1/3/3, Reports to the North Eastern Boundary Bureau Chairman, Report from Bolton C. Waller, undated.
68 Matthews, 'The Irish Boundary Crisis and the Reshaping of British Politics', p. 367.
69 NAI, NEBB/1/3/3, Reports to the North Eastern Boundary Bureau Chairman, Report from Bolton C. Waller, undated.
70 Murray, *The Irish Boundary Commission and its Origins*, p. 241.
71 E. Goldstein, 'Partition and Peacemaking after the Great War', in N.C. Fleming and J.H. Murphy (eds), *Ireland and Partition: Contexts and Consequences* (Clemson: Clemson University Press, 2021), p. 45.
72 Ibid., pp. 45–6.
73 Ibid., p. 45.
74 NAI, TSCH/3/S2027, Northern Ireland Boundary, Secret Document, 1922–1924, Report A, Memorandum on European Precedents for the North Eastern Boundary Bureau by Bolton Waller, undated.
75 Ibid.
76 Ibid.
77 Ibid., Memorandum from Kevin O'Shiel with details of reports from Bolton Waller on 10 January 1923.
78 Murray, *The Irish Boundary Commission and its Origins*, pp. 242–3.
79 NAI, NEBB/1/3/4, Reports to the North Eastern Boundary Bureau Chairman, Memorandum on English Attitude regarding Boundary Commission, B.C. Waller, undated.
80 Ibid., Report on Visit to South and East Down and Newry, Hugh A. MacCartan, 7 April 1923.
81 Ibid., Report on Visit to Derry and Belfast, Hugh A. MacCartan, 20 March 1923.
82 *Irish Independent*, 11 May 1923, p. 4.
83 NAI, NEBB/1/3/4, Reports to the North Eastern Boundary Bureau Chairman, Report on Visit to South and East Down and Newry, Hugh A. MacCartan, 7 April 1923.
84 NAI, TSCH/3/S1801 C, Boundary Commission: general, including appointment of Eoin MacNeill and request for completion of Commission, Minutes of Executive Council Meeting on 12 May 1923.
85 *Evening Herald*, 12 May 1923, p. 1.
86 NAI, TSCH/3/S1801 C, Boundary Commission: general, including appointment of

Eoin MacNeill and request for completion of Commission, Boundary Commission Memorandum, Secret and Confidential (June 1923).
87 Ibid.
88 NAI, TSCH/3/S2027, Northern Ireland Boundary, Secret Document, 1922–1924, Report from Kevin O'Shiel to each member of the Executive Council on 30 May 1923.
89 NAI, TSCH/3/S1801 C, Boundary Commission: general, including appointment of Eoin MacNeill and request for completion of Commission, Boundary Commission Memorandum, Secret and Confidential (June 1923).
90 Middlemas (ed.), *Thomas Jones: Whitehall Diary: Volume III*, p. 223.
91 NAI, TSCH/3/S2027, Northern Ireland Boundary: Secret Document, 1922–1924, Memo from O'Shiel to each member of the Executive Council on 21 April 1923.
92 G. J. Hand, 'MacNeill and the Boundary Commission', in F.X. Martin and F.J. Byrne (eds), *The Scholar Revolutionary: Eoin MacNeill, 1867–1945, and the Making of the New Ireland* (Shannon: Irish University Press, 1973), p. 200.
93 Ibid., p. 210.
94 Ibid., pp. 210–11.
95 For details of MacNeill's life, see C. Mulvagh and E. Purcell (eds), *Eoin MacNeill: The Pen and the Sword* (Cork: Cork University Press, 2022), and P. Maume and T.C. Edwards, *Dictionary of Irish Biography*, available from http://dib.cambridge.org/, accessed on 14 September 2024.
96 Hand, 'MacNeill and the Boundary Commission', p. 210.
97 D. Macardle, *The Irish Republic: A Documented Chronicle of the Anglo-Irish Conflict and the Partitioning of Ireland, with a Detailed Account of the Period 1916–1923* (London: Victor Gollancz Ltd, 1937), p. 898.
98 Matthews, 'The Irish Boundary Crisis and the Reshaping of British Politics', p. 212.
99 NAI, TSCH/3/S1801 P, Boundary Commission: index to dates and conferences, 1921–1925, 7 August 1923.
100 UCD Archives, Eoin MacNeill Papers LA1/F, 290, Speech by Eoin MacNeill in May 1927.
101 Hand, 'MacNeill and the Boundary Commission', p. 216, based on interview with McGilligan in 1967. Hand was McGilligan's student.
102 NAI, TSCH/3/S1801 C, Boundary Commission: general, including appointment of Eoin MacNeill and request for completion of Commission, Letter from Tim Healy to Duke of Devonshire on 19 July 1923.
103 Ibid., Letter from Duke of Devonshire to Tim Healy on 25 July 1923.
104 Middlemas (ed.), *Thomas Jones: Whitehall Diary: Volume III*, p. 223.
105 See, for example, NAI, FIN/1/2171, North Eastern Boundary Bureau: expenses in connection with Six-County elections, and NAI, FIN/1/1341, Publicity: estimated expenditure on propaganda work in connection with Boundary Commission for some of the costs involved for the Free State government.

CHAPTER 4

1 NAI, NEBB/1/3/4, Reports to the North Eastern Boundary Bureau Chairman, Report on Visit to South and East Down and Newry, Hugh A. MacCartan, 7 April 1923.

2 NAI, Department of an Taoiseach, S1955A, Boundary with Northern Ireland, Customs Barrier, General, 14 February 1923.
3 O. McGee, *Arthur Griffith* (Dublin: Merrion Press, 2015), pp. 173-4.
4 *Belfast News-Letter*, 15 January 1921, p. 4.
5 For a detailed account on the Belfast Boycott, see Moore, *Birth of the Border*, pp. 36-7 and pp. 119-26.
6 Bardon, *A History of Ulster*, p. 485.
7 *Binghamton Press and Leader*, 26 July 1921, p. 1.
8 *The Times*, 14 December 1921, p. 15.
9 *Belfast News-Letter*, 8 December 1921, p. 4.
10 *The Northern Whig and Belfast Post*, 8 December 1921, p. 5.
11 NAI, Department of an Taoiseach, S1095, Belfast Boycott, 30 January 1922.
12 See NAUK, CUST 49/617, Negotiations concerning setting up of Customs barrier between Irish Free State and Northern Ireland: transfer of administration of customs and excise services to provisional government.
13 See NAI, NEBB/1/3/3, Reports to the North Eastern Boundary Bureau Chairman, Memorandum by Joseph Johnston, 'The Boundary and a land customs frontier', November 1922.
14 Ibid., Memorandum by Joseph Johnston, 'Economic Unity between Political Areas', 28 November 1922.
15 Ibid.
16 Ibid., Memorandum by Joseph Johnston, 'Why Mr. Pollock's "Zollverein" is unacceptable', 28 November 1922.
17 *The Irish Times*, 30 July 1971, p. 11.
18 NAI, TSCH/3/S2027, Northern Ireland Boundary, Secret Document, 1922–1924, Memorandum from Joseph Johnston, 'Suggested modifications of schedules of Customs and Excise Duties and Free State fiscal policy and North East Ulster', February 1923.
19 PRONI, D921/4/5/1, Newspaper Clippings and Printed Booklets, 'If "Ulster" Contracts Out: The Economic Case against Partition', Undated.
20 *The Economist*, 4 November 1922, p. 843.
21 *The Economist*, 9 December 1922, p. 1067.
22 *The Times*, 1 January 1923, p. 12.
23 NAI, Department of an Taoiseach, S1955A, Boundary with Northern Ireland, Customs Barrier, General, 3 January 1923.
24 Ibid., 14 February 1923.
25 Ibid., 15 February 1923.
26 NAI, TSCH/3/S2027, Northern Ireland Boundary, Secret Document, 1922–1924, Memorandum from Kevin O'Shiel on 7 February 1923.
27 Hopkinson, *Green Against Green*, p. 273.
28 According to the Central Statistics Office, £30,000,000 in May 1923 is the equivalent to just under €2 billion in August 2024, see https://visual.cso.ie/?body=entity/cpicalculator, accessed on 16 September 2024.
29 Hopkinson, *Green Against Green*, p. 273.
30 *The Irish Times*, 10 March 1923, p. 7.

31 Ibid., p. 8.
32 *The Irish Times*, 3 March 1923, p. 7.
33 *The Northern Whig and Belfast Post*, 3 March 1923, p. 6.
34 Murray, *The Irish Boundary Commission and its Origins*, p. 150.
35 NAI, NEBB/1/3/3, Reports to the North Eastern Boundary Bureau Chairman, Memorandum by Joseph Johnston, 'Why Mr. Pollock's "Zollverein" is unacceptable', 28 November 1922.
36 NAI, NEBB/1/3/4, Reports to the North Eastern Boundary Bureau Chairman, Memorandum by Joseph Johnston on the effect of the Customs Barrier on marketing centres near the Border, March 1923.
37 Ibid., Memorandum by Joseph Johnston, 'Some Irish Commercial Centres and Their Hinterlands', 28 March 1923.
38 Ibid., Memorandum by Joseph Johnston, 'The Development of Donegal', March 1923.
39 NAI, TSCH/3/S2027, Northern Ireland Boundary, Secret Document, 1922–1924, Memorandum from Joseph Johnston, 'Suggested modifications of schedules of Customs and Excise Duties and Free State fiscal policy and North East Ulster', February 1923.
40 Ibid., Memorandum from Kevin O'Shiel to each member of the Executive Council, 19 February 1923.
41 Ibid., 2 March 1923.
42 NAI, NEBB/1/3/4, Reports to the North Eastern Boundary Bureau Chairman, Report by Hugh A. MacCartan on Visit to Derry and Belfast, 20 March 1923.
43 UCD Archives, Ernest Blythe Papers, P24/70, Memorandum by Ernest Blythe on Policy in Regard to the North East, 9 August 1922.
44 NAUK, HO 267/49, Customs & Excise, March 1923.
45 *The Irish Times*, 23 February 1923, p. 5.
46 PRONI, CAB 4/77, 16 April 1923.
47 C. Nash, B. Reid and B. Graham, *Partitioned Lives: The Irish Borderlands* (Surrey: Ashgate Publishing Company, 2013), p. 30.
48 NAUK, HO 267/49, Customs & Excise, March 1923.
49 Ibid.
50 D. Hall, 'Partition and County Louth', *Journal of the County Louth Archaeological and Historical Society*, vol. 27, no. 2 (2010), p. 264.
51 *The Irish Times*, 28 March 1923, p. 5.
52 P. Murray, 'Partition and the Irish Boundary Commission: A Northern Nationalist Perspective', *Clogher Record*, vol. 18, no. 2 (2004), p. 193.
53 Nash, Reid and Graham, *Partitioned Lives*, p. 30.
54 *The Irish Times*, 28 March 1923, p. 5.
55 *The Irish Times*, 7 April 1923, p. 3.
56 *The Irish Times*, 3 April 1923, p. 7.
57 *The Irish Times*, 2 April 1923, p. 5.
58 *The Times*, 13 September 1923, p. 11.
59 NAI, TSCH/3/S2027, Northern Ireland Boundary: Secret Document, 1922–1924, Report from Kevin O'Shiel to each member of the Executive Council, 17 July 1923.
60 Ibid., Memorandum from Kevin O'Shiel to each member of the Executive Council, 26 October 1923.

61 Nash, Reid and Graham, *Partitioned Lives*, p. 32.
62 PRONI, D1633/2/26, Diary of Lady Lillian Spender, 25 June 1923.
63 C. Nash, L. Dennis and B. Graham, 'Putting the border in place: customs regulations in the making of the Irish border, 1921–1945', *Journal of Historical Geography*, vol. 36 (2010), p. 423.
64 Nash, Reid and Graham, *Partitioned Lives*, p. 32.
65 G.J. Hand, *Report of the Irish Boundary Commission 1925* (Shannon: Irish University Press, 1969), p. 72.
66 NAUK, CAB 61-157, Principal Property Owners, Traders, Lodging House-Keepers & Residents, Urban District of Warrenpoint, 12 March 1925.

CHAPTER 5

1   NAI, TSCH/3/S1801 E, Boundary Commission: general matters, Memorandum by Kevin O'Shiel, 'Boundary Question and the Conference', 11 February 1924.
2   Bardon, *A History of Ulster*, p. 500.
3   O'Callaghan, 'Old Parchment and Water', p. 30
4   *The Irish News*, 8 May 1924, p. 5.
5   J. Bardon, 'Belfast at its Zenith', *History Ireland*, vol. 1, no. 4 (1993), p. 48.
6   Cousins, '"Without a Dog's Chance"', p. 313, and J. Thompson, 'A Century of Water from the Mournes: A Concise History', *Your Place & Mine*, BBC Northern Ireland, available at https://www.bbc.co.uk/northernireland/yourplaceandmine/down/A1068518.shtml, accessed on 21 September 2024.
7   *The Irish Times*, 11 October 1923, p. 7.
8   See NAUK, CAB 61-127, Portadown Banbridge Joint Waterworks Board.
9   PRONI, D1327/24/3, Bundle of Documents Relating to the Co-ordination by Unionist Headquarters of the Efforts of Local Unionist Associations to Gather and Submit Evidence to the Irish Boundary Commission, Loyalists case for Londonderry city by John Scott, Undated.
10 PRONI, D2991/B/1/23, Cahir Healy Papers, Minutes of Enniskillen Branch of National League, 1928–1939, Evidence of Cahir Healy before the Boundary Commission.
11 NAI, NEBB/1/3/4, Reports to the North Eastern Boundary Bureau Chairman, Report on Visit to South and East Down and Newry by Hugh A. MacCartan, 7 April 1923.
12 Trinity College Dublin (hereafter TCD), E.M. Stephens Papers, IE TCD MS 4239, File 1, Disabilities of Northern Minorities, undated.
13 *The Irish News*, 30 July 1924, p. 6.
14 TCD, E.M. Stephens Papers, IE TCD MS 4238, File 5, Possible basis for union, January 1924.
15 M. Farrell, *Northern Ireland: The Orange State* (London: Pluto Press, 1980), p. 25.
16 O'Leary, '"Cold House"', p. 822.
17 P. Buckland, *Irish Unionism 2: Ulster Unionism and the Origins of Northern Ireland 1886–1922* (Dublin: Gill & Macmillan, 1973), p. 142.
18 Farrell, *Northern Ireland*, p. 25.
19 Grant, *Derry: The Irish Revolution*, p. 94.
20 Buckland, *The Factory of Grievance*, p. 229.

21 PRONI, D2991/B/1/23, Cahir Healy Papers, Minutes of Enniskillen Branch of National League, 1928–1939, Evidence of Cahir Healy before the Boundary Commission.
22 PRONI, D1327/24/3, Bundle of Documents Relating to the Co-ordination by Unionist Headquarters of the Efforts of Local Unionist Associations to Gather and Submit Evidence to the Irish Boundary Commission, Statement for Irish Boundary Commission Chiefly Concerning Strabane and its Trade.
23 *Donegal News*, 3 February 1923, p. 5.
24 J. O'Brien, *Discrimination in Northern Ireland, 1920–1939: Myth or Reality?* (Newcastle upon Tyne: Cambridge Scholars Publishing, 2010), p. 10.
25 *Donegal News*, 3 February 1923, p. 5.
26 Bardon, *A History of Ulster*, p. 501.
27 B.M. Walker, *A Political History of the Two Irelands* (Basingstoke: Palgrave Macmillan, 2012), p. 51.
28 *Ulster Herald*, 7 July 1923, p. 5.
29 O'Brien, *Discrimination in Northern Ireland*, p. 12.
30 Bardon, *A History of Ulster*, p. 501.
31 J. Whyte, 'How much discrimination was there under the unionist regime, 1921-68?', in T. Gallagher and J. O'Connell (eds), *Contemporary Irish Studies* (Manchester: Manchester University Press, 1983), available at CAIN Web Service, https://cain.ulster.ac.uk/issues/discrimination/whyte.htm#chap1, accessed on 21 September 2024.
32 TCD, E.M. Stephens Papers, IE TCD MS 4239, File 1, Disabilities of Northern Minorities, undated.
33 *Ulster Herald*, 29 September 1923, p. 5.
34 B. O'Leary, *A Treatise of Northern Ireland, Volume II: Control* (Oxford: Oxford University Press, 2019), p. 41.
35 PRONI, D2991/B/1/23, Cahir Healy Papers, Minutes of Enniskillen Branch of National League, 1928–1939, Evidence of Cahir Healy before the Boundary Commission.
36 NAI, TSCH/3/S1801 E, Boundary Commission: general matters, Memorandum by Kevin O'Shiel, 'Boundary Question and the Conference', 11 February 1924.
37 NAI, NEBB/1/3/4, Reports to the North Eastern Boundary Bureau Chairman, Report on Visit to Derry and Belfast by Hugh A. McCartan, 20 March 1923.
38 NAUK, CAB 61-113, Newry Union (Armagh), Proposed Evidence of Reverend Felix Canon McNally, PP, Upper Kilevey, County Armagh and Catholic Chaplain to the Newry Union Workhouse.
39 PRONI, D921/3/6/1, John Henry Collins Papers, Boundary Commission, Preliminary Brief for Counsel on behalf of Inhabitants of Newry, Town of Newry.
40 NAUK, CAB 61-115, Newry Chamber of Commerce, Observations of Newry Chamber of Commerce, Newry No. Rural District Council (Down) and Newry No. 2 Rural District Council (Armagh).
41 NAI, NEBB/1/3/4, Reports to the North Eastern Boundary Bureau Chairman, Report on Visit to South and East Down and Newry by Hugh A. MacCartan, 7 April 1923.
42 Ibid..
43 Ibid., Report on Visit to Derry and Belfast by Hugh A. McCartan, 20 March 1923.
44 NAI, TSCH/3/S1801 C, Boundary Commission: general, including appointment of Eoin

MacNeill and request for completion of Commission, Letter from Kevin O'Shiel to W.T. Cosgrave on reply to British Government's boundary letter, 5 October 1923.
45   NAI, TSCH/3/S1801 H, Boundary Commission: appointment of Mr Justice Feetham as Chairman, Notes prepared for W.T. Cosgrave in connection with Seán Milroy motion and Thomas Johnson's amendment in Dáil Éireann, Delay in Carrying out Article 12.
46   NAI, TSCH/3/S1801 C, Boundary Commission: general, including appointment of Eoin MacNeill and request for completion of Commission, Extract from letter from Eoin MacNeill to Kevin O'Higgins from London, 2 November 1923.
47   See NAI, TSCH/3/S1801 P, Boundary Commission: index to dates and conferences, 1921–1925.
48   PRONI, FIN/18/4/309, Boundary Commission, Position Created by Proposed Establishment of The Ulster Boundary: Historical Outline by the Government of Northern Ireland, 8 October 1923.
49   Ibid.
50   Cousins, '"Without a Dog's Chance"', pp. 370–1.
51   PRONI, D2991/B/1/23, Cahir Healy Papers, Minutes of Enniskillen Branch of National League, 1928–1939, Evidence of Cahir Healy before the Boundary Commission.
52   NAI, TSCH/3/S1801 C, Boundary Commission: general, including appointment of Eoin MacNeill and request for completion of Commission, Memorandum by North Eastern Boundary Bureau, 'Uncertainty after British General Election', 13 December 1923.
53   Ibid.
54   Ibid.
55   Conservation with Denis Gwynn in the *Daily Herald*, February 1924, quoted in D. Torrance, *The Wild Men: The Remarkable Story of Britain's First Labour Government* (London: Bloomsbury Publishing, 2024), p. 179.
56   *The Irish News*, 25 January 1924, p. 5.
57   Murray, *The Irish Boundary Commission and its Origins*, p. 128.
58   Torrance, *The Wild Men*, p. 179.
59   NAUK, HO 463600/23, Irish Boundary: Publication of Correspondence, Letter from J.H. Thomas to Tim Healy, 24 January 1924.
60   Fanning et al., *Documents on Irish Foreign Policy: Volume 2*, Gearoid McGann (President's Office) to each member of the Executive Council, Hugh Kennedy and Diarmuid O'Hegarty, enclosing a memorandum (Copy) by William T. Cosgrave on the proposed Boundary Conference, 17 January 1924.
61   Matthews, 'The Irish Boundary Crisis and the Reshaping of British Politics', p. 244.
62   Fanning et al., *Documents on Irish Foreign Policy: Volume 2*, Gearoid McGann (President's Office) to each member of the Executive Council, Hugh Kennedy and Diarmuid O'Hegarty, enclosing a memorandum (Copy) by William T. Cosgrave on the proposed Boundary Conference, 17 January 1924.
63   UCD Archives, Ernest Blythe Papers, P24/156, Letter from (E.M. Stephens) Secretary of North Eastern Boundary Bureau on W.T. Cosgrave's memorandum, 18 January 1924.
64   Fanning et al., *Documents on Irish Foreign Policy: Volume 2*, Rough notes by Diarmuid O'Hegarty on the conference held to discuss the forthcoming meeting in London on the Boundary Question, 28 January 1924.

65 Hand, 'MacNeill and the Boundary Commission', p. 214.
66 Fanning et al., *Documents on Irish Foreign Policy: Volume 2*, Rough notes by Diarmuid O'Hegarty on the conference held to discuss the forthcoming meeting in London on the Boundary Question, 28 January 1924.
67 Matthews, 'The Irish Boundary Crisis and the Reshaping of British Politics', pp. 243–4.
68 Middlemas (ed.), *Thomas Jones: Whitehall Diary: Volume III*, p. 226.
69 NAI, TSCH/3/S1801 E, Boundary Commission: general matters, Executive Council Meeting, 12 February 1924.
70 UCD Archives, Eoin MacNeill Papers LA1/F, 295, Manuscript notes for a speech on the question of shelving the Boundary Commission at the English government's suggestion, undated.
71 NAI, TSCH/3/S1801 E, Boundary Commission: general matters, Executive Council Meeting, 12 February 1924.
72 PRONI, D1507C/7, Lady Carson Non-Irish Papers, Diary entry, 3 February 1924.
73 NAI, TSCH/3/S1801 E, Boundary Commission: general matters, Letter from High Commissioner's Office to Cosgrave, 15 February 1924.
74 PRONI, CAB 4/100, 15 February 1924.
75 *The Spectator*, 23 February 1924, p. 5.
76 See M.G. Valiulis, 'The "Army Mutiny" of 1924 and the Assertion of Civilian Authority in Independent Ireland', *Irish Historical Studies*, vol. 23, no. 92 (1983).
77 NAI, TSCH/3/S3342, North-East Boundary Bureau: weekly bulletin, North Eastern Boundary Bureau, The Weekly Digest, 24 March 1924.
78 PRONI, CAB 4/107, 26 March 1924.
79 PRONI, CAB 4/110, 15 April 1924.
80 PRONI, CAB 6/31 – Military and police, general correspondence file, October 1922 – December 1922, Letter from Arthur Solly-Flood to James Craig on 8 November 1922.
81 Matthews, 'The Irish Boundary Crisis and the Reshaping of British Politics', pp. 188–9.
82 PRONI, CAB 4/109, Notes of Interview in the Chancellor of the Exchequer's Room, House of Commons, 11 April 1924.
83 *The Morning Post* article quoted in *Belfast Telegraph*, 24 April 1924, p. 4.
84 Ibid.
85 Middlemas (ed.), *Thomas Jones: Whitehall Diary: Volume III*, p. 230.
86 Ibid., pp. 226–7
87 Fanning et al., *Documents on Irish Foreign Policy: Volume 2*, Rough notes by Kevin O'Shiel of a conference held in the President's Room with the Governor General, 30 January 1924.
88 M. Laffan, *Judging Cosgrave: The Foundation of the Irish State* (Dublin: Royal Irish Academy, 2014), p. 263.
89 Matthews, 'The Irish Boundary Crisis and the Reshaping of British Politics', p. 247.
90 NAUK, HO 463600/23, Irish Boundary: Publication of Correspondence, Letter from Tim Healy to J.H. Thomas, 15 March 1924.
91 Ibid., Letter from J.H. Thomas to Tim Healy, 1 April 1924 and Letter from Tim Healy to J.H. Thomas, 7 April 1924.
92 Middlemas (ed.), *Thomas Jones: Whitehall Diary: Volume III*, p. 228.

93   *Éire*, 8 March 1924, p. 2, and Matthews, 'The Irish Boundary Crisis and the Reshaping of British Politics', pp. 246–7.
94   Middlemas (ed.), *Thomas Jones: Whitehall Diary: Volume III*, p. 229.
95   TCD, E.M. Stephens Papers, IE TCD MS 4238, File 5, Possible basis for union, January 1924.
96   *The Northern Whig and Belfast Post*, 2 June 1924, p. 6.
97   C. O'Halloran, *Partition and the Limits of Irish Nationalism* (Dublin: Gill & Macmillan, 1987), p. 112.
98   *Westminster Gazette*, 2 October 1924, p. 2.

CHAPTER 6

1   K. Middlemas and J. Barnes, *Baldwin: A Biography* (London: Weidenfeld and Nicolson, 1969), p. 270, and Matthews, 'The Irish Boundary Crisis and the Reshaping of British Politics', p. 297 (quoting Lord Halifax Papers, Letter from Stanley Baldwin to Edward Wood, 6 September 1924).
2   Matthews, 'The Irish Boundary Crisis and the Reshaping of British Politics', p. 273.
3   Hand, 'MacNeill and the Boundary Commission', p. 217.
4   Middlemas (ed.), *Thomas Jones: Whitehall Diary: Volume III*, p. 230.
5   PRONI, CAB 4/114, 12 May 1924.
6   UCD Archives, Ernest Blythe Papers, P24/129, Letter from James MacNeill to W.T. Cosgrave, 13 May 1924.
7   Mansergh, *The Unresolved Question*, p. 234.
8   Matthews, 'The Irish Boundary Crisis and the Reshaping of British Politics', p. 274.
9   Hand, 'MacNeill and the Boundary Commission', p. 219. Hand spoke to Father John Ryan who made the claim, and who told Hand his source for this statement was MacNeill himself.
10   NAI, TSCH/3/S1801 H, Boundary Commission: appointment of Mr Justice Feetham as Chairman, Note, undated and unnamed.
11   D.J. Murphy, *Australian Dictionary of Biography*, available from https://adb.anu.edu.au/biography/givens-thomas-6395, accessed on 26 September 2024.
12   See Bodleian Archives, Richard Feetham Papers, MSS. Afr. s. 1793.
13   O'Callaghan, 'Old Parchment and Water', p. 31.
14   PRONI, CAB 6/97, Mr Justice Feetham (Chairman of the Boundary Commission): Background Papers, A correspondent in Johannesburg, September 1924.
15   Biography of Richard Feetham at South African History Online, available at https://www.sahistory.org.za/people/richard-feetham, accessed on 26 September 2024.
16   B.K. Murray, *WITS: The 'Open' Years. A History of the University of the Witwatersrand, Johannesburg 1939–1959* (Johannesburg: Wits University Press, 2022), p. 322.
17   Hand, *Report of the Irish Boundary Commission*, p. x.
18   Matthews, 'The Irish Boundary Crisis and the Reshaping of British Politics', p. 273.
19   NAI, TSCH/3/S1801 H, Boundary Commission: appointment of Mr Justice Feetham as Chairman, Letter from Ramsay MacDonald to W.T. Cosgrave, 27 May 1924.
20   Bodleian Archives, Curtis Archive, MS. Curtis 89: Ireland, 1916–1924, Letter from Curtis to Churchill, 19 August 1924.

21 Fanning, *Fatal Path*, p. 91.
22 PRONI, CAB 4/116, 12 June 1924.
23 NAI, TSCH/3/S3342, North East Boundary Bureau: weekly bulletin, North Eastern Boundary Bureau, The Weekly Digest, 9 June 1924.
24 PRONI, CAB 4/112, 5 May 1924.
25 UCD Archives, Ernest Blythe Papers, P24/129, Letter from James MacNeill to W.T. Cosgrave, 13 May 1924.
26 PRONI, D3099/3/20/1/1-21, Letters and one Telegram to Lady Londonderry from Ramsay MacDonald, Letter from Ramsay MacDonald to Lady Londonderry, 5 August 1924.
27 Ibid., 12 August 1924.
28 PRONI, D3015/3/B/2, Volume of press cuttings [Irish 2], including *The Morning Post* leak on the Boundary Commission, *The Morning Post*, 29 September 1924.
29 TCD, E.M. Stephens Papers, IE TCD MS 4238, File 8, Letter sent by Hugh MacCartan to Bolton C. Waller, undated.
30 I. Gibbons, 'The Irish Policy of the First Labour Government', *Labour History Review*, vol. 72, no. 2 (2007), p. 175.
31 Fanning et al., *Documents on Irish Foreign Policy: Volume 2*, Extracts from a letter by James MacNeill to Desmond FitzGerald (Dublin), 8 April 1924.
32 Ibid., Handwritten minute from W.T. Cosgrave to Desmond FitzGerald, undated, but mid-April 1924.
33 M. Kennedy, *Ireland and the League of Nations, 1919–1946: International Relations, Diplomacy and Politics* (Dublin: Irish Academic Press, 1996), p. 16.
34 See NAI, TSCH/3/S1801 P, Boundary Commission: index to dates and conferences, 1921–1925.
35 UCD Archives, Patrick McGilligan Papers, P35/173, Letter from S.P. Breathnach, secretary of Ministry of External Affairs to Desmond FitzGerald, 1 December 1924.
36 Middlemas (ed.), *Thomas Jones: Whitehall Diary: Volume III*, p. 226.
37 UCD Archives, Patrick McGilligan Papers, P35/173, Memorandum from Publicity Department with copy of *Morning Post* article, 17 December 1924.
38 Ibid., Letter from S.P. Breathnach, secretary of Ministry of External Affairs to Desmond FitzGerald, 1 December 1924, referring to Despatch from British Government, 4 November 1924.
39 Ibid., Draft of Suggested Reply to Despatch No: 628, 4 November 1924.
40 *The Scotsman*, 25 August 1924, p. 5.
41 Ibid., 27 August 1924, p. 6.
42 Ibid., 30 August 1924, p. 11.
43 *The Irish News*, 3 October 1924, p. 6.
44 M. Cronin, 'Projecting the Nation through Sport and Culture: Ireland, Aonach Tailteann and the Irish Free State, 1924-32', *Journal of Contemporary History*, vol. 38, no. 3 (July 2003), p. 396 and p. 401.
45 Ibid., p. 402.
46 *Daily Mail*, 3 July 1924, p. 9, and L. Schoen, 'The Irish Free State and the Electricity Industry, 1922–1927', in A. Bielenberg (ed.), *The Shannon Scheme and the Electrification of the Irish Free State* (Dublin: The Lilliput Press, 2002), p. 34.
47 Bodleian Archives, Archive of Robert Henry Brand, Baron Brand, Round Table: general

correspondence and articles, 1922–1925, MS. Brand 70/1, Letter from John Dove to Baron Brand, 12 April 1924.
48 J. Dove, 'Editor's Note: The Irish Boundary Question', *Round Table*, vol. 14, no. 55 (June 1924), p. 648.
49 Bodleian Archives, Curtis Archive, MS. Curtis 89: Ireland, 1916–1924, Letter from Curtis to Churchill, 19 August 1924.
50 Hand, 'MacNeill and the Boundary Commission', p. 220.
51 Bodleian Archives, Archive of Robert Henry Brand, Baron Brand, Round Table: general correspondence and articles, 1922–1925, MS. Brand 70/1, Letter from John Dove to Baron Brand, 2 July 1924.
52 NAUK, HO 463600/23, Irish Boundary: Publication of Correspondence, Letter from Arthur Henderson to the Duke of Abercorn, 29 April 1924.
53 Ibid., Letter from the Duke of Abercorn to Arthur Henderson, 10 May 1924.
54 *The Irish News*, 31 July 1924, p. 4.
55 Middlemas (ed.), *Thomas Jones: Whitehall Diary: Volume III*, p. 231.
56 *The Times*, 20 June 1924, p. 15.
57 Middlemas (ed.), *Thomas Jones: Whitehall Diary: Volume III*, p. 231.
58 PRONI, CAB 4/112, 5 May 1924.
59 Middlemas (ed.), *Thomas Jones: Whitehall Diary: Volume III*, p. 231.
60 *The Freeman's Journal*, 11 April 1924, p. 4.
61 Middlemas (ed.), *Thomas Jones: Whitehall Diary: Volume III*, pp. 231–2.
62 *The Times*, 20 June 1924, p. 15.
63 *The Irish News*, 23 July 1924, p. 5.
64 PRONI, FIN/18/4/309, Boundary Commission, Position Created by Proposed Establishment of, Letter from Wilfrid Spender to Hugh Pollock, 10 July 1924.
65 NAI, TSCH/3/S1801 H, Boundary Commission: appointment of Mr Justice Feetham as Chairman, Letter from Tim Healy to J.H. Thomas, 3 June 1924.
66 Ibid., Letter from W.T. Cosgrave to Ramsay MacDonald, 4 June 1924.
67 Ibid., Letter from Ramsay MacDonald to W.T. Cosgrave, 6 June 1924.
68 Ibid., Letter from W.T. Cosgrave to Ramsay MacDonald, 17 June 1924.
69 *Daily Mail*, 7 July 1924, p. 10.
70 *Belfast News-Letter*, 7 July 1924, p. 6.
71 PRONI, CAB 4/117, 4 July 1924.
72 Ibid..
73 Ibid.
74 Hand, 'MacNeill and the Boundary Commission', p. 224.
75 Bodleian Archives, Richard Feetham Papers, MSS. Afr. s. 1793, 7/2 1-5, Plebiscites Note by Lionel Curtis, 18 September 1924.
76 Matthews, 'The Irish Boundary Crisis and the Reshaping of British Politics', pp. 259–60.
77 Hand, 'MacNeill and the Boundary Commission', p. 240.
78 PRONI, FIN/18/4/309, Boundary Commission, Position Created by Proposed Establishment of, Memorandum by Richard Dawson Bates to Northern Ireland Cabinet, 'The Resources at Present at the Disposal of the Northern Government for Dealing with Disorder', 9 August 1924.

79 Ibid.
80 Ibid.
81 Ibid.
82 Matthews, 'The Irish Boundary Crisis and the Reshaping of British Politics', p. 261.
83 *The Irish News*, 31 January 1924, p. 5.
84 *Daily Mail*, 16 October 1924, p. 9.
85 *The Irish News*, 24 September 1924, p. 5.
86 *The Northern Whig and Belfast Post*, 26 April 1924, p. 12.
87 PRONI, CAB 4/112, 5 May 1924.
88 Matthews, 'The Irish Boundary Crisis and the Reshaping of British Politics', pp. 282–3.
89 PRONI, CAB 4/112, 5 May 1924.
90 PRONI, CAB 4/116, 12 June 1924.
91 *The Manchester Guardian*, 1 May 1924, p. 5.
92 NAI, TSCH/3/S3342, North East Boundary Bureau: weekly bulletin, North Eastern Boundary Bureau, The Weekly Digest, 3 May 1924.
93 NAI, TSCH/3/S1801 P, Boundary Commission: index to dates and conferences, 1921–1925, 11 August 1924.
94 *The Times*, 27 September 1924, p. 7.
95 Moore, '"I See All Your Difficulties"', p. 28.
96 Matthews, 'The Irish Boundary Crisis and the Reshaping of British Politics', p. 281.
97 Ibid., pp. 300–1.
98 *The Irish Times*, 23 October 1924, p. 7.
99 PRONI, D1507C/7, Lady Carson Non-Irish Papers, Diary entries, 28 and 29 August 1924.
100 PRONI, D3480/59/54, Arthur James Balfour to Robert Lynn, enclosing Letter from Lord Birkenhead to Arthur Balfour, 3 March 1922.
101 Ibid., Letter from Lord Arthur Balfour to Robert Lynn, 6 September 1924.
102 Matthews, 'The Irish Boundary Crisis and the Reshaping of British Politics', p. 302.
103 Ibid., pp. 305–6.
104 Middlemas (ed.), *Thomas Jones: Whitehall Diary: Volume III*, p. 233.
105 Hand, 'MacNeill and the Boundary Commission', p. 227.
106 Middlemas (ed.), *Thomas Jones: Whitehall Diary: Volume III*, p. 234.
107 PRONI, D1507C/7, Lady Carson Non-Irish Papers, Diary entry, 2 August 1924.
108 Ibid., 18 November 1924.
109 NAI, TSCH/3/S1801 J, Boundary Commission: agreement regarding composition of Commission, Résumé of the Proceedings of Conference in London regarding Boundary Question, 2 August 1924.
110 PRONI, FIN/18/4/309, Boundary Commission: Notes of Conference held at Colonial Office on the subject of the Irish Treaty, 2 August 1924.
111 NAI, TSCH/3/S1801 J, Boundary Commission: agreement regarding composition of Commission, Résumé of the Proceedings of, Conference in London regarding Boundary Question, 2 August 1924.
112 PRONI, FIN/18/4/309, Boundary Commission, Notes of Conference held at Colonial Office on the subject of the Irish Treaty, 2 August 1924.
113 NAI, TSCH/3/S1801 J, Boundary Commission: agreement regarding composition of

Commission, Résumé of the Proceedings of Conference in London regarding Boundary Question, 2 August 1924.
114   Ibid., Executive Council Meeting 3 August 1924.
115   Fanning et al., *Documents on Irish Foreign Policy: Volume 2*, Agreement supplementing Article Twelve of the Articles of Agreement for a Treaty between Great Britain and Ireland to which the force of law was given by the Irish Free State (Agreement) Act, 1922, and by the Constitution of the Irish Free State (Saorstdt Eireann) Act, 1922, 4 August 1924.
116   Matthews, 'The Irish Boundary Crisis and the Reshaping of British Politics', p. 293.
117   Ibid.
118   Middlemas (ed.), *Thomas Jones: Whitehall Diary: Volume III*, pp. 234–5.
119   Matthews, 'The Irish Boundary Crisis and the Reshaping of British Politics', pp. 296–8.
120   Middlemas (ed.), *Thomas Jones: Whitehall Diary: Volume III*, p. 235.
121   *The Times*, 30 September 1924, p. 12.
122   *Westminster Gazette*, 2 October 1924, p. 1.
123   *The Irish News*, 11 September 1924, p. 5.
124   *Daily Mail*, 9 September 1924, p. 8.
125   PRONI, D3015/3/B/2, Volume of press cuttings [Irish 2], including *The Morning Post* leak on the Boundary Commission, Press clippings of article from *The Morning Post*, 29 September 1924.
126   *The Times*, 7 June 1924, p. 12.
127   *The Irish News*, 3 September 1924, p. 5.
128   *The Times*, 13 September 1924, p. 12.
129   NAI, TSCH/3/S3342, North East Boundary Bureau: weekly bulletin, North Eastern Boundary Bureau, The Weekly Digest, 3 May 1924.
130   See NAI, TSCH/3/S1801 P, Boundary Commission: index to dates and conferences, 1921–1925, 13 August 1924 and 18 September 1924.
131   TCD, E.M. Stephens Papers, IE TCD MS 4238, File 8, Letter sent by Hugh MacCartan to Bolton C. Waller, undated.
132   NAI, TSCH/3/S1801 R, Boundary Commission: memoranda and statements by President and Ministers, Memorandum from W.T. Cosgrave, undated. *Hyacinth Halvey* was a comedy play by Lady Gregory about a man who tries unsuccessfully to attain a dishonourable reputation in a village but only succeeds in attracting praise and admiration.
133   TCD, E.M. Stephens Papers, IE TCD MS 4238, File 8, Letter sent by Hugh MacCartan to Bolton C. Waller, undated.
134   Ibid., North Eastern Boundary Bureau Memorandum, 1 September 1924.
135   *The Manchester Guardian*, 11 September 1924, p. 14.
136   *The Times*, 9 September 1924, p. 12, and *The Scotsman*, 9 September 1924, p. 5.
137   TCD, E.M. Stephens Papers, IE TCD MS 4238, File 8, Interview by Eamonn Duggan, Treaty signatory, on meaning of Article 12, undated.
138   NAI, TSCH/3/S1801 R, Boundary Commission: memoranda and statements by President and Ministers, Memorandum from W.T. Cosgrave, undated.
139   Ibid., Memorandum from Kevin O'Shiel to W.T. Cosgrave, 10 May 1924.
140   Ibid., Letter from Kevin O'Higgins to W.T. Cosgrave, 7 May 1924.

141 Ibid., Letter by Hugh Kennedy to W.T. Cosgrave, 9 May 1924.
142 Matthews, 'The Irish Boundary Crisis and the Reshaping of British Politics', p. 266.
143 Fanning et al., *Documents on Irish Foreign Policy: Volume 2*, Kevin O'Higgins to each member of the Executive Council, enclosing a memorandum on the Boundary Question, 25 September 1924.
144 Ibid., Report of the Committee appointed to consider an offer to Northern Ireland, with covering letter from Michael McDunphy to Ernest Blythe, 22 October 1924.
145 NAI, TSCH/3/S1801 P, Boundary Commission: index to dates and conferences, 1921–1925, 11 October 1924 and 13 October 1924.
146 Bowman, *De Valera and the Ulster Question*, p. 81.
147 *The Irish News*, 30 August 1924, p.4.
148 UCD Archives, Moss Twomey Papers P69/179, 123, 9 August 1924.
149 Cousins, '"Without a Dog's Chance"', p. 305.
150 Ibid., p. 373.
151 Bowman, *De Valera and the Ulster Question*, p. 84.
152 PRONI, D1507C/7, Lady Carson Non-Irish Papers, Diary entry, 31 October 1924.
153 Ibid., 28 September 1924.
154 PRONI, CAB 4/122, 30 September 1924.
155 Ibid.
156 Matthews, 'The Irish Boundary Crisis and the Reshaping of British Politics', p. 327.
157 Hand, 'MacNeill and the Boundary Commission', p. 230.
158 *The Northern Whig and Belfast Post*, 28 October 1939, p. 4.
159 See, for example, J.R. Fisher, *The End of the Irish Parliament* (London: Edward Arnold, 1911).
160 J.R. Fisher, 'Introduction', in *The Ulster Liberal Unionist Association: A Sketch of its History, 1885–1914* (Belfast: Ulster Reform Club, 1913), p. iii and p. v.
161 D. Ferriter, *Dictionary of Irish Biography*, available from http://dib.cambridge.org/, accessed on 3 October 2024.
162 *The Times*, 4 February 1924, p. 13.
163 *The Times*, 8 February 1924, p. 15.
164 St. J. Ervine, *Craigavon: Ulsterman* (London: George Allen & Unwin Ltd, 1949), p. 482.
165 NAUK, HO 463600/61, Remuneration of J.R. Fisher, Letter from R.R. Scott, Treasury to Under Secretary of State, Home Office, 15 January 1925.
166 NAI, TSCH/3/S4720 A, Boundary Commission: agreement with Great Britain, December 1925, Summary of Statements made at Meeting at Chequers between Stanley Baldwin, Kevin O'Higgins, Patrick McGilligan, John O'Byrne and James Craig, 29 November 1925.

CHAPTER 7

1 NAUK, CAB 61-161, Report of the Irish Boundary Commission, p. 26.
2 Ibid., p. 29.
3 UCD Archives, Eoin MacNeill Papers LA1/F, 290, Speech by Eoin MacNeill in May 1927.
4 Hand, 'MacNeill and the Boundary Commission', p. 231.
5 Matthews, 'The Irish Boundary Crisis and the Reshaping of British Politics', pp. 367–8.

6   NAUK, CAB 61-1, Boundary Commission Minute Book, 6 November 1924.
7   Ibid.
8   T. Hallett, 'Eoin MacNeill and the Irish Boundary Commission', in Mulvagh and Purcell (eds), *Eoin MacNeill: The Pen and the Sword*, p. 210.
9   Matthews, 'The Irish Boundary Crisis and the Reshaping of British Politics', p. 366.
10 Ervine, *Craigavon: Ulsterman*, pp. 498–9.
11 NAUK, CAB 61-1, Boundary Commission Minute Book, 6 November 1924.
12 PRONI, FIN/18/4/309, Boundary Commission, Position Created by Proposed Establishment of, Letter from Wilfrid Spender to F.B. Bourdillon, 7 November 1924.
13 *The Northern Whig and Belfast Post*, 8 December 1924, p. 7.
14 See PRONI, D1327/24/3, Bundle of Documents Relating to the Co-ordination by Unionist Headquarters of the Efforts of Local Unionist Associations to Gather and Submit Evidence to the Irish Boundary Commission.
15 NAUK, CAB 61-1, Boundary Commission Minute Book, 7 November 1924.
16 Hallett, 'Eoin MacNeill and the Irish Boundary Commission', pp. 210–11, and NAUK, CAB 61-1, Boundary Commission Minute Book, 28 November 1924.
17 NAI, TSCH/3/S1801 L, Boundary Commission: operations of Commission and preparation of Irish Free State evidence, Nov. 1924–Feb. 1925, Statement of Saorstat's Case sent to Boundary Commission, 20 November 1924.
18 TCD, E.M. Stephens Papers, IE TCD MS 4238, File 3, Shorthand notebook of E.M. Stephens, 4 December 1924.
19 NAUK, CAB 61-161, Report of the Irish Boundary Commission, Appendix I: Hearing of Counsel Representing the Government of the Irish Free State, 4 and 5 December 1924, p. 9.
20 Ibid., p. 8.
21 Ibid., p. 9.
22 Ibid., p. 22.
23 Ibid., p. 26.
24 PRONI, FIN/18/4/309, Boundary Commission, Position Created by Proposed Establishment of, Opinion of the Attorney General in Regard to the Boundary Commission. Presented to Northern Ireland Cabinet, 8 November 1924.
25 NAUK, CAB 61-161, Report of the Irish Boundary Commission, Appendix I: Hearing of Counsel Representing the Government of the Irish Free State, 4 and 5 December 1924, p. 29.
26 NAUK, CAB 61-1, Boundary Commission Minute Book, 7 December 1924.
27 Hand, 'MacNeill and the Boundary Commission', pp. 232–3.
28 PRONI, HA/32/1/21, Boundary Commission, Reports on Activities of Commission, Secretary, Northern Ministry of Home Affairs to Stephen Tallents, 6 December 1924.
29 NAUK, CAB 61-161, Report of the Irish Boundary Commission, p. 9.
30 *The Irish Times*, 19 December 1924, p. 7.
31 Cousins, '"Without a Dog's Chance"', pp. 312–13.
32 *The Irish Times*, 19 December 1924, p. 7.
33 Hand, 'MacNeill and the Boundary Commission', p. 234.
34 PRONI, HA/32/1/21, Boundary Commission, Reports on movements of Boundary Commission members, E. Gilfillan, DI for IG, IG's Office, RUC, Belfast, 15 January 1925.

35 NAI, TSCH/3/S1801 L, Boundary Commission: operations of Commission and preparation of Irish Free State evidence, Nov. 1924–Feb. 1925, Report by E.M. Stephens, 22 December 1924.
36 Ibid.
37 PRONI, HA/32/1/21, Boundary Commission, Reports on Activities of Commission, IG's Office, RUC, Belfast, 18 December 1924.
38 NAI, TSCH/3/S1801 L, Boundary Commission: operations of Commission and preparation of Irish Free State evidence, Nov. 1924-Feb. 1925, Report by E.M. Stephens, 22 December 1924.
39 Cousins, '"Without a Dog's Chance"', p. 316.
40 Ibid., p. 317.
41 *Belfast News-Letter*, 17 December 1924, p. 7.
42 PRONI, HA/32/1/21, Boundary Commission, Reports on movements of Boundary Commission members, E. Gilfillan, DI for IG, IG's Office, RUC, Belfast, 15 January 1925.
43 Hand, 'MacNeill and the Boundary Commission', p. 213.
44 *Derry Journal*, 22 December 1924, p. 5.
45 NAUK, CAB 61-1, Boundary Commission Minute Book, 27 January 1925.
46 Bodleian Archives, Richard Feetham Papers, MSS. Afr. s. 1793 – 7/2 1, Report of the Irish Boundary Commission: Representations Submitted.
47 NAUK, CAB 61-1, Boundary Commission Minute Book, 3 March 1925.
48 Hand, 'MacNeill and the Boundary Commission', p. 236.
49 NAI, TSCH/3/S1801 L, Boundary Commission: operations of Commission and preparation of Irish Free State evidence, Nov. 1924–Feb. 1925, Report by E.M. Stephens, 21 January 1925.
50 Ibid.
51 Ibid.
52 Ibid.
53 NAUK, CAB 61-124, Charles O'Neill, Statement from Charles O'Neill to Boundary Commission, 31 December 1924.
54 NAI, TSCH/3/S1801 L, Boundary Commission: operations of Commission and preparation of Irish Free State evidence, Nov. 1924–Feb. 1925, Letter from F.B. Bourdillon to Diarmuid O'Hegarty, 2 February 1925.
55 Ibid., Note by W.T. Cosgrave, 19 February 1925.
56 Ibid., Letter from Diarmuid O'Hegarty to F.B. Bourdillon, 19 February 1925.
57 PRONI, D1327/24/3, Bundle of Documents Relating to the Co-ordination by Unionist Headquarters of the Efforts of Local Unionist Associations to Gather and Submit Evidence to the Irish Boundary Commission, Letter from Wilfrid Spender to A.W. Hungerford, 12 February 1925.
58 Ibid., Letter from Wilfrid Spender to A.W. Hungerford, 2 February 1925.
59 PRONI, HA/32/1/21, Boundary Commission, Reports on Activities of Commission, IG's Office, RUC, Belfast, 23 February 1925.
60 Ibid., IG's Office, RUC, Belfast, 24 March 1925.
61 Bodleian Archives, Richard Feetham Papers, MSS. Afr. s. 1793 – 7/2 1, Report of the Irish Boundary Commission: Dates and Places of Sittings.

62   See, for example, a meeting where women were in attendance, PRONI, HA/32/1/17, Boundary Commission, General, Report by District Inspector's Office, RUC Enniskillen on Nationalist Deputation to British MPs, 15 September 1924.
63   P. Leary, *Unapproved Routes: Histories of the Irish Border, 1922–1972* (Oxford: Oxford University Press, 2016), p. 36.
64   Murray, *The Irish Boundary Commission and its Origins*, p. 108.
65   Ibid., p. 177.
66   NAUK, CAB 61-1, Boundary Commission Minute Book, 7 December 1925.
67   NAUK, CAB 61-120, Newry Urban District Council (Volume 2), 9 March 1925.
68   NAUK, CAB 61-158, Warrenpoint Urban District Council, 12 March 1925.
69   See NAUK, CAB 61-159, Summaries of Cases put forward in support of claims submitted to the Commission.
70   NAUK, CAB 61-119, Newry Urban District Council (Volume 1), 17 February 1925.
71   NAUK, CAB 61-113, Newry Union (Armagh).
72   NAUK, CAB 61-122, National Ex-Service Men of Omagh, 28 February 1925.
73   NAUK, CAB 61-67, Fermanagh Nationalist Committee, Volume 1.
74   NAUK, CAB 61-113, Newry Union (Down).
75   NAUK, CAB 61-115, Newry Chamber of Commerce.
76   NAUK, CAB 61-95, Londonderry Nationalist Registration Association.
77   *Fermanagh Herald*, 7 February 1925, p. 8 and PRONI, D2991/B/1/23, Cahir Healy Papers, Minutes of Enniskillen Branch of National League, 1928–1939, Evidence of Cahir Healy before the Boundary Commission.
78   NAUK, CAB 61-102, Rev. M. McGuire, Letter from Fr M. McGuire to Boundary Commission, 27 December 1924.
79   Ibid., Letter from Boundary Commission to Fr M. McGuire, 5 February 1925.
80   Hand, *Report of the Irish Boundary Commission*, p. 72.
81   NAUK, CAB-64, Fermanagh County Council: Volume 1, Evidence of Sir Basil Brooke before the Boundary Commission, 7 March 1925.
82   NAUK, CAB 61-115, Newry Chamber of Commerce, 24 March 1925.
83   NAUK, CAB 61-86, Kilkeel Rural District Council, 21 February 1925.
84   PRONI, D1327/24/3, Bundle of Documents Relating to the Co-ordination by Unionist Headquarters of the Efforts of Local Unionist Associations to Gather and Submit Evidence to the Irish Boundary Commission.
85   NAUK, CAB 61-115, Newry Chamber of Commerce, and CAB 61-157, Principal Property Owners, Traders, Lodging House-Keepers & Residents, Urban District of Warrenpoint.
86   Leary, *Unapproved Routes*, p. 31.
87   T.A.M. Dooley, 'From the Belfast Boycott to the Boundary Commission: Fears and Hopes in County Monaghan, 1920-26', *Clogher Record*, vol. 15, no. 1 (1994), p. 98.
88   NAUK, CAB 61-128, Presbytery of Raphoe, Resolution from meeting at St Johnston, Co. Donegal, 9 December 1924.
89   NAUK, CAB 61-159, Summaries of Cases put forward in support of claims submitted to the Commission.
90   Ibid.
91   PRONI, D1327/24/3, Bundle of Documents Relating to the Co-ordination by Unionist

Headquarters of the Efforts of Local Unionist Associations to Gather and Submit Evidence to the Irish Boundary Commission, Loyalists case for Londonderry city by John Scott, Undated.
92   Ibid.
93   NAUK, CAB 61, 155, Lt Col. F.T. Warburton, Letter from F.T. Warburton to Boundary Commission, 13 December 1924.
94   NAUK, CAB 61-67, Fermanagh Nationalist Committee, Volume 1.
95   PRONI, D2991/B/1/23, Cahir Healy Papers, Minutes of Enniskillen Branch of National League, 1928–1939, Evidence of Cahir Healy before the Boundary Commission.
96   NAUK, CAB 61-47, John Devine, Letter from John Devine and John O'Doherty to Boundary Commission, 27 February 1925.
97   PRONI, D1327/24/3, Bundle of Documents Relating to the Co-ordination by Unionist Headquarters of the Efforts of Local Unionist Associations to Gather and Submit Evidence to the Irish Boundary Commission, Representation from the Inhabitants of the City of Londonderry and the North West Liberties.
98   NAUK, CAB 61-161, Report of the Irish Boundary Commission, p. 61.
99   Dooley, 'From the Belfast Boycott to the Boundary Commission', p. 101.
100 PRONI, D1327/24/3, Bundle of Documents Relating to the Co-ordination by Unionist Headquarters of the Efforts of Local Unionist Associations to Gather and Submit Evidence to the Irish Boundary Commission, Letter from T.C. Wylie, Solicitor, 7, Castle Street, Londonderry to Hungerford on 11 February 1925.
101 Ibid., Statement of Committee of Donegal and Industrial Group for Boundary Commission.
102 NAUK, CAB 61-159, Summaries of Cases put forward in support of claims submitted to the Commission.
103 NAUK, CAB 61-106, Middletown, Committee of Inhabitants.
104 NAUK, CAB 61-157, Principal Property Owners, Traders, Lodging House-Keepers & Residents, Urban District of Warrenpoint, 12 March 1925.
105 NAUK, CAB 61-32, Bessbrook Spinning Company Ltd, 21 March 1925.
106 NAUK, CAB 61-115, Newry Chamber of Commerce.
107 NAUK, CAB 61-119, Newry Urban District Council, Volume 1, 17 February 1925.
108 NAUK, CAB 61-115, Newry Chamber of Commerce, 11 March 1925.
109 See for example NAUK, CAB 61-125, Pettigo Unionist Inhabitants.
110 NAUK, CAB 61-28, Belfast City and District Water Commissioners, 24 December 1924.
111 NAUK, CAB 61-76, P. O'Golain (Irish Free State Customs Service), Interview with P. O'Golain, 19 June 1925.
112 NAUK, CAB 61-109, Major R.L. Moore, 30 December 1924.
113 NAUK, CAB 61-125, Pettigo Unionist Inhabitants, 1 May 1925.
114 Dooley, 'From the Belfast Boycott to the Boundary Commission', p. 98.
115 PRONI, D1327/24/3, Bundle of Documents Relating to the Co-ordination by Unionist Headquarters of the Efforts of Local Unionist Associations to Gather and Submit Evidence to the Irish Boundary Commission, Loyalists case for Londonderry city by John Scott, Undated.
116 Ibid., Statement for Irish Boundary Commission Chiefly Concerning Strabane and its Trade.

117 See for example NAUK, CAB 61-119, Newry Urban District Council (Volume 1), 17 February 1925.
118 NAUK, CAB 61-24, Nationalist Inhabitants of Aughnacloy, Letter from T.J. Harbison to Boundary Commission, 1 June 1925.
119 NAUK, CAB 61-113, County Armagh Union Newry.
120 Ibid.
121 NAUK, CAB 61-115, Newry Chamber of Commerce, 11 March 1925.
122 NAUK, CAB 61-119, Newry Urban District Council vol. 1, Statement from Charles O'Hare, 17 February 1925
123 NAUK, CAB 61-110, Mullan Mills Limited, Letter from Francis O'Hanlon, Secretary Mullan Mills Ltd Boots Factory to Boundary Commission, 3 April 1925.
124 NAUK, CAB 61-81, Keady, Committee of Inhabitants of the Town End.
125 NAUK, CAB 61-119, Newry Urban District Council (Volume 1), 17 February 1925.
126 Ibid.
127 NAUK, CAB 61-55, Committee of Nationalist Inhabitants of East Down, 18 March 1925.
128 See for example, NAUK, CAB 61-146, Nationalist Inhabitants of Co. Tyrone, Volume 2.
129 NAUK, CAB 61-159, Summaries of Cases put forward in support of claims submitted to the Commission.
130 NAUK, CAB 61-74, J.M. Henry, Summary of Contentions to Boundary Commission from Joseph Henry as well as Maxwell I. Boyle and Samuel Cargill, 11 February 1925.
131 NAUK, CAB 61-134, Dr W.J. Smyth, Letter from William Johnson Smyth to Boundary Commission, 12 December 1924.
132 NAUK, CAB 61-108, Monaghan County Council, The Boundary Commission, Castleblayney Discussion, Newspaper cutting from *Impartial Reporter*, 7 May 1925.
133 Ibid., Letter from Boundary Commission to Monaghan County Council on 8 May 1925.
134 NAUK, CAB 61-157, Principal Property Owners, Traders, Lodging House-Keepers & Residents, Urban District of Warrenpoint, 12 March 1925.
135 NAI, TSCH/3/S1801 M, Boundary Commission: operations of Commission, March 1925 to May 1925, Report of E.M. Stephens, 24 March 1925.
136 NAUK, CAB 61-119, Newry Urban District Council (Volume 1), 17 February 1925.
137 PRONI, D2991/B/1/23, Cahir Healy Papers, Minutes of Enniskillen Branch of National League, 1928–1939, Evidence of Cahir Healy before the Boundary Commission.
138 PRONI, D1327/24/3, Bundle of Documents Relating to the Co-ordination by Unionist Headquarters of the Efforts of Local Unionist Associations to Gather and Submit Evidence to the Irish Boundary Commission.
139 O. Ozseker, *Forging the Border: Donegal and Derry in Times of Revolution* (Dublin: Merrion Press, 2019), p. 198.
140 PRONI, D1327/24/3, Bundle of Documents Relating to the Co-ordination by Unionist Headquarters of the Efforts of Local Unionist Associations to Gather and Submit Evidence to the Irish Boundary Commission, Statement of Committee of Donegal and Industrial Group for Boundary Commission.
141 Ozseker, *Forging the Border*, p. 200.
142 PRONI, D2991/B/1/23, Cahir Healy Papers, Minutes of Enniskillen Branch of National

League, 1928–1939, Some notes on the 'Case' presented to the Irish Boundary Commission from the Fermanagh County Council.
143 NAI, TSCH/3/S1801 M, Boundary Commission: operations of Commission, March 1925 to May 1925, Report of E.M. Stephens, 24 March 1925.
144 Ibid., Report of E.M. Stephens, 22 May 1925.
145 Ibid.
146 NAI, TSCH/3/S1801 N, Boundary Commission: operations of Commission June to July 1925, Report of Stephens, 2 June 1925.
147 Ibid.
148 Ibid., Report of Stephens, 22 June 1925.
149 NAI, TSCH/3/S1801 M, Boundary Commission: operations of Commission, March 1925 to May 1925, Report of E.M. Stephens, 28 April 1925.
150 Cousins, '"Without a Dog's Chance"', p. 323.
151 *Irish Independent*, 7 April 1925, p. 7.
152 Ibid., p. 6.
153 *The Times*, 8 April 1925, p. 8.
154 NAI, TSCH/3/S1801 M, Boundary Commission: operations of Commission, March 1925 to May 1925, Report of E.M. Stephens, 22 May 1925.
155 Ibid., Report of E.M. Stephens, 28 April 1925.
156 Ibid.
157 Ibid., Report of E.M. Stephens, 24 March 1925.
158 Hand, 'MacNeill and the Boundary Commission', p. 238.
159 NAI, TSCH/3/S1801 O, Boundary Commission: operations of Commission, including resignation of Eoin MacNeill, Résumé of Statement by Eoin MacNeill at Meeting of the Executive Council, 21 November 1925.
160 NAUK, CAB 61-73, H.D. Green, Evidence of H.D. Green, 30 June 1925.
161 Ervine, *Craigavon: Ulsterman*, pp. 498–500.
162 Ibid.
163 See TSCH/3/S1801 P, Boundary Commission: index to dates and conferences, 1921–1925.
164 NAI, TSCH/3/S1801 L, Boundary Commission: operations of Commission and preparation of Irish Free State evidence, Nov. 1924–Feb. 1925, Note by W.T. Cosgrave, 19 February 1925.
165 NAUK, CAB 61-131, Edward A. Saunderson and D. MacDonald, *Hard Border: Walking Through a Century of Partition* (Dublin: New Island Books, 2018), p. 16.
166 NAI, TSCH/3/S1801 M, Boundary Commission: operations of Commission, March 1925 to May 1925, Letter from Bourdillon to O'Hegarty on 7 May 1925.
167 NAI, TSCH/3/S1801 N, Boundary Commission: operations of Commission June to July 1925, Memorandums containing submissions with the Government of the Irish Free State, 9 July 1925.
168 NAI, TSCH/3/S1801 O, Boundary Commission: operations of Commission, including resignation of Eoin MacNeill, Provisional Copy of evidence given on behalf of the Irish Free State at Sitting of Boundary Commission, 25 August 1925.
169 Fanning et al., *Documents on Irish Foreign Policy: Volume 2*, Memorandum on the Boundary Commission (Probably by Hugh Kennedy), 19 September 1925.

170 Hand, 'MacNeill and the Boundary Commission', pp. 243-4.
171 Bodleian Archives, Richard Feetham Papers, MSS. Afr. s. 1793 – 6/1 29, Letter from Richard Feetham to his mother, 6 July 1925.

CHAPTER 8

1 NAI, TSCH/3/S1801 N, Boundary Commission: operations of Commission June to July 1925, Letter from F.B. Bourdillon to Diarmuid O'Hegarty, 8 June 1925.
2 NAI, TSCH/3/S4563 A, Boundary with Northern Ireland: administrative preparations in anticipation of determination of Boundary, Note of Meeting held at the Dominions Office to discuss administrative steps to be taken to give effect to the determination of the Irish Boundary Commission, 28 July 1925.
3 Ibid., Letter from Peadar MacMahon to Minister for Defence on 22 July 1925.
4 Ibid., Memorandum, A List of Statutory Rules and Orders administered by the Department of Agriculture and Technical Instruction, 2 September 1925.
5 Ibid., Letter sent from Deputy-Secretary of Department of Education to Diarmuid O'Hegarty, 15 September 1925.
6 Ibid., Memorandum from Department of Finance on Questions Connected with the Decision of the Boundary Commission, 11 September 1925.
7 Ibid.
8 NAI, NEBB/1/3/7, Reports of the North Eastern Boundary Bureau to the Minister for Justice, Memorandum from E.M. Stephens to Kevin O'Higgins, 'The Taking Over of Territory in Pursuance of the decision of the Boundary Commission', 12 October 1925.
9 PRONI, FIN/18/4/309, Boundary Commission, Position Created by Proposed Establishment of, Comments by Sir Ernest Clark on the Draft Letter addressed to Richard Best, undated.
10 PRONI, CAB/6/105, Colonel W.B. Spender, Opinion the Boundary Commission, Letter from Wilfrid Spender to C.H. Blackmore, 31 August 1925.
11 PRONI, CAB/9/Z/11/5, Boundary Commission, London Conference November to December 1925, Notes for James Craig for Interview with British Cabinet Committee, undated.
12 NAUK, CAB 61-161, Report of the Irish Boundary Commission, p. 14.
13 Ibid., pp. 65-8.
14 Murray, *The Irish Boundary Commission and its Origins*, p. 214.
15 Ibid., p. 217.
16 NAUK, CAB 61-161, Report of the Irish Boundary Commission, p. 32.
17 Hallett, 'Eoin MacNeill and the Irish Boundary Commission', p. 212.
18 NAI, TSCH/3/S1801 O, Boundary Commission: operations of Commission, including resignation of Eoin MacNeill, Résumé of Statement by Eoin MacNeill at the Meeting of the Executive Council on Saturday, 21 November 1925.
19 NAUK, CAB 61-161, Report of the Irish Boundary Commission, pp. 144-6.
20 Ibid., p. 146.
21 Rankin, 'The role of the Irish boundary commission in the entrenchment of the Irish border', p. 440.

22 Murray, *The Irish Boundary Commission and its Origins*, pp. 222–3.
23 NAUK, CAB 61-161, Report of the Irish Boundary Commission, p. 147.
24 Ibid., p. 150.
25 Hand, 'MacNeill and the Boundary Commission', p. 248.
26 Ibid., p. 250.
27 Hallett, 'Eoin MacNeill and the Irish Boundary Commission', p. 216.
28 Ibid., p. 216.
29 NAUK, CO537/1092, Letter by Stephen Tallents to John Anderson, 30 October 1925.
30 Middlemas (ed.), *Thomas Jones: Whitehall Diary: Volume III*, p. 236.
31 NAUK, CAB 61-1, Boundary Commission Minute Book, 5 November 1925.
32 See NAI, TSCH/3/S1801 P, Boundary Commission: index to dates and conferences, 1921–1925.
33 *Sunday Independent*, 6 September 1925, p. 1.
34 Matthews, 'The Irish Boundary Crisis and the Reshaping of British Politics', p. 390.
35 NAI, TSCH/3/S1801 O, Boundary Commission: operations of Commission, including resignation of Eoin MacNeill, Letter from Tim Healy to Eamonn Duggan, 10 October 1925.
36 *Daily Mail*, 6 November 1925, p. 9.
37 *The Morning Post*, 7 November 1925, p. 13.
38 Ibid., p. 12.
39 Hallett, 'Eoin MacNeill and the Irish Boundary Commission', p. 217.
40 *Derry People and Donegal News*, 14 November 1925, p. 4.
41 PRONI, HA/32/1/21, Boundary Commission, Reports on Activities of Commission, Strabane Nationalist Move, 19 November 1925.
42 *Strabane Chronicle*, 14 November 1925, p. 3.
43 See NAI, TSCH/3/S1801 O, Boundary Commission: operations of Commission, including resignation of Eoin MacNeill, Meeting of Executive Council, 11 November 1925, and *Irish Independent*, 14 November 1925, p. 7.
44 *Irish Independent*, 14 November 1925, p. 7.
45 *Daily Mail*, 16 November 1925, p. 9.
46 Middlemas (ed.), *Thomas Jones: Whitehall Diary: Volume III*, p. 237.
47 Dáil Éireann Debates, vol. 13, no. 2, 11 November 1925, available from www.oireachtasdebates.gov.ie, accessed on 15 October 2024.
48 Hallett, 'Eoin MacNeill and the Irish Boundary Commission', p. 218.
49 Hand, 'MacNeill and the Boundary Commission', p. 251.
50 NAUK, CAB 61-1, Boundary Commission Minute Book, 20 November 1925.
51 NAI, TSCH/3/S1801 O, Boundary Commission: operations of Commission, including resignation of Eoin MacNeill, Résumé of Statement by Dr MacNeill at the Meeting of the Executive Council, 21 November 1925.
52 Hallett, 'Eoin MacNeill and the Irish Boundary Commission', p. 221.
53 Bodleian Archives, Richard Feetham Papers, MSS. Afr. s. 1793 – 6/1 54-55, Letter from Richard Feetham to his mother, 20 November 1925.
54 Ibid., 6/1 56, Letter from Richard Feetham to his mother, 25 November 1925.
55 NAI, TSCH/3/S1801 O, Boundary Commission: operations of Commission, including

resignation of Eoin MacNeill, Letter from James MacNeill to Desmond FitzGerald, 24 November 1925.
56 *The Northern Whig and Belfast Post*, 23 November 1925, p. 7.
57 Ibid.
58 Ibid.
59 *Irish Independent*, 23 November 1925, p. 7.
60 *The Northern Whig and Belfast Post*, 23 November 1925, p. 6.
61 NAUK, CAB 61-1, Boundary Commission Minute Book, 23 November 1925.
62 Dáil Éireann Debates, vol. 13, no. 9, 24 November 1925, available from www.oireachtas debates.gov.ie, accessed on 15 October 2024.
63 Ibid.
64 Ibid.
65 Ibid.
66 *Derry Journal*, 25 November 1925, p. 4.
67 NAI, TSCH/3/S8378, Boundary agreement, 1925: messages of congratulations, Letter from Tim Healy to W.T. Cosgrave, 3 December 1925, forwarding letter from Fr McDonnell to Healy, 1 December 1925.
68 TCD, Diaries of Lily Stephens, IE TCD MS 11548/1/11, 24 November 1925.
69 NAI, TSCH/3/S1801 O, Boundary Commission: operations of Commission, including resignation of Eoin MacNeill, Letter from James MacNeill to Desmond FitzGerald, 24 November 1925.
70 Ervine, *Craigavon: Ulsterman*, p. 500.
71 Rankin, 'The role of the Irish boundary commission in the entrenchment of the Irish border', p. 445.
72 M. Tierney, *Eoin MacNeill, Scholar and Man of Action, 1867–1945* (Oxford: Oxford University Press, 1980), p. 274.
73 Ibid., p. 340.
74 Hand, 'MacNeill and the Boundary Commission', p. 264.
75 Hallett, 'Eoin MacNeill and the Irish Boundary Commission', p. 230.

CHAPTER 9

1 NAUK, CAB 61-1, Boundary Commission Minute Book, Letter from F.B. Bourdillon to Diarmuid O'Hegarty, 24 November 1925.
2 *Irish Independent*, 24 November 1925, p. 7.
3 *Belfast News-Letter*, 25 November 1925, p. 7.
4 Fanning et al., *Documents on Irish Foreign Policy: Volume 1*, Final text of the Articles of Agreement for a Treaty between Great Britain and Ireland as signed, 6 December 1921.
5 *The Irish Times*, 25 November 1925, p. 5.
6 NAI, TSCH/3/S1801 O, Boundary Commission: operations of Commission, including resignation of Eoin MacNeill, Telegram from Tim Healy to Leo Amery, 25 November 1925.
7 NAI, TSCH/3/S4720 A, Boundary Commission: agreement with Great Britain, December 1925, Conference in Downing Street on Boundary Commission, 26 November 1925.
8 Ibid.

9   Ibid.
10 Ibid.
11 Ibid.
12 Ibid.
13 Matthews, 'The Irish Boundary Crisis and the Reshaping of British Politics', p. 403.
14 Middlemas (ed.), *Thomas Jones: Whitehall Diary: Volume III*, p. 237.
15 PRONI, CAB/9/Z/11/5, Boundary Commission, London Conference November to December 1925, Draft Minutes of British Cabinet Meeting at Downing Street, 26 November 1925.
16 Ervine, *Craigavon: Ulsterman*, p. 501.
17 PRONI, CAB/9/Z/11/5, Boundary Commission, London Conference November to December 1925, Draft Minutes of British Cabinet Meeting at Downing Street, 26 November 1925.
18 Ibid.
19 Ibid.
20 *Belfast Telegraph*, 1 December 1925, p. 8.
21 Matthews, 'The Irish Boundary Crisis and the Reshaping of British Politics', p. 404.
22 PRONI, CAB/9/Z/11/5, Boundary Commission, London Conference November to December 1925, Letter from William Joynson-Hicks to James Craig, 12 November 1925.
23 Ibid., Draft Minutes of British Cabinet Meeting at Downing Street, 26 November 1925.
24 Matthews, 'The Irish Boundary Crisis and the Reshaping of British Politics', p. 407.
25 NAI, TSCH/3/S4720 A, Boundary Commission: agreement with Great Britain, December 1925, Cabinet Committee on Irish Affairs meeting, 28 November 1925.
26 Ibid.
27 Ibid.
28 Ibid.
29 Ibid.
30 Ibid.
31 Ibid., Summary of Statements made at Meeting on Morning on Sunday, 29 November 1925.
32 Middlemas (ed.), *Thomas Jones: Whitehall Diary: Volume III*, p. 240.
33 NAI, TSCH/3/S4720 A, Boundary Commission: agreement with Great Britain, December 1925, Summary of Statements made at Meeting on Morning on Sunday, 29 November 1925.
34 Ibid.
35 Ibid.
36 Ibid.
37 Ibid.
38 Middlemas and Barnes, *Baldwin: A Biography*, p. 364.
39 Middlemas (ed.), *Thomas Jones: Whitehall Diary: Volume III*, p. 242.
40 Ibid.
41 House of Lords Debate, 9 December 1925, vol. 62 cols. 1259–1260, available from http://hansard.millbanksystems.com, accessed 16 October 2024.
42 Middlemas (ed.), *Thomas Jones: Whitehall Diary: Volume III*, pp. 242–3.

43 Middlemas and Barnes, *Baldwin: A Biography*, p. 364.
44 Ibid.
45 NAI, TSCH/3/S4720 A, Boundary Commission: agreement with Great Britain, December 1925, Irish Boundary Commission, Draft Notes of a Conference held in the Board Room, Treasury, 1 December 1925.
46 Ibid.
47 Ibid.
48 Ibid.
49 Ibid.
50 Ibid.
51 Ibid.
52 Ibid.
53 Ibid.
54 Ibid.
55 Ibid.
56 Ibid.
57 Middlemas (ed.), *Thomas Jones: Whitehall Diary: Volume III*, p. 243.
58 NAI, TSCH/3/S4720 A, Boundary Commission: agreement with Great Britain, December 1925, Irish Boundary Commission, Draft Notes of a Conference held in the Board Room, Treasury, 1 December 1925.
59 Middlemas (ed.), *Thomas Jones: Whitehall Diary: Volume III*, p. 243.
60 NAI, TSCH/3/S4720 A, Boundary Commission: agreement with Great Britain, December 1925, Irish Boundary Commission, Draft Notes of a Conference held in the Board Room, Treasury, 1 December 1925.
61 Ibid.
62 Middlemas (ed.), *Thomas Jones: Whitehall Diary: Volume III*, p. 244.
63 Matthews, 'The Irish Boundary Crisis and the Reshaping of British Politics', p. 413.
64 NAI, TSCH/3/S4720 A, Boundary Commission: agreement with Great Britain, December 1925, Irish Negotiations, Draft Notes of a Conference held in the Board Room, Treasury, 2 December 1925.
65 Matthews, 'The Irish Boundary Crisis and the Reshaping of British Politics', p. 414.
66 NAI, TSCH/3/S4720 A, Boundary Commission: agreement with Great Britain, December 1925, Irish Negotiations, Draft Notes of a Conference held in the Board Room, Treasury, 2 December 1925.
67 J. FitzGerald and S. Kenny, '"Till debt do us part": financial implications of the divorce of the Irish Free State from the United Kingdom, 1922–26', *European Review of Economic History*, vol. 24 (May 2020), p. 818.
68 NAI, TSCH/3/S4720 A, Boundary Commission: agreement with Great Britain, December 1925, Irish Negotiations, Irish Boundary Commission, Draft Notes of a Conference held in the Board Room, Treasury, 3 December 1925.
69 Ibid.
70 Ibid.
71 P. Mulroe, 'The Free State's POWs', available at https://theborderkitchen.blog/the-free-states-pows/, accessed on 2 January 2025.

72 NAUK, CAB 61-1, Boundary Commission Minute Book, Notes on a Conference with Commission and three Governments held in PM's room, House of Commons, 3 December 1925.
73 NAI, TSCH/3/S4720 A, Boundary Commission: agreement with Great Britain, December 1925, Irish Negotiations, Copy of statement sent to Editors of *Irish Times* and *Irish Independent* signed by Cosgrave and O'Higgins, 3 December 1925.
74 J.M. Curran, 'The Anglo-Irish Agreement of 1925: Hardly a "Damn Good Bargain"', *The Historian*, vol. 40, no. 1 (November 1977), p. 50.
75 P. Bew, P. Gibbon and H. Patterson, *Northern Ireland 1921–1994: Political Forces and Social Classes* (London: Serif, 1995), p. 12.
76 *The Irish Times*, 4 December 1925, p. 6.
77 *Irish Independent*, 4 December 1925, p. 6.
78 NAI, TSCH/3/S8378, Boundary agreement, 1925: messages of congratulations, Letter from Kevin O'Shiel to W.T. Cosgrave, 4 December 1925.
79 *The Cork Examiner*, 5 December 1925, p. 10.
80 Dáil Éireann Debates, vol. 13, no. 16, 9 December 1925, available from www.oireachtasdebates.gov.ie, accessed on 17 October 2024.
81 Dáil Éireann Debates, vol. 8, no. 23, 15 October 1924, available from www.oireachtasdebates.gov.ie, accessed on 17 October 2024.
82 UCD Archives, Éamon de Valera Papers, P150/367, Diary from December 1925.
83 *The Times*, 9 December 1925, p. 15.
84 *Irish Independent*, 9 December 1925, p. 7.
85 UCD Archives, Éamon de Valera Papers, P150/591, Sinn Féin Standing Committee Minute Book, 11 December 1925.
86 N. Whelan, *Fianna Fáil: A Biography of the Party* (Dublin: Gill & Macmillan, 2011), p. 14.
87 Ibid., p. 14.
88 UCD Archives, Éamon de Valera Papers, P150/586, File on Sinn Féin from November 1925 to October 1926, 10 March 1926.
89 PRONI, D3015/2/100G, Box Entitled 'Boundary Commission', Memorandum from Memo from Douglas Savory, 9 November 1942.
90 Dáil Éireann Debates, vol. 13, no. 14, 7 December 1925, available from www.oireachtasdebates.gov.ie, accessed on 17 October 2024.
91 Dáil Éireann Debates, vol. 13, no. 16, 9 December 1925, available from www.oireachtasdebates.gov.ie, accessed on 17 October 2024.
92 For examples of co-operations between North and South after 1925, see M. Kennedy, *Division and Consensus: The Politics of Cross-Border Relations in Ireland, 1925–1969* (Dublin: Institute of Public Administration, 2000).
93 Dáil Éireann Debates, vol. 22, no. 5, 29 February 1928, available from www.oireachtasdebates.gov.ie, accessed on 17 October 2024.
94 TSCH/3/S4743, Boundary Bureau: formation and winding up, Letter from Stephens to O'Hegarty on 12 January 1926.
95 Ervine, *Craigavon: Ulsterman*, p. 507.
96 *Belfast Telegraph*, 4 December 1925, p. 10.
97 *Belfast News-Letter*, 4 December 1925, p. 8.

98 *Belfast News-Letter*, 10 December 1925, p. 8.
99 *The Manchester Guardian*, 11 December 1925, p. 7.
100 Dáil Éireann Debates, vol. 13, no. 17, 10 December 1925, available from www.oireachtasdebates.gov.ie, accessed on 17 October 2024.
101 See S.G. Beckton, *The East Donegal Border Petition and the Derry-Donegal Milk War, 1934-8* (Dublin: Four Courts Press, 2023).
102 P. Buckland, *James Craig* (Gill's Irish Lives series; Dublin: Gill & Macmillan, 1980), p. 110.
103 *Derry Journal*, 7 December 1925, p. 6.
104 *The Irish News*, 4 December 1925, p. 4.
105 Ibid.
106 NAUK, CAB 61-1, Boundary Commission Minute Book, Notes on a Conference with Commission and three Governments held in PM's room, House of Commons, 3 December 1925.
107 I. Gibbons, *Partition: How and Why Ireland was Divided* (London: Haus Publishing Ltd, 2020), p. 93.
108 *The Times*, 18 December 1925, p. 19.
109 Bodleian Archives, Richard Feetham Papers, MSS. Afr. s. 1793 – 6/1 61-63, Letter from Richard Feetham to his mother, 16 December 1925.
110 NAI, TSCH/3/S1801 O, Boundary Commission: operations of Commission, including resignation of Eoin MacNeill, Letter to James MacNeill from unnamed, presumably in British Government, 21 December 1925.
111 Middlemas (ed.), *Thomas Jones: Whitehall Diary: Volume III*, p. 246.
112 Hand, *Report of the Irish Boundary Commission*, p. xxii.

CONCLUSION

1 UCD Archives, Eoin MacNeill Papers LA1/F – 290, Speech by Eoin MacNeill in May 1927.
2 Ibid.
3 *Derry Journal*, 25 November 1925, p. 4.
4 Hand, 'MacNeill and the Boundary Commission', pp. 221–2.
5 NAI, TSCH/3/S1801 O, Boundary Commission: operations of Commission, including resignation of Eoin MacNeill, Résumé of Statement by Eoin MacNeill at Meeting of the Executive Council, 21 November 1925.
6 Murray, *The Irish Boundary Commission and its Origins*, p. 229.
7 O'Halloran, *Partition and the Limits of Irish Nationalism*, p. 155.
8 D. Ó Beacháin, *From Partition to Brexit: The Irish Government and Northern Ireland* (Manchester: Manchester University Press, 2019), p. 31, and M. Coleman, *Dictionary of Irish Biography*, available from http://dib.cambridge.org/, accessed on 29 November 2024.
9 NAI, TSCH/3/S1801 A, Boundary Commission: general matters, including correspondence between Michael Collins and Sir James Craig, Letter from James Craig to Michael Collins, 28 March 1922.
10 *An Phoblacht*, 27 October 1934, p. 3.
11 Bardon, *A History of Ulster*, p. 510.
12 *The Cork Examiner*, 15 February 1926, p. 7.

13 Irish Department of Foreign Affairs, available at https://www.dfa.ie/media/dfa/alldfawebsitemedia/ourrolesandpolicies/northernireland/good-friday-agreement.pdf, accessed on 4 January 2025.
14 E. Phoenix, E., 'Cahir Healy (1877–1970): Northern Nationalist Leader', *Clogher Record*, vol. 18, no. 1 (2003), p. 45.

BIBLIOGRAPHY

Primary Sources
Public Record Office of Northern Ireland (PRONI)
CAB/4: Cabinet Papers of the Stormont Administration
CAB 6/31 – Military and police, general correspondence file, October 1922 – December 1922
CAB 6/97: Mr Justice Feetham (Chairman of the Boundary Commission): Background Papers
CAB/6/105: Colonel W.B. Spender – Opinion the Boundary Commission
CAB/9/Z/11/5: Boundary Commission – London Conference November to December 1925
D640/7: Letters between Colonel Crawford and James Craig and Edward Carson
D921/3/6/1: John Henry Collins Papers
D921/4/5/1: Newspaper Clippings and Printed Booklets
D1327/24/3: Bundle of Documents Relating to the Co-ordination by Unionist Headquarters of the Efforts of Local Unionist Associations to Gather and Submit Evidence to the Irish Boundary Commission
D1507C/7: Lady Carson Non-Irish Papers
D1633/2/25-26: Diary of Lady Lilian Spender
D2991/B/1/23: Cahir Healy Papers
D3015/2/100G: Box Entitled 'Boundary Commission'
D3015/3/B/2: Volume of press cuttings [Irish 2], including *The Morning Post* leak on the Boundary Commission
D3099/3/20/1/1-21: Letters and one Telegram to Lady Londonderry from Ramsay MacDonald
D3480/59/54: Arthur James Balfour to Robert Lynn, enclosing Letter from Lord Birkenhead to Arthur Balfour
FIN/18/4/309: Boundary Commission – Position Created by Proposed Establishment of
HA/32/1/17: Boundary Commission – General
HA/32/1/21: Boundary Commission – Reports on Activities of Commission

The National Archives of Ireland (NAI)
Department of Agriculture
92/2/2305: Ordnance Survey Office; Preparation of Northern Ireland Population Map for North Eastern Boundary Bureau

Department of Finance
FIN/1/1341: Publicity – estimated expenditure on propaganda work in connection with Boundary Commission for some of the costs involved for the Free State government

FIN/1/2171: North Eastern Boundary Bureau – expenses in connection with Six-County elections

Department of the Taoiseach
S1095: Belfast Boycott
S1955A: Boundary with Northern Ireland – Customs Barrier – General
TSCH/3/S1801 A: Boundary Commission: general matters, including correspondence between Michael Collins and Sir James Craig
TSCH/3/S1801 C: Boundary Commission: general, including appointment of Eoin MacNeill and request for completion of Commission
TSCH/3/S1801 E: Boundary Commission: general matters
TSCH/3/S1801 H: Boundary Commission: appointment of Mr Justice Feetham as Chairman
TSCH/3/S1801 J: Boundary Commission: agreement regarding composition of Commission
TSCH/3/S1801 L: Boundary Commission: operations of Commission and preparation of Irish Free State evidence – Nov. 1924–Feb. 1925
TSCH/3/S1801 M: Boundary Commission: operations of Commission, March 1925 to May 1925
TSCH/3/S1801 N: Boundary Commission: operations of Commission June to July 1925
TSCH/3/S1801 O: Boundary Commission: operations of Commission, including resignation of Eoin MacNeill
TSCH/3/S1801 P: Boundary Commission: index to dates and conferences, 1921–1925
TSCH/3/S1801 R: Boundary Commission: memoranda and statements by President and Ministers
TSCH/3/S2027: Northern Ireland Boundary, Secret Document, 1922–1924: file containing mostly memoranda on proposed Boundary Commission by Kevin O'Shiel, Law Officers' Department, Ministry of Home Affairs
TSCH/3/S3342: North East Boundary Bureau: weekly bulletin
TSCH/3/S4563 A: Boundary with Northern Ireland: administrative preparations in anticipation of determination of Boundary
TSCH/3/S4720 A: Boundary Commission: agreement with Great Britain, December 1925
TSCH/3/S4743: Boundary Bureau: formation and winding up
TSCH/3/S8378: Boundary agreement, 1925: messages of congratulations
TSCH/3/S11209: Northern Ireland: deputation to Provisional Government, verbatim report of meeting relating to Boundary Commission

North Eastern Boundary Bureau
NEBB/1/3/1: Reports to North Eastern Boundary Bureau
NEBB/1/3/3: Reports to the North Eastern Boundary Bureau Chairman
NEBB/1/3/4: Reports to the North Eastern Boundary Bureau Chairman
NEBB/1/4/5: Six Counties boundary controversy
NEBB/1/3/7: Reports of the North Eastern Boundary Bureau to the Minister for Justice

Trinity College Dublin (TCD)
IE TCD MS 11548: Diaries of Lily Stephens
IE TCD MS 4238–9: E.M. Stephens Papers

University College Dublin (UCD)
P24: Ernest Blythe Papers
P150: Éamon de Valera Papers
LA1/F: Eoin MacNeill Papers
P35: Patrick McGilligan Papers
P7/A: Richard Mulcahy Papers
P197: Kevin O'Higgins Papers
P69: Moss Twomey Papers

National Archives of the UK (NAUK)
CAB 61/1–161: Irish Boundary Commission files
CO537/1092: Letter by Stephen Tallents to John Anderson
CUST 118/134: Ireland – land barrier and boundary commission (1923–1925)
CUST 49/617: Negotiations concerning setting up of customs barrier between Irish Free State and Northern Ireland: transfer of administration of customs and excise services to provisional government
HO 267/13: Land Registry Transfer of Documents
HO 267/49: Customs & Excise
HO 45/24812: Miscellaneous matters arising from the Partition of Ireland
HO 463600/23: Irish Boundary: Publication of Correspondence
HO 463600/61: Remuneration of J.R. Fisher

Bodleian Archives and Manuscripts
Archive of Henry Herbert Asquith
    MS. Asquith 39: Miscellaneous letters and memoranda on the Irish Question, 1913–1914
Archive of Robert Henry Brand, Baron Brand
    MS. Brand 70/1: Round Table: general correspondence and articles, 1922–1925
Archive of Lionel George Curtis
    MS. Curtis 89: Ireland, 1916–1924
    MS. Curtis 90: Ireland, 1924–1946, 1950
Richard Feetham Papers
    MSS. Afr. s. 1793 6/1 and 7/2

Newspapers and Magazines
An Phoblacht
Belfast News-Letter
Belfast Telegraph
Binghamton Press and Leader
Cork Examiner, The
Daily Mail
Derry Journal
Derry People and Donegal News
Donegal News
Economist, The
Éire
Evening Herald
Evening Standard
Fermanagh Herald
Freeman's Journal, The
Irish Independent
Irish News, The
Irish Press, The
Irish Statesman, The
Irish Times, The

Manchester Guardian, The
Morning Post, The
Northern Standard, The
Northern Whig and Belfast Post, The
Observer, The
Scotsman, The
Spectator, The
Strabane Chronicle
Sunday Independent
Times, The
Ulster Herald
Westminster Gazette

Books

Bardon, J., *A History of Ulster* (Belfast: The Blackstaff Press, 2001)

Beckton, S.G., *The East Donegal Border Petition and the Derry-Donegal Milk War, 1934–8* (Dublin: Four Courts Press, 2023)

Bew, P., Gibbon, P. and Patterson, H., *Northern Ireland 1921–1994: Political Forces and Social Classes* (London: Serif, 1995)

Bowman, J., *De Valera and the Ulster Question 1917–1973* (Oxford: Oxford University Press, 1989)

Bowman, T., *Carson's army: The Ulster Volunteer Force, 1910–22* (Manchester: Manchester University Press, 2007)

Buckland, P., *Irish Unionism 2: Ulster Unionism and the Origins of Northern Ireland 1886–1922* (Dublin: Gill & Macmillan, 1973)

Buckland, P., *James Craig* (Gill's Irish Lives series; Dublin: Gill & Macmillan, 1980)

Buckland, P., *The Factory of Grievances: Devolved Government in Northern Ireland 1921–39* (Dublin: Gill & Macmillan, 1979)

Burke, E., *Ghosts of a Family: Ireland's Most Infamous Unsolved Murder, the Outbreak of the Civil War and the Origins of the Modern Troubles* (Dublin: Merrion Press, 2024)

Churchill, W., *The World Crisis Volume 4: The Aftermath* (1923) (London: Rosetta Books, 2013, electronic version)

Cousins, J.A., *Without a Dog's Chance: The Nationalists of Northern Ireland and the Irish Boundary Commission, 1920–25* (Dublin: Merrion Press, 2020)

Dolan, A. and Murphy, W., *Michael Collins: The Man and the Revolution* (Cork: The Collins Press, 2015)

Ervine, St. J., *Craigavon: Ulsterman* (London: George Allen & Unwin Ltd, 1949)

Fanning, R., *Fatal Path: British Government and Irish Revolution 1910–1922* (London: Faber & Faber, 2013)

Fanning, R., Kennedy, M, Keogh, D. and O'Halpin, E., *Documents on Irish Foreign Policy: Volume 1: 1919–1922* (Dublin: Royal Irish Academy, 1998)

Fanning, R., Kennedy, M., Keogh, D. and O'Halpin, E., *Documents on Irish Foreign Policy: Volume 2: 1923–1926* (Dublin: Royal Irish Academy, 2000)

Farrell, M., *Arming the Protestants: The Formation of the Ulster Special Constabulary and the Royal Ulster Constabulary, 1920–27* (London: Pluto Press, 1983)

Farrell, M., *Northern Ireland: The Orange State* (London: Pluto Press, 1980)

Fisher, J.R., *The End of the Irish Parliament* (London: Edward Arnold, 1911)

Gaughan, J.A., *Austin Stack: Portrait of a Separatist* (Dublin: Kingdom Books, 1977)

Gibbons, I. *Partition: How and Why Ireland was Divided* (London: Haus Publishing Ltd, 2020)

Glennon, K., *From Pogrom to Civil War: Tom Glennon and the Belfast IRA* (Cork: Mercier Press, 2013)

Grant, A., *The Irish Revolution 1912–23: Derry* (Dublin: Four Courts Press, 2018)

Gwynn, D., *The History of Partition (1912–1925)* (Dublin: The Richview Press, 1950)
Hand, G.H., *Report of the Irish Boundary Commission 1925* (Shannon: Irish University Press, 1969)
Hepburn, A.C., *Catholic Belfast and Nationalist Ireland in the Era of Joe Devlin 1871–1934* (Oxford: Oxford University Press, 2008)
Hezlet, A., *The 'B' Specials: A History of the Ulster Special Constabulary* (London: Tom Stacey Ltd, 1972)
Hopkinson, M., *Green Against Green: The Irish Civil War* (Dublin: Gill & Macmillan, 2004)
Jackson, A., *Judging Redmond and Carson* (Dublin: Royal Irish Academy, 2018)
Jenkins, R., *Churchill: A Biography* (London: Pan Books, 2001)
Kennedy, M., *Division and Consensus: The Politics of Cross-Border Relations in Ireland, 1925–1969* (Dublin: Institute of Public Administration, 2000)
Kennedy, M., *Ireland and the League of Nations, 1919–1946: International Relations, Diplomacy and Politics* (Dublin: Irish Academic Press, 1996)
Kenny, C., *Midnight in London: The Anglo-Irish Treaty Crisis 1921* (Dublin: Eastwood Books, 2021)
Laffan, M., *Judging Cosgrave: The Foundation of the Irish State* (Dublin: Royal Irish Academy, 2014)
Laffan, M., *The Partition of Ireland 1911–1925* (Dundalk: Dundalgan Press, 2004)
Leary, P., *Unapproved Routes: Histories of the Irish Border, 1922-1972* (Oxford: Oxford University Press, 2016)
Lord Longford (Pakenham, F.), *Peace by Ordeal: The Negotiation of the Anglo-Irish Treaty, 1921* (London: Sidgwick & Jackson, 1935)
Lynch, R., *Revolutionary Ireland, 1912–25* (London: Bloomsbury Publishing PLC, 2015)
Lynch, R., *The Northern IRA and the Early Years of Partition, 1920–1922* (Dublin: Irish Academic Press, 2006)
Lynch, R., *The Partition of Ireland, 1918–1925* (Cambridge: Cambridge University Press, 2019)
Macardle, D., *The Irish Republic: A Documented Chronicle of the Anglo-Irish Conflict and the Partitioning of Ireland, with a Detailed Account of the Period 1916–1923* (London: Victor Gollancz Ltd, 1937)
MacDonald, D., *Hard Border: Walking Through a Century of Partition* (Dublin: New Island Books, 2018)
Mansergh, N., *The Unresolved Question: The Anglo-Irish Settlement and Its Undoing 1912–72* (Yale: Yale University Press, 1991)
Matthews, K., *Fatal Influence: The Impact of Ireland on British Politics, 1920–1925* (Dublin: University College Dublin Press, 2004)
McColgan, J., *British Policy and the Irish Administration 1920–22* (London: George Allen & Unwin, 1983)
McGee, O., *Arthur Griffith* (Dublin: Merrion Press, 2015)
Middlemas, K. (ed.), *Thomas Jones: Whitehall Diary: Volume III: Ireland 1918–1925* (London: Oxford University Press, 1971)
Middlemas, K. and Barnes, J., *Baldwin: A Biography* (London: Weidenfeld and Nicolson, 1969)
Moore, C., *Birth of the Border: The Impact of Partition in Ireland* (Dublin: Merrion Press, 2019)
Mulvagh, C. and Purcell, E. (eds), *Eoin MacNeill: The Pen and the Sword* (Cork: Cork University Press, 2022)
Murray, B.K., *WITS: The 'Open' Years. A History of the University of the Witwatersrand, Johannesburg 1939–1959* (Johannesburg: Wits University Press, 2022)

Murray, P., *The Irish Boundary Commission and its Origins 1886–1925* (Dublin: University College Dublin Press, 2011)

Nash, C., Reid, B. and Graham, B., *Partitioned Lives: The Irish Borderlands* (Surrey: Ashgate Publishing Company, 2013)

North Eastern Boundary Bureau, *Handbook of the Ulster Question* (Dublin: The Stationery Office, 1923)

Ó Beacháin, D., *From Partition to Brexit: The Irish Government and Northern Ireland* (Manchester: Manchester University Press, 2019)

O'Brien, J., *Discrimination in Northern Ireland, 1920–1939: Myth or Reality?* (Newcastle upon Tyne: Cambridge Scholars Publishing, 2010)

Ó Fathartaigh, M. and Weeks, L., *Birth of a State: The Anglo-Irish Treaty* (Dublin: Merrion Press, 2021)

O'Halloran, C., *Partition and the Limits of Irish Nationalism* (Dublin: Gill & Macmillan, 1987)

O'Leary, B., *A Treatise of Northern Ireland, Volume II: Control* (Oxford: Oxford University Press, 2019)

Ozseker, O., *Forging the Border: Donegal and Derry in Times of Revolution* (Dublin: Merrion Press, 2019)

Phoenix, E., *Northern Nationalism: Nationalist Politics, Partition and the Catholic Minority in Northern Ireland 1890–1940* (Belfast: Ulster Historical Foundation, 1994)

Sagarra, E., *Kevin O'Shiel: Tyrone Nationalist and Irish State-Builder* (Dublin: Irish Academic Press, 2013)

Tierney, M., *Eoin MacNeill, Scholar and Man of Action, 1867–1945* (Oxford: Oxford University Press, 1980)

Torrance, D., *The Wild Men: The Remarkable Story of Britain's First Labour Government* (London: Bloomsbury Publishing, 2024)

Walker, B.M., *A Political History of the Two Irelands* (Basingstoke: Palgrave Macmillan, 2012)

Whelan, N., *Fianna Fáil: A Biography of the Party* (Dublin: Gill & Macmillan, 2011)

Book Chapters

Barton, B., 'The Dáil cabinet's mission to Belfast', in Nic Dháibhéid, C., Coleman, M. and Bew, P. (eds), *Northern Ireland 1921-2021: Centenary Historical Perspectives* (Newtownards: Ulster Historical Foundation, 2022)

Fisher, J.R., 'Introduction', in *The Ulster Liberal Unionist Association: A Sketch of its History, 1885–1914* (Belfast: Ulster Reform Club, 1913)

Goldstein, E., 'Partition and Peacemaking after the Great War', in Fleming, N.C. and Murphy, J.H. (eds), *Ireland and Partition: Contexts and Consequences* (Clemson: Clemson University Press, 2021)

Hallett, T., 'Eoin MacNeill and the Irish Boundary Commission', in Mulvagh, C. and Purcell, E. (eds), *Eoin MacNeill: The Pen and the Sword* (Cork: Cork University Press, 2022)

Hand, G.J., 'MacNeill and the Boundary Commission', in Martin, F.X. and Byrne, F.J. (eds), *The Scholar Revolutionary: Eoin MacNeill, 1867–1945, and the Making of the New Ireland* (Shannon: Irish University Press, 1973)

Lynch, R., '7 December 1922: Ulster Opts Out of the Irish Free State – Partition and Power: Unionist Political Culture in Northern Ireland', in Gannon, D. and McGarry, F. (eds),

Ireland 1922: Independence, Partition, Civil War (Dublin: Royal Irish Academy, 2022)

Lynch, R., 'The Boundary Commission', in Crowley, J., Ó Drisceoil, D. and Murphy, M. (eds), *Atlas of the Irish Revolution* (Cork: Cork University Press, 2017)

O'Leary, B., '"Cold House": The Unionist Counter-Revolution and the Invention of Northern Ireland', in Crowley, J., Ó Drisceoil, D. and Murphy, M. (eds), *Atlas of the Irish Revolution* (Cork: Cork University Press, 2017)

Schoen, L., 'The Irish Free State and the Electricity Industry, 1922-1927', in Bielenberg, A. (ed.), *The Shannon Scheme and the Electrification of the Irish Free State* (Dublin: The Lilliput Press, 2002)

Whyte, J., 'How much discrimination was there under the unionist regime, 1921-68?', in Gallagher, T. and O'Connell, J. (eds), *Contemporary Irish Studies* (Manchester: Manchester University Press, 1983)

Journals and Periodicals

Anderson, J. and O'Dowd, L., 'Imperialism and Nationalism: The Home Rule Struggle and Border Creation in Ireland, 1885-1925', *Political Geography*, vol. 26 (2007), pp. 934-50

Cronin, M., 'Projecting the Nation through Sport and Culture: Ireland, Aonach Tailteann and the Irish Free State, 1924-32', *Journal of Contemporary History*, vol. 38, no. 3 (July 2003), pp. 395-411

Curran, J.M., 'The Anglo-Irish Agreement of 1925: Hardly a "Damn Good Bargain"', *The Historian*, vol. 40, no. 1 (November 1977), pp. 36-52

Dooley, T.A.M., 'From the Belfast Boycott to the Boundary Commission: Fears and Hopes in County Monaghan, 1920-26', *Clogher Record*, vol. 15, no. 1 (1994), pp. 90-106

Dove, J., 'Editor's Note: The Irish Boundary Question', *Round Table*, vol. 14, no. 55 (June 1924), pp. 643-8

FitzGerald J. and Kenny, S., '"Till debt do us part": financial implications of the divorce of the Irish Free State from the United Kingdom, 1922-26', *European Review of Economic History*, vol. 24 (May 2020), pp. 818-42

Gibbons, I., 'The Irish Policy of the First Labour Government', *Labour History Review*, vol. 72, no. 2 (2007), pp. 169-84

Hall, D., 'Partition and County Louth', *Journal of the County Louth Archaeological and Historical Society*, vol. 27, no. 2 (2010), pp. 243-83

Hopkinson, M., 'The Craig-Collins Pacts of 1922: Two Attempted Reforms of the Northern Ireland Government', *Irish Historical Studies*, vol. 27, no. 106 (November 1990), pp. 145-58

Moore, C., '"I See All Your Difficulties": Winston Churchill and the Irish Boundary Commission', *Finest Hour: The Journal of Winston Churchill and His Times*, no. 197 (2022), pp. 24-8

Moore, C., 'Reinforcing Partition Through Fiscal Policy', *Irish Political Studies*, vol. 39, no. 2 (2024), pp. 344-65

Mulvagh, C., 'Ulster Exclusion and Irish Nationalism: Consenting to the Principle of Partition, 1912-1916', *Revue Française de Civilisation Britannique*, vol. 24, no. 2 (2019), pp. 1-22

Murray, P., 'Partition and the Irish Boundary Commission: A Northern Nationalist Perspective', *Clogher Record*, vol. 18, no. 2 (2004), pp. 181-217

Nash, C., Dennis, L. and Graham, B., 'Putting the Border in Place: Customs Regulations in the Making of the Irish Border, 1921-1945', *Journal of Historical Geography*, vol. 36 (2010), pp. 421-31

O'Callaghan, M., '"Old Parchment and Water"; the Boundary Commission of 1925 and the Copperfastening of the Irish Border', *Bullán; An Irish Studies Journal*, vol. 5, no. 2 (2000), pp. 27–55

Phoenix, E., 'Cahir Healy (1877–1970): Northern Nationalist Leader', *Clogher Record*, vol. 18, no. 1 (2003), pp. 32–52

Rankin, K.J., 'The role of the Irish boundary commission in the entrenchment of the Irish border: from tactical panacea to political liability', *Journal of Historical Geography*, vol. 34 (2008), pp. 422–47.

Valiulis, M.G., 'The "Army Mutiny" of 1924 and the Assertion of Civilian Authority in Independent Ireland', *Irish Historical Studies*, vol. 23, no. 92 (1983), pp. 354–66

Wilson, T., '"The most terrible assassination that has yet stained the name of Belfast": the McMahon Murders in Context', *Irish Historical Studies*, vol. 37, no. 145 (May 2010), pp. 83–106

Electronic Sources

1911 Census of Ireland, available at https://www.cso.ie/en/statistics/historicalreports/census1911/

Australian Dictionary of Biography, available from https://adb.anu.edu.au/biography/

BBC Northern Ireland, 'Your Place or Mine', Thompson, J., 'A Century of Water from the Mournes: A concise history', available at www.bbc.co.uk/northernireland/yourplaceandmine/down/A1068518.shtml

Biography of Richard Feetham at South African History Online, available at www.sahistory.org.za/people/richard-feetham

Bureau of Military History, 1913–21, available from www.bureauofmilitaryhistory.ie/

CAIN Web Service, available from https://cain.ulster.ac.uk/

Central Statistics Office – Consumer Price Index Inflation Calculator, available from https://visual.cso.ie/?body=entity/cpicalculator

Dáil Éireann Debates, available from www.oireachtasdebates.gov.ie

Dictionary of Irish Biography, available from http://dib.cambridge.org/

Glennon, K., 'The Dead of the Belfast Pogrom', 18 May 1924, available at https://thebelfastpogrom.com/2023/04/22/the-dead-of-the-belfast-pogrom-updated/

Irish Department of Foreign Affairs, available at https://www.dfa.ie/media/dfa/alldfawebsitemedia/ourrolesandpolicies/northernireland/good-friday-agreement.pdf

Mulroe, P., 'The Free State's POWs', available at https://theborderkitchen.blog/the-free-states-pows/

House of Commons and Lords Debates, available from http://hansard.millbanksystems.com

Theses

Cousins, J.A., '"Without a "Dog's Chance": The Devlinite *Irish News*, Northern Ireland's "Trapped" Nationalist Minority, and the Irish Boundary Question, 1921–1925', PhD thesis, Simon Fraser University (2008)

Matthews, C.K., 'The Irish Boundary Crisis and the Reshaping of British Politics: 1920–1925', PhD thesis, London School of Economics and Political Science (2000)

Newman, S.B., 'For God, Ulster and the "B"-men': the Ulsterian revolution, the foundation of Northern Ireland and the creation of the Ulster Special Constabulary, 1910-1927', PhD Thesis, Birbeck, University of London (2020)

INDEX

Abercorn, James Hamilton, 3rd Duke of 110, 130
Agar-Robartes, Thomas 5
Agnew, P.J. 188
Aiken, Frank 72, 164
all-Ireland parliament 21–2, 113, 241; Glenavy's offer to Craig 59–60; Lloyd George and 16, 18, 19, 79; opposition to 15, 19, 30, 40, 72, 79, 119
Allen, William 107
Allenstein and Marienwerder 68, 69
Amery, Leo, Colonial Secretary 209, 216–17, 219
Anderson, John 223
Andrews, John M. 153
Anglo-Irish Treaty (1921), Article (5) 150, 216, 218, 220, 223–7, 228; waiving of 229, 230, 231, 236, 242
Anglo-Irish Treaty (1921), Article (12) 1, 2, 23, 47, 60; ambiguity of 27–8, 37, 38, 65, 124, 130, 149–50, 180–1, 239, 242; British signatories' views on 148–9; Cosgrave and 216, 242; de Valera and 23, 34; Feetham's interpretations of 161, 162, 180–1, 193, 200, 211–12; Free State government and 169–70; interpretations of 48, 129–31, 139–40, 145–6, 149, 156, 159, 161–2, 169–70, 180–1, 193, 200, 211–12; loose draughtsmanship of 27–8, 130, 195; MacEntee's views on 33–4; MacNeill's views on 75, 211–12, 238; NEBB's interpretation of 67; Privy Council and 130–1, 133, 141–2, 159, 244; Silesian precedent 55; Sinn Féin's lack of scrutiny 27, 239
Anglo-Irish Treaty (1921): anti-Treaty side 33, 35; Article (14) 57–8, 193; Bonar Law and 60, 146; breaches of 45, 51; British signatories 36, 38, 49, 139, 148; Collins's perception of 50; Conservatives' attitude towards 62–3, 138–9, 144; Dáil debates on 11, 33, 35, 151;

fiscal consequences of 82–3; international instrument 27, 126, 166, 193; Irish signatories 25–6, 46, 139, 148–9; League of Nations, registration with 126; Northern nationalists and 33, 35–6, 207; pro-Treaty side 33, 35, 74; ratification in the Dáil 39; republican perception of 118; signing of 25–6, 35, 36; Ulster unionists and 29–31, 58–9, 79–80, 244; *see also* Anglo-Irish Treaty (1921): Article (5); Anglo-Irish Treaty (1921): Article (12); Anglo-Irish Treaty negotiations
Anglo-Irish Treaty negotiations 1, 2, 11–13, 139; Boundary Commission 17–19, 27, 28; British delegation 13; Collins and 53, 140, 141; de Valera and 23; deadline date 22; draft treaty, British government and 21–2; Dublin Cabinet meeting, draft Treaty and 22–3; financial independence, symbolic significance of 94–5; Irish plenipotentiaries 11–13, 17–18, 20–1, 22–3, 27, 28, 94–5, 149, 156, 200; Lloyd George and 13, 14, 21, 22, 24–5, 79
Antrim 5, 37, 38, 67, 138, 189, 231; nationalist district in 20, 74; religious denominations (1911) 6
Archdale, Edward 90, 153
Armagh 15, 67, 163, 164, 165, 207; area transferred to the Free State 202; Boundary Commission hearings 171, 179–80, 185; Catholic minority in 6, 180; religious denominations (1911) 6; South Armagh 86, 155, 172, 173, 215, 237, 245
Armagh City 67, 179
Armagh Urban District 172
Asquith, Herbert Henry 5, 37, 109
Aughnacloy 44, 168, 182, 191
Aughnacloy Town Commissioners 170

Baldwin, Lucy 223

Index

Baldwin, Stanley 106; Boundary Commission and 120, 163, 204–5, 217, 222, 224, 237, 243; Cosgrave and 216, 217, 220; Craig and 138, 141, 144, 163, 223; Government of Ireland Act (1920) and 144; Ireland and 62, 63; O'Higgins and 220–2, 223; Ulster unionists, support for 120

Balfour, Arthur James 13, 140–1, 145, 148
Barton, Brian 39
Barton, Robert 20–1, 22, 148
Béal na Bláth 48
Beaverbrook, Max Aitkin, 1st Baron 121
Beerstecher, C. 163
Belfast 21, 39, 98, 184; Catholics, violence against 45, 46; religious denominations (1911) 6
Belfast Boycott 40, 78–9
Belfast City and District Water Commissioners 98–9, 181
Belfast News-Letter 30, 78, 79–80, 133–4, 234
Belfast Telegraph 31, 60
Belfast Waterworks 192, 193
Bennett, George 172
Beresford, S. 68
Bessbrook Spinning Company 180
Best, Richard, Attorney General 132, 162, 197–8
Birkenhead, F.E. Smith, 1st Earl of 124, 138, 218; Article (12), views on 38; boundary, rectification of 30, 36–7, 139; letter to Balfour 140–1, 145, 148; Treaty negotiations and 13, 21, 27
Blackmore, C.H. 226
Blanesburgh, Robert Younger, Baron 132
Blythe, Ernest 56, 74, 90, 112–13, 207, 210, 225, 232
Boger, Major Robert Albany 167
Bonar Law, Andrew 9, 13, 16, 62, 63, 72, 121; Boundary Commission and 32, 60, 61, 144; Treaty and 60, 146
Bonner, John 54–5, 56
Borden, Sir Robert 121
border poll 246
border/boundary: areas to be transferred 201–6, 219–20; Boundary Commissioners' tour of 163–7; British MPs tour of 146; Craig and 234; creation of 94; Feetham's conclusions on 199–201; Free State's views on 222–3; Government of Ireland Act (1920) and 230; nationalists and 36, 155–6, 164, 165, 183–4, 206–7; NEBB visits to 164–5, 167–9; rectifications to 36–7, 38, 49, 106, 116, 124, 135, 139, 140, 145, 146–7, 155, 156, 165, 217; referendum, de Valera's appeal for 232; stereotyping of 84, 241–2; *see also* customs barriers; Irish Boundary Commission
boundary commissions in Europe 22, 54, 68–71
boundary conferences 76, 105–6, 110–14, 117, 118–19, 130, 142–3
Bourdillon, Francis Bernard 68, 158–9, 163, 169–70, 192, 195, 204, 222
Bowman, John 10–11, 152
Boyle, Maxwell 185
British Army 135–7
British Empire 63, 125, 127, 128–9, 130, 216, 240, 241, 243–4
British Empire Exhibition (1924) 125–6, 131
British government: Boundary Commission, attitude towards 51; Chairman of Boundary Commission chosen by 22, 71, 118, 120, 121–2, 239; criticism of 30, 31; North East Ulster, attitude towards 46; Northern nationalists' perception of 245–6; Specials financed by 44, 45; *see also* Conservative government; Labour government
British press 46, 146–8, 149, 156
Brookeborough, Basil Brooke, 1st Viscount 106, 163, 166, 174–5
Brugha, Cathal 23
Buckingham Palace Conference (1914) 5, 38
Buckland, Patrick 35, 101–2, 236
Burns, Delisle 68

Cameron, A.R. 137
Cargill, Samuel 185
Carson, Sir Edward 5, 7, 15, 33, 39, 98–9, 140; Article (5), views on 223–4; Article (12), interpretation of 146; Boundary Commission, views on 8, 124; British government, criticism of 30; Conservative Party and 138; Craig, perception of 234; Free State government, views on 125; maiden speech to the House of Lords 30; Northern Commissioner nomination 32, 152–4; Treaty attacked by 30
Carson, Ruby, Lady 39, 113, 142, 152–3
Catholics 73, 108, 134, 171–3, 184, 225–6, 231; areas transferred 202–3; census (1911) 172–3; Craig, population exchange suggested by 218–19; Craig's attitude towards 236; in Derry city 177; discrimination against 40,

78, 100, 101, 173–4, 226; in East Donegal 176; emigration 100; Free State, seasonal work in 175; labourers, employment as 176, 177, 185; liaison officer for 228; mistreatment of 117, 174, 223, 227; nationalism and 172, 173; in the North-East 222, 224; political outlook 175; Protestant employers and 177; Ulster Special Constabulary and 17, 174; violence against 45, 46, 78

Cavan County 16, 106, 153, 165, 185, 192; religious denominations (1911) 6; unionists in 7, 34

Census of Ireland (1911) 6, 107, 159, 168, 172, 173, 176

Chamberlain, Austen 4, 19–20, 21, 45, 71, 141; Article (12), interpretation of 139; Cosgrave and 217, 218; Craig and 10, 15, 31–2, 219; Provisional Government and 44

Chartres, John 20

Childers, Erskine 27

Churchill, Winston 13, 14, 25–6, 44, 47, 48, 49; Article (5) and 224, 225, 226, 228, 229; Balfour's letter to Birkenhead 140–1; Belfast Boycott, views on 78–9; Boundary Commission and 38–9, 121, 123–4, 139–40; Conservative Party and 39, 139–40; Craig and 49–50, 138, 219; Irish Committee and 45; Liberal Party and 39, 139; Northern government, support for 49; Northern Ireland, finance and 220; report and award, suppression of 230; Treaty and 38–9; tripartite conference (1925) 224–30

civil rights campaign (1960s) 178

Civil War 48–9, 50–1, 52, 72, 80, 114; economic effects of 84–5, 181, 240; effects in Northern Ireland 54, 61, 175, 240

Claidheamh Soluis, An 74

Clann Éireann 243

Clark, Sir Ernest 115, 116, 197–8

Clogher, County Tyrone 102, 168

Clones, County Monaghan 55, 81, 87, 92, 165, 181, 191

Clough, County Monaghan 192

Clyde, James Clyde, Baron 32

Clynes, John 109

Collins, John Henry 57, 104, 187

Collins, Michael: Anglo-Irish Treaty, signing of 25–6; article in *The Times* 46, 47; Boundary Commission and 12, 22, 24–5, 35; Craig, meetings with 39, 40, 47; Craig, pacts with 40–1, 47, 48, 51, 80, 106, 223; death 48, 49, 148; kidnappings of loyalists ordered by 43–4; Lloyd George and 24, 28; Northern Ireland, obstructionist policies on 43, 51, 56, 57; Northern nationalists and 42–3; O'Shiel (director NEBB) and 53, 65–6; partition and 35, 43; plebiscite sought by 26–7; Six Counties, non-recognition of 43; Specials, views on 46; Treaty breaches, accusations of 45; Treaty negotiations and 11, 12, 17–18, 21, 22–3, 53, 140, 141

Colonial Office 20, 44–5, 68, 117, 131, 142, 166

Connolly, Patrick 173

Conservative government 62–3, 243

Conservative Party 5, 10, 13, 38, 62, 107, 108; Article (12), interpretation of 139, 156; Carson and 138; Churchill and 39, 139–40; Craig and 138, 141, 144; Treaty, attitude towards 138–9, 144; Ulster unionists, support for 14, 63, 109, 120, 138, 144

Cookstown, County Tyrone 57, 101, 168

Cooper, James 166, 191

Cope, Alfred 9, 10, 116

Corrigan, Thomas 152

Cosgrave, W.T. 36, 49, 57, 58, 105, 193, 207; Article (5) and 224, 225, 228, 229, 242; Article (12) and 216, 242; Baldwin and 216, 217, 220; Boundary Commission and 73, 76, 83, 121, 133, 169, 191, 210, 216–17, 237, 241, 242; boundary conferences and 110–11, 112, 117, 118, 142–3; British Empire Exhibition, views on 125–6; British press, criticism of 147, 149; Catholics in the North 226; Chamberlain and 218; Churchill, meeting with 224; Craig and 218–19, 220, 233–4, 235, 242; criticism of 215; customs barriers and 83–4, 85; Free State Commissioner, views on 74; Irish unity and 66, 111, 233, 234, 242; London Agreement and 230–1, 233, 235; MacNeill and 207–8, 210–11, 214, 217; *Morning Post* forecast, reaction to 209–10; NEBB and 242; negotiating skills, lack of 242; Northern nationalists and 233, 242; transfer of territory and 196, 207; tripartite conference (1925) 224, 225–6, 227, 228–9, 230–1

Council of Ireland 15, 40, 42, 223; abolition of 230, 231–2, 233, 234, 235, 242, 244

Index

County of Tyrone Boundary Defence Association 186
Craig, Captain Charles 42
Craig, Sir James 7–8, 9–10, 23, 33, 190, 204; all-Ireland parliament, opposition to 15, 40, 79; annual security costs for Northern Ireland 44; Article (5) and 223; Article (12), interpretation of 131; article in *The Spectator* 114; border areas, tour of 106; Boundary Commission and 29, 59, 131, 170; Boundary Commission, refusal to co-operate with 10, 32–3, 59, 65, 106, 107, 138, 160, 163; boundary conferences and 106, 113–14, 117, 118; British media and 46; Catholic minority, attitude towards 236; Chamberlain, correspondence with 32; Churchill and 49–50, 138, 219; Collins, meetings with 39, 40, 47; Collins, pacts with 40–1, 47, 48, 51, 80, 106, 223; Conservative Party and 138, 141, 144; Cosgrave and 218–19, 220, 231, 233–4, 242; customs barriers, views on 85; dominion status for Northern Ireland 16, 24; Feetham's appointment, views on 124; Free State Army mutiny, reaction to 115; Free State, voting out of 58; General Election (1925) 188–9; Glenavy's offer to 59–60; Government of Ireland Act (1920) and 112, 244; ill health 113, 142; Lloyd George and 10, 13, 15, 18–19, 25, 30, 31–2, 48; London Agreement and 234, 234–5, 244; loyalist kidnappings, reaction to 43–4; Northern Commissioner, Fisher as 154; Northern Commissioner nominee, Carson as 153–4; Northern nationalists, attitude towards 244; O'Higgins, meeting with 223, 224–5; population exchange suggested by 218–19; PR system, abolition of 48; Six Counties and 31, 32, 106, 154; Specials, financing of 45; Treaty negotiations, views on 31–2; tribunal suggested by 220; tripartite conference (1925) 222–9; Ulster Unionists and 204, 236
Crawford, Colonel Frederick 8, 16
Cronin, Mike 128
Crossmaglen, County Armagh 172, 182, 202
Culverwell, Edward 148
Cumann na nGaedheal government 66, 207, 230, 241, 243; *see also* Free State Executive Council; Free State government

Curragh Mutiny (1914) 135
Curtis, Lionel 20, 68, 116, 117; Article (12) and 118, 129, 130–1; Boundary Commission chairman suggested by 121; Collins, views on 44, 49; Feetham, friendship with 122, 123–4; Lloyd George, perception of 28; plebiscite, views on 135–6
Curzon, George Curzon, 1st Marquess 146
customs barriers 67–8, 76, 77–8, 79; border and 84, 94, 240–1; Boundary Commission, effects on 85, 90, 92, 96; consequences of 92–3, 181–3, 241–2; Cosgrave and 83–4, 85; Craig's call for removal 235; daily lives, effects on 90–1, 92–3, 181; introduction of 84, 85, 86, 90–2, 181; NEBB and 86–7; Northern Ireland and 88, 89–90; objections to 81, 85–7, 91, 164, 181–2, 235; partition, effects on 78, 80, 85, 87, 93–4; smuggling and 81, 88, 91; support for 183; tobacco manufacturers and 89, 91
customs stations 90–1, 92
customs union 81, 82, 89

Dáil Courts 52
Dáil Éireann 215; Belfast Boycott 40, 78–9; de Valera and 10, 232; Sinn Féin's abstentionist policy 232–3; Treaty debates 11, 33, 35, 151; Treaty, ratification of 39
Daily Mail 128, 147, 207
Daily Telegraph 147
Dalton, Charlie 114
Damage to Property (Compensation) Act (1923) 229
D'Arcy, Charles Frederick, Archbishop of Armagh 163, 164
Davison, Sir William 14
Dawson Bates, Richard 59, 136–7
de Valera, Éamon 14, 62, 121, 232; Article (5) and 216, 224; Article (12) and 23, 34; Clare election 74, 75; Cosgrave and 218; county vote option proposed by 10–11; Dáil Éireann and 10, 232; Document No. 2 and 34, 151; dominion status and 9, 10; Fianna Fáil and 233, 243; Lloyd George, meetings with 9, 11; Northern Ireland, policies towards 243; Oath of Allegiance and 23; partition and 151, 215, 232, 233; republican candidates (1924) sanctioned by 152; Sinn Féin and 4, 66; Treaty, opposition to 22–3

Derry city 86, 163, 168-9, 215; Boundary Commission hearings 171; Carlisle Bridge 98; Catholic lord mayor of 57; Catholics in 177; Craigavon Bridge, completion of 98; customs barriers and 89, 90, 92, 182; Donegal and 55, 179, 203; local elections (1920) 101; nationalists and 245; NEBB legal agent in 57; partition, effects of 169; political manoeuvres 98; Protestant wholesalers in 169; religious denominations (1911) 6

Derry City Corporation 36, 98, 99, 101, 173

Derry County 6, 67, 155, 173-4, 186, 187, 204

Derry County Council 98

Derry Journal 34, 166, 212, 239

Derry Nationalist Registration Association 173-4

Derry People and Donegal News 206

Devine, John 178

Devlin, Joe 60, 72, 77, 104, 228, 241-2; Northern Parliament and 188, 190, 245

Devonshire, Victor Cavendish, 9th Duke of 75-6, 105, 106

District Electoral Divisions 26, 102, 172, 176, 179, 184-5, 189

Dixon, Herbert 85, 109, 160

Document No. 2, de Valera and 34, 151

dominion status 22-3, 30; Free State and 9, 10, 28, 30, 126; Northern Ireland and 16, 18, 24

Donegal County 67, 87-8, 106, 155, 165, 192; area transferred to Northern Ireland 201-2, 216, 221; Burtonport Port 88; Catholics in 176; co-operative movements 87-8; customs barriers, effects of 92, 96, 182; deputation to Cosgrave 207; Derry City's importance to 179, 203; East Donegal 15, 59, 96, 155, 176, 221, 235; nationalists in 176; partition, effects of 186; Presbyterians in 176; religious denominations (1911) 6, 176; unionists in 7, 176, 187, 235

Donegal Protestant Registration Association 176

Donnelly, Alexander E. 186

Dooley, Terence 178-9

Dove, John 129, 130

Down County: Boundary Commission hearings 171, 181, 190; religious denominations (1911) 6; Silent Valley reservoir 98-9, 164, 181, 192; South Down 170, 172, 181, 185-6, 193, 215, 245

Drummully, County Monaghan 176, 185, 192, 202

Duff, Lyman P. 132

Duggan, Eamonn 139, 148-9

Dunedin, Andrew Murray, 1st Viscount 32, 132

Dungannon, County Tyrone 101, 168

Dungannon Urban Council 102

Dungiven, County Derry 99, 168

Easter Rising (1916) 7, 74

Economist, The 82-3

Éire (newspaper) 118

Emyvale, County Monaghan 92, 183, 209, 210

Enniskillen, County Fermanagh 57, 81, 189, 204, 206; Commissioners' visit to 163, 165; customs barriers and 87, 181; local elections (1920) 101; 'Nationalists of Fermanagh' 171; new ward boundaries 103; unionists and 137, 191

Enniskillen Urban Council 165

Ervine, St John 190, 213

European Union Single Market 235

Falls, Charles 152, 166

Fanning, Ronan 13, 25

Farmers' Party 187, 232

Farrell, Michael 101

Fawsitt, Diarmaid 39

Feetham family 122

Feetham, Richard 122-4, 200; apartheid, opposition to 123; areas to be considered for transfer 184; Article (12), interpretation of 161, 162, 180-1, 193, 200, 211-12; Baldwin and 205; bias 240; border areas, Commissioners' tour of 163-4, 165-6; Boundary Commission chairman, role as 120, 122-4, 129-30, 133-5, 143, 145, 155, 158, 159, 160, 172, 184, 185-6, 236-7; boundary, conclusions on 199-201; Catholics, assumptions about 172, 200; class distinction and 178; criticism of 193-4, 201; Curtis, friendship with 122, 123-4; customs barriers, views on 96, 181; Government of Ireland Act (1920), views on 211; interviews dominated by 190; MacNeill and 204, 209, 211-12, 213; majoritarian principle, abandonment of 203; nationalist perception of 239-40; nationalists and 189-90, 200; plebiscite, views on 162, 166-7; police protection and 207; Protestants, assumptions about 172, 200; report and award, suppression of 229-30, 236-7; report

(unpublished) 157–8; tripartite conference (1925) and 229–30
Fermanagh 4–5, 10–11, 16, 19, 86, 112, 165, 245; area transferred to the Free State 202, 215; Catholic majority in 5, 107, 173, 189; Churchill's views on 26; customs barriers, effects of 92; Free State counties, trade with 186; General Election (1924) 152; kidnappings of loyalists 43; Lloyd George and 37, 38, 46; loyalists in 170; nationalists and 33, 35, 178; Protestant minority in 6; religious denominations (1911) 6; Sinn Féin majority in 15; Specials, violence towards 174–5; unionists in 30, 31; voting register, Specials added to 97
Fermanagh County Council 36, 37, 101, 103, 166, 173
Fermanagh Herald 174
Fianna Fáil 233, 243, 246
Filene Prize (1924) 54
Fine Gael 246
First World War (1914–18) 7, 26, 98, 146, 167, 185; post-war boundary commissions 2, 22, 54, 70, 71
Fisher, Frank 180
Fisher, Joseph Robert: border envisaged by 155; boundary, Feetham's conclusions on 199–200; Commission's work leaked by 159, 190–1, 204, 206, 240; correspondence with Lady Florence Reid 190–1, 240; MacNeill and 204, 210–11; Northern Commissioner, role as 120, 151, 152, 154–5, 158, 190, 240; *Northern Whig* and 154, 155; plebiscite, views on 162; police protection and 207; report and award, suppression of 229–30; report (unpublished) 157–8, 174; tripartite conference (1925) and 229–30; Ulster unionists, information leaked to 240
FitzGerald, Desmond 56, 125–6
FitzGerald, John 229
Flynn, Charles Joseph 83, 84
Ford, Patrick J. 127
Forsythe, Robert 175
Foster, John 183
Free State: areas transferred to 201, 202, 203; British attitudes towards 127, 130, 243; British Empire and 125, 127, 128–9, 130, 243–4; constitution, drafting of 41, 47, 53; dominion status and 9, 10, 28, 30, 126; establishment of 58; fiscal autonomy 25, 28, 77, 78, 79, 80–1, 94–5; identity/independence 3; Land Act (1923) 168; Northern nationalists' perception of 71, 245; old age pensions 197; opting out of, Northern Ireland and 57–9; perception of in Northern Ireland 60–2, 164–5, 180, 181; Specials, perception of 222; submissions to the Boundary Commission 192; tariffs 25, 28, 79, 80, 82, 86, 183; taxation/cost of living in 181; unemployment insurance 197; *see also* Southern Ireland
Free State Army (National Army) 75, 196, 230; British assessment of 136, 137; mutiny (1924) 75, 114–15, 116; perception of in Northern Ireland 114–15, 137
Free State Executive Council 52, 61, 64, 75, 150–1; Boundary Commission and 72, 222–3; boundary conference proposals 113; customs barriers and 84, 90; MacDonald's legislation plan 143–4; MacNeill's resignation 211, 213; NEBB and 111–12; Northern nationalist deputation 207; O'Higgins's proposal 150; O'Shiel and 61, 62, 70, 73, 89, 97
Free State government 2; army mutiny 114, 116; Article (12), ambiguity of 149–50; British attitude towards 125; Department of Agriculture 196; Department of Education 196–7; Department of External Affairs 196; Department of Finance 197; Irish unity, commitment to 76, 244; League of Nations and 126–7; NEBB memorandum 118–19; payments for malicious property damage 230; perception of in Northern Ireland 164–5, 175; Ulster unionist 'mindset', failure to understand 66; *see also* Cumann na nGaedheal government; customs barriers; Free State Executive Council
Freeman's Journal, The 131

Gaelic culture 100–1
Gaelic League 74
Gallagher, Paddy (the Cope) 87–8
Gallaher's tobacco factory 89
Gavan Duffy, George 12, 46, 148
General Election (1918) 13
General Election (1921) (Northern Ireland) 188
General Election (1922) 50

General Election (1923) (Free State) 72, 75–6, 105
General Election (1923) (UK) 106, 107–8
General Election (1924) (UK) 152
General Election (1925) (Northern Ireland) 171, 188–9
George V, King 5, 58, 237
gerrymandering 71, 97, 104, 108, 117–18, 129, 150, 173–4, 189
Gibbons, Ivan 237
Givens, Thomas 122
Glaslough, County Monaghan 179, 185, 192
Glenavy, James Campbell, 1st Baron 59–60
Good Friday Agreement (1998) 246
Good, James Winder 148
Government of Ireland Act (1920) 13, 159; abolition of PR as violation of 48; Baldwin's views on 144; Conservative Party and 139; Craig and 41–2, 112, 244; Feetham's views on 211; Fisher's views on 155; Griffith's perception of 78; Ireland, arbitrary division of 1–2, 112; Northern Ireland and 14, 15, 34, 145, 156, 162, 230; Northern nationalists' perception of 42; primacy of 139, 155, 156; rejection by the majority 9, 112; Ulster unionists' perception of 41–2, 146
Government of Ireland Bill (1920) 7, 8, 106, 145
Great War *see* First World War (1914–18)
Green, H.D. 190
Greene, William Pomeroy Crawford 137
Grianán of Aileach 166
Griffith, Arthur 12, 15, 36, 44, 57, 66; Boundary Commission and 18, 19, 20, 22, 23, 25; de Valera, correspondence with 18; death 48, 148; fiscal autonomy and 25; Government of Ireland Act (1920), perception of 78; Lloyd George and 18, 19, 28; plebiscite sought by 26–7; Treaty, decision to sign 25–6; Treaty negotiations 12–13, 17–18, 21, 21–2, 139
Gwynn, Denis 33
Gwynn, Stephen 33, 66
Gwynne, Rupert 63

Hallett, Ted 201, 208–9, 213–14
Hamilton, Martin 180
Hand, Geoffrey 75, 121, 135, 190; Boundary Commission Report, publication of (1969) 237; Craig, views on 154, 163; Feetham, views on 239–40; MacNeill, views on 73–4, 111–12, 167, 194, 213
Hanna, Sergeant Henry 161
Harbison, T.J. 54, 60, 107, 152, 232
Harrison, Henry 148
Hayes, Richard 56
Healy, Cahir: civil rights, nationalists and 246; Fermanagh and 101–2, 103, 178, 186; General Election (1922) 107; London Agreement and 232, 236; loyalism, views on 127–8; Northern nationalists and 66, 152; unionists, views on 178, 187; voting register, Specials and 99–100
Healy, Timothy, Governor General of the Free State 72, 110, 116–17, 126–7, 132, 206, 213, 239
Hearne, J.J. 160, 161
Henderson, Arthur 110, 114–15, 130, 142, 143
Henderson, Gerry 189
Henry, Joseph 185
Hogan, Patrick 56, 234
Hogg, Sir Douglas 132, 138
Home Rule: Suspensory Bill 7; Third Home Rule Bill (1912) 5; unionist opposition to 1–2, 4
Home Rule Act (1914) 7, 8
Home Rule crisis 1–2, 4, 9, 146
Hopkinson, Michael 84
House of Commons (British) 8, 14, 37, 49, 60, 109, 143–4, 151
House of Lords 30, 144, 151, 223
Hungerford, Alexander Wilson 65, 160, 170, 179
Hyslop, Arthur 127

Imperial Conference (1923) 63, 105–6, 240
Inishowen, County Donegal 153, 166, 186, 206
Inskip, Sir Thomas 63
Inter-Allied Commission 68
internment 100, 107, 108, 151, 167
Irish Boundary Commission 1, 66, 103, 104, 188; Baldwin and 163, 204–5, 217, 237; boundary 199–202; British Commissioner, delay in appointing 117; British government and 51, 62–3, 117–18; British memorandum on 19–20, 25; British proposals on appointment of Commission 22; Carson's views on 19; Chairman, appointment of 122–3, 129–30; Chairman, British government and 22, 71, 118, 120, 121–2, 239; Chairman, Feetham as 122–3, 129–30, 133–5, 143, 145, 155, 158, 159, 189–90; Churchill and 38–9, 49–50, 139–40; Collins

and 12, 22, 24, 66; Commissioners appointed to 2, 22, 27-8, 73-4; Commissioners' tour of the border areas 163-7; Cosgrave and 73, 76, 83, 169, 191, 241, 242; Craig's attempts to obstruct 163; Craig's refusal to co-operate with 10, 32, 49-50, 59, 65, 106, 107, 133, 138, 160; Craig's views on 29, 134; customs barriers, effects of 85, 90, 92, 96; delays in convening 53, 62, 71-3, 76, 81-2, 84, 97-8, 105, 117-18, 132-3, 240-1; documents presented to 159; economic and geographic conditions 20-2, 23, 133, 157-8, 163, 168-9, 171, 178-9, 180, 182, 184, 186, 192-3; establishment of 155-6; first meeting of 158-60; formal hearings (1925) 171-2, 184; Free State Commissioner, MacNeill as 73-4, 75, 133, 155, 159, 160-1, 166, 194, 238-9, 242; Free State government and 61, 62, 71, 72, 135, 161-2, 169, 188, 191-3, 222-3, 241; Free State, submissions from 192; Griffith and 18, 19, 20, 22, 23; information leaked by Fisher 159, 190-1, 204, 206; inhabitants' wishes 1, 19, 20-3, 26, 27, 37, 64, 67, 70, 132, 133, 134, 149, 157-8, 161, 171-2, 175-6, 178, 184, 193; inhabitants' wishes, Feetham and 199-200, 212; inhabitants' wishes, MacNeill and 212; international dimension to 63, 70, 126, 141-2; Labour government and 110; Lloyd George and 24-5, 30, 32, 107, 145-6, 243; local opinion and 71; MacDonald and 124-5, 130, 133, 142-3; MacNeill's resignation from 138, 157, 207, 208-9, 211, 215, 217; MacNeill's views on 158; *Morning Post*, forecast of the award 206, 207, 208, 209, 214, 216, 221, 222, 233; nationalist submissions to 172, 173, 174, 178, 182, 186, 187-8, 194; NEBB and 64, 67, 70, 108-9; Northern Commissioner, Fisher as 152, 154-5, 158-9; Northern Commissioner, Labour's Bill to appoint 151; Northern Commissioner, Northern government's refusal to appoint 105, 118, 120, 130, 132, 133, 138, 141, 142, 152-4, 239; Northern government and 65, 97-8, 170; Northern nationalists and 33, 35, 40, 60-1, 108, 167, 245; perception of 3, 26, 124, 165, 187-8, 210; plebiscite and 26-7, 134-6, 162, 166-7, 172; press speculation about the award 205-6; pro- and anti-Treaty sides' support for 33, 35; proportional representation (PR), abolition of 102; report and award 174, 222; report and award, suppression of 230, 236-7; report, publication of (1969) 237; reservoirs in nationalist areas 99; Secretary, Bourdillon as 68, 158-9, 163, 169-70, 192, 195; Sinn Féin memorandum 21; submissions to 162-3, 167-8, 169, 172-86, 192; terms of reference 2, 65; territory, transfers of 139, 167-8, 169-70, 171-2, 184, 189, 190, 195-9; Ulster unionists and 3, 29, 30, 42, 79-80, 137-8, 165-6; unionist submissions to 65, 174-80, 181-2, 184-7; unpublished report 157-8; Waller's memoranda 68; *see also* boundary commissions in Europe; North Eastern Boundary Bureau (NEBB)

Irish Committee 45

Irish Free State (Agreement) Bill 44, 49

Irish Free State Constitution Act (1922) 58, 159

Irish Independent 71, 189, 207, 231, 232

Irish language 100, 177

Irish nationalists 2, 42, 79, 94, 239-40; *see also* Northern nationalists

Irish News 60, 71, 100, 205, 236

Irish Parliamentary Party (IPP) 5, 6, 7, 33

Irish Republican Army (IRA) 35, 42, 43, 114; anti-Treaty IRA 51, 72

Irish Times 81-2, 216, 231

Irish unity: Collins and 24; Cosgrave and 66-7, 111, 228, 233, 234, 242; Craig's views on 47-8, 66; Free State government and 76, 244; NEBB memorandum on 118-19; O'Shiel's views on 66-7, 241; Ulster unionist press and 78, 85-6

Irish Volunteers 74

Jenkins, Sir Lawrence Hugh 132

Johnson, Thomas 215, 231-2

Johnson, William 180, 185

Johnston, Joseph: customs barriers and 81-2, 86, 87, 88; customs union recommended by 88-9; NEBB and 53, 67, 68, 148, 184

Johnston, Thomas 181

Jones, Thomas 13, 18-19, 76, 112, 131, 204-5, 218; Article (12), views on 27; border rectification and 145; Boundary Commission and 17-18, 19, 20, 25, 117-18; Boundary Commission Report and 204; Lloyd George's achievement, summary of 28; MacDonald's proposed legislation, views on 144; O'Higgins, perception of 222; Privy Council's decision,

views on 141-2; Southern Parliament suggested by 18; Specials, maintenance of 116; tripartite conference (1925) 223, 227-8
Joynson-Hicks, Sir William 63, 163, 205, 220

Keady, County Armagh 164, 172, 179, 182-4, 204
Kennedy, Hugh, Attorney General 112, 150, 193-4, 201
Kennedy, Michael 126
Kenny, Colum 19-20, 25
Kenny, Seán 229
Kilevey, County Armagh 172, 173
Kilkeel, County Down 172
Kilkeel Rural District Council 173, 175
Kilskeery, County Tyrone 174
Klagenfurt 69
Knox, Sir Adrian 132, 133

Labour government 109-10, 121, 131, 141, 144, 151
Labour Party (British) 107, 109-10, 120, 125, 156
Labour Party (Irish) 215, 232, 234
Lamb, Edward A. 184
Land Act (1923) 168
Larne gunrunning 8
Lavery, Cecil 161
Lavery, Hazel, Lady 113
League of Nations 52, 63, 69, 76, 126-7, 221, 244
League of Nations Union 68
Leary, Peter 171, 176
Leech's Commission 102
Liberal Party 5, 13, 39, 109, 139
Limavady Council 98
Limavady, County Derry 101, 168, 191
Lisnaskea Rural Council 174
Lloyd George, David 4, 28; all-Ireland parliament and 16, 19, 79; boundaries, re-adjustment of 37, 38; Boundary Commission and 24-5, 30, 32, 107, 145-6, 243; Collins, meeting with 24; Conservative Party and 38; Craig and 10, 15, 18-19, 25, 30, 31-2, 48; de Valera, meetings with 9, 11; duplicity 24-5, 28, 41, 107; fiscal autonomy, Free State and 25; General Election (1918) 13; Griffith, meetings with 18, 19; Home Rule scheme 7; Northern government, executive powers transferred to 17; Northern Ireland, status of 13; Treaty negotiations 13, 14, 21, 22, 24-5; Tyrone and Fermanagh 37, 38, 46

local authorities: Carlisle Bridge, opposition to reconstruction 98; electoral boundaries, redrawing of 102-3, 174; nationalists and 173; Northern Parliament and 36; suspensions 36, 37, 173; unionists and 102-4, 173
local elections 101, 108, 173
Local Government (Ireland) Acts 104, 173
London Agreement (1925) 38, 230-2, 233, 234-5, 236, 244; tripartite conference and 222-31;
Londonderry, Charles Vane-Tempest-Stewart, 7th Marquess of 112, 124, 127, 142, 143, 153
Londonderry, Edith Vane-Tempest-Stewart, Marchioness of 124-5
Long, Walter 13, 145
Longford, Frank Pakenham, 7th Earl of 19, 20; *Peace by Ordeal* 11
Loughnane, Norman Gerald 117
loyalism/loyalists 29, 31, 32, 106, 134, 153, 170, 185; kidnappings and 43-4; perception of 127-8
Lynch, Michael 56
Lynch, Patrick 161, 193
Lynch, Robert 17, 29
Lynn, Robert 140, 159, 240

McAllister, Thomas 245
Macardle, Dorothy, *Irish Republic, The* 74-5
McCann, Matthew H. 183
McCartan, Daniel 104-5
MacCartan, Hugh A. 53, 72, 100, 104, 105, 125; border areas, visits to 167-8; British press, propaganda from 147, 148; customs barriers and 77, 86, 89, 90; NEBB and 71, 86, 148
McCartan, Michael 152
McCartan, Patrick 50
McCarthy, Timothy 71, 72, 104
McConville, Patrick 182
MacCurtain, Seán 230
MacDonald, Ramsay 109, 110, 115, 118, 121, 153; Boundary Commission and 124-5, 130, 133, 223, 243; boundary conference and 142-3; legislation proposed by 143-4; Northern Commissioner appointed 154; Privy Council, Judicial Committee 132, 141-2
McDonnell, Revd 212-13
MacEntee, Seán 33-4
McGilligan, Patrick 75, 208, 220
McGrath, Joseph 114
McGuckin, Basil 189

Index

McGuire, Revd M. 174
McKenna, Revd James 55
McKinney, Edward 47
McMahon murders 45, 47
McMahon, Owen 47
MacMahon, Peadar 196
Macnaghten, Sir Malcolm 191
McNally, Canon Felix 104, 172–3
MacNeill, Eoin 35, 74–5, 106, 111–12, 132; areas to be transferred, consent to 203–4, 207; Article (12), defects of 75, 238; border areas, Commissioners' tour of 163–4; Boundary Commission, resignation from 138, 157, 207, 208–9, 211, 215, 217; boundary conference proposals 113; Cabinet, resignation from 213; Cosgrave and 207–8, 210–11, 214, 217, 242; criticism of 212–13, 222–3; Department of Education and 196–7, 208; Easter Rising countermanding order issued by 74; Executive Council, resignation from 211, 213; Feetham and 193–4, 199–201, 210–12, 213; Free State Commissioner, role as 74–5, 133, 155, 158, 159, 160–1, 166, 190, 194, 238–9, 242; Irish Volunteers and 74; O'Higgins's defence of 221; perception of 166, 207, 213, 238–9
MacNeill, James 73–4, 113, 121, 125, 148, 209, 213, 237
McNeill, Ronald 63
MacPherson, C.J. 167
Madden, J.J. 187
Magherafelt, County Derry 57, 168, 172, 188
Mallaby-Deeley, Sir Henry 153
Manchester Guardian, The 148
Mansergh, Nicholas 8, 121
Marshall, Alfred 163
Martin, George 89–90, 105
Masterson-Smith, James 44–5
Matthews, Kevin 17, 18, 37, 111, 150, 153–4, 159, 205
Met Éireann 246
Middlemas, Keith 19, 25
Middletown District Electoral Division 179–80, 202
Midleton, St John Brodrick, Viscount 11
Miller, William T. 102
Milner, Alfred Milner, 1st Viscount 122
Milroy, Seán 53
Moles, Thomas 7
Monaghan County 16, 106, 154, 155, 168, 176, 179–80, 181; area transferred to Northern Ireland 202, 216; customs barriers, effects of 91, 92, 182, 183–4; deputation to meet Blythe 207; Gaelic footballers, arrest of 43; religious denominations (1911) 6; unionists in 7, 34, 184–5
Monaghan County Council 185
Montagu, Edwin 39
Mooney, Revd Isidore B. 165
Moore Boyle, J. 175
Moore, Major R.L. 181
Morning Post, The 14, 116, 126, 146; Commission's award 205, 206, 207, 208–9, 214, 216, 221, 222
Muff, County Donegal 92
Mulcahy, Richard 44, 47, 114
Mullan Mills, Emyvale, County Monaghan 183
Mullyash, County Monaghan 184–5, 192, 202
Murnaghan, George 161
Murney, Peadar 57
Murphy, D. St P. 54
Murray, Paul 20, 109, 172, 200, 203
Myles, Major James Sproule 235

Nash, Catherine et al.: land border, creation of 94; *Partitioned Lives: The Irish Borderlands* 94
National Archives of Ireland 64, 121–2
Nationalist Party 101, 164, 175, 188
Nesbitt, Revd S.T. 138
Newcastle, County Down 184
Newman, Seán Bernard 42
Newry Chamber of Commerce 175
Newry, County Down 86, 153, 164–5, 175–6, 180, 184; Catholic majority 172–3, 203; customs barriers, effects of 183, 242; Free State, omission from 203, 204, 206, 221, 222; nationalists and 187, 245; unionists' concerns about transfer 198
Newry Port and Harbour Trust 184
Newry Rural District Councils 173
Newry Union Workhouse 104, 172
Newry Urban District Council 172, 180, 183, 185–6
Newtownstewart, County Tyrone 163, 165
Nixon, John, RUC District Inspector 137
North Eastern Boundary Bureau (NEBB) 2, 49, 62–5; anti-partition pamphlet 82; army mutiny, 'Orange Press' and 114–15; Article (12), interpretation of 67, 241; articles/letters

to newspapers 148; B Specials, perception of 100; border areas, visits to 164–5, 167–9; Boundary Commission and 64, 67, 70, 108–9; Cosgrave and 242; customs barriers and 86–7, 89; director, O'Shiel as 52, 53, 55, 57, 62–6; economic advisor appointed to 53; fiscal autonomy, memorandum on 81; formation of 52, 53–4; Free State Executive Council and 111–12; *Handbook of the Ulster Question* 64; historical division 54; legal agents hired by 54, 57, 89, 105, 165, 188; memorandum 118–19; nationalists and 56, 108, 187; pamphlets issued by 62, 64, 148; publicity division 53, 71; research and investigation division 55; Six Counties and 55, 59, 71, 72; winding down of 234; work completed by 241

Northern government 2, 3, 15, 38; Boundary Commission and 65, 97–8, 159, 160, 170; Churchill's support for 49; details of Boundary Commission's work revealed to 159; executive powers/government services transferred to 15–16, 17; local authorities (nationalist), suspension of 173; National Army mutiny, reaction to 114–15; Northern Commissioner, refusal to appoint 27–8, 32, 105, 130, 132, 141, 142, 239; party system 168–9; Provisional Government's recognition of 56; Specials, control of 44, 174; transfers of territory 198

Northern Ireland 3, 24; ambivalent status of 9; annual security costs (1922) 44; areas transferred to 201–2, 203; atrocities 45; Collins's obstructionist policies 43, 51, 56, 57; customs barriers and 88, 89–90; dominion status and 16, 18, 24; electoral areas, redrawing of the boundaries 101–2; establishment of 11; finance 220; Free State, opting out of 57–8, 82–3; Free State, perception of 60–2, 164–5, 175, 180; Gaelic culture, erosion of 100–1; gerrymandering 71, 97, 104, 108, 117–18, 129, 150, 173–4, 189; Government of Ireland Act (1920) 162; internment without trial 100, 108; Lloyd George's perception of 37; loyalism of 127–8; nine counties, UUC's objection to inclusion 7–8, 106; prisoners convicted in 230; Provisional Government's policy towards 49; reservoirs in nationalist areas 99, 164, 181; road blocks 44; sectarian riots (1920) 245; Southern government policies towards 243; status, Lloyd George and 13; TV programmes, geo-blocking of 246; 'Ulster Month' 58; unemployment benefits 197; voting register 97, 99–100; *see also* Six Counties

Northern Ireland Labour Party 101, 188

Northern nationalists 3, 60, 64, 152, 229; abolition of PR system, impact of 54, 97, 174; border protest meetings 206–7; Boundary Commission and 33, 35, 60–2, 108, 167, 244, 245; Boundary Commission, submissions to 172, 173, 174; boycotting of elections and public bodies 104, 154; British governments, perception of 245–6; Catholic religion and 172, 173; civil rights and 246; Collins as spokesperson for 42–3; Collins-Craig pact, opposition to 40; Cosgrave and 233, 242; Craig's attitude towards 244; customs barriers, criticism of 86–7; Free State Executive Council, deputation to 207; Free State, perception of 71, 164–5, 246; Government of Ireland Act (1920), perception of 42; internment without trial 100, 108; local elections and 101, 108, 173; London Agreement, perception of 236; mistreatment of 117; Oath of Allegiance and 104; O'Higgins and 56–7, 221–2, 225; partition and 35, 36; PR, effects of abolition 54, 97, 101; Provisional Government, meeting with 54, 55, 56–7; reservoirs in nationalist areas 99; RUC reports on 170; Specials, perception of 17; Treaty and 33, 35–6, 207, 245; unionist mindset, understanding of 66; voting register, struck off 99, 100; *see also* Irish Nationalists

Northern Parliament 47–8, 232; Free State, opting out of 58; General Election (1925) 171, 188; local authorities and 36, 37; nationalists' boycott of 104–5; nationalists' decision to enter 188, 245; PR voting system, abolition of 48; six counties, confined to 8

Northern Sentinel 91

Northern Whig 80, 85, 140, 154, 155, 159, 210

Northern Whig and Belfast Post 30–1

Nugent, John D. 86

Oath of Allegiance 23, 28, 104, 173, 233

Observer, The 66
O'Byrne, John, Attorney General 23, 27, 134, 142, 143, 220; Boundary Commission and 161-2, 192-3
O'Callaghan, Margaret 9, 98
O'Doherty, Hugh C. 57, 101
O'Doherty, John 178
O'Doherty, Revd John 186
O'Halloran, Clare 119
O'Hanlon, Francis 183
O'Hare, Charles 183
O'Hegarty, Diarmuid 169-70
O'Higgins, Kevin 50-1, 56, 72, 106, 156, 196; Article (12), ambiguity of 149; Baldwin, Commission award and 220-3; boundary conferences 113, 119; Catholics in the North 226; Council of Ireland, views on 232; Craig, meeting with 223, 224-5; Executive Council, proposal presented to 150; Labour's Bill, resolution on 151; London Agreement and 230; MacNeill, criticism of 222-3; MacNeill, defence of 221; Northern nationalists and 56-7, 221-2, 225; PR, views on 226, 228; Specials and 222, 223; tripartite conference (1925) and 222-7, 228, 230
Old Age Pension Act (1924) 197
O'Leary, Brendan 103
Omagh, County Tyrone 36, 52, 57, 165, 171, 173, 190
Omagh Urban District Council 56
O'Neill, Charles 169
O'Neill, H.C. 68
O'Neill, Patrick 184
O'Neill, Ronald 38
Orange Order/Orangemen 12, 17, 32, 39, 46, 51, 54, 98, 102, 137-8, 218
Ordnance Survey Office 64
O'Reilly, Michael 170
O'Rorke, Robert 172
Orr, Edmund 175, 186
O'Shiel, Kevin 49, 52-3, 55; Article (12), ambiguity of 149; Collins and 53; customs barriers, views on 84, 86, 89, 92; Devlin, distrust of 60; Free State Commissioner, views on 73; Free State Executive Council and 61, 62, 70, 73; General Election (1923) 105; Glenavy's offer to Craig, views on 59-60; Irish unity, views on 66-7, 241; Labour government, perception of 109;

local elections, views on 104; NEBB, director of 52, 53, 55, 57, 61, 62-6

partition 2-3, 11, 70, 154, 175, 232; anti-partition pamphlet, NEBB and 82; Belfast Boycott and 78-9; business, effects on 169; Collins and 35, 43; consequences of 1, 3; customs barriers, effects of 78, 80, 85, 87, 93-4; Dáil Éireann debates and 33; de Valera and 151, 215, 232, 233; Donegal and 186; legislation enacted before 196; MacEntee's perception of 34; Northern nationalists and 35, 36; opposition to 1-2, 232, 236; perception of 228; pro- and anti-Treaty sides 33; Treaty negotiations and 12
Pettigo, County Donegal 71, 93, 181, 192, 201
Phoblacht, An 245
P.J. Carroll (tobacco) 91
Pollock, Hugh 79, 81, 95, 115, 116, 142, 143
Poor Law Unions 37, 172, 184, 200
Presbyterians 154, 176
Pringle, James 107, 152
prisoners: convicted in Northern Ireland 230; release of 220, 223
Privy Council: Article (12), interpretation of 130-1, 133, 141-2, 244; Judicial Committee 130, 131-2, 133, 134-5, 141, 244; Report of the Judicial Committee of the Privy Council 159
proportional representation (PR) 228-9; abolition of 48, 97, 101-2, 173, 242; impact of abolition 54, 97, 101, 173, 174, 226; local elections (1920, 1922) and 101; restoration, O'Higgins and 228
Protestants 172, 203; Boundary Commission and 134, 174, 184; Catholic employees 177; Craig and 218-19, 220; in Derry City 169; rates/taxes paid by 175-6; Specials, membership of 42, 100
Provisional Government Advisory Committee in Ulster 53
Provisional Government of the Irish Free State 38, 43-4, 46, 47, 52-3, 80-1; Chamberlain's warning to 44; Collins and 39, 41, 42, 45; Northern government, recognition of 56; Northern Ireland, policy towards 49, 51, 56; Northern nationalists, meeting with 54, 55, 56-7; *see also* Free State Executive Council; Free State government

Quinn, Canon 168

Rankin, Kieran 3, 213
Raphoe Presbytery 176
Redmond, John 5-6, 7, 236
Reid, David 159, 204
Reid, Florence (*née* Stiebel), Lady 159, 190-1
religious denominations (1911) in Ulster 6
Revenue Commissioners 83, 84
Roslea, County Fermanagh 165, 219
Round Table movement 122, 123, 129, 130
Round Table (periodical) 129
Royal Flying Corps 167
Royal Irish Constabulary (RIC) 16
Royal Ulster Constabulary (RUC) 137, 164, 170-1, 196, 227
Ruth, George A. 53-4

Sagarra, Eda 53
Salisbury, James Gascoyne-Cecil, 4th Marquess of 63, 205, 225, 227-8
Saunderson, Somerset 192
Schleswig dispute 68-9
Scotsman, The 127, 148
Scott, John 99, 177, 181-2
Seanad Éireann 53
Shannon hydroelectric scheme 128
Siemens-Schuckert 128
Silent Valley reservoir 98-9, 164, 181, 192
Sinn Féin 4, 19, 66, 74, 79, 188; abstentionist policy 232-3, 243; Belfast anti-Treaty section 36; Boundary Commission and 1, 2; Dáil Courts 52; fiscal policies 78; local elections (1920) 101; split within 36, 43; Treaty negotiations and 1, 11, 14, 17-18, 20-1, 79; Truce and 9; Ulster unionists' views on 78
Sinn Féin Advisory Committee for Ulster 53
Six Counties 3, 13, 14-15, 16, 18, 33, 90, 98; Article (12) and 162; British press and 147; Collins's non-recognition of 43; Craig and 31, 32, 106, 154; exclusion of 5, 7; Fermanagh and 174, 191; Long, Walter and 145; 'May Offensive' 51; nationalists and 12, 43, 48, 56, 98, 99, 101, 108, 225, 236; NEBB and 55, 59, 71, 72; Northern Parliament confined to 8; religious denominations (1911) 6; Specials and 100; *see also* Northern Ireland
Smuts, Jan 10

Smyth, William Johnson 185
Snowden, Philip 115, 116
Solly-Flood, Arthur 115
Southern Ireland 65, 79, 80, 127, 136, 142, 219; dominion status and 9, 10; fiscal autonomy 78; voting into 21; *see also* Free State
Southern unionists 7, 10-11, 59
Specials *see* Ulster Special Constabulary
Spectator, The 114
Spender, Lillian 31, 93
Spender, Wilfrid 31, 39, 65, 93, 159, 170, 231, 240
Stack, Austin 22
Stephens, Edward Millington: nationalist witnesses and 187, 188, 189-90; NEBB and 53, 111, 161, 164-5, 167-9, 185, 234; unemployed people, provisions for 197
Stephens, Lily 213
Strabane 87, 93, 178, 182, 204; nationalists and 101, 102, 163-4, 182, 206-7
Strabane Chronicle 207
Strabane Urban and Rural Councils 98
Sunday Express 205
Sunday Independent 74, 105

Tailteann Games (1924) 127, 128
Tallents, Stephen 44, 163, 204
tariffs 25, 28, 79, 80, 82, 86, 183
Templecrone Co-operative Agricultural Society (the Cope) 87-8
Thomas, John Henry, Colonial Secretary 109, 113, 115, 116, 233; Article (12), interpretation of 131; boundary and 115, 116, 124; Boundary Commission and 110, 112, 117, 121, 124, 132, 134; boundary conferences and 110, 112, 142, 143; British Empire and 125; legislation introduced by 143-4; Northern Commissioner, Fisher's appointment as 154; Specials, maintenance of 115-16
Tierney, John, Archdeacon 189
Tierney, Michael 213
Times, The 46, 47, 83, 148, 155, 189, 232, 237
Tobin, Liam 114
Tracy, John 57
Trimble, Egbert 165-6
Truce (1921) 9, 11, 14, 17, 68, 79, 230
Twomey, Maurice (Moss) 151-2
Tyrone 4-5, 10-11, 19, 24, 86, 186, 245; area transferred to the Free State 201, 215, 216;

boundary and 112, 116; Boundary Commission and 165; Catholic majority in 5, 107, 184; Churchill's views on 26; East Tyrone 168, 188; General Election (1924) 152; Lloyd George and 37, 38, 46; loyalists, kidnappings of 43; nationalists and 33, 35, 172, 188; Protestant minority in 6; religious denominations (1911) 6; Sinn Féin majority in 15, 16; unionists in 30, 31; voting register, Specials added to 97

Tyrone County Council 36, 37, 98, 101, 103

Ulster: Dáil debates and 11, 33; de Valera and 10, 11; Lloyd George and 10, 13, 14, 37; religious denominations (1911) 6; Treaty negotiations and 11–12, 13; *see also* Northern Ireland; Six Counties

Ulster Association 147, 198

Ulster Liberal Unionist Association 154

'Ulster Month' 58

Ulster Special Constabulary 16–17, 42, 47, 88, 97, 223; A class 17, 44, 136; B class 17, 100, 136, 196; C class 17, 100, 115, 136, 196; Catholics and 17, 174; Collins's perception of 46; demobilisation, Craig's concerns about 219; Gaelic footballers arrested by 43; maintenance of 44, 45, 115–16, 219, 222; members, number of 42; Northern government's control of 44, 174; Northern nationalists' perception of 17; perception of 46–7, 55, 217, 222; Protestants in 42, 100; violence towards 174–5; voting register, added to 97, 99–100

Ulster Unionist Council (UUC) 7–8, 39, 64–5, 106, 160, 240

Ulster Unionists 100, 136, 140, 159; Boundary Commission and 3, 29, 30, 33, 42, 79–80, 137–8, 165–6, 191; Carson and 30, 153–4; Craig and 204, 236; election (April 1925) 188; Fisher, Commission's work revealed by 204; General Election (1924) 152; PR, removal of 101; Treaty accepted by 58–9, 60; boundary, fortifying of 98; Collins's understanding of 39; Conservative Party's support for 14, 63, 109, 120, 138–9, 144; criticism of Lloyd George 38; customs barriers, opposition to 85; demonstration in Enniskillen 137; divisions 7; Dublin parliament, hatred of 24, 241; Free State, opposition to fiscal autonomy for 78, 79; Free State, opting out of 58–9; Government of Ireland Act (1920), perception of 41–2, 146; hatred for Dublin 119; Home Rule, opposition to 1–2; information leaks, Fisher and 240; Labour government and 109; local elections (1920) under PR 101; mindset of 66, 90, 241; Northern Ireland and 9; PR, abolition of 48, 97, 101; Treaty and 29–30, 58–9; Treaty, concerns about 29; United Kingdom, integration with 94

Upper Silesia 22, 27, 55, 68, 69–70, 158, 167

Upper Silesia Boundary Commission 158, 167

Vance, Henry 170

voting register (Northern Ireland) 97, 99–100

Walker, Brian M. 102

Waller, Bolton C. 54, 61–2, 63, 68, 69–71, 147, 150

Walsh, J.J. 56

Walsh, Stephen 115

War of Independence 114, 230

Warburton, Colonel F.T. 177

Warrenpoint, County Down 175–6, 180, 185, 203

Wedgwood Benn, William 60

Wheatley, John 109

Whelan, Noel 233

White, John 187–8

Wood, Edward (*later* Lord Halifax) 120

Worthington-Evans, Laming 8, 139

Wylie, T.C. 179